OVERLAND

OVERLAND

16 TOTAL STRANGERS TRAVELING THROUGH 8 COUNTRIES IN 1 BROKEN DOWN TRUCK

WELCOME TO AFRICA

Copyright © 2017 Pete Mandra
Front cover image and book design by Jessica Mandra

All rights reserved. No part of this book may be reproduced or transmitted in any form or by any means, electronic or mechanical, including information storage and retrieveal systems, without permission in writing from the copyright owner, except by reviewers, who may quote brief passages in a review.

ISBN 978-0-6928135-6-0 (Paperback Edition)

Library of Congress Control Number 2017908777

This is a work of fiction. Some characters and events in this book are fictitious. Any similarity to real persons, living or dead, is coincidental and not intended by the author.

Printed and bound in USA

Published by Ingram Content Group LLC
One Ingram Blvd.
La Vergne, TN 37086

*Dedicated to my wonderful wife Jessica,
whose spirit for adventure and travel has
made life's journey together priceless.*

PROLOGUE

It really started out as her dream but somehow I got sucked into it, as boyfriends in love with their girlfriends often do. And even though I promised her for a year-and-a-half that I would go—once I paid off a fistful of credit card bills and actually started saving some money—I don't think she ever believed it 100 percent. She even said as much, just as the taxi we flagged down at the Cape Town airport whizzed us past a depressing shantytown.

"I know I said I've wanted to do this trip," Megan began, keeping her gaze on a small, bare-chested boy swinging a stick on the side of the road, "but now that we're here it's kind of freaking me out."

As annoying as it was to hear her start moaning so early on, I knew what she meant. I couldn't believe it myself. After nearly a year of planning, we had finally arrived in South Africa, about to embark on a tour of the lower half of the African continent in a large, stranger-filled truck. By the time we'd finally reach our final destination, just outside of Nairobi in Kenya, it would be nearly six weeks from now.

Just as we pass a teetering, roadside hut made entirely of sheet metal, I start to ask myself why.

****

"It's called a walkabout—it's Australian," my girlfriend Megan explained, anticipating my follow-up question before it arrived.

"I've been planning it for years—first Australia for a few months, then Asia and most of Europe."

It figured, I told myself, while seated on her leather sofa as some bad Adam Sandler movie raced across the television. Since Megan wasn't the schizophrenic basket case or the man-hater like most of the women I had the pleasure of dating recently, it was just my luck that she was already planning an escape.

Though we had only been dating for a few months, I knew what Megan and I had was too perfect to let slip away. I mean, Megan had everything I was looking for, with her sexy, come-hither smile, gorgeous brown eyes, and chestnut hair that lightly touched her shoulders. She was that type of rare, elusive woman that men spoke about in legend in sports bars across the world; she was well-rounded enough to appreciate the musical genius of Bob Dylan and well read enough to discuss U.S. foreign policy. Not to mention, she actually appreciated my twisted and dark sense of humor, which I feared would get me locked up or, at the very least, slapped around one of these days.

"So tell me a little more about this trip of yours," I asked, intentionally looking away. I could just picture it—Megan on the back of a bright red Vespa, grabbing firm hold around the waist of a chiseled yet debonair Italian named Rico.

"...When you're going exactly...how long you'll be gone...."

I caught a brief spark in Megan's eyes—almost like she knew what would be coming out of my mouth even before I did. Maybe that was all part of her game, planting that seed of doubt deep inside me, testing me to see if I was willing to pick up and run off with her. (And they say men are sneaky.)

She hadn't settled on a specific date, Megan told me though it would be within the next year. The doubters in her family, who sometimes teased her about mentioning the trip and not yet doing it, were the only motivation she needed.

"The way I see it," she proclaimed, just after sipping from her glass of water, "now's the time for me to do this. I don't care for my job—I don't even know if I want to work in sales and marketing for the rest of my life. So why not?"

"And I have enough savings, you know."

Savings. Hearing that dreaded word should have been enough to make me pull the plug on my entire notion of worldwide travel. Instead of saving for an international excursion like Megan had, all of my money had been going towards paying off school loans and erratic eBay purchases. Sometimes I didn't know if I really wanted to add that golden age comic book to my collection or if I just wanted to see how high I could escalate the bid price without winning it. Damn you, eBay.

What happened after that is still sort of a mystery to me. I mean, I was there but I'm not quite sure how things progressed.

"Y'know, I've thought a lot about travel myself," I began nervously. The words escaped my mouth uncontrollably.

"I was thinking...I'd love to go along with you."

Throwing her arms up into the air in victory, Megan leaned forward and planted an excitement-fueled kiss on my lips.

Yeah, I guess I was in pretty deep.

****

"Do I feel warm to you?" Megan gasped, grabbing my hand and placing it on her forehead.

"I feel warm."

I bounced forward in my seat as the cab rolled forward through the intersection, the driver tapping on the brake only long enough to slow the lurching vehicle. Megan's forehead was cool. We had landed in Africa only a few short hours ago, and already she was convinced she wouldn't make it.

"What if I need a doctor?"

****

From the moment we started planning what at that point had become our worldwide trip, I made no illusion about my shortage of cash and how I'd prefer if we could wait until the following May, a little over a year from that moment, to begin. I could tell Megan was itching to go, so much so that she even offered to loan me as much as I needed if it meant we could leave sooner. I wasn't about to bite, however, since I didn't want to even entertain the idea of returning from the trip months later with a huge debt and the little savings I had exhausted. She agreed to wait—though I sensed she was slightly skeptical from that point on if I would deliver.

How we arrived at Africa as a destination, instead of Australia, Asia, and the other destinations Megan had planned on, was a game of 'if I only had six months to live, where would I go and what would I want to see.' Megan had lived in Europe and been to Asia on business so they weren't going to give her that buzz of being somewhere completely new. Africa, yes I would definitely want to see Africa before I die and Megan did too. The prospect of traveling to a land as exotic as Africa was very exciting, an unusual locale that's not exactly overrun with tourists but just wild and exciting enough to keep us on our toes. Much for the same reason I wanted to one day see bears in Alaska, I dreamed of finding myself in the middle of the Serengeti or some other far-off game preserve, witnessing the lives of lions, elephants, giraffe and the like in their natural habitat.

It didn't take a great deal of research to discover that Africa was not the sort of place where you could really get around by yourself. Public transportation seemed almost nonexistent, if not unreliable, and the immense, rural continent seemed the least likely place where you could expect to walk up the road to a gas station if your car happened to give out. Traveling by ourselves through Africa was not an option; it was something better left in the hands of professionals. Or in the case of African Wanderer, the overland tour operator we ended up selecting, primarily due to their affordable rate.

In Africa, overland touring, that is, touring the continent in a large, rugged truck with other adventurers, was one of the few affordable and therefore most popular ways to get around. The tour operators provided everything—food, shelter and an itinerary that included some of the most popular destinations in Africa—all for one low, all-inclusive price, though certain optional activities could cost extra. And best of all, the package offered by African Wanderer was the most inexpensive tour of its kind we managed to find, provided you didn't mind camping for nearly the entire duration of the six-week tour that started in Cape Town and slowly wound its way to Nairobi. I knew the old cliché about getting what you pay for usually rang true, but the surprisingly low cost of touring through Africa resonated even louder, a chiming gong ringing in relief for my bruised finances.

****

"We see a lot of tourists like you two come through Cape Town," the cabbie related as our car winded down a steep hill of asphalt. "On your honeymoon, are ya?"

I glanced over at Megan, her matted hair tangled over her face and held in place with drool as she slept hard against my shoulder.

"No...not like that," I replied over a loud, erupting snore.

"Uh-uh."

****

Megan yawned slightly as our cab headed down a confusing whirl of streets marked with numerous small hotels and hostels. In the immediate distance sat a large, rugged mountain shrouded in a thick, white mist, completely dwarfing the entire countryside.

"Table Mountain," our driver said, pointing to its base.

"You can hike up it or take a cable car."

Even thinking about performing a physical feat after the last 24 grueling hours it had taken us to get here left me exhausted. When the station wagon cab finally dropped us off at the hostel, a small yet cozy gated place where we'd be spending the next two nights before departing with African Wanderer, I was all too eager to tip the driver and send him on his way.

I just needed some sleep.

ORIENTATION

The sound of laughter emanating from down the hall woke me from my unbelievably deep sleep the following day. Tangled and twisted in black sheets, I carefully rolled myself free, trying to move as quietly as I could across the squeaky bed since Megan craved sleep the way a restaurant critic craved food.

Though the small of my back felt slightly sore from the limp mattress, there was little else to complain about physically. The sheer exhaustion of air travel seemed a distant memory.

Seated on the edge of the bed, I spied the small bottle of Lariam tablets I set on the end table before lapsing into my day long coma of sleep. I didn't need to worry about malaria just yet—at least not until we left with African Wanderer. I was hopeful that I wouldn't regret choosing Lariam—complete with its sometimes mind-warping side effects—over one of the alternates that Megan chose at the Travel Center's suggestion. She could deal with popping a tablet every day. With Lariam, once a week was all I needed. Besides, even if Lariam did invoke lucid dreaming, how bad could it really be?

The heavy, labored sound of something being dragged across the beige stone floor from the other side of our door—either a huge suitcase or a morbidly obese corpse—stirred Megan from her sleep a few minutes later, just as I was about to duck into the shower. Smacking her lips briefly while rubbing her eyes, she glimpsed quickly at the small clock radio on the night stand before turning her attention to me.

"We need to get going soon," she mumbled, burying herself deep into the bed and her cocoon of covers. "I knew you'd be up early."

****

I guess I never thought about how downright unpredictable a six-week tour could be until the actual day we had spent months planning for had nearly arrived. There was so much you had to prepare yourself for, both mentally and physically. And what if Africa wasn't the great place of adventure we figured it would be? I'd be sick if I decimated the little savings I had if all I had to show for it was a miserable time. After adding to that the risk of contracting some bizarre tropical disease or being attacked by a wild animal, the scenario became even more stressful. It was probably best I hadn't thought about all of the challenges of traveling through Africa until we were a few hours away from orientation.

We left the hostel and explored town a little bit, perfect therapy for my building apprehension. A sleepy craft market we wandered through, filled with indifferent hawkers more interested in local gossip than striking a deal, yielded 'it'—something so treasured I had been completely willing to abandon all tourist sensibilities in order to have it. That 'it' consisted of a large, cheery oil painting emblazoned with oranges, reds and blues. I loved it, making it easy to imagine proudly hanging in our Chicago living room.

"This one tells a story," explained the woman working the stall, sensing my interest while pointing out the canvas' abstract shapes "This woman — she knows the man over her wants to be with her, but she's shy."

Though admittedly I did not see every element of the story line the hawker had outlined, I knew I had to have it. Bargaining quickly on price, so I wouldn't attract a lot of attention from other hawkers, I rolled the thick canvas lengthwise and held it securely in my right hand.

"We're going to have to be really careful with that," Megan mentioned, inspecting the rubber band squeezing the painting's middle. "Six weeks on a truck!"

Unknowingly, with my purchase that afternoon, I had undertaken another mission, since surviving in Africa with my girlfriend amid a truckload of strangers apparently wasn't enough. That assignment? Protecting that painting, that wonderfully unique yet vulnerable painting, from spills, stains, tears, rips, careless fellow travelers, wild animals, corrupt warlords and roving gangs of thieves.

I had my work cut out for me, I guess.

Racing back to the hostel, we just had enough time to drop off the painting before scrambling to the trip orientation meeting place, which we guessed we could reach by foot. We quickly headed north, up the road to a deserted intersection.

"Darter's Road," Megan declared, pointing to a green sign just above the teetering traffic light. "I think it's this way."

I tucked the map I had been carrying in my right hand deep into my back pocket. Though the sun had just set, the streets were already dark and deserted, save for an old man hurrying crossing the street in the other direction.

"A little spooky, isn't it?" I commented to Megan as I noticed the absence of streetlights.

"Hopefully it's not too far," she replied, squeezing my hand in hers.

Passing several locked grocery stores as we wandered down the main street, it appeared that the only storefronts still open for business were the tour companies, where you'd typically see at least a couple people milling about inside. If Cape Town had a district for its touring companies, we had found it.

"It should be right around here," Megan commented as her eyes darted back and forth at the storefronts. "Safari Adventures...Serengeti Explorer....Desert Excursions...."

"There it is!"

With two human-sized, dark-wood carvings that resembled the monuments of Easter Island flanking each end of the enormously cluttered picture window, African Wanderer appeared cheesy but no worse than any other of the storefronts we had passed. And best of all, at least from the outside, it appeared packed with people, fellow travelers, young and old, who were prepared to begin the same adventure with us.

"Here goes nothing," said Megan, grabbing the loose, metal doorknob.

Despite the chiming 'ping' of the wind chimes that clanged against the door as Megan pushed it forward, few of the people seated in the semi-circle seemed to notice us. Tiptoeing carefully around the maze of chairs, the tiny store appeared filled with as many African mementos as it could hold. A medium-sized domed tent, looking completely out of place, sat by itself in the center of the room, while photos displaying all types of wildlife hung from a cheaply constructed wooden stand.

As Megan made some joke to me about the amount of crap scattered through the store, a tall, lanky, blond-haired guy who had spotted us as we walked in sprung up from a steel chair and rose quickly to his feet.

"I'm Aubrey," he said, through a thick Dutch accent as he thrust his hand forward.

"Paul," I said, slightly confused as I shook his hand. "And this is Megan."

After shaking Megan's hand, our greeter quickly returned to his seat without saying another word.

"Does he work here?" I whispered to Megan, as I watched Aubrey writing something in what appeared to be a journal.

"I don't know," she shrugged. "But we better sit down, too."

"We'll wait a few more minutes, guys," called out another blond guy holding an old clipboard near the front desk. "So we know everyone's here."

This blond guy, wearing a dark-green T-shirt and khaki shorts, retreated back to the small group he had been chatting with: a short guy in his twenties with a shaved head and a devilish laugh, a thin, young girl—eighteen years old, maybe—who frowned miserably as she glanced at her wristwatch, and an older, thin man with curly, brown hair who said very little.

"Those must be the guides."

"They look like they know what they're doing—don't they?" Megan asked.

Nodding my head, I began scouting out the group of strangers around us—strangers I figured I'd get to know pretty well by the time the tour ended. On Megan's right sat a blond, bird-like woman—Australian, I figured by the accent I overheard as she spoke with the thin, dark-haired guy next to her who introduced himself as 'Matt'. Next to Matt was someone he must have signed up for the trip with—a cheery, slightly goofy guy who passed the time by tracing the rim of a stocking cap between his fingers.

A single, empty seat separated him from Aubrey, our informal greeter, followed by a dark-complexioned, slightly stocky woman with dark, long hair. A short, barrel-chested guy with a bandana on his head had his nose firmly inside some book next to her, and rounding out the current crew was an elderly, white-haired couple, smiling politely as they waited for the orientation to begin.

"Do you think they know it's camping?" I whispered to Megan as I motioned with my head towards the old couple. "That old dude probably has a hard enough time getting out of bed in the morning!"

"Be nice," returned Megan.

I'd be the first to admit that sometimes I could be a little sarcastic, but I was also a little on high alert, too—particularly after Megan warned me that fellow travelers, particularly Europeans, may want to get into a hot debate regarding U.S. foreign policy. U.S. foreign policy. That's something I found about as interesting as looking through the hundreds of pictures my aunt snapped of the single trip to Italy she took with her new husband nearly ten years ago. Why couldn't we debate something relevant, like which export was worse for entertainment—the Spice Girls or any 'boy band'?

In looking around at the assembled group, I didn't detect anyone who looked too terribly interested in discussing weighty issues, though that could obviously change once all of our collective nervousness passed and we were well into the trip. Who knew—maybe after six weeks, I could become delirious enough to want to discuss politics.

A few minutes must have gone by before the blond guide who spoke earlier strode slowly towards our semicircle. Clasping his hands together after quickly glancing at a zebra-design clock on the wall, he cleared his throat.

"Alright, everyone," he began, spying over his shoulder at the three he had been speaking to earlier. As if on cue, the three moved forward, joining him at his side.

"I want to welcome all of you here to our office," the guide started, smiling as his eyes roved through the crowd.

"My name is Derek, and I am the tour coordinator here at African Wanderer. And it's my job to make sure all of you are ready for tomorrow, when you leave Cape Town with these people standing next to me."

The tall, thin guy standing near the back of the small crowd smiled politely. The young girl was still frowning about something, looking more annoyed than anything else, while the short dude with the shaved head looked indifferent, fumbling around his pockets for something.

"There's a sign-up sheet being passed around...." Derek mentioned as he quickly counted the number of heads in the crowd to himself.

"...And now's as good as a time as any to introduce your guides for your African adventure!"

"Van," the bald man mumbled as he looked down at the floor, kicking at something. "You can call me Van or 'Skonky'...whatever. I'm the driver."

Megan elbowed me softly in the ribs, probably wondering why anyone would want to be known as 'Skonky.' At least it was easy to remember.

After Skonky stepped back to where he originally stood, the young girl, smacking down hard on a mouthful of gum, crossed her arms in front of her and leaned back. With a terminally bored expression on her face, she looked like she'd rather be getting a root canal.

"Charlie. I cook."

You could just sense her enthusiasm bubbling over.

At least the tall, tanned man in the rear seemed excited. Extending his hand to give us a hearty wave, his voice bounced with enthusiasm when he was given the floor.

"Thanks for coming!" he chirped merrily. "My name is Rutger, and we're going to have a great time!"

Megan elbowed me again.

"How did he fall in with this bunch?" Megan whispered.

"Just lucky, I guess" I replied.

Derek stepped forward the moment Rutger had finished with his greeting, grabbing a copy of the sheet of paper that had been on our seat when we first sat down.

"Let's go over this first," Derek explained, raising his sheet high into the air. "There's a couple of things...."

Unexpectedly, the front door swung slowly open and a rather tall, pale-skinned man entered, smiling sheepishly. A dark blue cap rested on his head, covering long, straw-colored hair.

"Sorry I am late," the intruder said softly through slightly broken English, glancing around the room. "I am Dominick."

Derek smiled reassuringly.

"You didn't miss anything...Dominick, right? Please have a seat."

Returning a smile, Dominick carefully maneuvered his skinny frame over to Aubrey, finally settling in the empty chair between him and Matt's friend with the stocking cap. European, I guessed.

"Please read through this entire sheet," Derek continued, hoisting it in the air again. "I'm just going to go over the most important highlights."

Megan, prepared as always, handed me a spare pencil she had brought along.

"First off," said Derek in a commanding voice, as if he was prepping us for an invasion. "You need U.S. cash. Plenty of it, since you aren't going to be anywhere near currency exchanges for the most part."

Immediately, I sensed a collective 'What the hell is this guy talking about?' Cash? Who would travel anywhere with hundreds of dollars in U.S. cash on them?

The dark-haired woman, up to that moment sitting silently with her legs crossed, audibly sighed, "That can't possibly be safe...."

"But it is," Derek replied, noticing he had touched on a sore spot. "Our trucks feature elaborate safes that are impenetrable, so there's no danger of your cash being stolen."

"But what about us?!" Megan blurted out.

"All we brought were traveler's checks!"

Derek, unfazed, rested his hands on his hips.

"You'll need to get to a currency exchange before we leave, then," he stated. "Maybe that's something we should have told you about when you signed up...."

Looking around at the slightly annoyed faces in the room, I knew that everyone seated within the semicircle had also done the most responsible thing and brought everything in traveler's checks. Now, in addition to dragging all of our gear to the office tomorrow, each one of us had to worry about cashing in everything we had at a currency exchange before shipping out. Gee, maybe it would have been helpful if we had known that earlier....

"I hope you also brought plenty of goods that can be bartered with the locals," Derek continued. "Things like shoes, clothing with logos, anything that could be useful."

"Sometimes that's even more valuable than currency."

Derek paused again, not wanting to speak over a second round of grumbling.

"Maybe we should have told you that, too," Derek said apologetically as he threw up his hands. "You probably didn't know, did you?"

Great. Instantly I thought of all the bad Chicago tourism shops on Michigan Avenue selling cheapo Bulls jerseys four for $10 and the killing I could have made. Thanks, Derek. I was beginning to feel glad he wasn't coming along with us. Oh, you want to eat? I guess I should have told you to bring food.

"At least we thought of supplying you with enough water," Derek joked.

"Clean drinking water in Africa is sometimes difficult to find, but thanks to the tanks we keep filled at the rear of the truck, it should never be a problem for you guys. That's your water."

Clean drinking water. It was something, at least.

"Lastly, and most importantly, I can't stress to you enough how important it is to listen to your guides," Derek stated seriously. "Especially for those of you who are not leaving the tour in Victoria Falls and going on all the way up to Nairobi."

Victoria Falls. That was good news in a way, I thought. Our single opportunity for escape, should we want to take it, if the tour became too much. Or if the people with us did.

"Basically," Derek continued, pacing in front of us with his hands tucked behind his back. "You need to expect the unexpected—border crossings that can take a good part of the day if the guards feel like it, flat tires, engine failure...it can be anything. And after Victoria Falls, things become that much more unpredictable, almost to the point where complete flexibility is required."

Once again, a healthy dose of doubt crept over me. If the path to Victoria Falls isn't the easiest, could we even survive the entire route to Nairobi?

You just knew Derek had given these speeches enough to know when he needed to stop freaking us out and when he needed to start putting a positive spin on things. Sensing he was losing us once again, he stepped back to join his guides again.

"That's where the experience of all of these people comes in handy," Derek added. "Trust me; they'll take good care of ya!"

I studied the motley group of guides assembled in front of us, who stood awkwardly as if seeking out our approval. Perhaps feeling obligated to say something to prove his credentials, Skonky mumbled something about catching malaria on four separate occasions but 'had been feeling much better lately.' Charlie, the surly cook who looked more likely to bust a cast-iron pan over your head than be asked to cook with it, embraced silent boredom. I hoped Rutger, the happy-go-lucky one of the group, had enough knowledge to compensate for his companions.

May God have mercy on all of us.

After Derek had concluded, lastly reminding us to meet with all of our gear at 10 a.m. the next day, Megan asked me to hang back with her as the crowd began to disperse out the front door.

"I need to talk to Charlie," she told me. "I want to let her know that I'm lactose intolerant."

Lactose intolerance. Megan could be so much of a hypochondriac at times that I didn't know what to believe. One day I was certain she was going to tell me she had somehow contracted leprosy.

Charlie, still chomping forcefully at her wad of gum, had just finished whispering something to Skonky. She jumped slightly when she heard Megan move in from behind her.

"Excuse me, Charlie," Megan offered politely. "I just wanted to tell you that I'm lactose intolerant."

Shooting a look back at Megan that was part confusion, part "I don't give a damn," I suddenly felt like Megan and I were the modern-day version of the Howells from "Gilligan's Island."

"What?!?" Charlie questioned quickly, furling her eyebrows angrily.

"Cheese and dairy," Megan offered. "I can't eat a lot of that."

Charlie shook her head.

"I don't cook much with that," Charlie countered, turning back to Skonky as if we were no longer standing there. I gave Megan a knowing look—I just knew Charlie was going to be trouble.

The final thing we did on our last night before embarking on the trip through Africa that we had sacrificed so much for was to stop at the Internet café a few doors down. Aside from the usual junk mail about penis enlargements and helping a deposed dictator reclaim his inheritance by wiring him some money, I found a letter from my mother wishing us well and telling me to make sure I took care of Megan.

I shot her off a quick reply, reminding her that I'd try to write when I could but she'd be lucky to get something once a week.

"I have no idea what to expect," I wrote. "I just pray our guides do."

FEAR ITSELF

I kept waiting to wake up from the bizarre dream I found myself in the next morning. The one that found me halfway around the world in Africa, after spending all of the money to my name and leaving the only life I ever knew back in Chicago. But it wasn't a dream. In a few short hours, I'd be putting my trust in African Wanderer, where it would need to stay for the duration of our travels across the wild continent.

Shit.

After a quick breakfast of some croissants (the number one staple of any cheap traveler), we exchanged all of our traveler's checks into probably the largest pile of U.S. currency I had ever seen at an exchange off the main strip. With all of my gear awkwardly strapped on, I transformed from man to turtle, my shell being the bulky, 40-liter hunter green backpack stuffed to capacity. A smaller, school-sized backpack, strapped across my chest, counterbalanced the crushing weight on my back at the expense of anything resembling mobility. With my treasured painting rolled precariously in my right hand, I either resembled the consummate traveler or the easiest target a crook could ever lay eyes on. The only thing missing to make the outfit complete would be a big, bold sign that read, 'Rob the stupid American.' Hell, I would rob me.

"Damn, this is far!" cursed Megan, who was just as immobile and frustrated.

"If we have to carry all of this...."

We didn't say much after that, concentrating instead on keeping our balance as we struggled to African Wanderer's office, each of us knowing that we were both one slip away from resembling a flipped turtle.

By the time we arrived at African Wanderer, the office was already pretty full—a large contingent was hungrily swarming around the makeshift breakfast table near the back of the room (of course, they were serving bread, too). Dropping her gear next to me, Megan checked us in while I navigated across the sea of backpacks to add ours to the pile.

"Look!" Megan whispered, smiling as she pointed to a hard metal, baby blue suitcase set at the base of Backpack Mountain.

A suitcase. It had to belong to a chick.

A few minutes passed before Derek emerged, dressed in the same khaki outfit from the previous night. With a cup of steaming coffee in one hand and his reliable clipboard in the other, he spoke loudly over the din of activity.

"This is it," Derek boomed as his eyes roved over the crowd.

"Grab your gear and wait outside, because we need to get started."

I could feel myself shaking slightly as I handed Megan her pack, then a nervous rumbling in my gut as I dragged my gear out the door behind her. I really was in Africa. This was really going to happen.

Dragging everything as near to the behemoth, sputtering truck parked up against the curb as we could, I remarked to Megan how uneasy and anxious everyone looked. Aubrey, whose blond hair and yellow T-shirt gave him a Charlie Brown-like quality, nervously bit his fingernails as he peered into the truck on his tiptoes. Meanwhile the older guy, looking perplexed, fretfully removed the green cap from his head as he whispered something to his wife. At least I wasn't alone.

The truck selected by African Wanderer for our journey had been affectionately christened Ella by the staff. Specifically, she was named after Ella Fitzgerald, in tribute to the late singer. African Wanderer named all of their trucks after late entertainment personalities—the well-hidden garage in the rear of the office, we were told, housed such luminaries as 'Janis' and 'Jimi' among others. It was a cool way to pay homage, but I might be hesitant to step into a truck named after James Dean or any celebrity who died in a fatal crash anytime soon.

In any case, Ella was an impressive sight—a custom-built, white BMW truck with a square front that would make a great battering ram in a pinch, a trait that could possibly be useful. Not only was it solidly built but comfortable as well—no reclining seats, but ten aisles of cushy, black bench seats with plenty of leg room, more than enough room for the group. Built into the walls, high above the seats was a series of sturdy shelves designed for luggage storage, appearing to offer ample room for all. Even that silly, blue suitcase.

Best of all, Ella had also been equipped with the several security measures we had been told about, making me feel a little better after taking Derek's warnings about crime and safety so seriously. Two floor safes—designed to hold everyone's money belt, passports, and any other vital documents—with thick, steel main doors that looked like something out of a state penitentiary were outfitted with a sturdy lock that could be bolted from the inside. Leaning forward, I rapped hard on the imposing door.

"No one can get in there," I told Megan, who had been watching my inspection.

"Yeah," she countered sullenly. "Now we just had to worry about not getting mauled by a lion."

I spotted Skonky around the back end of the truck, smoking a cigarette and talking to Charlie, who looked even pissier that morning. Skonky reminded me of a dwarf—short, barrel-chested, and with a ruddy complexion. He had an almost sinister grin when he smiled—due primarily to his jagged and crooked teeth. A floppy white hat sat low on his shaved head, and he wore a pair of oversized, hunter green shorts—nothing else. Skonky, like most guides we met, had this thing against wearing shoes. They never did.

Taking a final drag from his smoke, Skonky tossed the butt underneath the truck and sauntered over to the group, studying our faces as he approached.

"We'll be there by eleven this morning—stopping at a place called Clan William. We'll get there in a few hours and then you have the rest of the day for yourself. They have some cave paintings and other stuff, I guess."

With those inspiring words, spoken so dryly they would make a chemistry textbook sound thrilling, our leader headed off, walking back to his territory around the other side of the truck, still fighting an itch.

Sure. Clan William.

At least we had Rutger, our other guide who seemed almost inspired with enthusiasm. While Charlie crawled slowly off to her seat in the truck cab, Rutger, after a final nod from Derek, bounced forward through our group and merrily called out.

"This is it, guys! Bring all your stuff aboard, and we'll throw it on top. Then grab a seat—we're takin' off!"

An initial mad dash onto Ella ensued after Rutger's announcement—either out of concern of getting stuck in a crappy seat or the luggage not fitting above—but things were fairly orderly. Rutger moved with the precision of a master bricklayer, building walls from luggage with tremendous speed and accuracy.

"I've been doing this a long time," Rutger said with a smile. "Haven't had to leave anything behind yet."

Megan and I chose to sit together in the second row on the left side of the truck. I was under the impression that our seat selection would be like selecting one on the first day of school—once it's yours, it's yours, meaning pick a spot that you can find manageable. The Dutch guy, Aubrey, was already in the seat in front of us, and he seemed harmless enough—maybe a little gabby, but not bad. The dark-haired, slightly husky woman claimed the seat behind us, an American woman named Stacey. Travel-snob Stacey.

Just what is a travel snob, you ask? A travel snob gets some enjoyment out of traveling, but gains more by trying to feel superior and make you envious. Example: 'You haven't been to [destination]? You absolutely must...I know this delightful little place, blah, blah, blah.' It just really annoys me.

I'll never forget London a few years back, where Megan and I met up with a friend and one of his acquaintances, a local travel snob (yes, they exist all over the world). Anyway, I guess he saw himself as some restaurant critic because he was talking up all of this exotic cuisine he had sampled in Asia and then ripped on the United States.

"Restaurants in the United States are terrible—you can't find a good place to eat there," he shared.

Buddy, you live in London, home of probably the crappiest food in the world. What's the matter—there wasn't enough mayo on it?

In short, I hate travel snobs because they have an elitist attitude. And they don't stop, even if they find out you also had the opportunity to visit some place they were bragging about. If you think that minimizes things, think again.

"Where did you stay when you were there? You know, the BEST place to stay is [where they stayed, naturally]."

Maybe Stacey was seeking some comfort sitting near us on the truck, being that we were the only other Americans on the tour among a gang of Australians, a Swiss-German (Dominick) and the older couple from Canada.

I didn't have to wait too long for Stacey to chime in. After sitting down, she popped out a little travel mirror, half checking her make-up, half listening to Megan and I attempt to privately discuss our post-Africa itinerary. Like Pavlov's dog, travel snobs react to stimulus. In Stacey's case, it was the word 'Europe' that caused her to slouch forward, resting her arms on the back of our seat.

"So, like, where else were you before South Africa?" inquired Stacey, pulling back her black, shoulder length hair. God bless travel snobs.

Megan fielded it, knowing that I never really cared for any penis measuring exercises.

"Just Cape Town—we only got in a few days ago," Megan said cheerfully. "After this, it's Europe—Italy, Germany, and Amsterdam."

Stacey had popped the mirror shut and tossed it on her seat.

"Have you ever been to Cinque Terra?"

Here it comes....

"We want to," said Megan, lowering her voice, "but I think money's going to be a little tight. We're flexible; we'll see."

Stacey's countenance became instantly smug. She smelled blood.

"Go, you have to go," Stacey ordered as she dramatically pointed at Megan. "That's all I have to say. Find a way, because a trip to Italy is a waste without it."

American or not, I figured Stacey to be the biggest potential pain in the ass on the tour. A dark-complexioned woman in her late twenties, she carried nearly all of her weight around the midsection, leaving two bony, chicken-like legs the unenviable job of supporting her frame. She was a few inches too tall to be classified as 'stocky', but at least she chose loose-fitting clothes to keep everything covered. The way she carried herself, however, led me to believe she considered herself a very desirable woman. I was always all in favor of positive self-image, though sometimes even I didn't get where it really came from.

I chimed in and told Stacey something about maybe checking out Cinque—I didn't want to seem unsocial, even in the eyes of a travel snob.

Talking some more, we got the scoop on Stacey—she worked in New York as a recruiter for Japanese companies in the United States but left the gig because she hated her boss. She planned to see more of Africa when the tour ended, including a trek through Uganda to track gorillas. If I had to guess her favorite hobby however I'd say it had to be prying into other people's business. After meeting us for only a few minutes, she seemed uncomfortably interested in Megan and me, grilling us about how we met, if we were getting married any time soon, the usual prying questions reserved exclusively for family.

When the truck filled and Rutger stacked the last of the luggage above, he took a quick head count. I didn't spot the blue suitcase, which had to have been wisely placed somewhere else in case it teetered off the shelf during travel. We were all aboard—it wouldn't be long now. With a heavy thud, our warden Rutger dramatically pulled Ella's steel door shut and bolted it. Our sentence had begun.

Giving Skonky a thumbs-up through the glass separating the truck cab from us, Rutger took his place on a bench at the front of the truck as we pulled away from the curb. Slowly, we lumbered out of downtown Cape Town and into the great unknown.

Megan flashed me a quick smile, grabbing my arm and squeezing it.

"Africa, baby!" she said excitedly.

Yeah. Africa.

Searching through the daypack beneath my seat, I grabbed Moby Dick—the novel I had picked up for the trip—but decided against cracking it open just yet. For one, I hated reading in a moving vehicle—it always gave me an intense headache—besides, I wanted to take in as much scenery as I could. After all, I was in Africa. If I blinked, I feared I might miss a lion taking down an antelope, an elephant stampede, a cheetah chasing down its prey, or a similarly stunning wildlife spectacle seen peppered throughout every nature documentary.

Yet soon, I didn't know if we were even on a road anymore. Things had gotten so bumpy and suddenly mountainous that it didn't even look like Ella was headed down a clean path, instead she was carving out her own through the rocky, rough terrain. I watched Skonky weave Ella between shrubs, occasionally weaving too far to the left or to the right and jolting her to one side. Thick, brown clay spat out beneath her tires, spraying the dry grass. This makeshift African road was worse than any expressway back home. Even in Detroit. If anyone had managed to sleep during the trip, they weren't doing it now.

This was nothing new to Skonky—you could just tell. Glancing back to us whenever we hit a particularly rough stretch, he'd flash a knowing smile that said, "You probably didn't expect this, did you?" Despite his perceived recklessness, I was relieved to have a driver with Skonky's experience at the helm. With Skonky, I figured we'd get there eventually, but where 'there' was still seemed painfully out of reach. The journey continued; Ella skirted along the sides of a crumbling cliff, rocked herself through yet another muddy bog and blazed trails through seemingly undiscovered land. After hours spent crashing through unforgiving road, there were few signs of life, let alone a campground.

Finally, the shrubs parted and gave way to what may have actually once been a road. It had been so long since I spotted one, I couldn't be absolutely sure. Green, sprawling vegetation now merged with the occasional grayish rock formation, the tallest being nearly fifty feet tall. I pulled up my window—a cool wind was blowing through. Finally, after driving for what had to be at least another twenty minutes, a bearded white man in khakis emerged from the rocks, waving.

"We're here," Rutger boomed excitedly. "This will be home tonight."

Ella slowed to a halt. 'Home' looked pretty deserted to me.

The man in khakis, our host on this barren stretch of earth disguised as a campground, was an unassuming man named Dave, who we learned had purchased the land from his father-in-law to develop into a tourist attraction. But let me say, I don't think the Disney people have anything to worry about. Despite being so remote, we found it striking in its own, lonely sort of way. The cool wind crept along the lush, rolling vegetation as it danced and climbed between imposing rock buttresses. The calming tranquility of nature couldn't be denied.

Dave paced anxiously as we all climbed off the truck, occasionally bending the rim on the white, worn pith helmet he carried in his right hand. For my money, he could not look any more like the stereotypical big game hunter—at least according to the image I had in my mind of what one SHOULD look like. A slightly tan man in his fifties with a patch of reddish hair on his head; his eyes were blue and cold, the eyes of a man who had stared down death on a daily basis. He appeared pleasant enough when Skonky and Rutger greeted him.

Skonky skulked forward with Charlie, arms crossed as she looked to the ground, in tow.

"Before ya go runnin' off," Skonky intoned, playing with his cigarette lighter, "ya better put up your tents. It'll be dark soon."

We followed a motioning Rutger to the driver's side of Ella, who unscrewed a latch beneath her belly that reveled a dozen or so dusty sacks, each one crudely numbered with black marker. I grabbed #9, Megan grabbed a bag of poles, and we set off to make our home for the night.

For the most part, the groups paired off as expected. Yep, every woman wanted to be in the enfeebled Canadian guy's tent but he chose his wife—what a guy. Aside from them, Matt teamed with Connor, his Aussie mate; Bill shared with Aubrey, Stacey and Mary, the Australian woman paired up, leaving Dominick on his own, which aside from setting up the tent by yourself, was probably the best choice one could make. Megan and I made sure we chose a tent site that was going to work (by the bathrooms, of course) and attacked it quickly. The slightly dusty tent had seen many days without a doubt, but it went up easy enough and was larger than any tent we had slept in before.

Once every couple erected their tent, attention was shifted to something of the most direct importance—food. Everyone wondered aloud about what Charlie would be preparing for our first, hearty African lunch. All three members of the African Wanderer crew had already begun moving the cooking equipment into a clearing surrounded by rock formations just west of our tents, and though we would let them retain their secrecy, we just hoped it would be an elaborate production.

"Mmmmm," started Mary, with stomach pushed forward and hands on her hips. "I'm looking forward to a big lunch."

"As long as there's meat," added Dominick. "I just need some meat." He craned his neck towards the clearing.

Megan reminded everyone about how African Wanderer talked up the meal preparation the previous night at the orientation meeting.

"I'm sure there'll be enough, because they must know how hungry we are," reassured Megan. "I can't stand this waiting, though."

One by one, the group slowly trickled into the clearing to sneak a peak at what the crew was preparing. I think Dominick went first. Though no one dared to ask, by all appearances it was promising, with Rutger chopping cucumbers and ripe, red tomatoes on a makeshift cutting board while Skonky shook a juice container like it was a can of paint. I couldn't see what Charlie was fussing over, but I could tell by her muttering it wasn't going well.

Before long, lunchtime was officially declared. I knew this day would be special—not only was it my 30th birthday, but it marked the inaugural appearance of a true African Wanderer classic—the TLC sandwich. TLC, as in tomato, lettuce and cucumber served on white bread.

I felt my stomach die. Is this it? IS THIS IT?!? Guys...did you forget the lunchmeat? Please tell me it's hiding somewhere....

Despite our ravenous hunger, we all traded confused glances with one another as we looked over the sparse lunch before us. We could have started taking food but the shock stopped us cold. Was this going to be as good as it gets?!? Why didn't I buy more candy at the airport? Travel snob Stacey gave one of her trademark "You have GOT to be kidding me" looks, complete with coy smile and hair flipping. Dominick, a man without the meat he had been craving, walked undetected to the makeshift kitchen area, searching for something, anything that might have walked the earth at one time to put between his bread. Megan let out a weak whimper.

Aubrey, the Dutch guy, tore into the food first, slapping down four slices of bread on his plate and stacking them high with everything he could find. If someone was going to starve, it wasn't going to be him. Bill followed with the same gusto, though it took him annoyingly long to prepare his sandwiches, resembling a gourmet chef who has to get that garnish just right. You could just feel the eyes of the group on whoever was up their preparing their food, watching, waiting, and planning. Luckily for Meg and I, we weren't too far back behind these guys, because who knew if there would even be enough food? I settled for one TLC and one peanut butter sandwich—I got on a protein kick when I started working out before we left and knew that peanut butter was really the only choice. After scarfing the two sandwiches down, I felt drained. And worst of all, still hungry. If this was a sign of things to come, we were all in trouble.

In a short time, the luncheon table was looted of everything edible. Both Skonky and Rutger showed tremendous constraint by waiting for the group to take their food and then help themselves, while Charlie munched away on a few tomatoes slices. Bill and Aubrey were assigned clean-up duties for the day, meaning they were to wash the items used for lunch and dinner meal preparation, and we were all individually responsible for cleaning our dishes. I just hoped that everyone would be as conscientious as I had planned to be when it came to washing what we used—the chilled dishwater would do little in the way of disinfection.

After lunch, we were on our own, so to speak—though in reality there is precious little you can do in the middle of the African bush. Megan and I did bring along our decks of standard playing cards and Uno, but after playing both games for hours on end on the flight to Cape Town, it didn't really seem like an option. We decided instead to join the milling crowd that had congregated near, conveniently enough, our tent site. Megan went ahead while I ducked into the tent to put long pants on—it was getting quite chilly, believe it or not.

By the time I met up with Megan, the bitch session regarding lunch was in full effect. Everyone was there except the guides, who climbed back on the truck to nap. I considered taking a short hike in the bush, but with my poor sense of direction and the lack of unique landmarks, I probably would never be heard from again.

Yes, the United Nations had assembled in Africa that afternoon, with delegates from the United States, Canada, Australia, the Netherlands and Switzerland all complaining about hunger in Africa—our own.

"A little meager, wasn't it?" asked Mary, scanning the group for affirmation. Maybe we were all still a little in shock or just down about it all—a collective mumble was the response.

It was during this first group meeting that I truly realized how annoying Mary, the Australian schoolteacher, could be. Did our collective grumbling shut her up? Of course not—there are people in this world—

everyone knows them—who talk only to be heard and have absolutely nothing to say. That was Mary, holding court and running at the mouth about everything from what a wonderful physical education teacher she was in Perth ("The kids just love me—I've been told I have a gift"), to her battles with acid reflux and a variety of other physical ailments, to the time she met Anson Williams, television's Potsie, during a visit to the United States. ("He's even more handsome in person!")

I had to wonder what life with Mary Rose is like on a day-to-day basis. That nasally, irritating voice that seemed to rise towards the end of each sentence; the underlying bitterness she had towards men (she was a single schoolteacher, after all), her inane conversations.... You couldn't listen to her without rolling your eyes—it was impossible.

Some good did come out of Mary's forced conversation that afternoon—everyone else then started talking, if for no other reason than to silence Mary. True, no one else could regale the group with an exciting, clandestine meeting with a star of "Happy Days," but the group was not lacking interesting characters.

Take Matt and Connor, for example, two of the Aussie guys who would be with us only through Victoria Falls. Both were onboard to blow off a little steam—Matt, a student in his early twenties, would be getting married to his girlfriend of several years when he returned home. Connor, a twenty eight-year-old diesel mechanic, was looking for space from his girlfriend back home, who had started turning up the heat and talking of marriage. I liked Connor—he had a goofy smile and a way about him that just made you feel welcome. There was something about Matt, though—he came across as sort of a pompous prick, lecturing Connor about how we shouldn't run from love and the like. Matt would come across like he meant well, but I suspected that whole pseudo-sensitive guy shtick was just an act. It was pretty transparent to me at least.

Bill, the remaining Aussie guy, made no qualms about his hopes for the trip. With Africa being the first stop on a worldwide journey that would last for nearly two years and carry him throughout Europe, South America, North America and Asia, he didn't even attempt to hide one of his obsessions.

"Women. This trip's gonna be a party just crawlin' with women," Bill said, biting his lower lip. He was eager to explain what he knew about overland tours like the one we were on, like how all the operators traveled the same route and there had to be another ten to twelve trucks easy we would be meeting up with over the next six weeks. Bill saw it as a chance to get to know female travelers pretty well.

"I'm ready for a good time," Bill added, adjusting the slipping bandana tightly around his head.

Bill didn't strike me as a lothario by his appearance—barrel-chested, wide-faced and dark, thinning hair—but he had the confidence, no doubt about it. Not to generalize, since I had never met anyone from the Australian quadrant prior to this trip, but the men all seemed to radiate machismo—or maybe I was confusing all of them for Paul Hogan.

Bill, though technically a New Zealander, was graciously allowed entrance into the Aussie clique of Matt, Connor and Mary. The opportunity never crossed my mind to counter with an American clique. For one, with Megan, Stacey and myself, we would still be outnumbered four to three. We could have made a North American clique I guess, which would give us a five to four advantage since we would gain the Canadians, but it wouldn't work. They were, after all, Canadians and pretty neutral.

Speaking of our friendly neighbors to the North, you did have to tip your hat to them. When the conversation did the occasional drift towards sex, drugs and the usual off-color comment, Helen just took it and smiled, arm wrapped around Abe's waist. Abe seemed a little cold and unemotional, taking it all in and probably wishing he could scold us and tell our parents. There was definitely a creepiness factor. The sensation that you were being chaperoned by your grandparents was inescapable. I mean, they were ripped straight from a Norman Rockwell painting. Helen, a registered nurse, was a little plump with stark white hair and a pair of tiny glasses perched on the end of her nose. Poor Abe was semi-retired and moved around like he was in a lot of pain—very stiff. He had the look of a stern grandfather—with piercing eyes that penetrated his wire-rimmed glasses. And like most old guys, he wore a pin-covered cap. I never understood the male fascination with hats, but thankfully, my hair wasn't close to becoming thin.

Abe stood very stiff during our post-lunch pow-wow, at times grimacing in pain while he reached behind his back. If he was in pain now, I figured he'd be pretty ferocious when we finally made it to Kenya, not to mention how sore Helen would be from doing all the work. There was no way tent life would agree with him; I could almost picture Helen unfolding him like a pair of pressed pants every morning, just one more of the long list of chores she probably had to do.

Dominick seemed a little shy—only nodding his head in agreement when the travesty referred to as lunch was mentioned. Picture an emaciated David Bowie, complete with blond, flowing hair drooped into his face, and that's Dominick, hardly looking like a guy with a voracious appetite. When I overhead him tell someone that he was a student in Switzerland and had been traveling through Africa for some time, I briefly wondered if his frail appearance meant he was already in starvation mode.

How I filled the time between lunch and dinner that first day was pretty non-eventful, split between hanging out with the group, unpacking some gear, and wandering around within the confines of camp. I soon found out this waiting was sometimes the norm. For personal safety concerns, you couldn't exactly go for an unguided walk through the African bush, and once the sun went down, a flashlight could only do so much. I'll never forget how completely dark it became at night with the absence of artificial light; they were the blackest nights I had ever witnessed.

As the sun began to set, I noticed campground host and opportunist Dave setting up a sad, makeshift bar inside our little cove that would have made Fred Flintstone proud, using a flattened rock as a counter and balancing beer bottles ever so gingerly on its layered surface. This too, we had been told, was also Africa—campsite managers constructing rustic taverns and doing whatever else they could to get a couple extra bucks out of us. I couldn't fault him—maybe all the heavy drinking was out of boredom like I'd heard went on in Alaska, too.

"Check it out," I told Megan, who briefly side-stepped from the debate she had been engaged in with Stacey about the best hotels in Japan.

"Good idea, but I can't say I really want to drink tonight."

"Ohmygod!" erupted Stacey when she noticed the bar. "They have Smirnoff! Bad ass!"

The great debate about the most decadent stays in Japan would have to wait. Megan shook her head and smiled as Stacey sauntered over to the bar, inspecting the label of an African beer before finally settling on her Smirnoff mixer. Drinking alcohol just didn't feel like something I wanted to do on the first night, not when I still didn't know what to expect entirely. Besides, I was the type of person who never saw the point to just having a beer or two—it was all or nothing, and tonight it would be nothing.

Maybe it was just the arrogance of youth, but some of the guys, particularly Bill, Matt and Connor, didn't share my sentiment one bit. They drowned away their concerns with the occasional vodka shot while sampling the local beers. Skonky, who along with Rutger had begun stirring again after their mid-afternoon nap, joined in, looking even more sinister with every sip.

If anyone could have benefited from a belt of alcohol, it was Megan, who grew more nervous as the sun slowly disappeared. I knew our first night tenting in Africa wouldn't be easy.

"I want you to sleep on the east side of the tent—just in case," Megan said with a touch of fear in her voice.

"In case? In case of what?"

"I heard there are leopards here!" she paused. "Dave told me. I want to be near the front, closer to the road."

"So what about me? What if the leopards come for me?" I asked, half-putting her on. "Then what?"

"Hey," she said cheekily. "This was your idea. I wanted to go to India!"

A smell of rich, exotic spice wafted through the air—it had to be dinner, and it smelled simply delicious. Megan had asked if I wanted to go and play cards in the tent, but we both decided it would be foolhardy to leave the kitchen area with the whole group already present and just as hungry as we were. Have you ever been tortured with the smell of food, compelled to walk up to the kettle and check on it yourself, hoping that your mere presence will expedite things and finally get you that meal of desire? That's exactly how I felt. C'mon, Rutger—fuck the bread...check on the pot...it may need more coals! What are you doing anyway, Skonky!

Abe stood like a soldier; his gaze fixed on the boiling brew inside the cast iron kettle. Aubrey and Dominick, our two biggest eaters, stood next to each other, keeping one eye on the food preparation and the other on one another. Mary, Bill, Matt and Connor stood as close to the serving table as possible—sometimes pretending to be engaged in conversation but always staying focused on the prize—food.

I thought about my birthday—reaching thirty years old in the middle of nowhere had a weird feeling to it. I guess on some level, even though I knew we would be in Africa on my birthday, I had expected things to be a little more comfortable. Yet here we were, shivering around a glowing pot with a group of strangers, hoping that the rain could at least hold off until we had a chance to eat. I had to laugh to myself—a few short weeks ago we would have handled such a day by renting a movie and curling up in bed.

As Rutger swaggered over the cast-iron pot, tending to it as a mother would her child, head cook Charlie finally made an appearance, dragging herself slowly through the hungry crowd before stopping just short of the wet, burning wood. Megan poked me lightly in the ribs.

"It's quite alright, Charlie," Rutger told her, just before dancing away from a long, reaching finger of flame. Rutger didn't believe in shoes, either.

"Whatever," Charlie mumbled as she rolled her eyes.

Retreating back through the crowd, Charlie dropped herself into a chair next to Skonky, who made himself busy by chopping a few celery stalks. Sitting on her throne like a pouting queen, Charlie kept her eyes on the dancing flames.

"Head cook, huh?" Megan said sarcastically. "Why's she even here?"

My attention remained fixed on Rutger, who had assumed the role of head cook for the time being with a great deal of gusto, darting back and forth through the wavering bonfire and laughing when the heat became a little too close. We all sat mesmerized—as entranced by the spectacle of the licking flames as we were with the fantastic, fragrant smells escaping from beneath the lid.

"You guys look pretty hungry," Rutger called out, grinning as he spun the ladle through the brewing contents of our dinner.

"Oops—ruined it!" he joked, pushing away from the pot on his heels. "No dinner tonight!"

Minutes that felt like hours painfully slipped by, with my hunger becoming more ravenous with every passing moment. Finally, after removing the ladle briefly to taste, Rutger threw his hands on hips, studied our hungry eyes one last time and took a long, deliberate step back.

"Food's done! Chicken curry for all!"

Dominick and Aubrey were on the fiery pot before Rutger even finished speaking. I think Dominick got there first, actually, as the promise of meat was all the motivation he needed to find the front of the line. Megan and I, boxed out by the others, brought up the rear, trying to block out the torturously tantalizing smells of the aromatic curry as we did our best to wait patiently. Pretty quickly, this concept got pretty old, especially after seeing how everyone seemed to dawdle once it became their turn to dish themselves up. What was so damn difficult? You take some noodles, throw them on the plate. Take some chicken curry, throw that on the plate. Done. Watching Bill was nearly infuriating, as he painstakingly layered the noodles evenly, then meticulously ladled on the chicken before dressing it all with salt, pepper and the like.

"C'mon, man," I said under my breath, though Megan heard me.

"Let's go, Bill," Stacey sternly barked, spinning the plate she had prematurely picked up through her hands. After a quick glance at her reflection in it, she took a deep sigh.

When our turn in line finally did arrive, I understood better what the hold-up had been; specifically how tricky it was to fish a ladle through the fiery mixture with only the light of Skonky's tiny flashlight as a guide. But if fishing out the chicken curry was tricky, then finding it with your fork and then transferring it to your mouth was downright difficult, requiring the same care I imagined a steel worker used to avoid getting burned by anything hot and molten.

For as difficult as it was eating in the pitch dark that night, the wonderful-tasting chicken curry made it worth the wait. The hot, nourishing dish was absolutely perfect for such a damp, cold night. And it was getting extremely cold. London winter cold.

"Do I have any on my face?" Megan would ask me every now and then through the darkness. I used to assume that when she asked that question of me, it usually meant that MY face was the one that resembled a used placemat.

"You're good…" I replied, quickly brushing my own face as I strained to locate her face in the darkness. "I think."

Surrounded in virtual darkness as Megan and I huddled close to one another to stay warm, our first night in Africa had already offered us the unexpected. Even with the fair amount of camping we had done in some of the more remote sections of the Midwest, it was nothing like the deep, dark night around us. I shivered momentarily, as I imagined getting lost, stumbling through the blinding, black night of the African bush alone.

The ladle echoed loudly as it banged against the quickly emptying pot, just as Dominick returned for a third, smaller helping. Before he got there Matt, Connor and myself attacked the chicken for seconds. I wasn't stuffed, but I was full in a nice way.

Aubrey was no slouch either, and I figured if anyone could challenge Dominick for the title of 'biggest eater' our friend from the Netherlands wouldn't be too far behind. As he scraped what appeared to be possibly a whole chicken off his plate, Aubrey addressed Skonky, who had since sat down with the group with a plateful of prized chicken curry for himself, leaving Charlie slumped back in her chair alone.

"So when are you going to tell us about tomorrow?" Aubrey asked bluntly, spitting small remnants of chewed chicken as he spoke. Like most Europeans, he got straight to the matter—perhaps out of necessity, perhaps unfamiliar with tact.

Skonky nodded in acknowledgement towards Aubrey as he swallowed a forkful of curry—he didn't appear to be bothered a bit by the cold weather, still barefoot and bare-chested but now wearing a black wool hat on his head. First taking a sip of water from the plastic tumbler at his feet, Skonky rose from his chair and addressed the group.

"I hope you're all enjoyin' your dinner," Skonky started, "but I just want to take a few minutes to tell you the plan for tomorrow." A hush fell over the group—this was still so very new to us that we all knew we'd better listen up. He continued, "We're getting up by six tomorrow—we got us a long day's drive into Namibia and have to be all packed and ready to leave at seven," he said with the authority of a drill sergeant.

He dug into his pockets for his lighter and lit the cigarette that had been resting behind his right ear. Skonky took a long drag, and then looked down.

"You're going to like Namibia—we're staying at a nice campsite, and you're going to go on a nice canoe trip the following day. Bush camping," said Skonky, watching an ash fall to the sandy ground. "Any questions?"

Connor, scraping the ladle inside the curry pot one final time, whirled around. "Yeah," bellowed Connor. "What's bush camping?"

Skonky smiled knowingly. He enjoyed questions like that.

"You're allowed one day-bag on the canoe, and we sleep under the stars—no tent, no sleeping bags, nothing extra."

"Any more questions?"

Silence, before Mary asked probably what we all thought but were afraid to ask.

"Is it safe?"

"Yeah," chuckled Skonky, throwing a smile towards Rutger who returned it. "There's nothing out there."

Skonky, lighting another cigarette, went on to tell us that the Namibia canoe trip was one of the highlights of the entire six weeks, complete with sleeping on a beautiful beach under an enormous, star-filled sky. I didn't know how I felt about not being in a tent—especially if it would be as chilly as it was tonight—but it sounded good to me.

So much for vacation, though...getting up at 6 a.m.? Though I was admittedly more of a morning person than most, hurrying out of camp just to sit on Ella for the better part of a day was not my idea of fun.

The group, at least for that night anyway, seemed interested in getting to bed early; it was so cold that few saw it worthwhile to shiver over the bar, despite the fact that some of the guys were still in that stage that they thought they had to prove something to one another. The group slowly dispersed—I think Helen and Abe were first, which didn't surprise me all too much. More bored than tired, we, too, decided it was time.

Megan and I split up to do our nightly toiletry thing—the tooth brushing, the pit stop, and the usual. Then, with that completed, we met back at the tent and prepared for our first night's rest in the middle of uninhabited Africa.

Immediately appearing nervous, Megan said very little once we zipped the tent shut, hunkering down on her "safe" side of the tent and listening for noises. The inside of the tent was almost as dark as it was outside—

the double-layered fabric doors blocked out every trace of light, making it necessary to temporarily string our lone flashlight up from the middle of the tent while we got situated.

Both burrowing into our sleeping bags—me in my comfy Nebo and Megan in a light purple-colored bag with a crappy zipper that she had bought overseas a few years back. The zipper was just the worst, getting split and stuck at the worst times, like whenever you used it. It could not have been warm. In fact, I knew it wasn't.

"Are you warm enough?" Megan asked meekly as she buried herself so deep into her bag that only the top of her hair protruded out of it.

"Yeah, I'm pretty good—this bag is nice," I said. I was afraid to ask, but I figured I had to—it was the boyfriend thing to do, after all.

"And you?"

"Can I come in?" Megan asked sweetly.

Nope, I thought to myself. No way! I couldn't sleep that way—I never could. I knew women like holding onto their men when they slept, but rarely did it work for me. All I ever got out of it was being too cramped, too crowded and being kept awake by someone breathing right into my face.

I heard Megan sigh deliberately from across the tent as I thought things over in my head. She knew she had me right where she wanted me.

"Sure," I mumbled. "C'mon in."

Damn, damn, damn!

Zipping my bag down to the bottom, Megan wedged her way into the base with her bag still wrapped around her, throwing the rest of my bag around herself. Tight and uncomfortable, even I grew cold as I contended with the open flap from letting her inside.

At least she was happy, I told myself, and I didn't mind taking a bullet every now and then for her, since she never asked me for much to begin with. Plus I had camped with Megan enough to know that I probably wouldn't be getting much sleep anyway.

Case in point: just as I could feel my body finally relaxing, Megan pushed off me and sat erect—clutching the sleeping bag in her hands.

"What's that!?!" she whispered excitedly. "I can hear it walking around!"

Flipping the flashlight on, Megan held her finger over her lips while we sat quietly and listened. Nothing.

"I don't hear anything," I whispered back.

"What did it sound like?"

"You never hear anything!" she barked with urgency in her voice.

"But I know what I heard. Something was breathing against the tent—a big animal."

OK, I thought to myself. You got me. I'll turn on the ol' charm—reassure her that nothing would come into camp with so many of us around, that we were safe in the tent, and that before we knew it morning would come. Then I heard it, too.

<vvvvvvvttttttttttttttttttt>

I stopped suddenly, feeling my heart pound hard in my chest. I heard something too—something that sounded like it was stealthily moving around outside. Could it be right outside the tent? It sounded like it was.

While my mind went racing trying to create a composite sketch of the marauding culprit, I heard that initial, startling sound again.

<vvvvvvvttttttttttttttttttt>

Breathing? Scratching? Oh God, we are so not ready for this!

"What should we do?" asked a panicking Megan as her breath pounded from her chest. "Should we make a break for the truck?"

I shook my head.

"It's probably not open," I countered. "And the last thing you want to do is be seen running from it."

"Let's just lie still and try to sleep."

We laid back down and before long, I heard the steady breathing of Megan's light snores. Once she was asleep, I knew I would be to. If I didn't have to go to the bathroom.

Holding it until morning was completely out of the question. I had to take care of things on my mind before I could fall asleep, whether it was wrestling with a dripping faucet or in this case, finding the nearest bush. And it was going to be a bush—it was too dark and too cold outside to begin an expedition for the elusive chemical toilet. I just hoped our tent was at the bottom of a slope or I'd end up drowning us.

Megan stirred a little as I extricated myself from the bag, throwing on my jeans and my sandals. Very little.

"Meg," I whispered. "I'm going to the bathroom."

She replied with a mumble and rolled over, taking the rest of my sleeping bag with her. That's my girl. The prospect of falling victim to the unknown terror outside had long been wiped away by sleep.

With slow precision, I carefully undid the tent zipper. I started to drag the tent bottom with my left foot as I climbed out, and then slowly emerged from the green tent flap and into the night with flashlight in hand.

Still in a crouched position, I maneuvered the flashlight beam around the entire perimeter of our tent. A tiny Duracell won't exactly light up a jungle, but I figured if the beam didn't return a set of watching eyes, I would make my move to the little bush about fifteen feet away. Taking a deep breath I made my move, attempting to walk to the bush confidently and with purpose but instead scurried to it just as I reached the halfway point.

But I made it. I let my member flop out just enough and got my hands in position—one hand to pull my pants up at a moment's notice, the other on the Duracell, which I used to keep scanning the entire area around me. Was that a leopard we heard back in the tent? Maybe it was watching me right now, I thought. Maybe it's in the bush—ready to slash me as soon as I begin!

I slowly crept forward into the bush with my exposed penis, eyes darting back and forth. Another deep breath and I let it flow, just hoping that I wouldn't suddenly see a pair of red eyes staring back at me or, worse yet, a clawed paw slashing down onto my manhood. I thought I heard something rustling in the distance—probably the wind, but I wasn't going to stick around to find out. I shook off when I finished and scampered back to the tent, vulnerable like I was being watched the entire time. Climbing into the tent feet first, I spun around and slowly zippered the flaps shut.

Megan jumped into a sitting position.

"There's that noise again! Something's out there!"

I paused for a second, and then realized I hadn't finished zipping up the tent so I pulled it in one quick motion.

<vvvvvvvttttttttttttttttt>

We found our leopard. It was the zippers on the tent.

ROUTINE

A dull, throbbing ache flooded my head when I rolled over to grab the alarm clock. Still completely pitch black inside the tent, it could have been the middle of afternoon and I'd have no way of knowing. Fumbling as I searched for the flashlight, I pried it gently from Megan's right hand, where I figured it had been clenched tightly the entire night. Poor Megan. Despite discovering that the tent zipper was the only thing spooking us, she still must have had a hard time relaxing and getting some rest. I stopped counting at one point, but I figured she must have woken up at least a half-dozen more times after that, scaring herself half-to-death each time.

"There's something outside!" "Do you hear that?" "What do we do?"

I think even Megan finally gave up after a certain point—maybe growing exhausted from being so afraid. But my sleep was just as restless—sharing my sleeping bag seemed like a tender moment but it was highly uncomfortable. My left arm, the one that served as Megan's impromptu pillow, fell asleep more often than I did throughout the night.

As I slowly clicked the flashlight on, Megan's eyes half-opened for the briefest second before, seeing it was me, she shut them tight again.

"What time is it?" she mumbled, rolling away in both sleeping bags.

"I'm checking."

Feeling with my hands around the interior of the tent, I searched for the elusive alarm clock I thought I had placed next to the laundry bag that doubled as my pillow. Camping with me was never pretty.

"It's 5:30," I told her in a quiet voice. "You got a half-hour."

I'm not sure if Megan heard me or not—her heavy breathing could have been sighs of disappointment or snoring.

With my entire sleeping bag now claimed by Megan, who looked like a large, purple jelly roll, I knew my chances of getting back to sleep wouldn't be very favorable. Now awake a full half-hour before anyone else, it was the perfect chance for a quick shower.

Gathering the clothes I had worn the previous night from the floor of the tent, I moved quickly. I reached for my shirt, piled in the far corner of the tent, and winced as I felt tightness in my back. God, I hated sleeping in tents. So much for being the outdoorsman.

By the time I got back to our tent, most of the tents appeared to be stirring with some sort of activity. Helen and Abe spoke in hushed voices; Helen asking Abe about how well he slept last night. The walls of Stacey's tent were expanding and contracting—she must've been getting ready, too. Bill was laughing about something—I couldn't see him but I heard his demonic cackling. And Megan? With our tent silent and unshaken, I figured she must still have been sound asleep—savoring every possible second of rest she could manage to wring out of the morning.

As I went to the truck to scrounge for a fresh change of clothes, I ran into Rutger, who was removing a plastic crate filled with cereal and the like from the back of the truck.

"Good morning, Paul," Rutger said, cheerfully as always. "Did we sleep well last night?"

Charlie, still looking half-asleep with her eyes nearly shut, seemed to at least be making an effort that morning, carrying a crate low to the ground as she followed Rutger.

"It was alright," I said. "But pretty damn cold. And Megan kept me up a little bit, too."

He let loose a sly, knowing smile. "We're going to have to keep an eye on you two!"

I figured I'd let him live with that illusion. Rutger mentioned that breakfast was ready and that he'd start waking everyone shortly so I figured I'd better get moving myself. I watched him carry the crate into the same cove where we ate lunch and dinner and spotted Skonky, who was slouched in a metal chair wearing only those same green shorts and a floppy hat covering his face.

I went back to the tent and climbed back in without even attempting to be quiet—I mean, it was time to get up, and I wanted to have a nice, long breakfast without having to worry about packing everything away at the last minute. And that meant Megan had to wake up.

"What time is it?" moaned Megan as I stumbled through the door flap. Blindly, she tried wiping away some hair from her mouth.

"Time to get up," I said as I pulled my fresh, blue shirt on over my head. "Breakfast is ready."

The tent started being shaken from the outside and we heard Rutger's booming voice.

"Alright you guys," Rutger said. "Let's get up and get out!"

Megan refused to stir, lying still like she always did when she teetered along that fine line between sleep and staying awake. I gave her a few minutes, then told her I was going to eat "while there were still pancakes left." A cruel trick, since I didn't see much more than dry cereal and some hard-looking bread.

Megan threw on her clothes from last night and laboredly climbed out of the tent behind me, probably picturing a Denny's breakfast. Instead she found one of the most unimpressive breakfasts around—a choice of rice krispies or bran flakes and white bread with the usual spreads of peanut butter, jam and butter.

The chairs, left out from last night and still in a circular shape, were about half-filled—Dominick, Mary, Helen, Abe and Matt. Proceeding to the dish tray to grab Megan and I some clean utensils, I quickly discovered finding a set you'd want to eat off of was the biggest challenge yet. That was the problem with putting everyone in charge of cleaning their own silverware and plates—not everyone had the same idea of hygiene. For some, hygiene is an immaculately sterile knife and fork—for others, it meant a knife that was probably licked a few times to get the bulk of the food off it then put in the tray for its next victim. After a few minutes of frustrating scrounging, Megan and I managed to find two knives and two forks that looked clean enough, though we still thought it best to wash them ourselves before we used them, anyway. If only it was that easy.

The "fresh" dishwater that morning—in the same green, rectangular tub from the previous night—was a foul, brackish, brown color with yellow, foamy bubbles on top. I didn't even want to stick my hand in it, let alone pretend that something dipped into it could possible be clean. The sour, sulfuric stench rising up from it would have probably made me lose my appetite if I wasn't already so damn hungry.

We ate breakfast rather quickly—Megan wanted to shower and I needed to tear down the tent. If only I had known how cold it could be in Africa, I would have brought along my thick, winter gloves. My fingers ached bitterly from the numbing cold made worse when it came to wrestling the heavy, wet canvas tent off from the metal grommets. Dismantling the metal frame first, I noticed Abe, the old Canadian guy, observing my progress as his wife, directly behind him, attacked their tent, wincing as she forced a rusted tent pole from its hole. He was unbelievable, hunched over slightly with his hands folded behind his back while Helen, on her hands and knees, resembled a hungry dog attacking a bone. That was Abe, I guess. Sore back or not, he wasn't even interested in pulling his own weight.

After ditching the tent into Ella's underbelly compartment, we lugged the rest of our gear onto the truck and climbed aboard to reclaim our spots, where we found Mary and Helen, each positioned in the middle of the aisle as they stuffed their gear overhead. And of course, even though both women could have stored their belongings anywhere, both had elected, for whatever reason, to use the space above our seats, completely blocking our path.

Though her back was to us, Helen must have heard us heading down the aisle, as she instantly flashed an acknowledging smile as she ducked into an adjacent empty row so we could pass. Mary, oblivious to us as she removed a yellow shirt from her green backpack, had continued on with some story she had been relating to Helen that we had thankfully missed the bulk of. After subtly clearing my throat, Mary sheepishly smiled and followed Helen's lead, bouncing herself further down the aisle until Megan and I ducked into our row.

"Get up there, guys," said Rutger, pushing on Connor's left shoulder as he approached the steps up to the truck.

Connor moaned a little during his ascent. His eyes barely open, he still looked asleep. Matt, not looking much better, playfully plucked Mary's straw hat from her head as he made his way to the back of the truck.

As Charlie climbed unenthusiastically into the truck, we gave our host, David, who stood on the left side of the makeshift road that brought us in, a final wave. My mind drifted slightly as Skonky guided the truck back through the unmarked bush, wondering how shitty things would get if our guides had managed to get us lost. As if on cue, a large, heavy bump shot Ella high into the air, rocking the entire cab and sending many of the sleeping bags that had been stuffed overhead spilling into the center aisle.

"This must be the right way," I told Megan as we covered our heads in fallout position.

Aside from the excitement of Rutger rushing over to re-stack the stray luggage, things were almost eerily quiet on the truck for the first couple of hours. A few of us cheered slightly the moment our truck met up with a bona fide, two-lane road again, but after that moment of jubilation, I think everyone became either sleepy or bored. Or, if they were like me, they were busy trying to figure out how they had gotten into this mess in the middle of nowhere in the first place.

"So," I said, slapping Megan on the knee. "This is Africa, I guess."

Laughing nervously, she then grabbed my knee.

"Baby," she began after a deep sigh. "I just hope we make it."

Megan drifted off to asleep soon after that. I couldn't really blame her—the scenery, about as interesting as a roomful of accountants, wasn't doing it for me, either. On this particular day, the theme outside the window appeared to be 'shrub'—one ugly, dry shrub lined up in single file after another across some of the most barren land imaginable. The oddest thing was that this land—as dry and sandy as it appeared—not only supported this shrub life, but that it was also entirely fenced off and used for grazing. As I saw what looked like a tumbleweed blow across a field and entwine itself in steel mesh, I couldn't help but wonder how well a farmer could possible do for himself here. According to Rutger, who never seemed to grow tired of watching the miles pass outside the window, the appearance was deceiving.

"Those little bushes out there," he said, extending a long, tanned arm toward the windows, "are very nutritious for livestock. They have these little green beads on them that animals find quite delicious."

Having Rutger in the rear of the truck with us was a godsend in those early days of our trek. He had so much enthusiasm for what he was doing—wanting to share every little African nugget he had with the entire group—that it almost became infectious. His eyes would light up like a child on Christmas morning when he would point out an usual native plant in the distance or recount some obscure tidbit about African history.

He always sat alert, perched on his bench with one knee resting beneath him, ready to jump up and point out the next landmark.

Even with Rutger, my enthusiasm continued to wane. The scenery never looked the slightest bit different—shrub, shrub and another shrub. And all of it looked way too sparse to find any sort of life lurking within it.

I think Skonky honestly thought he was helping relieve our tedium when he popped in that really bad cassette tape of techno garbage to take our minds off things. I guess it did work—instead of being depressed with the barren landscape outside, I wanted to murder Skonky for popping the short, horrible cassette back in as soon as it ended, making our audible assault an endless, horrible loop. Does anyone really need a hip-hop version of "Country Roads?"

I felt my eyes grow heavy as the outside scenery bounced past. Suddenly feeling a light tap on my shoulder, I turned quickly.

"Have one," Stacey said, lifting the small, mesh sack of oranges that shared the seat next to her.

"They're really juicy!"

"Those are safe to eat...right?" I said, leaning over my seat as I glanced at the innocent-looking sack, filled with maybe ten, small oranges.

Stacey smiled and shrugged.

"I guess so...yeah," she replied. "I'm not dead or anything, and I've been eating them all day."

Politely, I declined, just as I spotted Matt gingerly moved towards the front of the truck with a deck of slightly worn playing cards—he had now discovered the joys of spending the day barefoot, also. A bump from Ella nearly spilled him into Dominick's lap, who was fast asleep, but Matt righted himself and finally rested on Rutger's bench. I couldn't make out what he was saying to Rutger, but before long, Matt waved Connor up to the front and a card game broke out between Mary and the three of them. I didn't recognize the game but it seemed like a good time—lots of laughs while cards were tossed in a flurry of color. That is, until attention-starved Matt saw he had an audience and took full advantage.

"You really have no idea how to play this game, do you?" he asked Connor in a deadpan, disgusted tone. Connor pretended not to hear, but smiled sheepishly when Matt persisted.

"This is what I have to put up with," Matt explained to the other players. "Not even worth my time."

Matt threw down the three cards in his hand and removed his blue shirt, revealing his slight but toned build. I noticed how burnt his face was from the sun in comparison to how pale the rest of him was. I could have sworn I saw him glance at Stacey on the corner of his eye to see if she was paying attention.

Right around two in the afternoon, Skonky guided Ella to the right-side shoulder of the road for our lunch stop—a stop about as scenic as the journey thus far, complete with dust-laden fields and puny, fenced-in shrubs about. It was nice to not only get off the truck and stretch but to find the nearest bush and take care of business—no one had acquired the necessary nerve at that point to order Skonky to make an unscheduled stop. While the women headed off together towards the east, the men went just west enough to get some privacy.

Even in the African bush, women still couldn't go to the bathroom alone.

With lunch over, we headed out and made it to our campground for the night, Fiddler's Creek, a short time later. From the truck, we saw a tropical paradise that should be a part of everyone's vacation. Flowering vines of pink and red met thatch huts while the winding Orange River caught the sun just right, creating a magnificent sparkling haze. Even the showers and restrooms were housed in thatch, creating a Gilligan's Island–type feel to the place. I finally understood why the Professor never worked too hard to find a way off that Island in the first place—give me a radio made from a coconut any day if it meant staying in such a serene, beautiful place.

As Ella winded down the dust-laden road to our site for the night, it became pretty apparent that Fiddler's Creek was a popular destination with other overland tour companies. Just as Bill had predicted the other day, we passed probably a dozen other trucks just like Ella, brandished with various names and logos like 'Acacia' and 'Chimuga.' It made perfect sense—not only was Fiddler's Creek beautiful, but its location hugging the Namibia–South Africa border—made it a convenient way-station as well.

Ella slowed to a halt as we reached our campsite, grinding still just where the gravel-filled road met the grass of our site. The dry grass would make the ground a little hard for sleeping, but the site itself was very picturesque—about ten yards from the riverbank. While we assembled our tents, Skonky prepared the fire ring, located dead center in the middle of our site.

"Feel free to make some new friends with the other trucks," Skonky growled as he dragged a pile of dry timber to the ring. "You'll probably run into some of these guys later on, too."

The whole overland tour set-up became pretty obvious at this point. All of the different tour operators followed the same exact route, stopped at the same sights, and pretty much camped at the same locations. The main difference, of course, was price, which varied greatly in some instances depending on how much comfort you needed and how much cash you were willing to part with. In the case of Megan and I, we wanted comfort but settled for cheap, just because we had to make the money stretch if we planned on seeing Europe like we had planned.

It didn't take long for the Aussie guys to follow Skonky's advice and start mingling with travelers from the other trucks. Connor, Bill and Matt raced to put their tents up and then scaled the stone steps that led into the adjacent campsite, conveniently entering in the middle of a group of twenty-something girls. For all of Bill's bravado, he seemed almost shy, letting Matt take the lead.

"Look at that dog!" Megan whispered to me, watching Matt throw his arm around some giggling blond he had just met.

"I wonder what his fiancée would say about that!"

It was typical Matt to me. And quickly, I was growing to despise him.

"Who loves men from Australia?" yelled Matt, raising his arms above his head.

Absent from that scene was Aubrey, who I think saw himself as a kind of lothario, too, based on some of the teasing he made about how women always wanted his body. He wasn't interested in meeting women—at least not at the moment. It wasn't until I heard a steady splashing sound emanating from the Orange River did he reveal his presence.

"Eet's nice in 'ere!" yelled Aubrey, bobbing up and down in a slightly reed-filled area just off the riverbank.

"Hard current!"

Both Megan and I watched as Aubrey floated steadily, all the while being pulled towards the center of the river and drifting slightly downstream. Appearing to be a fairly strong swimmer, he disappeared into the dark waters after rolling into a dive, propelling himself back up moments later as if he had been shot from a cannon.

It was a very inviting scene, even for a not-so-strong swimmer like myself, to justify battling a little current for some refreshment on a humid, sticky day. This was one temptation that Meg and I knew would come one day, since we were both aware that taking a dip in freshwater also meant accepting the risk of getting the second-most common tropical disease in Africa—bilharzia. Caused by tiny, parasitic worms that lived in freshwater and burrowed unsuspectingly into the skin, bilharzia symptoms, which usually didn't show up until months later, included chronic fatigue, intense stomach pain, and bloody stool.

Naturally, the thought of swimming in the River lost much of its luster.

"The water doesn't even look that nice," Megan said, moving herself away from the shore and behind me as if it removed the temptation from sight.

"Probably filled with leeches."

"Screw the leeches," Bill said from behind us, stripping down to a blue bathing suit as he walked towards the riverbank. Stopping about five yards from the water, he ran and leapt high into the air, tucked into a perfect cannonball. Aubrey, who had again hid himself deep with in the waters of the Orange River, rose to the surface just long enough to feel the full affect of the tremendous, incoming splash.

"Tryin' to kell me, butty?" he laughed, wiping the water from his eyes. Jumping onto Bill's back, Aubrey pulled him under, the two tussling beneath the slightly brown current.

Though most of the group had gathered at the bank, no one else ventured into the water for fear of bilharzia. Two days into the trip was just too early.

Over dinner that night, Skonky, with beer in hand, shared the plans for the following morning.

"We're up at 8 a.m. tomorrow," he called out. "Have a long day of canoeing down the Orange River and then bush-camping."

Skonky trained his eyes on the ground, carving a line into the dry earth with the crease of his foot.

"Each group of two can only bring one small bag between them—take only what you need."

Yes, Skonky was a man of few words. But naturally, we had some questions.

"And our sleeping bags and tents?" Aubrey asked, probably realizing that the inflatable air mattress he'd brought with him to offset the hard ground might have to be left behind.

Skonky looked up from the ground and into Aubrey's eyes.

"You won't need 'em, sleeping on a soft, sandy beach under the stars," Skonky said.

Moving quickly, Skonky circled the fire ring, sidestepping to avoid Rutger, and stopped, crouching down to warm his hands.

"Charlie and I are going with, but Rutger's staying behind to keep an eye on the truck."

Great. Charlie and Skonky. We were going to starve.

"So let me get this straight," Stacey said, waving her left hand into the air as she spoke. "No tents, no sleeping bags...are there showers, at least?"

A low laugh came from Skonky—he probably got that from Americans all the time. Rutger smiled and chimed in.

"That's bush camping, Stacey! Very primitive. No showers, no toilets... you won't miss showering for a day. Everyone will stink!"

Rutger crept in closer towards the fire, moving a loaf of bread from the coals with a pair of blackened tongs.

"Believe me, guys—it's worth it. The night sky is just amazing and it's one of the few times you can sleep outdoors here without worrying about malaria just yet."

I didn't know how much I was looking forward to sleeping outdoors—completely uncovered and even more remote than the previous night. But what could you do? I figured my comfort zone would be tested a little on the trip. Yeah, I could do it—I'd just make sure my six-inch hunting knife managed to find a way into the bag we were bringing.

The group continued buzzing about bush camping the entire night—it was one of the first great unknowns we were to encounter. When he'd overhear our concerns—which ranged from everything to 'smelling gross' (Stacey) to being attacked by a lion (Megan), Rutger interjected as best he could to ally any fears, standing firm on his insistence that we'd be fine. Dominick, our hungry Swiss friend, was the funniest—not as worried about being outdoors all night as he was about food.

"We're a big group," Dominick blurted out in Skonky's direction, catching all of us a little off guard. "How can you feed us?"

The poor guy genuinely looked concern, like a child worried that Santa Claus would forget his house on Christmas Eve.

Skonky mumbled something back about packing enough food on the canoes for several days—nothing to worry about, he said. He was pretty toasted, his feet flanked by empty beer bottles.

Mary chimed in, naturally. It had been a few minutes since we had to endure her annoying voice.

"I'll bet it's just lovely," she said with a smile, scanning the entire group. "We back-country all the time in Perth—just lovely." She licked some rib sauce off her fingers.

The Aussie guys didn't seem too concerned. Connor, Matt and Bill disappeared shortly after Skonky briefed us, hunting for some fellow overlanders from a neighboring truck to bellying up next to the thatch bar across the way.

The rest of us hung out by our own fire, chatting and taking turns commandeering the stereo with our own music. Finally some good music. We put on one of our Bob Dylan albums we brought with.

After some of the magical punch—prepared by Skonky—I had sampled earlier was starting to hit me, I chose to instead retreat to the tent than risk getting hung-over. Megan joined me, and we ducked out—leaving the party that kept seeming to wind down but wouldn't quite die, finding new life with each new batch of punch.

We actually slept well that night, much to my surprise. Megan felt safe; I was exhausted and we had a nice, filling dinner. I woke up briefly in the middle of the night—I always did—and heard some kind of commotion, probably the guys retreating to their tents. Nothing major. Not in our tent, at least.

BEACH?!?

I never got back to sleep that morning. Once that annoying bird started screaming around 5 a.m., that was it. Fucker. It started this shrill call, almost like a high-pitched whine, just before sunrise and then stopped, maybe realizing that it was too early for even a bird to start the day. I would have welcomed a little more sleep now that it was particularly more peaceful, as the trickling water of the river echoed with a calming, bucolic resonance.

As I usually did when I thought about everything on my mind, I got a little down. I could be pretty dramatic if given the opportunity. Yet as much as I knew Megan was great about listening to me vent, even I get tired of listening to me rant about the same old things, like being homesick, worrying about money and the like. Still, she got more than her fair share of bitching from me.

Rutger broke my fun-filled morning of despair, I guess, or whomever it was who shook the tent to get us moving. I let the mysterious shaker know that we were awake and, after Meg and I threw on some clothes, we made our way to the breakfast table.

As the gang trickled in one by one, noticeably absent were Connor and Matt, who were last seen sometime last night, according to Dominick, having a spirited and rowdy conversation about rugby at the bar across camp.

"They looked to be enjoying themselves," Dominick deadpanned with a slight smile.

"Didja all hear Connor last night, then?" whispered Mary to the group, looking like a child sharing a secret on the playground.

"Came home so drunk last night, almost stumbled over my tent!" she smiled as she scanned over our expressions, then took a sip from her cup.

"That punch was pretty bad," said Megan, her back turned to the group as she scoured the dish rack in search of a clean cereal bowl.

"Punch, nothing," Mary called out. "It didn't stop there. He closed out the bar with Matt—don't know what time it was!"

That Mary—if she couldn't run her mouth about something, the poor girl would have nothing to do.

Still hunting, Megan jumped briefly as Bill moved in from behind and grabbed a spoon.

"That's Connor for ya!" he cackled. "Boy's outta control!"

We kept our eyes fixed on Connor and Matt's tent during breakfast that morning, wondering if our two Lazaruses would rise from the dead yet again. The question was not when they would emerge but in what shape they would be in when they finally did. At the moment when Skonky started preparing to pack breakfast away and the guys were still no-shows, Rutger had enough as he skipped over to their tent, resembling a scarecrow on his way to school.

"C'mon, boys," Rutger chided as he lifted the front of the tent a foot off the ground. "Up and at 'em!"

A groan—possibly Matt, yet still indistinguishable. Showing approval, Rutger playfully backed away from the tent with a smile on his face and jogged back to the breakfast area, putting a few, hard biscuits aside for the guys while Skonky cleared away the rest.

Though the tent door remained shut, the morning sun revealed silhouettes pressing against the inside tent walls, stumbling as they attempted to right themselves. After a quick tug at the zipper, a shirtless and shoeless Matt emerged: Lazarus had indeed risen, but not looking so well. Truth be told, Matt looked nearly lifeless, his pallid face a stark contrast to the half-burnt complexion he sported yesterday from the intense red sun beating through the truck windows. His eyes were barely open, mere slits that struggled to handle daylight once again, as he seemingly limped to the breakfast area.

"Morning all," he mumbled as he approached, studying us through partially glazed-over eyes.

"We're leaving," Skonky said bluntly, watching Charlie as she ran a crusty rag over the breakfast table.

"Where's Connor?"

Stacey, standing to the right of Matt, sniffed the air.

"What's that horrible smell?"

Discretely, I smelled my shirt. You can only get it so clean in a sink with soap. When I found out it wasn't me, even I could smell what our little drama queen had detected. The smell of sick.

"Oh man, that's bad," Megan proclaimed disgustedly, crinkling her nose.

Looking a little embarrassed, Matt, remaining silent, backed up and limped towards the tent. He climbed back inside, and after a brief exchange between he and Connor, emerged with a green towel over his shoulder and a pile of clothes in his hand, darting off to the shower.

Emerged from the tent himself moments later, Connor resembled a bear that had just ended a season of hibernation, crawling on all fours before rising and reaching around to his back in order to scratch himself. He put on a brave face, too—popping to his feet as he flashed a knowing smile to the audience, greeting us with one of those "I got plowed last night but I survived" type of looks.

The novelty of the Connor and Matt show ended shortly after the guys had cleaned up—even that pompous dick Matt was hurting too much to relish in it. Plus he had bigger things to worry about. Not only was that foul odor we initially smelled coming from Matt, who we discovered had puked in the tent at some point last night, but he had inadvertently immersed his heavy sleeping bag in his own sick, too. Needless to say, I remained skeptical with Matt's claim later that morning that he had cleaned out the tent and it didn't smell anymore, which luckily was easily identified thanks to a big #6 etched across the stuff sack. Cleaning his sleeping bag was another matter entirely. After first soaking the heavy, pink chunks that floated away like lily pads in the Orange River, he flung it over a makeshift clothesline left by the group who had the sight before us, bowing under the weight of the dripping wet back. For Matt's sake, at least Rutger would be around to keep an eye on it until we returned.

As we all stood close to the shore, a small, muscular woman approached, twirling a canoe paddle in her right hand. Giving Skonky a playful push from behind, she moved through the crowd until she was in its center.

"This is Esther, everyone," Skonky called out as he chased her, looking to return the push. "She's your guide today."

Esther looked like the typical girl next door, looking more like a California beach bunny than an African guide. Her blond, sun-bleached hair hung just over her shoulders and she had a pretty smile. Yep, the girl next door—though the girl next door in Africa with a canoe to call her own could mean trouble. I just sensed it.

"This is not going to be the easiest canoe trip, people," Esther boomed as she stalked in front of us, almost resembling a drill sergeant with her determined gait.

"If you listen to me and follow directions, you'll be fine. If you don't, you'll go under—the rocks and rapids will see to that."

Did she say rapids?

"There's little danger of running into any wildlife here," she continued. "No crocs, no poisonous snakes...."

"...But me? I'm dangerous. And if you go off on your own or even so much as splash me, you're getting tipped. And I'm serious."

Esther laid down the paddle in a nearby canoe and deftly tightened her life jacket.

"I need to know who can't swim before we head out," she said, briefly loosening the black strap across her chest.

Helen and Abe's hands shot up—I figured that. Me? I was paralyzed—I could not and would not do it. I glanced at Megan from the corner of my eye, but she didn't look towards me. How could I, a big, strong guy, admit that I wasn't the greatest swimmer and risk being couched in with the oldsters? It was suicide.

I tried to reassure myself. I had a life jacket on and I wasn't a hopeless swimmer, I told myself. But then again, the last thing I wanted to happen was to inadvertently panic and strike someone else's canoe, grounds for our lovely guide to toss Megan and me overboard. That sweet exterior wouldn't fool me—she was the Terminator.

Megan gave me that knowing look of hers, the one that said, "Why don't you let her know that you scream like a little girl in the water, just to be safe?" I did, but I made sure I did it as everyone else was too busy bringing their canoes down to the water to hear anything.

"Hello," I mumbled sheepishly. "I'm not that confident of a swimmer, either." God, how embarrassing.

Though she smiled a little, she didn't break free of that hardened exterior.

"Just a few rapids—nothing to worry about."

I felt a little foolish after that, I admit, but at least I covered my ass. Esther probably saw Helen and Abe and figured they weren't exactly athletes and wanted to reassure them by letting them know she would look out for them. And then you have me—she probably figured I just wanted her to rescue me.

With that out of the way, Megan and I each grabbed an end of the canoe and descended the slight hill that led into the riverbank. Everyone was paired off with their tent mate and it already looked like the trip would be a joy to behold—Bill and Aubrey were bickering over who should sit in front; Helen and Abe couldn't quite crouch down enough to actually sit in the canoe without it almost teetering over; Stacey and Mary were trying to talk over each other about some nonsense, neither one doing much listening to the other; Dominick, sharing a canoe with Esther, drooled as he eyed the large trunk of food strapped down in front of him; Matt and Connor looked dead—drawn, pale, and silent; and Megan and I were both a little nervous about dying. Yep, fun on the Orange River.

Skonky and Charlie stuffed their canoe with the remainder of the supplies. I even saw Charlie actually smile, as she wrestled with Skonky over who would get to sit in the front of the canoe. Meanwhile, our green dry bag, snuggly fastened with a cord, served as a makeshift wall that divided the front of the canoe from the back, separating my domain from Megan's. Taking a deep breath, I lowered the tip of the canoe into the water with Megan, who we decided would take the rear since she had canoed more than I did and could actually steer. Lowering herself in first. I then handed her a small plastic bag I had kept separate from the rest of our gear—filled with two jugs of clean water, a few snacks, and sunblock.

We pushed off and steered our canoe directly in line behind Esther's lead canoe—making sure, of course, not to pass her or risk facing her wrath. Initially, she kept a watchful eye on each canoe, stopping and turning her boat around once we were about a half-mile down river so she could get a full view of the procession. Helen and Abe's canoe looked drunk, following a wavy, circular path that spun them through several reed patches before righting itself and lurching towards the rest of the group.

"We may need to change groups," said Esther in a low voice so only the canoes around her could hear. She yelled to Helen and Abe, "You guys all right? We can switch if you want!"

Abe looked stoic as always. He still seemed like a very proud guy who didn't want anything from anyone if he could help it. Why should he, when his wife would do everything for him, anyway? I think seeing him in the canoe with paddle in hand was the first time I saw him lift a finger on the trip, though he looked to be really struggling, his flailing limbs looking like machine parts in need of some heavy duty oil.

Helen wasn't doing much better, but she was probably used to her husband's stubbornness and didn't want any special treatment, either. She smiled and waved off Esther, fighting a current that threatened to spin the canoe once again.

"I'll keep an eye of them," Skonky called out to Esther. At about thirty feet away, the canoe he commandeered with Charlie was the closest to the elderly couple.

The scenery during the canoe trip was really nothing special—the riverbanks were surrounded with either assorted trees that blocked the entire horizon or barren rock cliffs that looked like we were in Afghanistan.

Though Esther warned us that the day would be hot, and we could take a dip in the river later on, it didn't seem like something I wanted to do. The water looked almost muddy it was so dark, and I never jumped into anything if I couldn't see its bottom.

Even though the scenery proved unspectacular, the jutting rocks that appeared to sprout up through the water, and the quick-moving rapids kept things interesting. The real obvious rocks, the ones that spiked up in plain sight, weren't too difficult for us to avoid as long as we continued to follow Esther in a straight line—she always made sure she steered us clear around them. More difficult were the flat, long ones that waited just beneath the water that we sometimes had no choice but to go over, occasionally stranding ourselves on the craggy, hidden island. And let's not forget the rapids—not as formidable as your Colorado River-type, but enough of a nuisance to require you to grip the paddle extra tight while paying close attention as you approached them and battled your way through. The trick, according to Esther, was to paddle through it. If you let the rapid take control, you would almost certainly get tossed.

Our canoe procession drew a bit of an audience as we made our way down the river. Occasionally you'd see some children at play who would drop everything to catch a glimpse of us, running alongside the shore for a little bit while waving to us. Or we'd see livestock, lazily grazing along the river and basking under the afternoon sun.

Before long I could feel my arm muscles and my lower back starting to get a little sore; it had been three hours since we'd shoved off. I probably paddled more than I needed to, but it's a guy thing.

We continued along the river for a little while longer, all of the groups pretty much holding their own. How Connor and Matt were managing seemed almost inconceivable—I knew how terrible and dehydrated I felt when I was hungover, not to mention adding physical exercise on top of it. How they were surviving under this hot afternoon sun was beyond me. Even more surprising, Helen and Abe were getting the hang of canoeing—occasionally getting stranded on a rock or two like the rest of us but always wiggling themselves free while maintaining that slow but steady pace.

I really had no idea how long we paddled through that completely barren landscape—at some point, you get so tired and bored that you just stop caring. Though it wasn't excruciating slave labor, I just didn't see the point of thinking about it anymore, instead electing to just let my mind wander. I daydreamed about everything that afternoon, from telling off ex-bosses from previous jobs to conjuring up a name for a rock band I planned on forming when I got a little more practice with my lead guitar. Anything but the constant paddling.

Esther, still at the front of the canoe procession, whistled back to Skonky when the river narrowed again and then pointed to the left, about a mile upstream. This was going to be home for the night, I figured, and it looked just as bare and sparse as everything we had just passed the past couple of hours. The exception was that this was the pre-arranged pick-up point for tomorrow—when a couple of Esther's associates, we were told, would make their way in with four by fours to drive us back to civilization as we knew it. What distinguished this particular spot from all the rest was lost on me—no road leading to it, no landmarks, nothing. But she seemed to know what she was doing and that was good enough for me. And if it meant getting out of these damn canoes for the day, even better.

The line of canoes broke suddenly as we approached the beach, each one splitting off to grab enough land to keep it from drifting away. The relief of finally being out of the canoe rushed over me once I stepped foot on land once again; it was good to stretch my legs and even better to have made the entire trip without incident. Esther was all right, it turned out—a little brash initially, but probably just to get our attention.

"Here's the beach," Esther called out as she dragged her canoe up through the sand.

"Make yourselves at home!"

Home. Maybe my trip to the Bahamas a few years ago spoiled me, but when someone tells you that you will be spending the night on the beach, certain images come to your mind—sparkling water; rich, white sand; peace and tranquility. Granted, I knew that the sparkling water thing wasn't going to happen as soon as we traveled through the murky waters of the Orange River in our canoe, but the beach I found myself standing on wasn't exactly going to find itself on the cover on 'Conde Naste' any time soon.

"Welcome home," I told Megan, kicking at a small rock resting on the dark and gritty dirt ground.

"This isn't a beach!" Megan declared, her voice rising in disbelief.

"Does this look like a beach to you?"

"Oh yeah. Figured I'd build a large sand castle of mud right there," I sarcastically replied, pointing to a large, man-sized boulder that jutted up from the river.

"This is not a beach," Megan repeated, waving her arms.

"Does this look like any place you'd want to sleep on, this black dirt?!??"

"Now we know why there aren't any resorts along the Orange River."

I was happy to see that Megan and I could at least laugh at our accommodations for the night. Aubrey, stamping his left foot down onto the hard ground, looked like he was going to cry, probably wishing he hadn't listened to Skonky and smuggled his air mattress along. Standing with his cap pulled down almost over his eyes and with his hands on his hips, he surveyed the rocky land like an archaeologist searching for a lost tomb.

"How am I supposed to sleep on this?" he said aloud as he spun towards Dominick. "I need my air mattress!"

Stacey tilted her head down, bobbing her hair forward until it covered her eyes and hid the crappy beach from sight.

"This is hardly Ft. Lauderdale."

Maybe Skonky felt prompted to brief us after hearing our rumblings and dissension, though his always-present lackadaisical attitude hadn't changed as he strode towards us from across the beach, kicking the sand high into the air with his bare feet.

"You have the next couple of hours to yourself," he said, watching Esther as she bent over to untie her gear from the canoe.

"It's too hard here!" Aubrey shouted, sounding like an upset child. "We can't sleep here!"

"Grab a canoe," Skonky replied, unfazed by Aubrey's emotional outburst. "Tip it over and let a little air out—they make great sleeping pads."

Megan and I grabbed our canoe and began the difficult assignment of finding that perfect spot to sleep in. Attempting to climb inside the mind of a would-be predator, it didn't take us long to convince ourselves that no place was safe.

We don't want to be the closest ones to the mountains, right? But what if something swims up the river? Under that tree? Don't spiders live in trees?

In the end, it was all about compromise. After growing more frustrated and arguing with one another, we picked a spot near a little patch of underbrush in front of Matt and Connor but behind Bill and Aubrey—if something was hungry that night, we'd at least be protected by a perimeter of meaty Aussie appetizers.

Taking a short nap, I woke up shortly before dinner, in time to help Bill and Dominick round up some more wood to keep the fire that Skonky had started raging. Dry wood wasn't hard to find, but I looked at everything a couple of times before picking it up, just in case of scorpions or spiders. As the utter darkness of night began to creep in, everyone minus Stacey had gathered around the fire, waiting for Charlie to put the finishing touches on that night's meal of pasta.

"Who's seen Stacey?" Skonky called out.

"Megan?"

Megan shrugged, a little bewildered.

"She told me she wasn't feeling well and she was going to lie down," related Megan, "but I haven't seen her since."

"Maybe Aubrey knows!" yelled out Bill, rolling on his belly towards the fire like a snake.

"How 'bout it, Aubrey?"

Turning a little red, Aubrey said nothing, pouting his lips in anger.

"Actually," chimed Mary, with a knowing look in her eyes. "I think she's not feeling so well. I've seen her headin' off for the loo quite a bit."

"I'll take a look-sie," declared Esther, pushing herself off the sand and heading down the rocky path to the chemical toilet.

Megan's eyes grew wide, turning towards me as Esther disappeared over the ridge.

"Maybe it was those oranges she offered me," I suggested, shrugging my shoulders. "She ate nearly the whole bag by herself!"

Esther returned a few minutes later with the report—Stacey had severe stomach cramping but would try to eat something later, prompting Skonky to immediately ladle a pile of noodles aside for her before turning us loose. We completely devoured the rest—the canoe trip really worked up an appetite for everyone and Charlie, believe it or not, actually did an acceptable job with the tasty meat sauce. For once, Charlie even actually appeared to be enjoying herself, surprisingly sliding herself in between Skonky's spread legs and smiling gleefully once he subtly threw his arm around her. Maybe those first few days alone together in the cab had brought the two together. Maybe Charlie just needed to get laid.

As the black, night sky settled above us, I couldn't help but appreciate it—every bit as magnificent as Rutger led us to believe. It stretched endlessly, thousands of flecks of illumination shining through the pitch-black night. You could not help but feel a little insignificant in its splendor.

After the group began to break up, Megan and I decided to put the finishing touches on our canoe for the night. It wasn't exactly large enough for us to sleep side-by-side on—that alone made me curious about what sleeping arrangement the guys would choose, though I doubted if the canoe was bigger we'd find Aubrey spooning Bill in the morning.

Megan and I decided that each of us lying flat on our backs and head-to-head would probably work best. I slept facing away from the fire ring, of course, providing her with the added comfort of knowing that I would, once again, serve as a sort of human shield for her that night. Still, I didn't blame her –it would be a little spooky trying to sleep feeling so vulnerable and exposed. I certainly wouldn't try it on the 12th St. beach back home in Chicago—I'd wake up robbed of everything, if I woke up at all.

After brushing our teeth and performing a quick critter inspection around the canoe, Megan climbed aboard the bouncy canoe and settled in.

"It's really nice," she said, squirming back and forth. "Like a big pillow."

The canoe rocked a little when I put my left foot in it—holding steady, finally, when I grasped the sides with my hands and hoisted myself up. It was cushy, without a doubt—probably more comfortable than the mattress we had at home.

I settled in firmly with my back to Megan's, staring up at the wondrous night sky. No, the dirty beach was not my favorite, I didn't appreciate canoeing the entire day, and I would have killed for a hot shower, but even I had to admit that the nocturnal sky show above us made it all worthwhile. I don't know how long Megan and I spent on our backs staring into the panoramic night above us, but at that moment I felt like I could lie awake all night, looking for constellations (or creating my own), tracking a shooting star as it raced beyond the mountains, or just enjoying the sheer peacefulness. I slept well that night.

STUCK INSIDE NAMIBIA WITH THE AFRICA BLUES AGAIN

I woke up a little before our planned 8 a.m.

"You sleep alright?" I asked, reaching into the plastic bag we had set in the sand that housed our toothbrushes.

Megan yawned.

"What time is it?" she mumbled as she rolled over.

"Time to get up," I said. "I slept like a baby."

Megan mumbled her reply into her sweatshirt pillow.

"I heard you—you were snoring pretty bad," she said, sitting up. "I didn't sleep well, but it was OK—I kept watching the stars shift across the sky."

I walked over to the head of the canoe, stroking her head with the back of my hand.

"You must be tired, then. Hope you're ready to canoe back!"

She shook her head and laughed. It was good to hear her laugh again.

"We're getting picked up," Megan said. "I don't think we have all day to canoe back upstream, do you?"

She swung her legs around and hopped to the sand, brushing the dirt from her slacks. Handing her a toothbrush, we stopped behind a tree to prepare for another day in Africa.

By the time we headed off to breakfast, it looked like the entire group, minus Helen and Abe, had gathered back around the fire ring. Dominick, seated adjacent to the breakfast table, looked like a guard dog, ready to bite if necessary. Skonky gave a wave of acknowledgement when he spotted us, moving near the fire ring.

"Let's go over the plan for the day," he said, taking a sip from a coffee cup and flashing a quick smile at Charlie, seated near his feet and smiling widely.

"We get picked up in ten minutes, then we go back and have a real breakfast—bacon and eggs. After that, a border crossing into Namibia and Fish River Canyon. Any questions?"

I liked what he had to say. Real food, a change of scenery, and best of all, no more canoeing. After my standard bowl of cereal, I dragged our canoe to the projected pick-up point, a sandy patch crisscrossed with multiple tire tracks about thirty feet from camp. Just as eagerly, Megan grabbed our bag after finishing breakfast and joined me, waiting for our ticket back to civilization.

If nothing else, our rescuers were timely, as the unmistakable sound of the climbing vehicles echoed throughout the entire valley shortly after the last of us had gathered to wait. Then, almost magically, the three lumbering beasts appeared, and our tiny caravan instantly sprouted up from the sandy floor of the desert. Stacey let up an enthusiastic cheer, feeling better than last night and more than ready to put the whole bush camping experience behind her. I still think it was all those oranges.

Appearing a little rough for wear but otherwise sturdy, the caravan of three, sand-covered, military-style trucks looked more than prepared to tear through the rocks and sand dunes and deliver us back to camp. Each driver sported that "rough African" appearance that we were also growing accustomed to—shirtless, unshaven, and disheveled. One driver actually looked like a handsome enough guy until he smiled—the few teeth he had in his mouth reminded me of a bottle opener I lost in college.

We worked as a team to load all of the canoes into the largest of the three trucks, and then a few members of the group—Charlie, Helen, Abe, Connor and Mary—climbed aboard into the back, looking like the most bizarre envoy in military history. The driver, after checking his cargo from the front seat, gave thumbs up to Skonky and peeled out, kicking a trail of sand in his wake. A few seconds later, they disappeared over the horizon as those of us remaining longingly looked on.

"Now for the rest of ya," said our chauffeur through a toothless grin. "Up ya go!"

We split into two, makeshift groups—one for each truck. I wasn't too interested in actually sitting inside the truck—it looked very hot and uncomfortable. Instead, Megan, myself, and Matt climbed into the back of the first truck; the one with the toothless driver, while Skonky and Stacey took the cab. Esther, Dominick, Aubrey and Bill settled into the last one, the largest of the three and the one saddled down with the most gear.

I held tight to the wooden slat sides of the truck, expecting a bumpy take-off. Despite hearing the rhythmic spinning of the massive, worn wheels in the sand, we didn't move—not even a little. Revving the engine more only netted the same result—nothing.

"Not to worry," shouted our driver after mildly cursing to himself. "We need to get a little weight off until we get moving. Everybody off!"

One by one, we climbed down from the truck. But even with the truck entirely emptied of her cargo and the driver flooring her accelerator, she still refused to move through the deep sand. I looked over my shoulder at the other truck enviously, pissed if they decided to take off without us.

The driver of the third truck, a thin, sandy-haired guy, popped out of his cab and ran to the window of our truck, speaking to our driver in Afrikaans. After a few minutes more of our driver still ramming down on the accelerator, he smoothly cut the power to the engine and emerged from the cab, looking a little frustrated but still keeping his humor.

"We'll get it, guys," he said with a slight smile. "I promise."

Racing back to our truck with some heavy chains, the thin driver attached them somewhere beneath the front bumper of the stranded truck, leaving the other end momentarily strewn across the sand. Then, pulling his own truck forward and then reversing it so only ten feet or so separated the two vehicles, he attached the free end of the chains to the rear of his truck.

"Cross your fingers!"

For several seconds, the two beasts groaned approvingly as their drivers fed them. It was suspenseful, waiting to see if the last-ditch effort to free the wallowing creature from its sandy trap would work.

"C'mon," I mumbled to myself. "Let's go."

The very instant we heard the lead truck shift into gear, all of us sprung into action, lending the muscle that we could muster to the backside of the idle truck. Engines roared. Sand flew. Bodies strained. Yet despite all of the efforts of man and machine, the truck still would not budge; its wheels seemingly locked against its will.

"Keep pushing!" rallied Skonky. "I think we're close!"

Then, the worst that could happen did. The heavy steel chain that connected the two trucks, the one that we were certain would give us that extra edge, snapped in two. And my hope that we'd be getting out any time soon, snapped right along with it. Damn.

Camp was a good half-hour drive away, so even if we waited for the lone truck that had departed to come back for the rest of us, it would still add up to be a very long, very miserable day. Both drivers turned their attention to what passed for the gearbox of the second truck; a worn, weathered instrument panel that looked like it held many secrets, the most relevant being what gear you were actually in because of the layer after layer of caked on dirt covering it. After a little more communication in Afrikaans between the guides, our driver wrestled briefly with the stiff gearshift.

"Once more time, guys," our driver called out. "We need one more big push!"

One more big push by us, but still nothing. No dramatic roll forward, no collective cheer, no nothing. The big behemoth would not budge from its sandy grave.

After the drivers and Skonky spoke privately for a few minutes, it was decided that the third truck would go on ahead with half of the group and then send the first truck back for the rest of the group. The stalled truck would stay behind for now, getting a closer look later, more likely at Skonky's insistence because he knew we couldn't spend much more of the day off schedule.

Somehow, Megan and I lucked out—the group we were a part of—with Matt, Skonky and Stacey—was the one chosen to return to camp in the lone, functioning truck while the others waited behind. It probably had something to do with Skonky being in our group and him needing time to take care of some things back at camp before we headed out. Whatever the reason, I wasn't about to complain.

We climbed aboard and waited again—Skonky and Stacey in the cab while Megan, Matt and myself held on tight in the back. With fingers crossed, I let out a brief sigh as the truck slowly lumbered ahead through the sand. We're on our way back...hot showers, hot food...just hang on.

As the truck slowly made its way through the sand, I felt compelled to meet the envious eyes watching us leave. So long, losers! Maybe I'll save some hot water for ya!

"You'd better hold on, sweetie," Megan warned as she tapped me on the shoulder.

"Look at the size of those rocks!"

It was almost startling, the way the dense sand quickly gave way to craggy, sharp rocks lying ahead, resembling carving knives as they jutted forth from the ground. I felt my teeth shake in my mouth as the truck lumbered over the path in front of it, plastered with piercing, dark stone. Headed right for what looked like an extremely narrow pass, I was convinced that the two towering and shattered, black rocks waiting to meet us on either side would attack.

<POP>

Without warning, a tremendous jostle rocked the truck, its momentum surely flinging me headfirst into the cab had I not been holding on so tight. Noticeably, we limped along the few feet we managed after that, until the driver, noticing the rocking ride, stuck his head quickly out the window to looked behind and then slowed to a halt. First slamming his fist into the steering wheel, he grudgingly got out of the cab and glanced at the rear tire.

"We got a flat, guys," he laughed, removing his hat and then wiping the steady stream of sweat from his brow.

"Fuckin' unbelievable!"

"We don't have a spare," the driver said sheepishly, almost laughing at the theater of mishaps unfolding before us.

"I'm going to race back to the other truck and get theirs. Just be a bit, then I promise we'll get you out of here."

We watched him disappear over the ridge towards the other truck, and then watched him reappear about twenty minutes later with the spare, rolling it in front of him as best he could through the uneven sand. At least they had a spare. This couldn't get any worse, but at least they had a spare.

Releasing the spare so it spun shakily to the ground next to the rear flat, he danced to the cab and returned with a circular lug wrench he had stored behind the front seat. Bending down in the sand, he looked at the wrench, then at the tire, then back to the wrench. Silence, then laughter.

"I can't believe this!" he shrieked, dropping back into the sand before popping up to his feet. Grains of brown sand clung to his sweaty back.

"I have the wrong kind of wrench," he cackled. "It won't fit my tire!"

Shit. We're never getting out of here.

Any trace of energy I had managed to maintain through all the disappointments of the day was drained from my body. What was the point anymore? We'd probably get back quicker if we canoed.

Sharing in the laugh with Skonky, the two then turned the truck upside-down looking for some kind of tool that could get the job done. All kinds of crap littered the interior—torn plastic tarps, assorted containers, yellowed newspapers—so it wouldn't be a total shock if the right wrench had been inadvertently tucked somewhere. After a few minutes, after rummaging through the rear seat like a raccoon in a trash can, Skonky emerged victoriously, the steel wrench reflecting the gleam of the sun as he hoisted it high above his head like a trophy. We cheered, we laughed and we cried until the new tire was finally secured to the truck and we sped off for camp. I wouldn't believe we made it back, I told Megan, until we could actually see camp.

The ride back was bumpy and a little frightening at times, with every expansive sand dune being a potential hazard that could again leave us stranded; this time leaving us completely isolated from everyone else. Through all the winding roads and rugged terrain, however, the driver handled her as well as could be expected. Again, I wondered how on earth anyone could really find his or her way around such a barren place. Take a right at the second large dirt pile? It seemed more complicated than following tire tracks—in some cases, several branched out into all sorts of directions.

We didn't arrive at camp until nearly a half-hour later, where the long-departed group from the first truck had already showered and begun feasting on their breakfast. Damn that Dominick! If he ate all the bacon....

We got in line behind Matt, who was wrestling with a couple of sunny-side-up eggs in probably the greasiest frying pan I ever laid eyes on. Everyone else had not only eaten breakfast, but had also used the same frying pan for all of their cooking. My stomach actually felt a little queasy as I watched Matt's eggs swim from side to side in the filthy pan, occasionally reaching the completely white pieces of bacon also sizzling away in the foul brew. I don't think you could legally call the white strip presented to us for breakfast 'bacon' since bacon tends to at least have a little meat on it.

Retreating with his blackened eggs, I waited until Matt completely cleared the area until I dumped what little grease I could manage to get out of the pan onto the ground, then cracked a total of four eggs off the side. They didn't swim as much as Matt's but quickly acquired a greasy brownish color along their edges. And though I am not proud to admit it, yes, we also threw in four strips of that so-called bacon into the pan as well. Desperate people, desperate times. Breakfast wasn't great that morning, but a change of pace was always appreciated.

Unfortunately for Megan and I, we drew the shitty end of the stick that day since it was our assigned day for dish duty. My attempt to scrub all the grease from the frying pan was ritualistic at best—a few hours of caked on grease couldn't exactly get wiped away with the half-eaten sponge soaked in tepid water available to me.

By the time we finished our chores, it was time to board Ella and depart South Africa for what would be our first border crossing into Namibia. I didn't realize until we had left the campsite that we were so close to the Namibian border—about a ten-minute ride.

Ella eased to a quick stop once the dilapidated border shack came into view. The steel door gave a heavy thud after Rutger unlatched and swung it open. Skonky, having hopped down from the cab under Charlie's romantic gaze, slowly scaled up the ladder leading into the truck and handed Rutger a beige sack.

"A few things to remember before we go in," Skonky began, pausing to glance quickly out the window.

"One—be respectful. Remove your hats, be polite, and say 'please' and 'thank-you.'"

"Two," Skonky continued. "Fill in everything on the immigration sheet accurately. Copy off ours, if you aren't sure."

"And three—you need your passports. Rutger has those."

As we lined up in the aisle single file, Rutger dug his bony arm into the beige sack, haphazardly pulling out the blue, red and black passports. Rutger, after handing Mary hers, looked as surprised as we must have when she suddenly made the event a race, sprinting into the immigration office as if someone had dropped a checkered flag. That was Mary—annoying to a fault.

The border office was kind of what I expected minus the Edi Amin look-alike I had expected to see at every border crossing and attitude. The woman behind the counter, wearing a white, neatly pressed uniform and a small cap, handed Mary a stack of white cards while directing us in a soft-spoken voice to fill them out carefully. The cards asked the obvious questions—name, country of origin, etc.—along with the less obvious—like destination address in Namibia, number of days we'd be staying, etc. While Stacey and Connor were busy trying to borrow a pen from someone, the rest of us were harassing poor Rutger about what to write down.

Rutger, accompanying Skonky and Charlie inside, left the couple at the front desk with the bulky black vehicle registration book to help us. I felt like I was asking a parent for help with my homework. Where are we going? Where did we come from? How many days? Thank God for people like Rutger and Megan—two souls willing to help a geographically challenged person like myself.

Mary raced through her form, making her the first to add the prestigious Namibian stamp to her passport. Admittedly, I was a little envious at first, but then less than enthused when I actually saw the drab-looking stamp, a simple, blue ink square that read 'Namibia' and the date. I wasn't turning into a dreaded travel snob, mind you, but would it be so difficult to put a lion or an elephant on your country's stamp? Instead of inquiring about where I could find the complaint department, I kept my mouth shut.

Once we received our stamps, we waited outside in the hot sun for Skonky, Charlie and Rutger to emerge. We could have waited in Ella, I suppose, but a slight breeze made it more comfortable outside. Besides, observing the group interacting outside of the truck was becoming a pretty interesting pastime, sort of like having your own traveling Animal Kingdom.

Observe the creature called 'Matt,' sauntering past the females and attracting only the most desperate by singing some crap techno song in his whiny voice. He is clearly the leader of his pack of Aussie males, as Connor and Bill have all given way. The female known, as 'Mary' looks particularly desperate, so needy for attention she'd be happy with anyone. But Stacey, another female, was having none of that. She had limited her search, now seemingly turning her attention to another species, a Dutchman named Aubrey.

Seeing Stacey and Aubrey flirt together, which had only really begun that day but was already getting pretty obvious, was a little weird, to say the least. For all of his unabashed comfort, I liked Aubrey, a nice guy in a goofy sort of way. He reminded me of what having a little brother would probably be like—a little annoying, sometimes clamoring for attention, sometimes pissy, but a good guy. The thing that got me, though, was how Stacey could find him sexually attractive.

"He just doesn't have it, y'know?" Megan explained as Aubrey began chasing Stacey around a dying, black tree. "When I look at him, I see nothing even remotely sexual. Nothing!"

I agreed. Nice guy aside, Aubrey was basically an over-grown boy who spit when he talked and liked getting people to laugh by making stupid references to his body.

Clearly, Stacey was applying all the pressure, however. She had done pretty well in sales back home and charming Aubrey, a guy who liked attention no matter where it was coming from, did not seem like the most difficult thing to do.

"I had a feeling Aubrey and Stacey would hook up," I said to Megan, nodding my head in their direction.

Megan turned towards them and then back at me.

"That? That's nothing," she said. "What makes you think there's something going on?"

Stacey, ducking quickly from Aubrey's grasp as he snuck around the tree, suddenly began her pursuit by attempting to pull on Charlie Brown's yellow shirt. "She'll hook up with him before this is all over," I said. "You'll see."

As good as the border crossing was at breaking up the morning, it became all too clear to me when we boarded the truck once again that we were racing to get back on some sort of schedule, even if it did only exist in Skonky's mind. I guess even though you always had to plan for something unexpected to slow you down—be it a flat tire, a border crossing, or a random animal mauling—you still had to get from Point A to Point B in a given day. Even if that did require you to hold on for dear life and put all of your trust in God. And Skonky.

Skonky, more than capable to handle the driving duties, punished Ella at times, leading me to wonder on many occasions how much more she could endure before expiring. Sometimes the entire shell of the truck bounced continually off the radials with bench seats swaying into the aisle and back again like spring-loaded jack-in-the-boxes. Yet no matter how bumpy the ride got, I knew I could always look back and see either Bill, Connor, or both spread out and fast asleep.

"We lost a lot of time this morning with everyone getting back so late from canoeing," Rutger mentioned nonchalantly as he cleaned his sunglasses with his shirt bottom. "Don't know if we'll have time to visit the Hot Springs or not."

"Hot Springs?!?" Megan said excitedly. "Where?!?"

Rutger smiled.

"Easy, Megan—if we have time, we'll stop. Just outside of Fish River Canyon—very good for sore muscles and all that."

Stacey, trying to get through the thick "Lord of the Rings" hardcover she had brought along, dropped the book dramatically in her lap and sat up.

"We have GOT to make it there," she said. "I haven't been in a hot spring since I visited my friend on the West Coast."

Rutger promised us that Skonky would stop there for a little while if time permitted, emphasizing that we needed to reach Fish River Canyon by sunset to get the whole experience. The Canyon, according to Rutger, was not only the oldest known canyon in existence but also the second largest behind the Grand Canyon. Thank God for Rutger—he had such a passion for guiding through Africa. Without him, our trip through Africa would resemble nothing more than a race across the continent.

We motored on for well over a long, uneventful hour before Rutger spoke up again.

"There you have the Hot Springs, guys!" Rutger exclaimed, pointing East towards a small clearing boxed by a newer chain link fence.

"Biggest attraction in these parts, though not so crowded today."

Megan's eyes grew wide. She loved all things related to body massage, so the hot springs had to be a blessing to her after the drudgery of tenting the past few nights.

"How long do we get here?" she asked Rutger excitedly, checking the time on her watch.

Rutger smiled.

"That's all up to Skonky—I'm not really sure what he has planned."

When the truck slowed to a halt, Rutger unlatched the door and kicked it open. Climbing up the ladder just enough to stick his head through the open doorway, Skonky scratched the top of his shaven head as he spoke, "You got twenty minutes here. You can change in the restrooms."

After letting up a collective cheer, the scramble was on for everyone to locate his or her swimsuits. My pair was buried so far down into my backpack I found myself forced to haphazardly dump everything out onto the seat to find it. It was chaos for a few moments; the entire aisle was jammed with bodies grasping overhead in desperation. Abe was always the most annoying during times like this. Barely able to move as it was, he did so as if he was in a vacuum, completely oblivious to those of us who needed to pass him in the aisle. I almost wished he had left that chore for Helen, too.

Throwing our suits on quickly in the changing area, Megan and I waded through the shallow end of the hot springs pool. I could feel the appeal, even on a 90 plus degree day. The therapeutic waters attacked my sore back instantly, loosening upon the stiffness derived from my hard earth mattresses from the past couple of nights. Megan, meanwhile, resembled a ray as she propelled herself effortlessly over the floor of the pool. Aside from us, only Connor, Bill and Aubrey chose to frolic in the pool—the rest settled for dipping their feet into the pool on one end or relaxing in a lounge chair.

Perhaps sensing that most of us would have rather stayed at the Hot Springs, Rutger did his best impression of a pitchman. "You guys will be stunned when you see Fish River," Rutger said confidently as Ella bounced across the gravel parking lot before merging back onto the main road.

"Like we've been telling you—every bit as spectacular as the Grand Canyon."

As the late afternoon sun began to wane and turn a deep, burnt orange color, Skonky pushed Ella even harder, kicking up cloudbursts of gravel dust as she hugged the shoulder of the climbing, hill-laden roads.

"I hope this is worth it!" Megan screamed into my ear over the sound of Ella's squealing tires as Skonky banked a hard left.

"There's gotta be a payoff, right?"

I nodded in reply.

It became increasingly apparent we were near Fish River Canyon when a whole collection of parked overland trucks appeared over the horizon, all spread out over an expansive lot of black pavement. No matter which overland tour through Africa you were on, Fish River Canyon was one of the few highlights of Namibia.

Weaving Ella between two green behemoths, Skonky somehow squeezed into a makeshift parking space only twenty yards or so from the paved walkway that inclined to the Canyon's lookout point. Shooting a quick look back at Rutger, Skonky flashed a 'thumbs-up' through the window before killing the engine.

"Hurry, guys!" Rutger ordered, before swinging the heavy steel door open. "Only a few minutes left before sunset!"

Racing from the truck with our cameras and binoculars, our entire crew sprinted enthusiastically up the path, blending in with a few stragglers from the other tours who also risked missing the much-heralded sunset. When the observation point came into view, it was packed; filled with so many camera-clad bodies that they surely would have spilled over into the canyon if the thick, steel gates surrounding the area weren't in place.

"I think everyone's here now," huffed Connor. "We'll have to squeeze our way in."

Aiming for a tight area that overlooked the east side of the Canyon, the neighboring groups adjacent to us politely gave way so we could all fit in. Only then, once I stood just behind the protective barrier, did I finally take a moment to peer out on Fish River Canyon, just as the sun started to dip behind us.

It was alright. I guess.

Maybe I was a little tough on Fish River Canyon—one of the 'most magnificent spots in Namibia' according to Rutger—though I figured there'd be a little more payoff after spending the better part of a day trying to reach it before the sunset. Though I hadn't visited Grand Canyon up to that point, I had seen enough photographs of its deep, multi-colored valleys to have an idea of what to expect out of Fish River, the so-called 'Grand Canyon' of Africa.

In that sense, Fish River Canyon was a disappointing letdown, bathed entirely in dirty sand color that offered little in the way of wonder and inspiration. The Canyon didn't even seem that impressively large to me, making me wonder if it was all those Grand Canyon documentaries or my desire to have remained at the Hot Springs that spoiled the experience for me.

Megan, snapping only a handful of photos, admitted the Canyon wasn't as impressive as she thought it might be either. My expectations of what I believed Fish River Canyon should look like tempered my enjoyment; something I needed to get under control to avoid complete and utter disappointment on the tour.

What if Fish River Canyon truly was the best Namibia had to offer? If it was, it'd be a grueling six weeks. I knew that much.

After noticing that our three guides were absent from the overlook, we returned as a group to the parked truck and discovered where they had disappeared to. For whatever reason, Skonky decided we'd eat dinner that evening in the parking lot, probably because it'd be pitch dark by the time we arrived at camp for the night.

It didn't matter to me. I was starving.

"I hope there is enough!" Dominick told Charlie as he gripped a plastic plate tightly in his hand.

"Sometimes I worry we might run out."

Looking up from the large, silver pot she had been scrubbing clean, Charlie scowled angrily as Dominick dug the spoon into the heaping mound of pasta.

"Why are you always complaining, man?!?" barked Charlie, tossing the scrubby into the pot.

"All you people do is whine!"

"I...I didn't think I was," Dominick replied, looking stunned at the outburst.

"Whatever!" Charlie sniped, pushing the pot out of her way as she stomped out of sight behind the truck.

"She's just...miserable," Dominick stated, shaking his head as he walked to his chair with dinner.

"Such an angry woman!"

Though the group conversation steered in a variety of directions, it somehow always got back to Mary. When Connor would begin a story about his experiences camping in the Australian outback, Mary would interrupt with some inane story about a field trip she chaperoned at her school. When Aubrey would tell us about his life in Amsterdam, Mary would butt in and take the moral high ground regarding drugs and sex, grinding the whole works to a halt.

The cap on the evening, however, had to be when Mary unabashedly volunteered to the group that she had not had a bowel movement since we left Cape Town nearly a week ago. Now that's good dinner conversation—I hope we're having chili!

"It's the oddest thing," she explained, sipping on a plastic mug of coffee, I think.

"I can feel it up in there, but try as I might, nothing. A few pebbles, but that's it."

Matt, not missing an opportunity to be a jerk, began referring to Mary from that point on as 'Pebbles'—a nickname that Mary seemed to get a kick out of, for whatever reason. She finally got the attention from the Aussie guys that she sorely craved—and all it took was for her to share an embarrassing story about how she couldn't pinch a loaf.

As we cleaned our plates under Charlie's watchful, scowling eye, Skonky walked towards the impromptu fire he'd built in the dirt and demanded the group's attention. For some reason, I had a real bad feeling.

"Tomorrow is one of the highlights of Namibia—a walk through the Namibian desert with a bushman," Skonky started, walking delicately around the fire with his bare feet very close to the ashy wood.

"He'll show you things in the desert that'll amaze you—all the life, animal tracks, you name it."

Standing silently for a second, Skonky dug deep into the front pockets of his shorts and continued.

"But first, we're going to see the sun rise in the Namibian Desert," he smiled wickedly. "And the best place to see it is on top of Dune 45."

"That's 4:30 a.m., guys," Rutger added apologetically. "We need to leave when the front gates here open at five, since there may be traffic."

Traffic? HERE?!?

"When you get down from the top of the Dune, we'll have a real breakfast for ya—bacon, eggs, and the works. And have a change of clothes ready, too—the hike up the Dune in the morning will be chilly, but if you don't change for the Bushman walk, you'll bake for sure."

The dinner silence was broken soon after that—interspersed with the excitement of climbing the famous Dune 45 coupled with the dread of waking up early to watch the sun again.

IT'S ONLY SAND!

Who gets up at 4:30 a.m. anyway? Farmers, maybe. Or at least that's what I always thought. There's something so very depressing about waking up in total darkness—I always grudgingly picture everyone but me tucked into their little beds and enjoying the deepest sleep imaginable. At least misery had company that day—every overland group in the entire campground had begun stirring early with the sole purpose of making it to Dune 45 on time.

Despite the early waking hour, Rutger was as chipper as always. Surprisingly, everyone responded to Rutger's initial wake-up call—after we broke down our tents in the darkness, we climbed aboard Ella single-file in zombie-like obedience. If I was to ever start my own cult, I would borrow heavily from the whole African Wanderer experience—little sleep, less food and plenty of boredom.

Ella silently rumbled towards the campground gate, trying to sneak away without alerting the rest of the herded overland trucks still grazing in the deep grass. No such luck. Even by the time we arrived at the locked campground gate, just a few minutes before 5 a.m., we found ourselves in queue behind three trucks at least as large as ours and a couple of vans. All that was missing was the checkered flag to signal the start of the race. I just knew all hell was about to break loose.

"I'll be damned!" Bill exclaimed from the back of the truck. "Someone actually got up before we did? Impossible!"

"You'd be surprised!" replied Rutger through a stifled yawn. "It becomes a mad rush out of here to get to the dune on time."

Before the guard emerged from the shack next to the gate, several more trucks and various other vehicles continued lining up behind us. It resembled a scene somewhere between a NASCAR race and 'Mad Max,' with vehicles of all shapes and sizes being commandeered by all sorts of frightening guys, each driver willing to pull out all necessary stops to be first.

I'm sure the Skonkys in this world loved this sort of thing.

The flame of Skonky's lighter illuminated his ghoulish-looking silhouette in the darkness for a brief second—making him look even more sinister than usual. Revving in unison, the elderly guard checked his watch one last time and slowly sauntered over to the gate as the engines belched smoke and noise. Fumbling briefly for the key to the padlock, the guard gave a final, slightly timid look in the direction of the convoy, swung the gate open, and danced deftly out of the way.

The checker flag was down. The race had begun.

Rather than peel away amid an exciting scene of squealing tires and burning rubber, the heavy, lumbering vehicles more accurately crawled away, initially resembling a slow-moving elephant stampede. For all of the chest beating and engine revving, it was kind of funny watching those big behemoths slowly slink away once allowed to actually leave the campground, sleepily ambling down the narrow, rocky road. This didn't last, however, and as soon as Ella stirred to life, we began tearing up the road at the same reckless speed we had grown accustomed to, except this time we were completely sandwiched between identical vehicles in front and behind us. If you were either claustrophobic or a nervous driver, this was not the place to be since Skonky's sudden, relentless braking was the only thing keeping Ella from resembling an accordion.

The madness of the makeshift road race continued for almost a half-hour that morning until we finally arrived at Dune 45 just as the darkness of the previous night began to give way. After finally seeing that heaping mound of fiery red sand extending high into the sky and decorated with scores of footprints, I truly understood what all the excitement was about. Dune 45 was THE sand dune of the Namibian desert, instantly recognizable thanks to the sheer number of documentaries that existed on Africa. And with the sun just starting to peak in the East, we'd have to hurry if we wanted to reach the top by sunrise.

Parking as close as he could to the starting point up the Dune, Skonky nodded approvingly as we ran off, merging into a quick, makeshift line that streamed upwards towards the summit. From top to bottom, Dune 45 was already completely filled with people, hundreds of tiny ants orderly marching to the highest ridge.

Taking a deep breath, Megan and I began our ascent. Almost instantly, my stomach became queasy and I grew mildly nervous. I hated heights, and everyone was moving so quickly up the dune that I struggled to keep the image of me losing my footing along the thin ridge and tumbling to my death. Making matters worse, I had worn my sandals that morning, not terrible for traction, but not as good as the hiking boots I had left on the truck.

Concentration was key I told myself; though I probably concentrated so much on every precise step I made along the narrow ridge that I made things worse, catching my breath each time one foot slipped a little or temporarily lost my balance. As I scaled higher, I found myself walking in a way that either looked like I was poorly imitating a duck or I had to use the bathroom very badly, bending my knees slightly while extending my arms at my side. If I tumbled over the side, I told myself, my gravity would be low enough where maybe I could dig myself quickly in or, at worst, roll safely down. With each deliberate step, I focused only on the path in front of me, daring not to look down even once.

Though I never claimed to be the most patient guy, common courtesy at the very least should dictate moving off the path to let people pass if you feel compelled to stop and gaze or even catch your breath. In my mind, it was a simple notion: GET OFF THE DAMN PATH. Yet the three older, beefy Germans in front of us—two women and a man—seemed oblivious that they were holding up probably a couple hundred people who were still racing to the summit to beat the rapidly rising sun. Trekking straight up through sand is a difficult task, but walking fifty feet, coming to a complete stop, and making the path impossible like they were just seemed pretty selfish and rude. And after it became more persistent the higher up we got, I grew annoyed, first sighing loudly (a 'Paul' classic) and then starting with the usual, slightly audible phrases ("C'mon!" and "What's the hold-up?" among others). Meg always stepped in when she saw me getting annoyed—I think part of her was afraid I was going to totally lose my cool one day and murder someone. When even her sweet "Could you excuse us?" did not work, she let loose a frustrated sigh of her own, finally prompting the three to move to the side so we could pass.

I began to get more winded as I hurried up the ridge, though I still managed to focus on every step I made into the well-worn footpath. Despite my constant anxiety, the last thing I wanted to do was stop. Stopping meant scurrying out of the way of the mass of people behind me while digging into the side of the dune, a prospect that seemed far more precarious. I did not want time to study the ground below me or to follow the path ahead of me, which fluctuated between gradually leveling off at times to jutting straight up into the sky at a frightening angle. I concentrated on the crumbling red sand beneath my boots and little else, though I felt sick in the pit of my stomach when I figured that the thin ledge of sand I was trudging along had easily carried me at least 200 feet into the air.

Still, I continued on with great determination. And if the sun rose without me at the top, so be it. I just wanted to get up there. Still marching right behind me, Megan faintly called out to me just as we approached the final leg up.

"Go on without me," she gasped. "I need a few minutes."

The group's speed seemingly picked up as the sun jutted out from behind a valley in the distance. Even with the glowing, orange light of a new day dancing brightly in the corner of my eye, I wasn't about to take my mind off the path before me. Step after careful step. I fought on, until a couple hundred feet later, when there finally was no higher up I could go, I could safely look down at the red ground so far below me. I had made it—I reached the summit.

Seeking out familiar faces, I dug in near Connor, Thom and Bill, who had reached the top for at least a few minutes.

"Team America just made it," teased Connor. "Haven't seen any sign of Team Canada yet, though."

I took a deep breath.

"No man," I said, looking across the valley towards the rising sun. "That's a long way up for them, maybe."

As soon as those words left my parched mouth, Megan staggered in, looking very flushed. With one hand still over her heart, her cheeks were emblazoned red. The water bottle she had been clutching was nearly empty.

"I guess we should have brought more water," I said. "How do you feel?"

Plopping herself down into the sand next to me, Megan dug the water bottle deep into the sand between us.

"Did you have a hard time breathing back there?" she asked nervously. "I think something's wrong."

"It's a workout," I said, grabbing the water bottle out of the sand. "Everyone was moving so fast that you had to keep up."

"How would you know if you had a heart attack?"

"What?!?"

"I think you'd know right away, right?" Megan asked shyly.

I once joked that we would never buy a medical encyclopedia since I was convinced Megan could randomly turn to any page and discover she had contracted wherever her finger landed.

"It wouldn't be a heart attack," I reasoned. "You would have collapsed."

Megan said nothing as she placed her hand on her heart for a few moments, listening to its beat. Her spirits picked up once she removed her camera from its case and snapped several photos, catching the vibrant orange sun just as it came into full view over the red mounds of sand. The view from the dune was absolutely breathtaking.

After a few minutes of socializing with the group, we joined the mass of people now headed down—the exact same way we headed up. I prayed we wouldn't come across any latecomers now on their way up since the path wouldn't be wide enough for two.

We could smell breakfast was ready as we made our way back to the truck. While we stuffed ourselves with scrambled eggs and breakfast sausage, Rutger squatted onto a seat near the middle of the group, conducted a quick head count, and started briefing us on the rest of the day. He seemed to be clutching his breakfast plate especially tight; I could swear he was watching Dominick from the corner of his eye.

"When we finish up, we hit the road for the Bushman walk," he said, scarfing down a forkful of eggs. "This is one of those optional activities, mind you, so if you don't want to pay the $10, you can stay back at the truck with Skonky and Charlie. Anyone?"

The group was silent except for the sound of Aubrey chewing loudly. Either pay $10 to get away from the truck for a few hours or witness some drama between Skonky and Charlie play out firsthand.

The $10 price was a bargain in any country.

Rutger seemed pleased everyone had opted in. 'Bushman' sounded like a figure of legend to me—an elusive and crafty master of everything. I pictured a proud, stouthearted African warrior, forced to learn desert survival skills that allowed him to adhere to the traditional ways of his people. And that left me both excited and a little intimidated at the prospect of our impending meeting.

We boarded the truck after breakfast to reach our rendezvous point with 'Bushman'—a spot deep within the Namibian desert named Sousseveli. Before departing, Skonky popped in briefly and reminded us that even though we weren't taking the walking tour of the desert in the heat of the day, we'd better carry plenty of water with us and wear warm weather clothing.

"It's going to get hot out there, guys," Skonky warned. "And you're going to be doing enough walking to make things really miserable if you aren't prepared."

For most of the group, a change of clothes wasn't necessary—most of the men, at least, had already braved the hike up Dune 45 wearing nothing more than shorts and would be more than suited to take on the heat of the desert as a result. At the other extreme was Abe, for the moment looking quite comfortable in stiff-looking blue jeans and a heavy red sweatshirt with a big bass on the front of it.

"Someone's going to get some CPR practice in later today," I whispered.

But the strangest sight of all had to be Stacey, decked out like she was going clubbing on a Saturday night rather than hiking through the scorching desert. From head to toe, she had completely covered herself in black, looking like a woefully lost Goth chick. Plus make-up, of all things—spackled layer upon layer over her entire face to attract Aubrey, no doubt. Yes, this was the same travel snob who bragged about exotic journeys into Hong Kong and trekking through the Himalayas—wearing a hardened cake of poorly-applied cosmetics and an outfit that would probably bake her alive.

We climbed into one of three pick-up trucks and pushed through the high sand drifts. There were no roads where we were headed, only partially covered tire tracks crushed into the sandy earth. Precarious and bumpy, the bouncing made you feel like you were going much faster than you probably were, while the constant weaving back and forth by the driver to avoid the largest drifts only made matters worse. Admittedly I suppose, my mood had begun deteriorating since the rush of scaling Dune 45 had subsided. Crammed into a shaky, uncomfortable pick-up truck while hard sand pelted your face could do it to anybody.

All three pick-up trucks seemingly stopped in the middle of nowhere, on the lip of an enormous, barren clearing surrounded by mountainous sand dunes. Though none appeared as big as Dune 45, most had to be at least thirty feet tall. Without a well-worn footpath dug into any them, none could be easy to climb. At our feet rested an assortment of green shrubs, some only knee-high, some slightly larger. But aside from the occasional, seemingly misplaced rock, there was nothing. A cool breeze calmly whipped past my ear, then utter silence. This was the desert.

Climbing out of the driver's seat of one of the pick-up trucks, a muscular white man, dressed completely in khaki with a tan pith helmet pulled down low over his eyes, moved towards the center of where we had gathered. He had a friendly look in his dark eyes, a warm confidence that made you feel instantly comfortable.

"Hello," he said, removing his hat to wipe the small beads of sweat from his brow. "I'm Bushman, and I'll be your guide in the Namibian desert this morning."

Bushman?!? He's a white dude!

"There's lot of life here in the barren-looking place. It's my job to show it to you."

Bushman?!?

Admittedly, I felt a little foolish for assuming that the name 'Bushman' would belong to a native black African man—not the well-spoken, unassuming English-looking guy standing in front of us. But 'Bushman' was definitely the real deal—as someone who had survived in the unforgiving Namibian desert for years, he spoke to us with a casual, almost humble, sort of confidence.

In short, the guy was amazing. Where we saw little, insignificant-looking markings in the sand before, 'Bushman' saw the tracks of jackal and sidewinder snakes, recently hunting for food in the very spot where we now stood. He could tell so much from so little, like approximately the time of night that jackal had arrived, where it stopped, and where it probably continued on in search of a nighttime snack.

Most impressive to me was the abundance of life in the desert. There was lots of edible life, according to 'Bushman.' With one knee resting on a small mound of sand, 'Bushman' gently plucked a single sprig of green that sprouted out of the sand with his fingers. Resembling a thin needle, the tiny base of the vegetation held nourishment—tiny and juicy potato-like fruits that could sustain both man and animal.

"The key to survival out here," Bushman declared, "is water. Whether you get it from food or by drinking blood, it is absolutely essential."

'Bushman' added later that if drinking blood wasn't your thing, you could always just eat the eyes of whatever you had killed for the fluids. This guy was hardcore.

The intensity of the sun increased noticeably as the tour progressed. It became rather obvious why all tours ceased before the heat of the day began. Barely past 10 a.m., the blazing sun made it feel upwards of 90 degrees. And Megan and I had a few empty water bottles to show for it, making me thankful for having a girlfriend so determined about having enough on-hand if we needed it, even if it meant briefly trudging along like a pack mule.

As expected, it didn't take too long for the rising heat to strike Abe, forcing him to remove the long-sleeved sweatshirt and tie it around his waist. Personally, I didn't need to see Abe's sagging, pasty body, but if it saved him from a heart attack, it was okay. I guess.

Try as I might, I couldn't really feel sorry for Stacey, who, looking like she belonged in a wax museum as layer after layer of cosmetics melted off her face, dug her feet firmly into the sand while the tour continued. Wiping massive streams of sweat from her forehead, she had had enough climbing through the misleadingly dense sand dunes and plopped herself to the ground.

"I told you to dress comfortably!" Rutger lectured, popping over to Stacey briefly.

"There are two ways to get through these dunes on foot," the Bushman said, temporarily distracted by the sight of Stacey, as we gathered in front of a 20 foot wall of sand that extended across the entire section before us.

"The long, unnecessary way, and my way—straight up."

With his large, bare feet extended straight out, almost resembling the webbed feet of a duck, 'Bushman' dug them directly into the sand mound in front of us, scaling it in a few, short seconds as we looked on with amazement. Waving his hand in front of him with a grin, 'Bushman' indicated that it was now our turn.

I worked out, I told myself—no problem. Digging my first foot in, I struggled instantly, wrestling to maintain my balance as I extricated my other foot from the soft sand and into the same dune. Each small step I could muster up the wall triggered a sandy avalanche, quickly covering each foot and making each subsequent step that much harder. After two steps up the dune I was utterly exhausted, nearly sliding back to the point from which I started. Slowly, I fought my way up determinedly with the rest of the group until I finally breached the sandy wall. 'Bushman' and maybe Rutger were the only two that had an easy go of it. Maybe there was something to wearing no shoes after all.

The view from the top of the mound was breathtaking, however—as we looked down onto a salt flat that contained several fossilized trees, which had remained well preserved despite being thousands of years old thanks in large part to the dry climate. Eerily beautiful, the blackened trees were desert sentinels, perpetually on watch. We learned they filmed a scene from "The Cell" here. Stopping, I suddenly felt the scorching burn of the sun beat hot against the back of my neck. As noon approached, things really began to heat up.

Leading us back a different way, 'Bushman' brought us up a fairly level ramp of sand that culminated atop one of the larger dunes in the entire valley, easily fifty feet tall. When the entire group reached its summit, 'Bushman' held out his right hand and paused.

"This is probably what some of you've been waiting for," he started, craning his neck deliberately down the other end of the dune, which was a 45-degree angle straight down.

"You can get down this dune any way you want," he continued. "Slide, run, walk. Just have fun."

As if on cue, Connor, waving his arms back and forth over his head, screamed as he dove forward into the sand, sliding on his back the rest of the way down. Bill followed similarly but not as graceful, rolling the more he tried to right himself.

Matt, as expected, made sure things were at most dramatic, waiting until his Aussie buddies had gotten down from the mound to ensure that everyone's attention was focused on him. Backing up about fifteen feet, Matt let loose with a low-pitch scream and charged forward, trying to cartwheel down, but instead he was gracelessly dumped into the blazoned red sand, rolling down the entire length of the mound like he had been tossed out of a bar. When he did hit bottom, Matt sprung to his feet merrily, pretending that the slightly embarrassing way he headed down was exactly the way he planned.

For his efforts, Matt was completely covered in warm, red sand, adhering to his sweat-covered face and arms like it had been glued on. With the red sand stuck to him, Matt became a fiery demon—his face, back, neck, arms and hair took on a crimson glow. Spitting a couple of times into the sand to remove what he could from his mouth, Matt tried vainly to brush off the clinging sand from his face.

Seeing Matt's misery quelled the aspirations of any other would-be-daredevils, myself included. Walking down the mound with Megan suited me just fine, though if I knew Matt was waiting for us to reach the bottom, maybe I would have taken the leap—and aimed for him.

"Could I have some water, please?" he pestered Megan as he eyed the half-empty water bottle she had been clutching.

"I seem to be all out."

Damn, these people pissed me off. What do you say or do? I knew we had enough—she had half a liter in her hand and I had one more full one in the bag. But it was the damn principle of the thing—if you didn't bring enough, why should we give you ours? And aside from that, neither one of us wanted to start some kind of precedent where every famished, ill-prepared traveler came to us when they needed something.

Megan hesitated. I knew she felt the same as I did, but she was in another tight spot. Biting her lip, she handed the water over to Matt—I would have, too. But as soon as she did, she wanted to leave him to rot in the desert like I did.

Unscrewing the cap from the water and placing it into the sand, Matt lifted the water bottle high over his head and poured it directly over his head, arrogantly wasting the water Megan had agreed to share because we figured he needed a drink, not a bath. For all he knew, that was all of the water we had with us—not even considering how vital water is in the middle of the desert.

His shower didn't last very long, at least. As soon as Meg and I realized what he was doing, we both yelled an angry "Hey" forcing him to quickly tilt the bottle upright.

"That water's for drinking," Megan yelled, snatching it from his hand.

"Sorry," replied Matt with a sheepish smile. "Just gettin' off the sand!"

Rutger, who had been standing behind us and witnessed the whole thing, chimed in.

"You're in the middle of a DESERT, Matt...I can't believe you!" he said incredulously, sounding like a disappointed parent.

"You NEVER waste water here!"

I think Rutger's comment got to Matt the most, causing him to silently put his shirt back as he quietly joined Connor and Bill. Rutger watched him with his hands on his hips and a look of disbelief on his face.

"Some people just don't get it," Rutger mumbled to himself.

With that, the tour ended, and we thanked 'Bushman' before preparing to head back. Just in time, too, if you ask me—the sun was really starting to warm things up, with small waves of heat rising up off the sand in the immediate distance. It had become downright sweltering. Stacey looked a little better after tying her long sleeve top to her waist but still appeared to be struggling in the rest of her all-black outfit.

A single though slightly large truck pulled up to return us to Ella, pelting us briefly with sand as it rounded and faced the direction it came from. By the time the truck .agonizingly crawled and jostled us back at a turtle's pace. I was in a pretty foul mood. The Bushman tour was excellent, a true highlight up to that point, but getting from point A to B just made me focus on how my misery of being in Africa and putting up with everything else that came with it was getting to me. It brought back a whole flood of things I didn't like about the tour: Skonky's lack of interest; Charlie's downright surliness; the routine of sitting on the truck all day; sleeping in tents every night; lousy food; and, for the most part, little excitement save for a few, shining moments. Part of me wished I had never left Chicago.

During the drive to our next campsite for the evening, I wondered how exactly I was going to make it through the next five weeks. Six weeks in Africa didn't seem like a long time when I read the colorful brochure that made everything seem so exciting, cloaking the actual reality thus far of experiencing a few flashes of excitement buried beneath a great deal of boredom and routine.

And the people were really starting to annoy me. After spending an entire day doing everything with them, from eating all of our meals together to riding with them for all those endless hours on Ella, the last thing I really wanted to do was hang out with them any longer than I had to at some sad campsite bar after dinner. Retiring to the tent to read, even sleep, was a much better option.

Being away from home and Chicago was much more difficult for me than I ever would have anticipated. I yearned for that freedom to do whatever the hell I wanted, when I wanted to do it.

SOME PARADISE

Ella rolled out at nearly 10 a.m. that morning. At least the landscape was a little more interesting as we drove closer to the shore of the Atlantic Ocean. A spooky, grayish mist blanketed the horizon, wrapping black, gnarled trees that jutted out along the beach in haunting fashion. The sour, salty stench of the ocean also became more prominent, which somehow always managed to make me feel a little queasy.

"You're looking at Cape Cross," yelled Rutger, his voice battling the whipping ocean winds that blasted through the windows. "It's home to the seal colony, but you won't miss it."

"I thought we were stopping," I said. "It was in the brochure."

Rutger looked like he was caught a little off-guard.

"They're just seals," he answered, directing his gaze out the window.

"Stinky, smelly seals."

Megan returned with an incredulous look. Rutger sat silently for a second, then sprung up quickly and projected through the entire truck.

"Who wants to stop at the seal colony?"

Rutger's request was met with a variety of responses, all wanting to see the creatures for themselves, smell or no smell. Some of the Aussies seemed like they could take it or leave it, claiming they saw seals fairly frequently, but the masses had spoken, and I thought then that maybe Rutger had regretted even bringing it up until after we were well past Cape Cross. Oh well. What did he expect after spending over a week in Africa and only having a few, fenced-in ostriches to show for it?

"Next stop, smelly seals!" Rutger yelled, plopping back into his seat.

Minutes later, Skonky pulled Ella onto a small road with a red, rusted sign that read 'Seal Reservation.' The sign almost seemed unnecessary—the increasingly sour smell in the air said we had to be close. I could hear the barking of a symphony of ceaseless, bellowing voices in the distance, somewhere through the mist.

Cutting through the sour air until we were about thirty feet from the ocean shore, Ella grinded to a halt.

"Ladies and gentleman," said a smiling Rutger, flinging the door wide open as he playfully covered his nose.

"Welcome to Seal Country!"

The intense stench hit me like a sledgehammer as I climbed down onto the beach, probably the most sour and salty smell ever. Almost immediately, several in the group—Helen, Mary, and Stacey—pulled up shirt collars or stuck handkerchiefs over their mouths and noses in a vain attempt to make it a little more palatable. You could only do so much—it was that type of eye-watering stink that you could only hope wouldn't stick in your clothes and follow you around all day.

At least you didn't need to step very far across the slimy beach to see the masses and masses of seals crowding the beach area, each one seemingly barking and baying for that total sensory experience. I could only guess how many there were—hundreds, thousands, ten thousand, maybe—packed in so close that it was virtually impossible to spot the sand they rocked back and forth on. Through the masses of slick black skin was a panoramic spectacle.

Groups and groups of seals barked and challenged one another for a coveted couple of feet of space, sometimes using the sheer might of their rubbery bodies in a never-ending battle to slam their opponent away. The cleverest seals, I believed, avoided all the conflict and lazily warmed themselves beneath the obscured sun, precariously positioning themselves over a jagged and jutting rock gathering and finding deep sleep. A great number of seals, however, chose to live the sort of carefree and idyllic life that would make anyone envious, riding the waves of the ocean like professional surfers until they gently crashed into a spray of foam along the beach. Through all of the life, though, you could still find death, in the form of battered, young pups and aged veterans who lacked the strength to survive.

For me, the key to surviving the stench was to breath through my mouth—taking a long, deep breath through my nose bordered on suicide. In spite of the stench, I was very excited to finally see something worth getting excited about; something on the trip that had actually lived up to my expectations. Maybe it was selfish for me to think in such a way, since my expectations might have been so high in the first place. Still, witnessing the seal colony was extremely exhilarating; it filled me with the sensation that perhaps we had finally turned that corner of boredom. I made a mental note to have my binoculars on the seat next to me from that point on as I daydreamed about herds of elephants and prides of lions straddling the road.

We probably spent nearly fifteen minutes observing the seal colony that morning—eventually we reached a point where the nagging, noxious odor just got to be too much regardless of what clever way you chose to breathe. Neither Skonky, Rutger nor Charlie had ever left the truck. Only later did Rutger mention that African Wanderer had considered eliminating the stop at the seal colony altogether due to lack of interest, something he confessed may need to be reconsidered judging by our reactions.

Heading back to the truck, Skonky didn't miss the opportunity to get in a joke about the intense smell.

"This looks like a good spot, guys," he said seriously from the safety of the cab.

"Charlie, let's set up lunch right here!"

****

Our journey through Namibia that afternoon was very similar to that first day when we left Cape Town, complete with diverging, winding roads that hugged mountainous passes that seemed to be trail blazed as we went along. The sun was getting pretty intense, too—not as hot as the desert, but uncomfortable enough to significantly diminish our water supply. Megan and I were down to about one liter between the two of us before we finally reached the campground in Spitzkoppe, landmarked by a little wooden shack that almost seemed to sprout from the middle of the desert.

A kind looking black man, smiling through a mouth of broken, gnarled teeth and waving heartily as he raced to the cab, greeted us. I peered into the shack and noticed a woman—probably his wife—with a small child rocking on her knee.

To say this campsite was the sparsest we had been to at this point in the trip would have been an understatement. I didn't even know if you could legally call this 'camping'—there was nothing there! I guessed the guy who greeted us owned the land we would be spending the night on, but that was as far as his obligation to the entire camping experience went. The few, dry shrubs that existed on the plot of land conveniently rose from the only level ground available to pitch our tents. The remainder of it was littered with rough boulders, strewn all over as if they had been randomly dropped some time ago. A lonely pit toilet, nestled behind the only life form that could be mistaken for a tree, hid itself nearly seventy five feet away from camp, across a barren field that just screamed 'snake haven' to me. Getting bit by a venomous snake would be bad enough—getting bit in the middle of nowhere could be lethal.

Finding a good place to put the tent was our most difficult task to date. Both of us were a little hinky about putting it too near a bush for fear of snakes, and finding flat land without roots jutting out from it was impossible. Finally, we settled on a small, slightly slanty patch that placed us nearly on top of Stacey's tent, which wouldn't be so bad if she didn't sound like an eighteen-wheeler truck when she snored.

The swarms of insects weren't much better; they buzzed directly into our ears as we hurried to erect the tent poles. Throw the stifling heat of the afternoon into the mix, and you had one miserable experience.

"We need water," said Megan in a dry voice. She took a long sip from the bottle and glanced nervously as another bee whizzed past us.

"Doubt we'll find any here," I said. "From the truck. I guess."

Megan sensed the hesitancy in my voice. As much as African Wanderer had made it a point at orientation to mention how the water in the truck's tank was available to all of us, our guides never mentioned it. No one asked and no one ever used it, except for those couple of times Megan and I took a quick blast of it to clean our dishes before a meal. It was unchartered water that needed to be crossed, no pun intended.

I felt silly, convinced I was making a big deal out of nothing. We were in the middle of a desert. Even if we did stop some place earlier in the day for water, we'd still need to fill up to fight the sweltering heat.

I grabbed a single two-liter bottle; I didn't want to come across as a greedy, selfish bastard and cheat anyone else out of water—and sought out Charlie. I didn't need to, and in retrospect, Rutger or even Skonky probably would have been a better choice to ask. Still, if nothing else, I thought asking would be best, if only to make them aware that I realized that water was not to be wasted.

I spotted Charlie standing by herself, arms crossed as she watched Rutger and Skonky unload the red, plastic crates of food from the truck.

"Charlie," I said in a polite yet firm voice. "We're going to fill up a little water from the truck, if that's okay."

Charlie stood silent for a few seconds, spinning on her heels quickly to reveal her sour-looking expression.

"We need it for cooking, man!" she exclaimed incredulously. "And for cleaning!"

Yeah, Charlie. Cleaning. We're in the middle of a desert, and you're worried about dirty dishes.

"But we're totally out and I don't see anything else around."

Maybe she thought I was being a typically difficult American. I didn't want to come across that way—I hated people like that myself. She said nothing as she turned her back to me.

"Take it, then," Charlie growled.

I bit my tongue sharply as I proceeded to the tank, scraping the dust off the spout before opening it just enough to let loose a thin, steady stream. What a bitch.

When I returned to Megan with the full bottle, I did my best to downplay the whole confrontation. Megan was not amused.

"That little shit!" she screamed. "What does she mean, 'for cooking'?!? Did she forget we were in the middle of a fucking desert?!?"

"But she didn't say 'no,'" I reminded Megan. "We'll just be a little sneaky in the future, that's all."

Once everyone was settled in and had their tents up, it was time to visit "Bushman's Paradise"—a name we had heard repeatedly that day but were still very unclear as to what it exactly was. 'Paradise' was such a vague term to begin with. When I thought of 'Paradise' for example, I thought of a lush, Caribbean-type getaway, complete with tropical plants and flowing waterfalls. Somehow, I doubted we'd find a rushing, stream of crystal blue water in this 'paradise.'

We boarded Ella and Skonky tore through probably the rockiest and most uncomfortable road to date—if you could even call it a road. Skonky stopped the truck when we saw a series of metal poles connected with chains that led to the top of the cliff—at least a good fifty sheer feet straight up. At first I couldn't tell if Skonky, staring up towards the top, was considering the ultimate suicide run and attempt to cart us to the top. When he turned off the ignition, it all became clear we would be on our own the rest of the way.

"Right up there," said Rutger, pointing to the top of the cliff, "is what's known as 'Bushman's Paradise'—a fertile area that offered great protection years ago when they lived here."

"You'll see ancient cliff paintings and dwellings, but you won't see them from here," he added, flipping down the mirrored sun glasses that rested within his curly hair.

"It's a straight climb up, so hold on tight to the chains."

God, I was really growing to hate all of this 'extreme' bullshit. I knew this trip wasn't going to be a day at the shopping mall, but for once I would have welcomed a nice, safe path all the way to the top—not something that looked like a certain, rocky death if you slipped even slightly. And I thought Dune 45 was bad—at least that would have been a somewhat soft landing. All that would cushion my falling here would be sheer rock, and I had a feeling it wouldn't do a very good job.

I looked over at Megan, partially for support, but primarily to see how she was doing. Her face appeared to be a mix of anxiety and fatigue; I grabbed her hand and squeezed it. She smiled slightly and squeezed back before we started the climb.

At least I had the chain to hold onto, I repeatedly thought, as I started my ascent. If I started to slip, I could just grab hold and stop myself. Like Dune 45, I concentrated solely on making sure my two feet were making firm contact. The rocky earth made it a little easier for traction, but the steepness made things a little more treacherous. We stopped once or twice along the way up to catch our breaths, but it wasn't as bad of a trek as I thought it would be.

Without offending the many 'Bushmen' out there who are surely reading this, the so-called 'paradise' left a little to be desired. Through my eyes, I saw nothing more than another barren stretch of rocky land, not the fertile, green stretch of beauty I had imagined. I guess it was all relative. To a Bushman, maybe it was 'paradise', if only because the numerous caves and cliffs that lined the area were absolutely perfect for hiding from enemies or hunting game. Though I saw the practicality and resourcefulness of 'paradise', I still couldn't get too excited. To me, it represented another example of desolate Namibia that only made me more restless to spot wildlife.

We snapped a couple of pictures of the ancient drawings that lined a small portion of the cliff walls, faded remnants in brown and red hues of animals, mostly. At least there was a sort of payout for climbing as high as we did.

This particular night, Charlie was in probably her all-time pissiest mood. Maybe she was still sore with Skonky, but Charlie looked fiercer than any wild animal you could expect to find lurking in the Africa wild. Beneath the glow of the evening campfire, with the flame of the fire ring casting devious shadows against her already piercing eyes, Charlie cursed angrily as she readied the meal under our hungry eyes.

"Don't know what you people all expect from me," she mumbled as she flipped the wire grate of raw chicken under the flame. "Ingrates. All ingrates."

Even with Charlie's unbridled surliness, it was refreshing to spot chicken on the menu instead of those greasy sausages again. I had a sort of love-hate relationship with them. Eventually, Charlie's cursing must have gotten to Rutger. Whispering something to her, Rutger disappeared briefly and returned with several loaves of bread wrapped in aluminum foil, which he carefully poked with a long stick until each was nearly adjacent to the warm flame. Dinner always seemed to take so long, but mainly because there was little else to do except watch it being prepared. Though I had seen the ritual more than I had cared to, I was bored. And judging from the turnout at the fire, the rest of the group shared in the same struggle.

I didn't stay up very late that night—I felt like I wanted to be left alone to escape into sleep. Maybe it was the Lariam I was taking to keep from getting malaria, which supposedly could make you depressed, but I suspected more that it was the realization that if this trip continued the way it had, it would be nothing short of a total bust.

I spent my life savings on this?!?

I knew I was never much fun to be around when I got depressed. But once I was in the mood, I just went with it. I thought about how much I missed being home. How hard it would be to find work when I returned home. Most of all, I thought about the strain that the trip had begun putting on the relationship I had with Megan, transforming our intimate relationship into one where each of us really just wanted to be left alone.

Africa sucks.

FUN WITH JACKALS

As I sat with the group during breakfast, I paid special attention to the expressions around me. Maybe Megan and I were the only ones disappointed with the way things were going in Africa. I knew it wasn't the guide's fault if we were going through a particularly barren section of Africa, they were just getting us from point A to point B. I mean, if you were to take a road trip across the entire United States, I imagine it'd be much the same way—a decent amount of interesting sites sometimes lost between the miles and miles of boredom that is in Indiana and Iowa.

Over breakfast, I continued studying the faces in the group as an expert card player would study his opponents during a poker game, looking for that one subtle 'tell' that would reveal what they were trying to hide. Helen and Abe weren't cracking—they always had the same, accommodating expressions, smiling and nodding along to anything being discussed. Mary? That same, blank stare matched with the smile that she carried from day one. She wasn't bright enough to be upset about anything—she was like that big, dopey dog you could lead anywhere, and it would patiently sit until a tug on the leash. The Aussie guys—Matt, Connor and Bill—always seemed to be yucking it up about one thing or another, lately the sport of cricket. Even hung-over, they seemed in better spirits than I did most of the time. Aubrey was like Mary—not as dopey, but trying very hard to get people to like him through off-color comments about sex and such. And Stacey? She never got much play from men back home, so with Aubrey as a possibility, she had to be loving life. Maybe Dominick. I couldn't tell if the slouched way he sat and his tired expression merely signaled fatigue or annoyance, but I knew he didn't much care for Charlie at all. Given his appetite, it was no surprise, as Charlie's lack of passion must have really irked him.

It dawned on me then that maybe Megan and I had a harder time handling the trip simply because we were a couple and had laid all our cards on the table already, and having little desire to mask over the little things that annoyed us. I wasn't trying to impress anyone through manly acts of bravado or drinking contests at the bar. And Megan wasn't flirting with any guy she had been thrown together with to have a summer romance. Helen and Abe aside, everyone else had more to gain by maintaining a front about what a great time they were having. We were all strangers, and for this trip, you could try to become whoever you always wanted to be.

Skonky reminded us over breakfast that the reason for the early start was to get to the Etosha game preserve in time for dusk; the time of day when the animals were most active. Even for as ignorant as I was about some of the areas we were traveling through, even I had heard of Etosha—home to some of the best game viewing on the continent.

As usual, the day long ride in Ella to our next destination was very unspectacular—most of us spent the time to ourselves reading, resting, or a combination of both. Aubrey had begun reading 'Long Walk to Freedom,' the autobiography of Nelson Mandela, pausing through the thick book only to ask Megan or myself to define a few English words he was unfamiliar with. He had begun the habit of then writing the Dutch equivalent of those same unfamiliar words above in pen, so he could re-reference them if necessary.

Stacey was sleeping, and the thing about her that I found particularly weird is that she never moved from her seat behind us to the seat in front of us to join Aubrey. Maybe she was waiting for him to be a little more assertive and make a move—she would have loved the pursuit. As briefly as I knew Aubrey, however, I could tell this really wasn't his style. I could see right through all of the sexual innuendos he put out there and the off-color jokes. Like most men in the early twenties, he was a nervous little boy around women.

Mary, unfortunately, never gave into falling asleep on the truck too often. If anything, she became more and more aggressive with the Aussie guys as the days passed, occasionally dancing her way to the back of the truck to join her countrymen or squeezing her way into a vacant seat. Matt, who didn't mind attention no matter where it came from, seemed to almost enjoy her banal observations on life, though Bill and Connor would often roll their eyes at her approach and give her a hard time. Mary still gushed when the guys referred to her as 'Pebbles.'

I admired Helen and Abe the most, however. How two people could spend several hours with their noses buried in boring books like 'Trees of Africa' and its stirring sequel 'Wildflowers of Africa' was beyond me. It made me envious to see them pass the time so effortlessly, though Abe was the type of dullard who could spend the better part of an afternoon reading the back of a Cheerios box.

We arrived at camp in late afternoon, and judging from the number of people and vehicles we spotted when we first pulled in, our campground had to be where the action was. Dozens of overland-type trucks—most new and unfamiliar to us—orderly lined the parking area like soldiers waiting for an assignment. But this just wasn't a haven for overlanders, however. Cozy, moderately sized chalets also lined the campground, complete with electricity, running water, and individual pit grills. Though we were told when we departed that we would have the opportunity to upgrade to chalets at certain campsites, this was not one of them—Rutger quickly squelched our interest by telling us those chalets could run as high as $100 U.S. per night.

We set up our tents in a grassy area lined with thick, green bushes and a chain link fence in the rear. I never liked setting up our tent too close to the fire ring since I was a light sleeper and wasn't into the drinking scene that could sometimes ensue, so Megan and I began to set up pretty far back towards the bushes. Until Rutger spoke up.

"You guys are brave," said Rutger, half-joking and half-serious. "Make sure your tent is zipped up tight at night!"

Rutger was always so jovial that it wasn't easy to tell when he was pulling your leg or being legit. We stopped trying to bully the last rusty tent pole into the grommet to face him.

"It's the jackals," he said nonplussed, dumping his tent from its stuff sack. "At night, you'll see them run through camp and steal whatever they manage to get their greedy little hands on."

"Jackals?"

"Oh yeah, Paul," Rutger replied seriously. "They're the size of dogs and not aggressive to people, but they hide in bushes like the ones behind you."

"Sometimes they get bold when they're hungry."

Rutger's warning was enough to get us to strike our tent and move it closer towards the fire ring and away from the bushes. The threat of animals in the area would switch Megan's anxiety into 'high.' And even I wasn't too keen with the notion of our tent being raided by marauding jackals.

Skonky gave us the lay of the land and the way things would go down once we finished putting up our tent. Leading us all in a quick walk to the far side of the campground, he pointed out a huge, man-made watering hole that made this campground one of the most popular in Africa.

"As soon as the sun sets, they come out," Skonky explained.

"Elephants, rhino, wildebeest—you name it."

The watering hole itself, a good 100 feet wide and fifty feet across, was designed to appear very natural and unobtrusive, save for the large, film-like spotlights that rose high above on steel arms and illuminated down on the water. Yet the arms of those towering lights were hidden just enough along the side of the separation wall, behind some small rock formations, to make them almost unnoticeable. Though the late afternoon sun still hung high in the sky, people were already staking out their places on the many benches that lined the watering hole area, maybe hoping to get a glimpse of animal who wanted to get an early jump on everybody else.

The crowd grew steadily as the sun began to dip lower towards the west. Still, aside from the occasional hushed conversation, the silence remained. When Megan finally arrived, I waved her over to the seat next to me and we waited together, while the suspense continued to build, both of us hoping that the payoff would be huge.

We didn't have to wait very long.

A symphony of hushed gasps coming from the crowd on the right effectively killed the silence, and when several people began pointing to a wooded area still out of our view, I knew the payoff was near. Time stood still, as the sound of rustling trees and heavy feet plodding over ground were my only signals that something big was about to happen. Then, resembling a gray, arched periscope, the trunk of an elephant slowly emerged into view through the leaves.

"Oh my God!" whispered Megan. "Look!"

I'll never forget that sight, the sight of an entire, formidable herd of at least twenty five elephants uniformly marching to the watering hole, looking almost close enough to reach out and touch. It was completely awesome.

With an enormous female leading the way, the elephants advanced with quiet precision until they were almost flush with the low lip of the watering hole, each one no doubt eyeing a small section for themselves. I couldn't believe how quiet they were—so quiet that I could still hear the faint sound of the whipping wind through the trees above us. Then, spreading themselves thin, the caravans formed a massive, mighty semicircle around the far edge of the water, their way of telling any other thirsty animals that it was their turn. You could sense their raw power and confidence with every stride made; the elephants were seemingly aware that even the most feared predator didn't stand much of a chance against their sizeable herd. Even if they were aware of our presence, I doubt they would have behaved any differently.

Yet for all their power, the elephants appeared so noble. The several young, awkward calves flanked between massive adults as they eyed their anticipated drink.

When every elephant had managed a spot on the bank, the female signaled the herd by raising her head and trumpeting softly, prompting each one to step carefully down from the bank and into the water below. It was unlike anything I had ever seen before except in nature documentaries. I knew there'd be no going back to a zoo from that point on.

The long-standing silence of the elephants had soon given way to playful trumpeting and splashing. Mammoth behemoths, first employing their trunks as hoses, spouted water high into the air and onto their clay-covered backs. Then, quite unexpectedly, the same cows crouched down on their knees, dropping to the soft ground and rolling with little grace onto their bulky sides, the water covering them with a slick, blackened sheen. Calves, maybe a quarter-size of the largest cow, joined in the fun as well, trumpeting with the same, cheery enthusiasm as they bathed and drank their fill, sometimes losing their footing momentarily or tripping on their overgrown trunks and stumbling forward. Two young male calves battled one another for dominance, each putting their heads down while struggling to push forward in a show of force.

I felt so very lucky to have seen all of this unfold right before my eyes. Though the elephants had probably always traveled within the same herd, it seemed like they didn't really cut loose and interact on a social level until they had cause to celebrate.

Maybe that was what the rigors of life in Africa did to everyone.

I completely lost track of how long the elephants staked out the watering hole. I honestly believed I could have watched them all night. Ultimately, though, it was the same huge female who led the herd going in that decided it was finally time to move on. Slowly backing up towards the bank, she signaled the herd with another knowing bob of her head, quickly being met with a few short trumpets by several neighboring elephants. Then, spinning on her heels, the towering female slowly and methodically scaled the bank to firm ground, with each elephant falling diligently in line behind her. Within seconds, the entire herd drifted from our view, just as silently as they had entered.

The murmurs of the crowd became more audible but never above a slight whisper as the elephants lumbered off.

"That was just unbelievable!" I whispered to Megan, squeezing her hand. "I hope you got a lot of pictures!"

"Mmm-hmm," she said, digging for a fresh roll of film from her camera bag. "Who knows if we'll even see something like that again here."

Seeing the herd did do a lot to improve the pessimism towards Africa that both Megan and I had been feeling. Once again, I wanted to believe that we had turned some sort of a magical corner where we would see nothing but wildlife, versus the nondescript and not very impressive cliffs and canyons that took up so much of our discovery.

As I played those thoughts through my mind from our seat on the bench, a tiny jackal scurried towards the watering hole, scanning the ground in front of it before dipping its tongue in for a quick drink. Looking like a cross between a fox and a dog, with a mangy reddish-orange coat and a slender body, it boldly stood by the bank, waiting for something.

"I'm glad we listened to Rutger," I said, nodding towards the lone jackal. "It just looks like it might try something stupid."

The jackal danced back and forth along the water as the sun completely disappeared to the west, though the watering hole remained visible thanks to the large, film-like spotlights that flanked either side. It was approaching 6 p.m., the time Rutger had tentatively set for dinner, so Megan and I, with the other members of our group, made our way back to camp.

That night's feast of hamburgers was surprisingly good—meaty, juicy and with real cheese. I attacked mine quickly—not only was I hungry, but I knew I'd be upset if something spectacular was happening at the watering hole and I was back in camp stuffing my face.

The jackal we had left at the watering hole while we went for dinner hadn't left; he was still darting along the banks and keeping its nose close to the ground as it searched for whatever scraps it could find. I sat spellbound with anticipation, continuing to wait anxiously with the rest of the crowd for another nocturnal visitor. There was just that undeniable, inescapable feeling in the air. Suddenly, as it happened before with the elephant herd, hushed voices silenced suddenly. Megan, craning her neck towards the far-right corner, squeezed my hand twice and readied her camera.

"Something's coming! I can just tell!"

The whistling wind picked up through the leaves, the way it always did just before a summer storm. I could hear a slight crunching of earth coming from the right, a slow yet steady rhythm. The bright glare of flashbulbs danced through the night.

"Oh my God!" whispered Megan excitedly. "I didn't think we'd even see rhinos!"

Just as the elephants had done before them, the pair of black rhinos slowly sauntered over the edge of the watering hole, this time choosing the far right side closest to the jackal as their chosen spot. The lead rhino, nearly twice as big as the one behind it, stopped just short of the watering hole, paused briefly, and lowered its head, lapping with a long, twisting tongue. The accompanying rhino then did the same, maybe needing that bit of reassurance from his more formidable companion.

The silhouetted rhinos projected a spooky presence, wrapping themselves so well within the black night, sometimes so much so that all you could really focus on were their deep, penetrating eyes. True remnants of the prehistoric age, their stocky, compact bodies were adorned in heavy, layered armor, tiny tanks standing low to the ground. Most surprising to me was the reaction—or lack of reaction—of the jackal, never budging from its original position and now a mere fifteen feet or so from the huge creatures. A rhino taking out a jackal had to be the equivalent of stepping on an ant. What was the point?

As the crowd of people observing the watering hole swelled to at least a hundred, few had left before the rhinos finished drinking and disappeared into the night. Though they weren't the rare white rhinos that had been driven to the edge of extinction as a result of mass poaching, I was still left with the sensation that I had seen something extraordinary.

It was approaching 10 p.m. when the crowd finally began to dwindle, a good couple of hours since the rhinos had vanished. Feeling tired, Megan related she was headed off to bed, though I figured, after brushing my teeth, I'd check the watering hole out one last time.

"You're, like, obsessed with it," Megan teased. "I'm going to find you out there tomorrow morning with your sleeping bag!"

"It's all Skonky's fault," I replied. "He's the loser who could only find a few ostrich!"

THE GAME IS ON

The time was exactly three minutes before 5 a.m., the situation nearly identical to the impromptu road race to Dune 45. Like that morning, we waited inside Ella, along with several other trucks of all shapes and sizes, for a lone, rickety gate to open in the wee hours of the morning. But unlike the inspired madness that was the Dune 45 experience, the mass, heart-pounding exodus from the campground, this morning we waited to bust in, not out. Our destination? Etosha National Park—site of our first, full-fledged game drive.

According to Skonky, the best times for game viewing were either at dusk, when most animals began their day, or first thing in the morning, when that same busy day was winding down. Secretly, I wished that for just once, every single attraction for that day could be done according to our schedule. A glorious sunrise at 9 a.m.; animals showing up roadside at 10 a.m. to pose for photographs; you get the idea.

Through my sleepiness, I couldn't deny the excitement I felt building in anticipation of my first game drive in Africa, really the primary attraction, as far as I was concerned. Sleep was so difficult to come by the previous night, however. It was filled with several disturbing instances that I couldn't remember clearly enough, save for the undeniable force that roused me awake. It was nothing I heard outside the tent—rather, it was dreams and sensations, haunting my sleep in ways I couldn't even recall. Though I wasn't sure what threw me into such a panic that it forced me awake several times during the night, what I was certain of was the vertigo-like sensation greeting me when I sat up from my sleeping bag in fright, struggling to catch my breath. I battled back and forth all night to get back to sleep, sometimes finding a little success, sometimes keying in too much with the noises around me to tune anything out and relax.

When I thought I had finally gotten myself relaxed enough to fall back asleep that morning, that's when the tent-rattling began, which had almost become as routine as picking through the dirty dishes for clean ones. It was too early to wake up, it was too early to shower, and it was even too early to eat. After a little over a week, life in Africa had changed me. I'd never consider leaving the house without showering and putting on some clean clothes, yet in Africa, I wore the same clothes so often they almost became like a uniform, and I would sometimes go a few days without showering if one wasn't available, leaving my long hair in dry, matted knots.

After rubbing the sleep from my eyes, I grabbed several breakfast biscuits, about as tender as tree bark, and stuffed them into my pockets. I downed about a liter of water in anticipation of another warm afternoon, and then worked with Megan to filter all we could before heading out. If the game drive lasted into the heat of the day, we'd be miserable without it.

Not surprisingly, an almost somber quiet, second only to death, filled the truck as we journeyed to the game reserve. Someone snored pretty steadily from the rear of the truck, rhythmically sawing through the silence with a nasally buzz. Megan leaned over towards me and slept on my shoulder, taking short, whistling breathes through her mouth. Even the sun appeared to struggle as it woke itself, the sky resembling dusk.

"This is the time," Rutger said excitedly, peering out the window.

"Just dark enough to make the animals feel safe to explore."

At the urging of Skonky, Ella rolled slightly forward resting just in front of the shackled gate of the game park. Skonky, no doubt, started making designs on our sprint ahead. The guard at the gate, who all the while had stood with arms at his side like a statue, suddenly extended his right arm into the air, as if signaling to the throngs of gurgling vehicles that the time was near. Then, scanning the horizon for a little added drama, the guard mechanically lowered his arm, turned and unlatched the ramshackle gate, pulling it open wide while spinning his right arm in a pointed, circular motion.

The race was on. Sort of.

I guess you couldn't really consider it a race, since most races I had seen didn't abide to speed limits.

"Speeding is Grounds for Ejection! Speed Limits Strictly Enforced!" a sign just past the guard station angrily warned.

"Speeding is silly through here, anyway," Rutger agreed. "Move too fast and you could miss something huge."

With roads wide enough for any size vehicle to pass, many behind us seized the opportunity to do just that, without Skonky putting up much of a fight. When I noticed that every single vehicle, even ones larger than Ella, had whipped past us with abandon, no doubt headed off somewhere exciting while we lumbered along slowly, I was certain we wouldn't see much of anything that morning.

"They're going to scare everything away!" Stacey complained loudly. "Why aren't we going faster?!?"

"There's hundreds of miles here, Stacey," Rutger reassured her, before carefully rising to his feet to address the group.

"It's all luck, guys. They're unpredictable to a large degree and it's just being in the right place at the right time."

As if on cue, our first glimpse of wildlife on the game drive that morning appeared in plain sight, well clear of the small trees and high grass that could offer the perfect cover. A small herd of springbok, which to me looked like small, lean antelope had gathered about fifteen feet from the road, nosing through the brush and skipping over the occasional branch. As the truck slowed to a halt for the photo opportunity, we flocked to the windows like we had just seen Bigfoot. Springbok. About as common in Africa as a road kill raccoon back home.

Unconcerned with the presence of our hulking truck and the dazzling displays of flashbulbs, the springbok still seemed timid and guarded by nature, lifting their eyes as they listened through the light breeze for anything unusual. Nothing against our friends the springbok, but I secretly wished for a lion at that opportune moment, one that would appear out of nowhere for one of the wildest photos ever to adorn a picture album.

When we had gotten our fill, Rutger shouted to Skonky through an open window to continue on. It was the perfect system. If there was anything off in the distance, we knew we'd get there with Skonky, even if it meant him taking out an entire ecosystem. I doubted that Charlie, in her customary perch in the cab, would bring much, but we made up for that with the sharp eyes of Rutger, who did nothing more than scan every area we passed for subtle, covert movements.

"They like remaining hidden, guys," Rutger, related in a low voice, glancing back and forth from the corner of his eyes.

I was convinced that Rutger knew so much about animal behavior and instinct that we'd easily snap through the twenty rolls of film we had brought with us.

Following the springbok, we then spotted some impala (another unremarkable antelope-type species) and a small herd of zebra, nervously on watch. Several of the zebras had paired off, with each standing face-to-face but then lowering their heads onto the backs of their partners. This allowed the herd to stand watch in all directions while relaxing at the same time. There had to be a way to incorporate this crafty lookout system at the office.

We slowed a short time later after spotting a lone, shading wildebeest, probably 100 feet away but close enough with binoculars to see the threatening look it flashed while it laboredly chewed on some vegetation. Though the sun had just fully risen, perhaps it had already hunkered down to prepare for what would probably be another Namibian scorcher. The wildebeest was so far off that we weren't terribly optimistic about how well the photos would even turn out.

Then, the action started.

It all began innocently enough, with Skonky guiding Ella onto a sharp, dust-laden road that resembled the rest we had been down to that point. The important exception became immediately obvious—the shoulders were littered with several parked vehicles, all watching something in the immediate distance. Just like the fisherman who sticks his pole in the spot on the dock where everyone else is, so is the savvy tour guide, and Skonky had been around long enough to know that a small caravan of stopped vehicles meant something was going down.

As Skonky slowed Ella down to a spot behind a slightly larger, hunter green overland truck, Rutger quickly scanned the area, on a mission for one of those signs that would reveal all and tell the story. Bushman would have been proud.

"Jackals!" Rutger exclaimed, pointing to the two scruffy creatures that darted in front and past our now-idle truck. Stopping to glance curiously back at us once they had moved about ten feet from the trucks, the jackals raced with purpose across the green, slightly barren field.

"Guys!" announced Rutger, still scanning the horizon. "There's something big going on here! Look sharp!"

From the little I knew about jackals, they were bold little bastards who lived for opportunity—particularly, the opportunity to scavenge a free meal. Something had to be going on.

In silence, every pair of eyes in the truck gazed in the direction of the fleeing jackals, which in an instant had disappeared through a small patch of thicket.

"Look at that!" yelled Bill, pointing in the opposite direction.

A pair of hyena, brazenly galloping on the tips of the feet, darted past the truck, following the same route taken by the jackal. They had an eerie quality to them, their upper lips seemingly etched into permanent, twisted smiles. Both moved with surprising speed, more concerned with what was going on across the green field in front of them than our truck.

"This is huge, guys!" said Rutger, now standing and stretching back and forth between both sides of the truck windows, resembling a caged bird planning an escape.

"Hyena and jackals means a fresh kill. And that means lions."

Rutger tapped on the glass window to get Skonky's attention, gesturing with his hands to get him to inch forward past the truck in front of us. We didn't have a great view of the field where the scavengers had disappeared to—it seemed to drop off over a largely obscured ridge blanketed almost completely with low-lying shrubs. Heeding Rutger's orders, Skonky rolled Ella forward. The King of the Jungle had arrived.

Though it took me a few, long seconds to decipher what exactly it was I was looking at, it soon become unmistakable. A large, muscular male lion, with its paws and mane drenched in the freshly spilt blood of its foe, lay a mere 200 feet away in a small clearing. What exactly was on his menu that morning was not distinguishable, though Rutger speculated that it was some form of antelope, probably springbok, and that it happened fairly recently, judging by all of the scavenger interest. The jackal and hyena we saw scampering to the area moments ago had disappeared, no doubt waiting patiently under cover as the lion gorged. It was probably best not to interrupt.

Even at the considerable distance we found ourselves at, the command and confidence of the powerful creature was apparent. The lion was that notorious prizefighter, toying with its opponent and delivering that knockout before the audience could even find a seat. Dining completely exposed and unprotected, the lion seemingly sent a message to all would-be challengers, almost daring the truly foolish to tempt its rage.

My binoculars provided me with a great view, which the lion's piercing eyes managed to cut through even from so far away. Meg and I switched viewing between the binoculars and her zoom lens, which brought the beast so close that soon the entire truck begged for a view. I said it once and I'll say it again: why go to Africa if you only bring shitty gear?

Like all game parks we eventually visited, Etosha strictly advised that you stay in your vehicle at all times. Rutger, propping the door of the truck open only long enough to allow those sitting on the other side an unobstructed view, quickly snapped it shut when he thought the lion, who still had not budged since we first spotted it, started growing annoyed.

"You could never get me out there," Rutger laughed, latching the bolt on the thick steel door. "They cover so much ground so fast you wouldn't have a chance."

We snapped our fill of pictures and waited patiently for what was probably a half-hour—hoping for more action but coming to the quick realization that the lion wasn't going anywhere, at least not until the carcass had been picked clean. They weren't the quickest eaters, according to Rutger, and from what we could see, this one fit the bill perfectly. Sometimes it seemed like the lion was interested in doing anything but eat, he parked his enormous head briefly onto the ground as if he was resting and scanned the horizon through lazy-looking eyes. Probably having eaten its fill, the lion still was not about to abandon the fruits of his morning labor just yet.

We slowly puttered away down the nondescript road as most of the trucks that had alerted us to the lion stayed behind, hoping for more excitement. Either Skonky had a comprehensive road map in the cab or had driven this path hundreds of times before, because so many roads seemed to sprout off one another that it would appear very easy to get lost.

In the minutes following the lion sighting, we spotted: a lone giraffe, who quizzically stared at us through black, rounded eyes; a small herd of timid springbok, perhaps patting themselves on the back for surviving another night amid the lions; and a tiny bunch of zebra that darted behind some shrubs at our approach. It was approaching 9 a.m., on the cusp of that time of inactivity for the majority of African wildlife, when resting and conserving one's energy beneath shade made more sense than battling the heat of the day in search of food.

We pulled into a tiny-gated rest area to stretch our legs, use the restroom and then boarded the truck once again to eat lunch while we continued the game drive. My enthusiasm waned steadily over the next couple of hours, however, when we really didn't see much of anything except a springbok or two. Skonky seemed very persistent for one reason or another—maybe our next campsite was so close to Etosha that he figured he could waste most of the day driving in circles, or maybe he knew how bad we wanted to finally see something living and tried to make up for it.

"We're spending the night on the other side of Etosha," Skonky mumbled through his mouthful of lettuce and tomato.

"Namutani campground is a lot like the one we spent the night at yesterday. Huge watering hole and pretty new, too."

"How 'bout a pool?" shouted Connor from the luncheon table as he prepared another sandwich, slathering on a huge slice of mayonnaise onto his bread.

"Nice pool," answered Skonky. "And nice showers."

Being able to dip in any African water was still a privilege, as far as I was concerned, and even a working, warm shower was good enough for me.

Just as Skonky was about to discard the stained tub of long leftovers, two young boys appeared out of nowhere, remaining silent and stoic as they cautiously approached the truck. Rutger, greeting the pair with a warm smile, dumped the contents of the container into a plastic bag and handed it to the smaller of the two boys, who we watched dart behind a tree and dig into the pouch using their fingers. It still amazed me, how all you had to do was break out a little food in the most remote of places to discover an entire village worth of people.

Skonky's claim that we would not be on the truck long after lunch surprisingly rang true—it didn't even take us an hour to reach our campground for the night. At first appearance, the campground appeared nearly as expansive as the one we had just left, a maze of neatly paved asphalt roads and scattered whitewashed buildings. Spying the pool from the truck, Megan hugged me tightly and flashed me a smile, bouncing up and down on the seat in excitement.

As nice as the oval-shaped pool looked as its navy waters rippled under the sun, my thoughts primarily centered on breaking free from the whole forced group dynamic and getting some time to myself. Matt had become so damn annoying, laying down his whole bravado act pretty heavy and thick. I think Mary had to be the only one who believed his fabricated camping stories in Australia.

"...Of course, no man wants to stare a dingo down, but sometimes you just have to stand tall and strong...."

Aubrey, too, had become a bit of a stroke, a self-realized Casanova made even more unbearable by the 'secret' affair he had been carrying on with Stacey.

"Hey! Lookit my arse! Aren't I sexy?!?"

Seeing himself as a super-stud, Aubrey had begun doing the most outlandish things for attention, topped off by the time one recent morning when he climbed aboard Ella wearing only his boxers and exposing his thin, chicken legs. By laughing at his lame jokes early on, we had created a monster.

The top spot on my 'Most Annoying' list, however, switched on an almost daily basis between Abe, our crotchety neighbor to the North, and Stacey, who, like Aubrey, flaunted this whole, weird sexuality that oozed creepiness. Maybe I'd be crotchety like Abe, too, if I had to lay my already bad back on the ground every night when I went to bed. But why Abe annoyed me went way beyond his sometimes pissy mood. The way he treated Helen, who seemed to merrily do everything for him, was really grating and thankless, like when his idea of washing the dishes with his wife that night consisted of him shining a flashlight into the water while she toiled in the putrid water. Or the way, without fail, you'd always find him under foot, blindly parked in the middle of the truck's main aisle unpacking.

Though Stacey hadn't become quite as bold as Aubrey, she, too, had begun displaying a Aubrey-like sense of cockiness that she had kept in check since we left Cape Town. Even after realizing that the desert wasn't the best place to glam up, Stacey somehow could still rationalize applying a heavy cake of make-up most days in that same, unflattering manner, spreading a coat of cover so thick you could spackle an entire wall with it. People who never learned a lesson always seem to annoy me the most.

****

When Skonky finished circling the campground and parked the truck on a patch of dried-grass, we disembarked in complete silence, battle-weary soldiers going only through the motions of combat. We had done this routine so many times that there was really no need for words: grab tent from beneath truck; erect tent; pile in gear. One by one, the tents went up. And one by one, the entire group began to appear at the small square pool just to the left of the main drive we arrived on.

The campground's pool, though filled with frigid water, remained a nice diversion nonetheless. Despite my vow to separate myself from the group that afternoon, I dipped in briefly to cool off then laid poolside with my eyes shut and in complete silence, trying to even out the bad tan I had acquired on my arms and face by sitting next to the window.

Meg sat on the edge of the pool, legs dangling in the cold water. She looked great in her blue bikini, filling everything out beautifully in all the right places.

God, I loved being a guy.

BARFLIES, BOOZE & ALL-AROUND DEBAUCHERY

Rundu. Great. Two questions: when the hell would we be getting there and why was it so damn far away?

Without a doubt, the day we took off for Rundu seemed like one of the longest days on Ella, which, given the amount of time we spent on the vehicle, was really saying something. There's precious little you can do to prepare yourself for the sheer misery and boredom that was a cross-country drive across the shittiest roads known to man. Sometimes I felt so trapped.

It all began innocently enough.

As we exited the campground that morning, Skonky did a quick loop through the game park, where we unexpectedly spied three, tiny hyena cubs, all looking very hungry and vulnerable as they waited for their mother to return with dinner. The size of kittens, they fearfully ducked in and out of a small mound of earth as they anxiously passed the time, instinctually aware of just how vulnerable they were, yet trying to muster up enough courage for the sake of sheer hunger. I didn't know much about hyenas before the trip, but they were quickly becoming some of the more interesting animals in all of Africa. I admired their fearlessness when it came to getting what they wanted, sometimes even challenging lions if it became necessary to eat. Plus the way they skirted along on the tips of their feet was pretty wild and unique—much more interesting than the assorted antelope we saw that hopped back and forth.

Understandably, we didn't stick around long enough for the mother to return to her cubs. According to Rutger, it could be the better part of a day before she would return, having gorged herself to the point where she would then feed her brood through regurgitation. Okay—so hyenas weren't perfect.

"We need to leave, anyway," Rutger added. "Rundu is not close, you know."

Rundu. All I knew of it was Ngepi, our campground destination for the evening and that is was supposedly Skonky's all-time favorite place to stay during the tour.

"They really know how to treat ya well there," Skonky cackled with a wicked smile over breakfast. "Great African hospitality."

Inexplicably, a chill crawled down my back.

Megan borrowed Helen and Abe's multi-fold map of Africa to find Rundu on it—a small spot pretty far northeast from where we currently were, which naturally meant plenty of hours on the road. The journey to Rundu was made slightly more interesting by daredevil cows and donkeys, who were oblivious to the fact that a several ton truck was screaming down the same road they chose to stop in the middle of and graze. Most of the time, a quick honk of the horn and some timely braking was all it took to get the road clear, though we actually passed one donkey who clearly didn't move out of the way in time for somebody; its head was twisted around and facing behind him in a ghoulish grin.

Skonky drove with as much determination as always, hitting bumps and holes in the road with the same, reckless abandonment that had become his trademark. Skonky must have really wanted to get to Ngepi bad. In an instant, though, something felt different, as the ride became even shakier than we had grown accustomed to. There was no loud pop like you would have thought, but it became painfully clear that something was wrong, as the rough roar of Ella striking the road became increasingly audible. Our second flat tire.

We piled off the truck once Skonky forced it to the shoulder and Rutger climbed into the rear of the truck to remove the spare—full-sized, thank God. At least we had Connor this time. Though his expertise was with repairing transmissions, I took some solace in knowing we had someone who knew something about trucks available.

"It's a blowout," Connor called out from under Ella, having crawled halfway under her frame for inspection himself.

"It's just completely destroyed!"

To my surprise, Skonky and Rutger worked extremely well with one another in replacing the mammoth tire, demonstrating great precision and a touch of humor. "See, guys," Rutger said with a wink, referencing the shirt he was wearing which commemorated a previous African Wanderer excursion, one highlighted by no less than four flat tires during the duration of the trip.

"We owe you at least two more before we're all said and done."

As Skonky tightened the lug nuts of the fresh, black wheel, I took a brief sigh of relief. Maybe the flat wasn't such a bad thing after all, since at the very least, it provided us with enough time to take a needed bathroom break and stretch a little. Judging by Skonky's determination to reach Ngepi, there wouldn't be many more.

Just after 3 p.m., Skonky pulled the truck through what looked like a barren field of grass, which later revealed to be the access road to Ngepi campground. As soon as we crossed the sprawling field, our path, which then brought us through pointed trees and thickets, narrowed considerably, wide enough to fit only a single vehicle through in either direction. And even that made things extremely tight, made even worse by the sharp, stray branches that attacked us through open windows as we passed. A single, pointed branch dug a deep, red scratch into my shoulder before I managed to shut my window.

The jagged branches of death were only part of the excitement—the wet, muddy road made even Ella's slightest movement an adventure, as she seemingly battled to stay upright and steady with every careful lurch forward. As we jostled back and forth on our seats, grabbing on to whatever we could to keep from spilling into the aisle, I prayed that another vehicle wouldn't need to get through from the other direction and force us onto the shoulder. That would be a recipe for disaster.

We probably traversed that muddy bog intent on impersonating a road for less than a mile total, though the pace we navigated over it made it seem much longer. Finally, the road opened up wide as we came to a clearing and saw our tropical paradise—Ngepi Campground.

Spotting Ella instantly, an older, heavy-set guy with a white beard smiled and yelled something as we pulled up, then he nearly pulled Skonky's arm out from its socket as he shook his hand with tremendous vigor when he leapt merrily from the cab.

"Welcome back, lad—make yourself at home!" our white-haired host chirped, still pumping Skonky's arm up and down.

"Got a big night planned for ya!"

Ngepi's appeal was obvious—it was beautiful. Ngepi was much more than a campground. It was a campground done right, surrounding by lush, tropical greenery along a lazily flowing river. It sort of reminded me of the campsite we stayed at before departing on our canoe trip, except Ngepi was more private and secluded.

Megan and I scoped the place out to get the lay of the land as soon as we constructed our tent. The huge bar that rested on the far end of the campground actually appeared inviting, with dozens of pictures of previous guests strewn along the wall in different poses of drunken revelry. Megan even spotted a recent-looking photo of our fearless leader, Skonky—getting a haircut, of all things. The entire bar area was tastefully decorated in a subtle but striking tropical theme, with drums of assorted shapes and sizes pushed up against the walls and bright, festive lights hanging from the ceiling.

A towering termite mound rested just outside of the bar area, near a small fire pit. About twenty feet to the right of the fire pit was a deck that overlooked the entire river valley and sometimes afforded a pretty good view of crossing elephants or hippos, we were told. Ngepi seemed to have it all. Relaxation was in order.

Megan and I split up to shower—it had been a long, smelly day on Ella and I knew I'd feel more like having a good time if I knew I wasn't as stinky. I met back up with Megan and we headed over to the dock, where we noticed Rutger, sitting with legs crossed and looking out into the water. A few other guests were attempting to fish but coming up empty. Rutger spotted us as we approached and slid over to give us room to sit.

"Are you here to see the elephants?" Rutger asked, gazing at the river.

"You'll probably hear them at night, at least."

He pointed to a small lip on the edge of the riverbank, almost completely covered in high, green grass.

"That's where you'd see them, probably," Rutger added. "Feeding first, then maybe a swim."

"They were so cool the other day, by the watering hole," Megan remarked.

"Yeah," I added. "I was starting to think we might not see anything!"

Rutger laughed.

"A lot of people who come here think they're going to see animals everywhere," he said, picking up a small branch and breaking it into smaller pieces. "If you're patient and keep a keen watch, you'll see them."

"You two are having a good time, then?"

Megan glanced at me and I back at her. She was better at diplomacy than I was.

"Oh yeah, Rutger," Megan replied, in a tone tailored to make her answer seem obvious.

"...Though it does get hard being away from home sometimes—missing creature comforts and all."

"Yeah," said Rutger in a quiet voice. "You need to really be away for a while to get used to that."

Rutger evasively turned his attention back to the river.

"So how long are you guys gone at a time, then?"

"It depends," Rutger answered somberly. "This time, we do the first three weeks with you, drive back to Cape Town on Monday, and start all over again the following Sunday."

Picking up a small stone off the pier, Rutger winged it into the river.

"I should have about three days to myself, though."

Megan moved in closer which she always did when she was about to get personal.

"That must be hard for you and your girlfriend," Megan stated.

Rutger chuckled slightly and began in a serious tone, "Well, it's been nothing but hard for us, these past couple of years, so we're used to it. Even with apartheid over, the notion of a white man and a black woman being together still isn't looked on very kindly."

Megan and I sat silently, not wanting to pry but wishing he'd continue.

"My family was the worst, you know," Rutger said, snatching a small twig off the deck floor and rolling it between his palms.

"Not one of them agrees with the way I live my life, so I don't even bother with them anymore."

That sounded like family to me.

Looking up to the sky, Rutger continued.

"The only life they think is suitable is the one they lead, and I guess I just can't fit in like that." Rutger went on in some detail about getting started in guiding through Africa—which was all he had really considered doing after a several-year stint in the Army. With his unbridled enthusiasm for Africa and the knowledge to go with it, he knew as well as we did that he should be leading the whole excursion. But since Rutger was on his inaugural tour with African Wanderer, he unfortunately had to prove himself all over again.

"Couple more times here and there after this first one," Rutger philosophized. "Then we'll see. I'm a patient man."

Rutger was patient, but much more than that, he was a man who personified the free spirit and adventure of Africa. A place, he told us, where you had the ability to try anything you wanted to just because the structure was so loose. Maybe he'd do something like Jackie, our host at Ngepi. Jackie, a former guide himself, led a group through the area where we now stood and fell in love with the land, eventually deciding to open Ngepi Campground a few years later. That, related Rutger, was the appeal of Africa.

While the three of us sat momentarily in reflective silence, the slight sound of a trumpeting elephant echoed somewhere in the distance. Rising quickly to my feet, I spotted a gray, bulky figure disappear into the rippling water, near the far edge of the riverbank. The very tip of its trunk jutted up from the murky deep, like a World War II submarine on the prowl.

"That's the way an elephant crosses the river," Rutger instructed as he peered across the river. "Don't be surprised if you hear them trumpeting tonight. Or hippos, I suppose."

Hippos. Next to lions, I really wanted to see hippos, regarded as the biggest killers of humans in all of Africa. From a distance, naturally.

The three of us kept our eyes on the river for a little while longer before I excused myself and headed to our tent for our deck of Uno cards. Passing the half-full bar on the way back, I noticed the tour's designated drinkers—Skonky, Connor, and Bill –all bellied up to the bar and cackling loudly. Several empty shot glasses lined the small area near the group.

"'Ey, beautiful," Skonky yelled to the thin, raven-haired waitress behind the counter.

"I've thought about comin' back to you the entire time I was away."

Smiling politely, the waitress said little as she sopped up a mess of spilled beer in front of the trio. She surely noticed the sinister gaze of

Skonky, watching her every move. Listening to the nonsense of drunk people had to be probably the worst part about bartending.

Matt, also at the bar, had kept his distance from the group, hanging back with Charlie, of all people, at a small table in the corner. With his hand resting on hers, Matt was definitely working it, listening to Charlie as tears welled in her eyes. Matt. What a shallow prick.

As I moved past the bar, I suddenly heard Skonky and Connor get very loud with one another, overhearing Skonky chide Connor about some sort of challenge.

"We'll just see if you can last with me, then," Skonky demanded.

"If you have the guts!"

The sun had just begun setting when I made my way back with the cards, and by the time the game started, Megan, Aubrey, Stacey and myself all battled the shadows and dimming light to squeeze in a few hands of Uno before the blanket of darkness arrived.

We quit playing after a few hands, joining Rutger by the fire pit as he scurried back and forth to get dinner ready. At least Charlie was there, too, still looking weepy about something but tending to the percolating pots just the same. Finding Skonky was relatively easy—the position of the fire pit offered a nice, clear view of the bar. A little more crowded since I last noticed, the bar was probably two-thirds full, with a small group from another tour company thrown into the mix.

What remained constant, however, was the African Wanderer trio of Skonky, Connor and Bill, each riding that slow train to total inebriation. Connor, with a white knot hat pulled over his ears and still seated next to Skonky, appeared to be taking the express, pausing slightly after nearly spilling a shot glass of sticky, brown liquid in front of him.

"C'mon, you pussy!" growled Skonky. "Yer not a man!"

Connor, teetering slightly in his seat, righted himself. A smile, albeit one of those dopey, oblivious, drunken smiles, came to his dry lips before he hoisted the shot high into the air.

"This is for you, Skonky!" Connor yelled, lowering the shot glass to his mouth and dumping the liquid back.

Grimacing hard as we swallowed, Connor quickly chased the concoction down with a mouthful from a nearby beer. A few brown droplets raced down his chin, though I didn't even think Connor was aware. Wrestling the empty shot glass free from Connor's hand, Bill added it to the top of a small pyramid of empties being constructed in front of his Aussie mate, which I counted to be at least fifteen.

"Fuckin' amateur!" laughed Skonky, goading Connor.

"You're not going to be able to keep up with me, boy!"

Snatching the full shot glass of dark brew in front of him, Skonky downed it in a quick, single gulp, and then shot a cocky glare towards Connor.

"I guess they're having a drinking contest," I related to Megan, who I had been watching with me from the safety of the fire ring.

Megan shook her head.

"I got a really bad feeling about this."

Alcohol poisoning wasn't anything to take lightly, and with a mounting pile of shot glasses in front of him, I didn't know how much more Connor could take.

"That Connor is hilarious," observed Mary, as the antics at the bar suddenly became everyone's source of entertainment.

"He's going to be hurting tomorrow!"

Megan gave her an incredulous look.

"I don't think it's very funny," Megan said firmly, almost buried beneath the whooping and hollering coming from the chanting bar spectators, now in on the act, too.

"I think it's dangerous and needs to stop!"

Mary shut up. All she had to do was glance around the fire pit to see the concern on everyone's face. Fifteen shots?!? Did Skonky simply not know any better, or was he just so determined to prove something and win his little contest that he didn't care what happened to Connor in the process? And this was the guy we were entrusting our safety to as we navigated through a potentially dangerous land, who was encouraging a tourist to drink himself sick in the remotest of places?

Skonky proved himself far more reckless than anything we had encountered in Africa thus far.

Rutger glanced over towards the bar now and then to catch a glimpse of what was going on—it was hard to tune out the commotion when another shot found its way down. Though he must have heard our concerns, Rutger seemed completely uninterested in getting involved. I guess I couldn't really blame him. As much as I thought Skonky's encouragement was inappropriate and dangerous, I wasn't about to get on my soapbox and close down the bar for the night, either. Of all of us, Rutger probably found himself in the toughest spot—if he spoke up, he'd almost assure himself an uncomfortable ride the remainder of the way.

Surprisingly, Rutger's announcement that dinner was ready served to briefly interrupt the shot-drinking contest. Being guided steadily by Matt, Connor stumbled over to the fire pit only. After being steered to the nearest vacant chair, his body fighting for balance, he dropped himself hard into the chair, sinking lower and lower until his head hung down into his lap. Skonky hadn't left the bar.

"C'mon Connor," pleaded Matt, dishing up a small plate of the beef stew dish and steaming rice for the conquering hero. "Just have a little."

Lifting his head quickly before letting it sway from side to side, Connor attempted to steady the fork Matt placed in his fist, pecking at the mounded pile of food like a bird before spilling most of the rice into his lap. Grabbing the fork more firmly, Connor managed to get a few bites of rice into his mouth.

"How are you feelin' Connor?" asked Mary, finding a touch of concern in her voice.

"...Just...havin' fun...Mar," Connor warbled through the queasy expression on his face.

"If Connor considers puking fun," I whispered to Megan, "he's gonna have a great night."

I moved behind Bill as I watched Connor for a little while longer, belching back his downed liquor with each tiny bite of dinner.

"How many?"

"Seventeen, man...I think," Bill replied discreetly.

"But I think he's about done, though."

Just seeing Connor made my stomach a little queasy—it reminded me of too many of those nights spent drinking. Those days were long over for me now. Despite the challenges from drinking buddies to keep up, I didn't chase that ever-lengthening finish line any longer. When you're drunk, you're drunk.

Matt held Connor steady as he slowly spilled forward from the chair and stood on wobbled knees, knocking the plate of rice still resting on his lap to the ground below. With a firm grip, Matt grabbed Connor by the left arm and began dragging him back to the bar while Connor goofily grinned, completely numb.

Not a word was exchanged around the fire ring as Connor, with Matt's assistance, went back to reclaim his spot at the bar, with Bill chasing close behind. As Connor's best friend, it was Matt's responsibility more than anyone else's to try to talk some sense into his friend and convince him to end the contest. Instead, despite trying to get him to eat, Matt was no better than the rest of those drunken slobs at the bar, motivating a guy who straddled a dangerous line already to keep at it. Maybe you needed to be completely sober to see just how dangerous things were getting. Or possess common sense.

As Connor hunkered back down onto the vacant bar seat next to Skonky, I noticed that Aubrey and Rutger had ducked away at some point after dinner. Maybe both had seen enough, though I would have loved to see Rutger, with all of his wisdom, pull Skonky aside to quell things before they really spiraled out of control.

The bar became completely electric as another bartender, a blond, poured two shots of that same, vile brown liquid, and placed them carefully in front of each contestant. I didn't think that any one of the probably twenty spectators had any question what the outcome of the contest would be. On one stool sat Skonky, downing the last shot as easily as the first while looking no worse for wear. Next to him, Connor—eyes glazed, stomach churning, mouth grimacing. The only question, really, was just how much longer Connor could actually last.

Gripping a shot on the bar while dangling a cigarette between his fingers, Skonky moved in eye-to-eye with Connor, baring his mangled teeth.

"'Ere's to you, Connie!" he smiled, before letting it slide down the back of his throat.

Following Skonky's lead, Connor slammed the shot down almost as fast as his opponent, closing his eyes as he brought his head back in one, quick burst. Then it hit him.

Staggering to his feet, Connor found the ground just enough to make a blind charge towards a tree-covered area behind the bar, with Matt in hot pursuit. Tripping and then falling to his knees, Connor was within clear sight of everyone at the bar when he started puking, his mouth spraying a chunky mixture of clear liquid on the grass around him.

I really felt sick then.

"At least that should do it," Megan related, peeking through the hand covering her eyes like she was watching a horror film.

I hoped that was the end of it. I knew I never felt like drinking anymore once I puked. But I just had a bad feeling when I saw Connor and Matt, amid the cheering crowd, emerge a few minutes later and make their way up to Skonky and the bar once again. Wiping his stained mouth with the back of his hand, Connor slumped back into his seat.

"Why the fuck doesn't he just quit?" I muttered.

Seeing Connor behind the tree even made some of the bar patrons start to have reservations about the contest. Quite a few shot bewildered looks when Connor demanded another shot from the bartender. Granted, some jerks still cheered him on, but Skonky didn't even bat an eye, maybe so drunk himself that he had no idea how bad Connor was and how close the whole situation was to becoming dangerous. Somehow, I doubted it. Skonky just didn't give a damn.

After three more labored rounds, Connor had still somehow managed to match Skonky shot for shot, making the grand total twenty one—if you included the several Connor must have puked out. Connor, too stubborn or proud to quit, propped his back against the edge of the bar, just to obtain enough leverage to sit upright.

"He's going to need a doctor," Megan nervously stated as we watched Connor, smiling one instant, and then collapsed onto the bar like a rag doll the next.

The way I saw it, Connor was fucked if he needed medical attention. Helen was a nurse by profession, but I doubted she packed a stomach pump to bring to Africa with her. And that telephone behind the bar? I didn't think one, panicked call would bring an ambulance racing through the rough Namibian roads for such an emergency.

The nervous tension of eyeing Connor as he flailed in the barstool had finally reached a crescendo when, after lifting his slumped head from the small pool of spilt liquor, slammed the first empty shot glass he found down in front of him.

"One more," Connor belched to the bartender, swallowing back a mouthful of puke. "Just one more."

Thankfully, the bartender had seen enough.

"Sorry, mate," the bartender replied calmly, wiping down the area with a white cloth.

"That's it. Game's over."

Initially looking stunned at being denied, Connor soon smiled and nodded, probably garnering some satisfaction that he wasn't the one who quit the contest. Me? I just felt relieved. At the very least, Connor had stopped drinking.

As an assortment of barflies emerged to offer Skonky a congratulatory slap on the shoulder, Matt, with Bill's aid, slipped over and dragged the lifeless body to a glass-filled table in the rear. Skonky, unflinching, lit a fresh cigarette and smiled arrogantly, laughing and pointing over his shoulder. For what it was worth, a few spectators congratulated Connor for his unyielding effort, though even he had to be wondering why he had even bothered in the first place.

The bar was rife with a lot of debauchery that night. Not only did we witness Connor and Skonky's tribute to Bacchus, but a whole creepy scene went down between Jack, the white-haired owner of the campground, and this fat red-head from another overland group who looked young enough to be his daughter. After some alcohol-inspired close dancing, the heavy grinding soon followed, topped off with the old letch digging his pudgy hand down the fat girl's top. His dance partner must have dug it, because then the floodgates really opened, with the unusual couple completing groping each other in the middle of the dance floor— and right in front of the old dude's real daughter, a cute brunette girl home from college for the week.

His daughter was completely livid, angrily lashing out at the redhead as Pop stumbled off to the bathroom sporting a huge erection. Hell, I was disgusted and I wasn't even related. Watching him grab her fat, saggy breasts while she reached her hands down into his tighty-whiteys would turn anyone's stomach.

We hung out with the group a little while longer around the fire, laughing some more about the events of the evening and venting a little about Skonky, who hadn't even moved from that same barstool all night to check on Connor. Connor had disappeared somewhere—at some point, someone must have helped him to his tent.

I grew angry watching Skonky, sloppy drunk but still laughing about his victory amid the cheers of the loser entourage he had acquired during the evening. Sure, Connor's an adult who has to make his own decisions, right or wrong. But as the leader of our expedition, how could Skonky goad him on in such a way, helping bring Connor to such a dangerous point? Skonky was the head guy, the one responsible for all of our safety, yet this was his idea of harmless fun?

"Connor could easily have died," argued Megan to the group. "It's almost impossible to get medical help out here!"

"It's reckless," agreed Stacey, who seemed more down-to-earth and actually pleasant when she wasn't pandering to Aubrey.

"As a guide, he's crude and irresponsible. And I think I'm going to let African Wanderer know, too," Stacey assured us.

Megan and I were becoming increasingly tired and departed soon after that, with Stacey vowing to everyone she'd send off a letter to the head office the moment she returned to the United States. We made our way back to our tent to prepare for bed, where we saw Rutger cleaning some of the cookware from dinner.

He nodded to us as we approached.

"How'd you guys like dinner?" Rutger asked, scraping some dried food from a pot.

"It was great," I said. "You ducked out before we could thank you."

"Yeah, I know," he replied sheepishly. "Aubrey's in pretty bad shape, and I've been checking in on him. Hasn't eaten all day and probably's got some kind of bug."

"He didn't look that good, now that you mention it," Megan chimed in.

Rutger placed the pot on the ground and picked up a smaller one.

"It's quite normal, really," reasoned Rutger. "It'll probably happen to all of you at some point here."

"Well, he probably won't be as bad as Connor tomorrow," I said. "Did you see that crap, or did you leave before it all got so bad?"

Rutger paused for a second and placed his hand on his hip.

"I had a feeling things would turn bad. I wouldn't have stuck around, anyway. It's not my business but it's not for me, either."

I could understand his predicament. I was a paying customer, and I didn't want to rock the boat. Here he was, recently employed with African Wanderer and seconding Skonky, who probably could make things really miserable if you got on his bad side.

We helped Rutger finish the dishes and got ready for bed. I was grateful that our tent was far enough from the bar to only hear the slight din of music. I made sure I went to the restroom because I didn't want to run into any hippos in the middle of the night, which Rutger reminded us sometimes scale the riverbanks during the night to graze. That's Africa.

CRY FREEDOM

"My stomach—eet just couldn't handle things. I spent most of the night in the bathroom."

"Well over ten days for me and still nothing more than a pebble."

Ladies and gentleman, welcome to another installment of 'Toilet Talk,' where guests from all corners of the world discuss their bowel dysfunction over a bowl of corn flakes. Today we're joined by Aubrey, who looks much better today after a restless night of tummy trouble, and the one and only Mary Rose, who has insisted on sharing daily updates with the group about her loaf that refuses to be pinched.

Yeah, we were quite a piece of work that morning. Mary was particularly annoying—going on and on about her family's history of intestinal blockage and how she'd try anything at this point to get a little relief. If only she'd try shutting her mouth first.

At least Aubrey looked a lot better after a good night's rest. He told us he felt a fever and chills coming on during dinner, and though he still felt a little drained, the fever had since passed and his energy was returning. I could swear I saw Stacey's eyes light up when she heard that.

Maybe Mary was particularly annoying because she sensed Connor would steal the spotlight that morning, coming off that high-profile drinking contest that thankfully didn't kill him. Skonky, who met us at breakfast with Rutger as usual that morning, didn't look any worse than normal. Though he moved around a little slower and said little he didn't appear hung over, either out of personal pride or because he knew it would be a dick move to make Rutger do all the work while he recovered.

My opinion of Skonky hadn't changed much from the previous night, however, and I got the sense through the occasional whispering I heard throughout the day that neither had anyone else's. I don't know what I was expecting from him that morning to try to make things right—I didn't think he'd address the situation and apologize in an attempt to restore our faith in him. If anything, he was completely oblivious to the fact that he had crossed the line.

I had to admit, however, that for as bad as Connor looked last night, he looked surprisingly well. Like Skonky, he moved a little slowly and talked very little, yet he'd flash the occasional smile and joke about how crazy things had gotten.

"I'm not looking at another shot again on this trip," he said with a slight smile while shaking his head. "If I even see another shot of Jaeger, I'll lose it."

Connor was lucky he bounced back as well as he did—Skonky had huge plans for us that day. Not only were we finally leaving Namibia, a country that I swear we had traveled every single mile over, but it was also the day of the optional trip to the Okavango Delta. A trip that Megan and I had decided to pass on.

Our reasons for passing to visit the Delta were as numerous as they were obvious—at least to us. Per person, the cost was $140 U.S., which included two nights of bush camping in probably one of the worst malaria zones on the entire continent. Of course, Skonky played it up as so much more than that, naturally—describing a village walk with resident guides as a 'once-in-a-lifetime' experience.

"And don't forget the mokoros," Skonky noted, referring to the carved-out canoes steered by skilled locals that had been commissioned to take each person into the Delta.

"You'll probably see all sorts of wildlife, then."

The high cost, the bush camping, and the malaria risk weren't the only things that made the Delta excursion less than appealing for Megan and myself. If we chose not to join the rest of the group, we would still go into the Delta but not quite as deep, staying at a scenic campsite complete with hot showers until the returning group joined us three days later. Ultimately, what tipped it in was hearing that everyone else had planned to take the optional trip into the Delta, meaning we would then get almost three full days for ourselves.

God, what a glorious thought. Three full days of not hearing Mary's shrill voice. Or not having to endure Stacey's sex kitten act while she tried to find a way into Aubrey's pants. A mini-vacation from Matt's cockiness, Abe's crankiness, Charlie's surliness and Dominick's insatiable appetite. What wasn't to like?

Climbing back on Ella once our border crossing was complete, we drove past scores of mini-villages along the way. Following Rutger's friendly cue, we got into the habit of waving to the many people we passed on the roadside, though it seemed like only children were more than willing to wave back. Turning down a narrow dirt strip that seemed more like we were cutting across someone's backyard than taking a road through town, we barreled over a stretch of land that carried us no further than fifteen feet from a series of huts stacked one on top of another. Swerving carefully to avoid running down several wandering goats and chickens, which roamed freely and without fear, Skonky slowed down considerably and continued taking us through cautiously.

Ella slowed to a halt after Skonky pulled her up a small drive that carried us to the center of a small village. Several women and children, emerging from straw huts to inspect the racket, barely looked surprised when they saw it was only us. After spotting another overland-type truck parked nearby, we realized this had to be a common rendezvous point. Small children in bright clothes played while adult women hung laundry on makeshift clotheslines or cooked over smoky fires. A few mangy dogs strolled through, wagging their tails gently and looking like they needed a friend.

Rutger rose to his feet just as Ella's engine fell silent.

"OK guys—listen up," he started, briefly waving his arms in the air to get our attention. "This whole area that we're sitting in has to be empty—no one's going to be here to watch the truck."

"...Whatever isn't going with you is getting locked up in the back where it's safe."

"Only one daypack, guys," added Skonky in a low-sounding bellow. "No sleeping pads allowed, but you'll need your tents and sleeping bags."

"No sleeping pads?" Aubrey whined. "And my mattress?"

Skonky shook his head.

"Won't need it. Trust me."

Right.

Before long, we had managed to completely empty the front part of Ella of everything, even the countless empty chip bags that floated under our feet.

"Take extra good care of Aubrey's blue suitcase, Rutger!" teased Matt as he dropped his pack into the pile.

"You're really going to carry that through Nairobi?"

Like a masterful carpenter, Rutger's expertise and experience made the difference, as he gingerly stacked one bulging, bulbous bag on top of another, constructing tight walls that leaned just enough without toppling. I handed him the painting I purchased in Cape Town—I knew it'd get crushed on the bottom if I didn't—and Rutger slammed the door with an authoritative 'thud.' It didn't mask the sound of everything shifting and falling from behind the locked door but at least everything was now locked behind a thick, steel door.

I just prayed it would remain there until we returned.

Climbing into the cab one last time, Skonky, looking like a master safe-cracker on the biggest heist of his life, emptied the steel lockbox containing our wallets and passports into a cloth sack.

"All of your wallets will be with me," Skonky told us quietly. "That way, they'll be safe."

"I hope our campground isn't like Ngepi," Megan joked. "Or he'll blow through it in one night!"

As Skonky, looking like an evil, miniature Santa Claus, threw the cloth sack over his shoulder, a big, rickety, transport vehicle roared through the village, raining clouds of dust down on the scattering livestock. To me, it looked exactly like a military assault vehicle, the type you'd spot during Third World newscasts when some rebel group would attempt a palace coup, complete with a pair of vertical benches running down the back of and housed by wooden sideboards that wrapped completely around the vehicle. If we were a makeshift guerilla army, then the aging, red-haired guy who called himself 'Billie' was our commander, I guess.

"Skonky!" chided Billie. "It's been a long time, lad!"

Billie greeted Skonky pretty warmly, instantly stirring more flashbacks from that drunken night in Ngepi. Megan and I just wanted peace—not an intervention. Something about Billie, though, made him seem like a no-nonsense-type of guy. His instructions were very methodical, coaching us on the best way to load our gear onto the transport ('tuck the tents below the seats—more leg room') as well as offering plain common sense ('If you go into the Delta without repellent, you're just asking for malaria.') Overall, Billie seemed okay. Maybe a little cold, but definitely better than that old drunk pervert at Ngepi.

Billie crawled the truck over these stretches cautiously, unable to determine just how deep the water was until we inched through it. We were never more than tire-deep into it, but this careful approach left us very vulnerable to a mosquito attack, slowing us just enough for the entire swarm to descend.

"I didn't think they'd be bad until the Delta!" Aubrey whined, slapping one off his shoulder.

"At least these don't spread malaria," Matt interjected, brushing a mosquito from his leg.

The end of the road came at a small swampy inlet, at the same point where we spotted several villagers washing their laundry. You can't slap at a mosquito in Africa without thinking about the rare diseases you could catch from one. They were ferocious, even battling through clothing in order to feast.

We weren't going anywhere until the canoes arrived, the ones designated to take us into the Delta. To pass the time, we unloaded the truck onto a small, dry patch of land after I got the much-needed opportunity to dig into my daypack for that coveted canister of insect repellent. It was nearly full, thankfully, since it was the single can we brought along, and it didn't take long to realize that we could possibly use all of it during our short stay in the Delta.

"Let me help," Megan called out, leaping over a few stray backpacks to maneuver to my side.

We took turns completely spraying each other—bare skin and clothes alike. Dealing with the sheer number of mosquitoes in a malarias zone just had 'disaster' written all over it.

As we sat around and ate a lunch of TLC sandwiches and some unidentifiable leftover from a previous night, I was very excited about the next couple of days. I knew I needed a break from bush camping and the predictable routine that had been making my time with African Wanderer so trying. I yearned only for beautiful, unscheduled freedom; ready to completely throw my arms around once we headed in an opposite direction from the rest of the group. No Mary, no Stacey, no Matt, no Abe—just Megan and myself at Moquena Lodge, our campground for the next couple of days. It all sounded so good.

"I think our ride's here, guys," declared Connor, pointing in the distance. "Look!"

What began as a slight buzzing sound off in the distance grew measurably louder and louder, revealing a single motorboat slowly driving towards us through the expansive river.

"This is you two," Skonky told Megan, nodding to the boat. "I'll be by a little later."

"Well," started Megan, addressing the group members seated nearby on a fallen tree.

"Have fun in the Delta and we'll see you when you get back!"

I couldn't hide my grimace as I waved to the group. Suckers.

"Yeah," chirped Mary with a goofy smile. "Take care, now."

When the craft, with its power cut, gently floated to the bank, the man who had been steering held the tiny craft steady as we carried our gear aboard, instructing a second man to take our gear from us as we carried it aboard. I didn't mind not being on a canoe—with crocs, hippos, and snakes around, that'd be quite an experience.

With a final wave to the group as our driver revved the engine, we slowly drifted away. Once the boat came to a small clearing, the driver took a hard right, entering what appeared to be a tunnel-like path cut right through a massive wall of towering green reeds. Uniform and dense in appearance, the reeds would be nearly impossible to see through, yet we sped through the narrow path with enough sheer reckless to prompt me to grab hold of the life jacket beneath the seat. The path through the reeds was almost maze-like. Though there appeared to be only one path, it wasn't straight and easy-to-follow by any means, requiring hard-angled turns on the occasionally choppy current throughout. Our driver had done this too many times to be interested—a look of boredom was etched all over his hard features.

After our craft navigated through the reeds safely, the entire Okavango Delta seemingly opened up, a vast, blue stretch of the largest swamp I had ever seen dotted with small patches of tall grasses and reeds. The driver headed straight for a small, unassuming dock set in a small clearing, killing the engine as we were about twenty feet away to allow the lazy current to take us in the rest of the way. Meg and I climbed out slowly once the craft was secured against the pier, with the driver and his assistant handing over our belongings when we stood on firm ground. Thanking them, we watched the vessel slowly disappear through the reads once again, until the sound of the buzzing motor completely disappeared.

"We made it!" Megan shrieked over the silence as she hugged me.

"Life is good."

Grabbing our gear and the slightly damp tent, we climbed over a short ridge and found ourselves in the middle of Moquena Lodge—though 'campground' would be a little more accurate. Moquena was better than most of the places we had camped, with its grounds nicely shaded from the towering trees above, thatch-encased restrooms featuring private, hot showers, a bar area that featured board games and some newer magazines, and best of all, privacy. The entire campground was empty, save for the two local women villagers hired by Moquena, I assumed, to maintain the grounds, though sharing gossip seemed to be their true passion. Megan and I had the lay of the land completely to ourselves, with the lazily flowing Delta provided the perfect backdrop for what we hoped would be a few days of tranquility.

Taking a few minutes, we quickly walked the grounds to familiarize ourselves with everything and to locate a host to introduce ourselves to. We didn't find one—Skonky and Billie hadn't arrived yet, and no one else appeared to be around either. Probably the nicest thing about being the only ones in a campground is the ability to put up your tent wherever you felt like it.

Even beneath the shade of the trees, the air was rather warm and moist. Even unzipping every window so that the mosquito net remained our only barrier didn't help much. I was getting wet and uncomfortable.

"Maybe reading in here isn't the best idea," I said, placing my book down and pulling my shirt off over my head.

Flashing a quick, sexy smile, Megan eyes jumped open wide. I knew that look. I liked that look.

Sliding across the floor of the tent towards me, Megan reached forward and began lightly stroking my chest.

"I forgot how good your touch feels."

"Good," she replied.

As she continued touching me, I lightly caressed her neck, moving my hand downward until it reached the small of her back. Placing my other hand on her inner thigh, she moaned slightly as I moved up her shorts, legs squirming. I felt like I was going to explode as it was. Nothing gets me hotter than seeing her excited.

The sexual tension between us hung heavy, just like it had when we first started dating but had refrained from doing anything about it. Moving her hands, Megan caressed me around the neck. Torture.

My brain was no longer in control of the situation, relinquishing all power to the enticement of physical pleasure. Sometimes you just have to throw all practical thought completely out of the window, and we were both so starved for one another that we were willing to do just that. That's typical of sex, though—at least as my experiences went. Sex wasn't rife with bad judgment necessarily, but sometimes you just had to stop worrying about everything else on your mind and let loose. You could talk yourself out of anything if you're too practical. Would anyone hear us?

Things escalated so quickly between Megan and I in that steamy tent that there wasn't even time to be practical. With the tent windows still completely open, Megan ripped at my shorts like they were on fire, a favor I returned in between kisses of deep passion. The air was humid and sweltering as our naked, sweaty bodies entwined, two people enjoying one another without a care in the world.

Megan and I always had a great sex life—comfortable in the sense that you knew what to depend on but wild enough to keep things interesting. That afternoon in Africa immediately shot to the top of my 'most memorable' list, an instance so urgent and primal, I felt like we had become one with the African jungle. I remember the minutest details, like the two of us clothed in only our sandals before the urge became too much for even us to sustain.

"Get a condom!" she gasped urgently. "In the bag!"

I fumbled through the many tiny pockets arranged on her day bag before I finally found one. I still muse about the two entire boxes we brought with us. So much for wishful thinking.

Without divulging a whole lot of detail, I can safely report that our afternoon at Moquena Lodge wiped clean all of the frustration I had felt to that point. It seemed like such a long time since we felt so connected with one another that it was divine to experience that once again.

After our amorous session, we noticed another tent had sprung up next to ours—Skonky's. Peaking inside through the half-opened outer flap, we saw nothing except his sleeping bag and several plastic crates full of food.

"He must be around here somewhere," Megan said. "Maybe at the bar."

"As long as he remembers to feed us tonight."

Hearing someone stirring in the bar area of the campground, we decided to check things out, thinking that maybe Skonky or one of our camp hosts had finally made an appearance. It was on that afternoon that we first met Wendy, Billie's young girlfriend and co-host of Moquena Lodge.

"Hi," she said, looking up from a book she was reading behind the counter.

"I've been expecting you! I'm Wendy."

We each took turns shaking her hand.

"I'm Megan and this is my boyfriend Paul," she said, looking around. "Do you know where Skonky is?"

Wendy smiled.

"He's helping Billie transport some more people into the Delta, but they should be back this evening," Wendy said. "But please make yourself at home, by all means. It's a little quiet, but there are things to do."

I didn't exactly need or want to even think about doing anything today—just getting away from the group and relaxing sounded good to me. Wendy mentioned a path leading out from behind the campground through an old, abandoned airstrip—perfect for a small hike.

"But whatever you do," she warned, "don't cross water. It's too easy to get lost going back, and there are animals in the area."

"Animals?" asked Megan nervously, glancing at me quickly.

"What animals?"

"Well," started Wendy. "There are hippos and crocs in the Delta—you may even see them surface if you're lucky."

"And the leopard," Wendy added. "Can't forget about her. She's harmless, really."

Leopard?!? Harmless?!? It didn't matter where you traveled in Africa. Locals didn't seem afraid of anything.

"A harmless leopard?" I asked.

If it meant staying in the tent all night, I wanted to know before I drank that glass of water before bed.

Wendy flashed a reassuring smile, maybe regretting she told us so much so early on.

"I was in a tent with my mom once and I heard her breathing outside—right up against it. You probably won't even see her. She's quiet timid, you know."

You could only relax so much in Africa—at least in my mind. As we basked beneath a shaded tree and listened to the playful chirping of birds, all I could think about was how I needed to stay alert. Would the leopard wander into camp, casting even more doubt on its reputed shyness? Maybe a microscopic insect, intent on burrowing into my skin and using me as a host? I glanced up at towering, craggy tree we sat beneath. What a perfect place for a snake to jump out on you.

The sound of a several, distant motorboats broke my train of thought, thankfully, slowly growing louder and louder until the small fleet finally came into sight. It was Billie and Skonky leading the way in a rusted, red-metallic boat, followed by two additional boats filled with campers like us. Welcome to our island.

****

Dinner that night was great, one of the best I had in Africa, if only because there was plenty of food and I felt no shame in mounding heaping piles of pasta on my plate twice. And dessert. You had to love dessert. Though nothing more than canned fruit cocktail cooked inside some sort of pudding, it brought me immediately back home, reminding me of all the sweets I so sorely missed. I would kill for a slice of German chocolate cake.

SNEAKY SNAKES

I'm enveloped in complete darkness—totally devoid of light.
Where am I?
...Moving...why am I moving?!?
Groping through the darkness, I reached for Megan in a panic.
"Are we moving?!?"
"What, honey?"
Megan mumbled something into the darkness as I frantically searched for the door.
"I got to get out of here!"

In escalating panic, I fumbled for the tent zipper where I imagined it should be, clawing at the front wall like a wild animal. I had absolutely no sense of reference: tent walls were spinning while my mind raced in fear, leaving me struggling to comprehend my unusual sensations of motion. My heart beat heavy. I needed light. I needed to see.

After scrambling to another tent wall in search of a way out, Megan, hearing my commotion, had found the flashlight, landing its glowing yellow beam on me while revealing the zipper, a few short feet above me.

"What's wrong?!? Paul?!?"

Lurching forward at the zipper, I tugged it straight down to open the front flap on and stuck my head out into the cool night air. Taking a few deep breaths, I slowly regained my senses. We weren't moving—we never were moving. Everything was fine.

I felt a little foolish ducking back into the tent. I was never one for having bad dreams, and I kind of felt a sense of added responsibility to be the level-headed one since Megan was still getting frightened at every turn. Megan, sitting up in her sleeping bag with concern, deserved an explanation.

"This tent," I started. "It gets so dark sometimes that I forget where we are. and I could swear we were moving."

Megan sat silently, half-sasleep, attempting to understand my ramblings.

"Was it a dream?" Megan asked, fighting a yawn.

"Not that I can remember, no," I said, drawing another deep breath.

Moments later, we both lay back down, though it was a while before I managed to calm myself enough to fall back asleep. My first thought was that the Lariam was finally kicking in, unfortunately messing with my mind and preying on my phobia of being in confined spaces. Things like elevators didn't bother me because they never tended to get completely packed, but I hated the feeling of not being in control. The worst was being pinned against a wall in a place like a crowded, smoky club, where people continued to pour in and envelop the lone exit on the other side of the room. That was the sensation I had in the tent when I awoke from my sleep. Somehow, I felt trapped with no way out.

I got back to sleep eventually that night and woke to the sound of steady rakes being brought down on the dirt around us. It was the two local women we had seen yesterday when we arrived, still gossiping about God only knows. I threw my shirt on and slowly climbed outside the tent, smiling at the women who were moving about. Our visitors the previous night had already left, presumably in the early morning hours to get a jump on things as they headed south. Good luck to them.

Skonky's tent looked exactly how we saw it the other day—with the exterior flap open slightly to get a little air inside but minus our fearless leader. I guess it was foolish to assume that breakfast would be any different from the ones we had been growing accustomed to since we left Cape Town. I crawled inside his tent to poke around at the green dairy crate that housed our food—loaves of bread, peanut butter, some cereal, a carton of milk, and a can of sardines. If this was also our dinner, we were in trouble.

Our first wildlife sighting in the Okavango Delta was a band of small vervet monkeys, tan in color and especially bold. We had been told to watch our stuff very carefully because they were opportunistic enough to snatch something if your guard was down. The moment we cut into the loaf of bread, the monkeys took immediate interest, hopping from limb to limb and tree to tree with lightening quickness, leaving shaking branches in their wake.

****

It had turned out to be a nice morning for a hike.

"You can't miss it," she told us, washing a dirty beer glass. "Just head out behind the restrooms and you'll see a well-worn path—it's the same one the ladies take to their village."

Megan looked at her quizzically.

"It's safe, right?"

Wendy smiled reassuringly. She was one of the few locals we had met on this entire trip who seemed to understand that not everyone was looking to encounter some man-eating predator.

"Oh yeah," Wendy said, nodding her head slowly. "Just don't cross any water so you can find your way back and you'll be fine."

Since the whole warning about crossing the water kept coming up, we decided to press Wendy on it, who shared a pretty wild story about a guy and a girl who went wandering around the airfield one day and got completely lost. Warned not to go too far, the couple instead crossed onto so many of the little, lush land masses that bobbed in the Delta that they had no idea where they were; they were forced to spend the night in the middle of the wild area without food, shelter, or even a flashlight. They found their way back the next day, but endured an entire, exhausting night of snorting hippos and hungry crocs. Warning received.

After stopping by the tent to grab a couple liters of water and some insect repellent, we headed towards a small clearing—the only clearing—and our African hike began. Wow—'hiking through Africa.' It just sounded so cool and dangerous. I never considered myself a hardcore hiker, but I did enjoy doing it every now and again. I didn't expect to grow fat sitting on my ass in Africa, but I knew I needed some sort of physical release through exercise or something.

We probably walked around 100 feet before the clearing completely opened, finding ourselves in the middle of a dry, tree-laden field. The slight, breezy wind, whistling gently through a massive, old tree on my left, sent a slight chill over me. It wasn't the wind, though. All I could think about was coming face to face with the leopard.

I think Megan and I were both pretty nervous about trekking through the African wilderness on our own, but we kept it to ourselves until later. As much as I questioned Skonky's leadership, at least he'd have an idea of what to do if we came face to face with a wild animal. That came with the territory, and I was convinced that instinctually, all native Africans knew how to handle themselves in such a situation.

It didn't even seem unlikely that we would spot a wild animal of some sort roaming through the abandoned airstrip. Small pebbles of animal dung, probably from an antelope of some kind, littered the area, and the tall grasses and full trees would provide the perfect hiding place for a predator. We walked silently but vigilantly, glancing in all directions for any kind of movement.

"Could you imagine being stuck out here all night?" I asked, hoping that a little conversation might take my mind of off things. "Like that couple?"

Megan stopped in her tracks. I looked ahead, thinking she had spotted something, but realized she only needed a drink of water.

"Where would you go?" she asked, unscrewing the pink lid from the bottle and taking a long sip. "I mean, it must be completely dark out here."

"I have no idea," I said, surveying the landscape around us. "That tree, maybe." I pointed to a tall, black tree we had passed just before stopping. Its branches looked sturdy but bare.

"We'd be safe up there, no?"

Megan turned and studied the tree, inspecting it almost as if she had planned on climbing it later that afternoon. Walking towards it, she semi-circled it and nodded with approval.

"Yeah," she confirmed. "I guess staying above makes more sense."

Could you tell Africa was making us both a little paranoid? Here it was, a perfectly sunny, comfortable day, and we were examining trees to decide which one we should run up in the event of an animal attack.

The dry, straw-like grass became even taller and bushier as we headed down the only thing that resembled a path—two, slight markings carved out at one time by wheels of some sort. The perfect hiding places for snakes. I picked up a long, black branch at one point and poked it forward, hoping to warn any resting snakes of my presence. What would happen, God forbid, if a venomous snake bit me? Even if I was able to make it back to camp, then what? I tried to put it out of my mind. I started to think that maybe this hike wasn't such a good idea after all. It's hard to enjoy yourself when thoughts of death completely consume your mind.

"Wait!" whispered Megan. It was one of the whispers that meant there was trouble.

"What's that?!?"

I stopped in my tracks and quickly looked to wear she pointed, far across the field towards a small patch of trees. I didn't see anything—until something brown and furry poked up in a sprawling patch of grass. Then another. And another.

We both stood silently for a few seconds, trying desperately to decipher what was out there watching us before it charged. Sometimes the brown, furry things would disappear, sinking beneath the grass, and then rise up again, curiously. I remembered what Rutger told us about how the large cats like lions could be ten feet in front of you but completely hidden within tall, tawny grasses, but that couldn't be a lion. Or a leopard, for that matter. Could it?

The budding tree behind the brown fuzzies began shaking, the occasional leaf floating gently to the ground beneath. We watched another brown fuzzy disappear deep into the grass and then the tree shook slightly again. The mystery was solved—the brown fuzzies were nothing more than the same mischievous vervet monkeys we spied earlier in camp, just as curious with us as we had become with them.

I took a deep sigh of relief, feeling slightly foolish for getting so worked up over a small party of monkeys. Oh well—at least we didn't need to go scuttling up our tree to wait it out.

With the fear of coming across a venomous snake still fresh in my mind, Megan and I removed ourselves from the carved-out trail we had been following and began to slowly pursue the monkeys instead, who had all timidly retreated to the shelter of the tree branches. There must have been at least ten in that single tree, alertly watching us and chirping to one another as we slowly approached. When we came to within thirty feet, slightly further than we wanted to but necessary for a good photo, several tree limbs shook and the monkeys scattered to the ground, rejoining one another fifty feet away in another grassy pile.

"I don't think they want their picture taken," I deadpanned.

"Yeah," started Megan. "We could end up chasing them all over."

She paused.

"I've seen enough, have you?"

I laughed a little. It was a laugh of relief.

"Yeah, let's head back. It's a little creepy out here for me."

Megan nodded. She knew exactly I meant.

The walk back to camp almost seemed the most unnerving aspect of our hike. Like that scene in every slasher film, I just couldn't shake that eerie feeling that my every move was being watched; almost certain that at the very moment when I let my guard down, something horrible would happen. Megan and I probably glanced over our shoulders as frequently as we looked ahead, both half-expecting to see the elusive leopard charging us across the open field. Or worse. Luckily, nothing happened, and I felt a tremendous sense of relief come over as me as the surroundings became familiar once again when we arrived back in camp.

We decided on lunch shortly after we returned—we weren't so much starving as we were bored, needing to break up the day at least a little bit. Still no Skonky, who was either working his ass off somewhere with Billie or passed out underneath a bar somewhere. With Skonky, you could never be too sure.

Peanut butter. God—even I was getting absolutely tired of peanut butter and jam sandwiches. I could imagine how poor Megan felt.

"There's that can of sardines in there, too, you know," I said. "If you want something else."

She smiled a wry, sarcastic smile.

"Yeah," Megan said. "I'll have what you don't finish."

The monkeys started stirring excitedly in the trees above us the instant I reached inside Skonky's tent for the food supply. Restless and hungry, the small cluster of monkeys chirped loudly, daring one another for an early afternoon raid. I wasn't in the mood for scarfing down my meal while on monkey patrol.

"C'mon," I said, motioning to Megan as I rose to my feet.

"Let's eat at the bar."

The single path through the campsite had become very familiar to us, winding around the entire grounds in a complete circle and crowded with trees and green, string-like vines. The sun reflected beautifully off the water that day, while birds noisily chirped away.

As we approached the site of the tattered volleyball net, something gray and quick darted through the grass on our immediate left, no more than fifteen feet away. Both digging our heels into the ground, we spotted our first snake, a shiny, gray one approximately six feet long that glided just behind a nearby tree.

"Our first snake!" I exclaimed, leaning forward from my still position in the hopes of spotting it in the grass. Those were the exact terms that I wanted to spot a snake by: it spotting us and fleeing rather than me stepping on it or getting bitten.

"What kind was it?"

Megan grabbed my hand and we continued down the path towards the bar, both of us focusing on the area near the tree where our little friend had disappeared. The tree was approximately fifteen feet behind us when Megan, still searching the perimeter, quickened her pace and tugged at my hand.

"There it is!" she cried out. "It's watching us!"

I tried to stop to get a glimpse but Megan wouldn't let go of my hand, dragging me along like a mom trying to get her child out of a toy store. In a brief second, I quickly spun around and spotted it, wrapped halfway up the tree and watching our every move beneath an eerie, intimidating smile.

Megan didn't need to hurry me along after that—I had a weird feeling about things, too. We didn't stop speed walking until we reached our safe haven, the bar, where Billie, Wendy and Skonky were all seated around a long table for an afternoon drink. So much for my theory that Skonky was off helping Billie.

"Well," said Skonky in a friendly voice, looking up from a half-full glass of beer. "It's the Americans!"

"How was your hike?" asked Wendy with a sweet smile. You could tell she was new to Africa.

Megan took a deep breath.

"Alright," she sighed. "We got a scare from a snake, though, on the way back. It sort of followed us from behind a tree."

"Oh yeah," Billie stated, rising from the bench and walking towards the bar with his empty glass for a refill.

"This whole area is full of snakes, though most are completely harmless. Mambas and adders are very rare. Mostly grass snakes and such."

"This one was pretty spooky," I added. "It just kept watching us. Gray, right?"

Megan nodded.

"Sounds just like a grass snake," Billie related. "Nothing to be afraid of."

Wendy rose to her feet.

"Billie?" Wendy asked, tossing her yellow napkin to the table. "Is that snake book still behind the counter?"

Without saying a word, Billie ducked behind the rustic-looking bar and popped back up with a bright, thin book in his hands.

"Your snake is probably in here," he said. "Take a look."

Megan snatched the book from his hands, and we sat down on an empty section of bench, flipping through the volume entitled 'Snakes of Africa.' Minutes later, we had our answer.

"There it is!" Megan cried, pointing to a photo.

"That's it!"

Yeah, I was positive we had found our snake: the wicked smile, the almost metallic-gray coloring, and the sinister eyes. And as little as I knew about snakes, I had heard of the species 'Black Mamba' before—the most dangerous snake in all of Africa, if not the world.

A Black Mamba. Part of me was completely unnerved that we confronted one, while the other part couldn't wait to tell everyone I knew about the chance encounter. I mean, these snakes were the real deal; one of the few species that would actually pursue its prey by aggressively chasing it down. And when mambas did attack, they'd bite repeatedly, emptying venom-filled fangs of perhaps the deadliest toxin in the world. Bite victims weren't completely hopeless, but not a second could be spared, as the venom moved very quickly through the bloodstream, slowing down and eventually shutting down the major organs.

With another mug of beer in hand, Billie walked over to spy the photograph of what Megan had shouted at and shook his head approvingly.

"Yeah," Billie stated matter-of-factly. "Mamba's are very rare right here, but you do see them every now and then."

Unimpressed, Billie walked back over to the bar. Nothing surprised someone living in Africa. It was impossible.

Skonky's gaze caught the loaf of bread and jar of peanut butter we had placed down on the ledge when we arrived.

"Didn't you see the sardines in there? I brought them for ya."

"Not a big fan of the sardines, man," I replied, shaking my head.

He laughed.

"Well, we're having a big feast tonight," he said, leaning forward like he was telling us a secret. "You can't tell the others, but all of us are going to sit down together and have one of the best meals yet!"

"Mmmm," said Megan. "Sounds good."

I didn't know how much Skonky smoked, but he never seemed to be without something burning dangling from his lips. And even though I seriously questioned the guy's judgment at times, I was willing to bite my tongue since we'd only have to put up with him through Victoria Falls, anyway.

At least he was right on about dinner that evening,—it was easily the largest feast I had in Africa, a collection of fresh salads, barbecued ribs, slow-cooked chicken, fresh bread and even grilled cheese sandwiches.

"Don't tell anyone else about this guys," Skonky warned.

"The guys in the Delta are stuck eating whatever slop Charlie felt like putting together!"

FUN WHILE IT LASTED

I rubbed my stomach pleasurably as I woke the next morning, still nice and full from that huge dinner the previous night. To my surprise, I also enjoyed one of the best nights of sleep I had in a long time, without a trace of Lariam-induced delusions. Best of all, Megan didn't make a peep.

"What time is it?" grumbled Megan, eyes still shut.

"About ten," I answered. "Are you up?"

She moved her hands to her face and rubbed her eyes slightly, then let out a yawn.

"Yeah. Are you hungry?"

"I could eat," I replied. "But I think we're on our own again."

Megan rifled through the pile of clothes at the foot of the tent, slipping into her pair of dusty khakis.

We climbed out of the tent and headed straight for Skonky's—empty again except for the dwindling crate of food. He had positioned the sardine can prominently in front of the crate, either being a smartass or pointing out to us that we had more options than the same tired sandwiches we had been making for ourselves the past several days.

I pulled out a new loaf of bread from the crate while Megan dug through our tent for our camping knife, perhaps the most useful things we decided to bring with us on the trip. Not only would it make short work of the bread, but it was the weapon of choice against any particularly bold predator.

Using a tree stump as a makeshift picnic table, I set the peanut butter, jam and bread down while I waited for Megan, who crawled from the tent a short time later with the knife.

"It's a little dirty," she declared, wiping something off the blade with the bottom of her shirt.

"Have we even washed it yet?"

I shook my head.

"I doubt it. But we should."

Removing the green plastic vial of camp soap from my front pocket, I motioned for the knife.

"I'll go too," Megan said. "I need to use the restroom."

In retrospect, we were pretty foolish leaving the food on the tree stump completely unattended when we left camp. After witnessing just how bold the vervet monkeys could be the previous day, what happened after that seemed inevitable.

"EEEEEEEEEEEEEE"

Instinctively, I spun on my heels towards the direction of the woman's scream that came from our camp.

Hippo?!? Leopard?!?

Without even thinking about what peril could be awaiting us, I jogged back to camp with Megan, witnessing one of the funniest 'only in Africa' scenes imaginable. The campground's two women caretakers, instead of raking the ground, now angrily swatted their tools high into the air.

"He took it, Missus," one woman said. "Very quick."

Looking up through the twisted collection of gnarled branches, I spotted it. The sneaky vervet monkey was taking huge, hurried bites into the middle of our loaf of bread.

Lowering their rakes, the local women surrounded us and continued to speak excitedly, one pantomiming the devious manner in which the money crept down the tree and then scampered back up. Big crumbs of bread showered us from above as the monkey continued to gobble up its treasure, devouring what it could before its scampering partners arrived.

A huge hunk of the loaf, nearly half of it, fell to the dusty ground with a thud. Megan and I both looked at each other and then down at the bread, decorated with about a dozen little bite marks all around it.

"You don't think we can still eat it, do you?" Megan asked sheepishly.

"Monkeys throw crap at one another," I said, shaking my head. "We can do better than this."

Luckily, it wasn't the last bread loaf Skonky had brought along. After depositing the mess of crumbs into a secure trash can, we brought out a new loaf of bread and kept a watchful eye as we cut it into thick slices, though I think we both felt really stupid for letting our guard down. Unlike our run-in with the mamba, at least witnessing a monkey steal your breakfast was relatively harmless.

Today, we had decided, was just going to be a lazy day—especially since it all started up again as usual the following day. Megan felt Billie out about taking us out to spy on the hippo family that dwelled in the Delta but he brushed her off, telling her to bring it up after he returned later that afternoon. I didn't care when it would be, but I knew I wanted to see hippos.

I didn't expect to second-guess my decision not to join the group for the excursion into the Delta but I found myself doing just that, even though the past couple of days alone with Megan were probably some of the most enjoyable of the entire trip. Secretly, I hoped the group hadn't see anything too spectacular or unusual to make me regret not going. It'd almost seem criminal for someone like Stacey, who usually showed no interest at all, to get a glimpse of a pride of lions or something equally cool. Plus I just knew someone like Mary would like nothing more than to rub it all in. Over time, a weird sort of tension existed between she and Megan, with my theory being that Mary was just jealous to see that Megan had such a studly boyfriend like me.

With the bright afternoon sun high above us, Megan and I spent the better part of the afternoon seated on the dock overlooking the Delta, alternating between reading our books and simply taking in the view. Many birds of all shapes and colors hovered just over the lazily flowing water, looking for that perfect mosquito lunch. My favorite bird, though, was a dark blue one that we first spotted after hearing a slight rustling in the bushes in front of us. After noticing us, the little guy, who seemed to prefer the ground instead of the sky, tore out of the bushes on its two tiny legs faster than any ground creature could, racing across a small section of riverbank before hiding itself in another bush.

Turning her attention back to the water, Megan spotted a large ripple about fifteen feet from the shore, followed by a series of small bubbles.

"Is that a branch?" she asked, pointing to a dark form that almost appeared to be drifting along with the current.

"I can't tell."

It looked lifeless to me—just another piece of debris, maybe some bark or a plant. I returned to my book, noticing out of the corner of my eye the intentness with which Megan continued to track the object.

"Oh my God!" she screamed. "Look!"

Bubbling up slightly from the depths of the Delta was the unmistakable eyes and upper jaw of a crocodile, rising into sight for a few seconds before sinking back down into the murk. I'd guess it was about five feet in length—not the huge size you sometimes see devouring entire antelopes, but formidable enough.

Our eyes remained fixed on the dark form of the crocodile, watching as just enough of its head rose above the waterline like a periscope, surveying its surroundings through cold, steely eyes. I would have loved to see that mouthful of sharp, jagged teeth but that wasn't going to happen unless some form of prey had unknowingly wandered in front of it. Eerily waiting, the croc floated back and forth, remaining close to the shore.

"I'm going to move," Megan nervously stated. "And I don't think you should stay here, either!"

Springing from her chair, Megan backed up to the main footpath behind us, never taking her eyes off the water.

"It doesn't even see us! It doesn't care," I reasoned. "It might do something cool!"

"They come out on land, you know."

"I know," I snapped.

"I'll hear it if it comes—I'm not going to fall asleep here."

"Well," Megan started. "I'll be at the bar, so if it starts chasing you, don't bring it by me."

I watched her walk away and sit in a small shaded grove just behind the bar, where she gave me a quick wave and began reading again. I turned my attention back to the croc, still vanishing and then materializing just on top of the water. It proved to be difficult to track after a while—sometimes I'd see a bump that resembled its dark shape in the far reed patch, but then I wasn't so sure, as the Delta at times seemed brimming with shadowy objects. Finally, after losing sight of the croc for several minutes and losing patience with the bees that curiously buzzed near my hair, I retreated to the grove and joined Megan.

"I knew you'd be back," she smiled. "I just knew it."

"He knows where you are," I countered. "He'll get you tonight!"

Aside from lunch, that was how we spent our final day in the Delta—completely relaxed and without a care in the world. In the late afternoon, everything changed, signaled unceremoniously by the hard, chainsaw-like grind of approaching motorboats, growing louder and louder. Through the trees, two small boats drifted slowly towards the dock. After two days of peace, we were no longer alone. The group had returned from the Delta.

Inexplicably, my stomach sank and I grew apprehensive about seeing everyone again. When I mentioned it to Megan afterwards, she said she felt the same way. Even now, it's hard to explain why, but I guess I felt a little violated to see the group 'invading' our little island paradise. The instant Billie latched his boat to the pier, all those feelings of being annoyed by each and every one of them stirred anew. And worst of all, they arrived so suddenly and without warning. One minute Megan and I were enjoying the peacefulness around us, and the very next we heard Matt rallying his Aussie buddies to the bar for an afternoon drink. It brought me back to my first day of high school, when I was the lone graduate of my grade school who didn't opt for attending the private Catholic high school down the road. Like then, I felt very much the outsider, completely detached from everyone else.

Not everyone was so bad, though.

"There you guys are!" Connor said cheerily, approaching us with his daypack blanketed in plastic. He looked more life-like than I had seen him in about a week.

"We thought you guys would have gone on without us."

I grabbed him on the shoulder.

"Yeah," I started. "We thought about it, believe me...You look a lot better, man."

He rolled his eyes slightly.

"I'm done drinking on this trip," Connor said, nodding his head. "I thought I was going to die on that makoro ride. Lots of weaving through reeds and shit."

"So how was it?!?" asked Megan excitedly. "What did you see?"

Connor paused thoughtfully, setting his pack down at his feet and crossing his arms.

"Let's see...," he began. "Hippos, then we saw a few antelope on the guided walk...that's it."

"Don't forget Stacey," Bill chimed in. "She said she saw a few lions on her canoe trip."

As selfish as it sounds, I felt relieved we hadn't missed much. I could handle one person seeing a few lions, but I was grateful I hadn't missed a trip highlight.

I quickly glanced at Megan—she knowingly smiled back.

"You didn't miss much," Connor reassured.

"Besides, you must have had it pretty good yourselves here. Better than bush camping."

"It was alright," I said, playing things down. "We just needed some down time. Hiked a little and just relaxed."

The rest of the group began trickling around us to catch up on what we had been up to, with Megan sharing our adventures with the black mamba and the breakfast-stealing monkey, second only to the excitement Stacey had experienced. Stacey had lucked out, spotting the lions when she chose to take a guided canoe trip by herself instead of the nature walk with the group. See—there was something to breaking free of that group mentality.

"I wouldn't say they were super-close to me," Stacey explained modestly, recounting her canoe trip. "But there were three of them, and they just kind of watched as we floated by. Maybe about thirty feet away or so."

The group looked like recently liberated prisoners of war, with the happiness of returning to civilization cloaked behind sheer exhaustion and disheveled appearances. And they all needed to shower. Badly.

Surprisingly, Mary didn't seem to be her usual chipper self, as she quietly headed directly to the showers once she recovered her pack from the boat. She looked the worst of the entire group—seemingly asleep on her feet; her face was completely devoid of all color to the point of being ashy white.

"I don't think she's feelin' very well," Bill told Matt, pulling close.

"I think her stomach's upset now, too."

Matt knowingly shook his head and returned with one of those 'what do you expect' sort of looks.

"Is Mary okay?" asked Megan, not missing a beat. We knew there was a story here somewhere.

Connor swallowed a smirk then stepped forward and briefly looked at the ground.

"She went on and on to some of the locals about her stomach problems," recalled Connor, shrugging his shoulders.

"Y'know...about her pebbles."

"Anyway," Bill added, tightening his blue headband. "They gave her some sort of root drink to help her, but I think it made things worse."

I had to bite my tongue. If I had heard of something more stupid on the entire trip, I couldn't think of it. It seemed incredulous to me: your stomach is messed up for nearly two weeks and your first instinct is to consume some exotic, unknown root offered to you by locals?

"Well," I started, "I hope she gets well, anyway."

We went back to the tent soon after to find Aubrey, fresh from his shower, who had started setting up his tent on the dry patch behind us. After first throwing the sack hard to the ground, Aubrey cursed loudly to himself as he stabbed each tent pole through the heavy, canvas shelter.

"Fuckin' Skonky!" Aubrey cursed. "Cocksucker!"

Imagine the surrealism of an R-rated Charlie Brown cartoon special and you have Aubrey, sourly cursing as he readied camp. There was just something about a blond, dopey-looking guy in a bright yellow shirt that made things more comical then threatening.

Pushing myself up off the ground, I held the far end of Aubrey's tent steady as he awkwardly drove the last support rod into place, struggling to contain my laughter.

"Fucking Skonky," Aubrey growled again, just as the last leg of the tent hit the ground.

"And bush camping!"

I stifled a smile as I bent to the ground, looking away as I pretended to examine one of the tent poles.

"Oh, don't worry, Aubrey," he angrily mocked. "You don't need your mattress—the ground is nice and soft."

"This ground is worst than last night!" Aubrey declared, stomping down hard on the dirt like a spoiled child.

"How am I supposed to sleep tonight?!? How?!?"

The more I got to know Aubrey, the more he really did remind me of a spoiled, bratty younger brother. Nice enough guy, but he had issues. You would think he left a king-sized imperial mattress behind with the way he was behaving, not an inflatable, plastic mat.

Megan looked about as amused as I did during Aubrey's tirade, burying a smirk into her knees. I guess she was trying to be helpful when she offered her advice, but I think we both knew her plan for Aubrey would fail miserably.

"Aubrey," began Megan. "There's a big sofa in the bar. Maybe Billie will let you spend the night on it."

Instantly, Aubrey's demeanor transformed—from one of total, consuming anger to sudden calm and tranquility. Maybe the baby would get his bottle after all.

"Yes," Aubrey proclaimed, stepping back as if to admire Megan's solution. "I will do just that."

As Aubrey took off towards the bar, Megan and I took our customary seats around the fire ring, which Rutger had begun just as the setting sun began to disappear behind the trees. When Charlie wasn't assisting with the meal, chopping some green vegetables on a wood cutting board, she was seated next to Matt, giggling about something or staring longingly into his eyes. At least it got Charlie out of her surly mood.

If death had a face that evening, it was Mary. Lying horizontally across a fallen log, Mary moved sparingly, occasionally forcing herself into a sitting position to rub her shoulders before lying back down again. She looked completely miserable, and certainly feeling ill in the middle of nowhere did nothing to alleviate her anxiety.

Though it wouldn't do Mary any good, I took some comfort—seeing her in that sorry state—that Megan and I had been so careful about things. As anal as we had been about food and water, it was beginning to look like it was paying off. First Stacey fell ill, then Aubrey, and now Mary, her condition made worse after consuming whatever root she had been given in the Delta.

Mary was beginning to look more and more restless as dinner drew near, sometimes grabbing her stomach as she picked herself up off the log long enough to pace back and forth beneath her shivering. Helen, our lone medical professional of the group, sat and talked with her quietly about how she was feeling, but there's only so much you can do in a situation like that. Something had to give, and give it did.

With Helen's arm around her waist, Mary slowly rose to her feet, stepping gingerly at first until she unexpectedly broke free of Helen's grasp and darted to the restroom, slamming the door hard behind her. Helen, by this time lightly jogging in pursuit, rapped lightly on the door and then slipped inside, closing it behind.

As far as the restroom had seemed from where we were cooking dinner, the two seemed adjacent that night, as Mary's guttural burps and moans echoed throughout camp. My own stomach grew queasy, convulsing slightly with each retching sound.

"Uuuhhh," moaned Megan, her upper lip sneering in disgust. "That's just foul!"

I could only shake my head in bewilderment.

"Why would she even take that root?" I said over the splash of toilet bowl water.

"She probably didn't even know what it was!"

Bill, seated on the other side of the fire, wiped his hands into his shorts as he rose to his feet.

"Now if only she could do that from the other end," he quipped, "we'd all be a lot happier." Mary's 'pebbles' act was wearing thin on everyone.

Helen returned to the fire circle minutes later, quietly badgered by scores of questions about how Mary was doing. It was nothing we didn't know or didn't hear for ourselves—she was in bad shape.

Rutger, at times almost obscured by the heavy smoke of our fire, anxiously watched for any signs of life emerging from the restroom, looking considerably calmer when Mary, appearing paler than ever, stumbled out. Mary was in complete agony as she loped forward, looking barely able to stand as she meandered back to the fire circle, plopping down with a heavy thud back on the reclining log. The only one who seemed completely unfazed by all of this was Skonky, whose interaction with the group that evening consisted largely of him popping by with a beer in his hand to check on dinner before retreating back to the bar.

As he continued studying Mary through concerned eyes, Rutger decided he'd seen enough and tiptoed over to Mary, who was lying motionless on her log. Then, wrapping one of her arms around his shoulder, Rutger gently supported her weak frame long enough to carry her to her tent and help her inside.

"She's not doing so good," offered Rutger when he returned, grabbing the long stick he had been using to poke the fire. "If she's no better, she's going to have to see a doctor."

"A doctor?" quizzed Aubrey. "There is nothing around here, right?"

Rutger hunkered down low in front of the fire, pushing off his knees to rise fully to his feet.

"Probably Jo'burg is her best bet," he declared. Only later did I realize 'Jo'burg' was Johannesburg—I was a little clueless.

Rutger's statement brought a shocked, bewildered expression to Megan's face. Seeing Mary ill enough to get evacuated really made Megan's fears of contracting a disease really hit home.

"You mean, all the way to Johannesburg?" Megan asked softly.

"She'd have to fly, then."

"That's the way it is, unfortunately," replied Rutger. "Only your large cities have good medical facilities, and with Mary's other problem, she needs attention."

Mary's other problem. If Mary didn't look so poor, I would have made some smartass joke about knowing that she was always full of shit.

Mary's sorry plight that evening, combined with the ravenously hungry swarms of mosquitoes that infested camp for that one, unprotected spot to nibble on you, served as constant reminders of how no amount of precaution in Africa was too much.

Maybe the mosquito swarm was so thick that night because of Stacey, who was once again practicing her own, unique brand of safety and self-preservation. In a light blue, short-sleeved shirt and white shorts, she single-handedly advertised her delectable vulnerability to every mosquito that called Africa home. Without a trace of insect repellent applied to her exposed flesh, Stacey's hands were constantly flailing, slapping away at the dozens of mosquitoes that landed on her at a time. Finally, it became too much.

"Megan!" Stacey exclaimed, spitting as she chased an errant mosquito out of her mouth.

"Can you give me your repellent? I ran out late yesterday in the Delta."

As I watched Stacey slap away at a mosquito that began digging into her right shoulder, I remembered the old saying that God looked out for children and fools. For Stacey's sake, I hoped it was right.

Still, just as she did by mooching water off us on the truck, Stacey, through her rampant lack of planning, managed to put us in another bind. I was about to say something but stopped when I saw Megan passing our half-empty can over, though I knew Megan wouldn't let it go at that. She was always more diplomatic than I could be.

"You know," stated Megan as she eyed Stacey's revealing outfit. "You really should cover up. Don't you have slacks?"

Stacey started liberally spraying herself, stretching out her legs as she zapped them from behind.

"They're dirty."

They're dirty. Megan just had one of those 'what the fuck?!?' looks on her face. People often confused the Okavango Delta with a trendy, hot nightclub.

With a quick swipe, Megan's hand struck like a snake and latched onto the almost empty spray can as it hissed air.

"That's all we have, Stacey," Megan declared, placing the can at her feet.

"You should probably get those slacks on."

I expected Stacey to walk away in a huff, but she didn't, surprisingly gracious as she thanked us and strolled to her tent, returning in her slightly dusty khakis. They looked fine to me. During dinner, she managed to mooch a little more repellent from Matt.

With the entire group now back together, things were relatively normal—or as normal as you could consider them. Skonky left the bar long enough to eat and slur the usual something about driving all day tomorrow; Rutger got screwed once again, doing nearly all of the cooking despite Charlie's presence while still maintaining his trademark chipper disposition; Helen and Abe sat completely silent and motionless, probably wondering why the hell they blew their retirement on this; Aubrey and Stacey flirted some more after he went on and on about how rude it was for Billie not to allow him to sleep on the sofa in the bar; while the Aussie guys and Dominick laughed about some obscure cricket reference I didn't really get. Oh yeah—and Meg and I began dreading going out on the road again with these knuckleheads.

Like I said—business as usual.

A RETURN TO THE CRIME SCENE

"If one of you doesn't want to, then we aren't going to do it," boomed Skonky as he flipped the cigarette lighter in his hand. "But we've done it a ton of times...."

"...And the military escort is completely safe."

I think we all felt a little blind-sided that morning as Skonky selected being escorted through the Caprivi Strip as the topic of breakfast conversation. Let's face it: the words 'African military' never really paint a rosy picture. The whole point of bringing it up, according to Skonky, was that taking this armed escort would shave off an entire day of dull driving, giving us one more day to ourselves when we'd finally reach Victoria Falls.

I had to bum Abe's map off him to get an idea of what this Caprivi Strip was that Skonky was talking about. The Strip, explained Rutger, was a small hunk of land between Namibia and Angola currently being contested by the Nambian military and a small band of rebels. The rebels had attempted to claim the strip as their own for the past dozen years, so the conflict wasn't new by any means, but the military, through a show of force, still arranged for an armed convoy twice daily to escort vehicles through. And passing through it meant picking up an extra day in Chobe National Park, Botswana's famed game reserve.

"I've taken that route at least a dozen times myself," Skonky said, clearly rallying for us to join the convoy.

"Nothing's ever happened, though you guys need to decide as a group what you want to do."

No one said anything for a few seconds—a combination of still being half-asleep and thinking about worst possible scenarios involving the African military. Skonky, grabbing a small stone off the ground, pelted it towards a vervet monkey that danced along a tree branch above us. Ricocheting off the metal roof of a nearby shelter, the <ping> echoed throughout camp.

"Let's do it," I said aloud.

"Yeah," seconded Bill, looking at the others. "No big deal, right?"

Rutger chimed in.

"We need everyone to agree, guys," reminded Rutger. "Does anyone not want to take the escort through the Strip?"

Silence. Skonky cracked a smile.

"You made a good choice," reassured Skonky. "When we take the Strip tomorrow, you'll see."

Skonky headed to his tent while the rest of us finished our breakfast. If anyone would have objected, it would have been Mary, whose naivety at times must have made her go through life like a scared little rabbit. She didn't have a vote, though. Mary wouldn't be going with us.

Though she looked better that morning, smiling and even laughing on occasion, the guides still thought it best that Mary receive medical treatment, especially after she confided in Rutger that bowel blockages were a part of her family's medical history. And I thought eczema was bad.

With Billie's help, the plan was in place. When Billie returned us to Ella, he would then drive Mary into town where she'd get air-lifted to a hospital in Johannesburg.

Surprisingly, Mary seemed to be in good enough spirits about the whole thing, though she wouldn't concede leaving the tour permanently.

"If I get fixed up in Johannesburg," she promised, "I'll definitely see you all in Vic Falls."

I felt like taking her aside and trying to convince her that she shouldn't hurry back, making sure she got time to rest and convalesce. Please, Mary.

As we broke camp, Skonky kindly shared with everyone the day's agenda: a return to Ngepi Campground, the scene of Skonky's unbridled debauchery, Connor's brush with alcohol poisoning, and the old, sleazy campground host who boned a fat chick younger than his visiting daughter.

May God have mercy on our souls.

From a purely logical perspective, returning to Ngepi did make sense, though I half-wondered if that was the primary reason why Skonky rallied so hard to use the escort through the Strip. According to Skonky, Ngepi sat barely half-a-day from where we currently were and barely an hour from the Strip—crucial since we needed to join the convoy at 9 a.m. sharp the following morning. Ngepi—good times laced with bad memories. I thought I saw Connor dry-heave at the mere mention.

We crowded ourselves next to our stowed gear and returned to the same muddy riverbank that we started from days earlier, this time unloading our stuff into the big military-type vehicle waiting for us. Matt became particularly annoying, barking out orders the whole time while he struggled to lift packs that were a little too heavy for him.

The road back to Ella was about as pleasant as it was on the way in—not very. The water that had collected on the muddy, makeshift roads looked like it had actually risen, sometimes nearly immersing the fat tires of our truck completely as it slogged through. I could appreciate Billie taking things slow, easing into the wet and muck versus charging forward into it, but that also made things painfully bumpy as I sat with my back against the slatted wooden side of the vehicle. My three days of rest, relaxation and mending were gone, all but forgotten, as I braced myself against the truck's frame while slapping away at the hungry mosquitoes.

The monster crawled along for nearly an hour, bringing me to that point where I became convinced I could actually get out and walk quicker rather than subject myself to the vehicle's slow pace. Vervet monkeys, picking at pieces of long, plump fruit, scurried up tree branches at our approach, their timid eyes fixed on us until we passed. I knew we were getting close when I smelled the unmistakable odor of wet, burning wood—that unmistakable telltale scent that life was nearby.

"Well, I'll be," said Bill, nodding his head. "She's still in one piece."

A few curious children rushed outside when they heard our approach, though life in the tiny village largely continued unabated by our presence. Women cooked in heavy metal pots or tended to their laundry, barely noticing us, while dogs and chickens wandered aimlessly.

Skonky had an aside with Billie once the truck came to a labored halt while we all unloaded, working in tandem this time and making quick work of it. This had to be how it was in the military. At least, it seemed about as depressing.

Rutger slide over to the rear of Ella and unlocked the thick steel doors, slowly cracking one door open while holding the onslaught of assorted backpacks at bay with one hand. I glanced over and noticed that my painting was still on the very top of the pile—a very good sign. With one hand, Rutger began dismantling the wall of luggage, mounding our bags in a small pile in front of him.

"You know the drill, guys," he bellowed. "Take a few minutes to re-pack your things, then back on the truck. Don't leave anything behind."

Rutger popped over to Mary, who had been waiting quietly at the foot of the mound. He slung the two bags that she pointed to over his back and carried them over to Billie's truck, tossing them into the front seat.

"Well guys," Mary said with a sigh. "Maybe I'll see you all in Vic Falls."

Matt and Helen gave her a hug—the rest of us just settled for wishing her luck. Personally, I hoped it was nothing too serious and that she'd be back in good health shortly after some medical attention. But I also had to be honest with myself. I knew I wouldn't miss Mary's grating behavior if this truly was the last time I ever saw her.

"There she goes," Megan said, as Mary settled into the passenger seat of Billie's truck.

"Think she'll be back?"

"I don't know if I would," I shrugged.

Here I was, after a few relaxing days in the Delta and only a few hours back into things full-force, and I was already beginning to question if coming to Africa had been a good choice, not to mention if I could even imagine putting up with this for an additional four weeks. At least, I thought it was four weeks. Most of the time, I didn't even know the date or the day of the week, going only by the highlights mentioned on our itinerary that sometimes changed as well.

I think a lot of us were growing frustrated. And Skonky didn't help.

"I am notifying the office on him," warned Stacey at our lunch stop, a nondescript shoulder of road in the middle of somewhere. "He's crude, he's rude, and we shouldn't have to put up with his swearing all of the time."

Megan just kind of looked at me, then at Stacey.

"I don't know," Megan said. "I mean, you get what you pay for, and I kind of figured anyone who'd do this for a living would be a little rough."

"Well," continued Stacey in a huff. "I spent good money on this trip and I demand a little more professionalism. It's just not acceptable."

Stacey was a weird one—getting weirder as the days progressed. She liked to put on this sophisticated heir at times, like she was so much above any sort of hardship on this trip. The reality, though, was that she was just as cost-conscious as the rest of us, and I saw nothing in African Wanderer's brochure that made me mistaken them for the Ritz-Carlton. We passed those beautiful lodges often enough through the many miles we logged—white, sprawling complexes cradled in the afternoon sun that offered more to its visitors than most five-star hotels back home. Not once did I think Skonky would detour up even one of those driveways, not even if we were hopelessly in need of directions.

When Stacey wasn't acting like a snob, she'd flirt with anyone with all the grace of a mountain gorilla in heat. When Aubrey wasn't the poor victim, Connor, Bill, even Skonky—the man she found so despicable and disgusting—proved just as inviting. Typically, she'd approach her hapless subjects from behind and wrap them in what amounted to be a death grip while she'd bat her eyes and rattle off a variety of sexual innuendos, like about how a 'good lay would really help my back' and other similarly grotesque images. As a representative of the male species, it is important to note that only the most desperate of men (Aubrey) showed anything resembling interest.

The road actually started looking very familiar shortly after lunch. Once we came to the clearing and slowed down, the white-haired owner that we spied making time with the fat redhead last time spotted Skonky from a short distance and began striding our way, wagging his finger and smiling.

"Skonky," he teased excitedly. "I knew you couldn't stay away."

Having a good part of the day to ourselves was mind-blowing to me. As much as I hated the routine of the entire trip, it did grow on you, much like being brainwashed. Often, I was left bewildered when we were told we had time for ourselves, as if Skonky was the prison warden releasing us for the afternoon. Even with unstructured and unplanned time, it often meant nothing more than time on our hands, as the top three activities of every campground were 1) drinking; 2) napping and 3) waiting to eat. Myself, along with most everyone else, opted for the second choice: napping.

I had never been much of a napper, but I quickly became one while in Africa. The afternoon sun felt so good when I spread out my sleeping mat near the river, with its trickling water providing the ultimate in relaxation. The Aussie guys began whacking a cricket ball near me so whenever I heard them yelling a great deal I expected the ball to strike me. It never did, though, and before long I was in a deep slumber.

It must have been about an hour before I woke up and spotted Megan, lying about fifteen feet away and reading her 'African Disease' book. She was beyond hiding it from me as she tried to read it—I guess she was in her own survival mode.

Loud Irish music blared from the bar, getting noticeably louder as Megan and I approached. Skonky, the King of Ngepi himself, had resumed his throne on the second bar seat from the left. Though Bill and Matt milled around him, each with a beer in hand the subdued nature of things indicated that there were no drinking contests going on.

We sat down on a bench just outside of the bar area by Aubrey, Dominick and Connor.

"So you're laying off things?" I asked Connor.

"Yep," Connor replied firmly with a slight head nod. "They gave me a lot of shit when I first got here, but there's no way I'm doing that again."

Almost on cue, a portly female bartender with auburn hair appeared with a knit stocking cap in her hand, stopping in front of us.

"I am here at the request of the owner," she began, "to name the bearer of the Notty hat tonight." She held the hat high above her head and showed it to us for approval.

"The bearer of this hat must uphold the spirit of Notty and be prepared to drink," she said. "And I choose you".

Her crooked finger landed on Aubrey, who lowered his head slightly and smiled a little.

"No, no, no," he said, as flecks of saliva sprayed from his mouth. "I'm not interested in that."

The bartender, looking to Connor and then me, got the same response from all of us. No way.

"Hey, I'm just communicating what my boss said to," she stated, a little upset that we were so quick to brush her off. I was convinced—these people were drunks.

I knew Aubrey and Connor wouldn't bite at the offer—I found out that Aubrey was fairly religious and didn't go in for excess, and Connor was a given. Dominick, always mysterious, would have been a small possibility, but I noticed that he wasn't looking particularly good when I sat down next to Connor. He looked very cold, wearing heavy, long sleeves with his arms clutched close to his body despite being bathed in the warmth of the sun. Like Mary and Stacey before her, his face was colorless, almost ashen, and you could see tiny beads of sweat collecting near his forehead.

"Are you feeling alright, Dominick?" I asked, prompting the entire group to collectively turn and look.

"No," he said, forcing a smile. "I need to lie down."

Rising slowly to his feet, Dominick trudged to his tent slowly, forcing himself to walk steady and true. Megan walked over to Rutger, enjoying a soft drink at a table by himself in the bar, and let him know, not wanting a repeat of the whole Aubrey scene the last time we were here. Rutger, looking genuinely concerned, thanked her and said he'd look in on Dominick in a little bit. Good, reliable Rutger—at least we knew he could stay sober.

Surprisingly, at least for that particular night, Skonky was not acting as unruly as I had suspected he might—but running low on cash usually makes even the most raging drunk sober. Though Skonky was never without a drink in his hand the entire night, he seemed to be pacing himself a little better, thanks to a cute, shapely brunette sitting next to him at the bar. It was a little amusing to watch—tough-as-nails Skonky acting like the perfect gentlemen, rising from his stool when the brunette excused herself and rising again when she returned. I always had to remind myself that the guy was in his middle-twenties—younger than myself—and still trying to get his game together.

The brunette would smile politely every now and then, but I don't think she really saw Skonky as lover potential—it would be hard to get past his troll-like appearance no matter how many drinks you consumed. I couldn't help but wonder, what kind of conversation a guy like Skonky would strike up to impress a woman. I chuckled when I pictured Skonky dressed in a tuxedo with no shoes, waiting at the altar for his bride.

But while Skonky was almost charming that night, Matt, the same Matt who was engaged and getting married when he returned to Australia, was up to his usual, pretentious games. Seated at a far table with Charlie, who gazed longingly as some thin, blond-haired guy hung on one end of the bar, Matt appeared to lack anything resembling sincerity.

Charlie was a piece of work, an emotional basket case just as likely to be found weeping silently in the corner of the truck as she was screaming at someone who dared place a dirty dish in her bus pan. That particular night, as she sat with Matt, she was in one of her weeping modes.

"I'm never going to find love...," she cried to Matt. "...Love is bullshit anyway, who needs it."

Charlie hung her head low and slumped to the table as tears rushed from her eyes. The heartbreaks of teenage life.

Leaning back in his chair, Matt sprung forward and put his hand on hers, giving it a slight squeeze.

"There, there, Charlie," he began. "You'll find love."

"We all need love."

We all need love?!? Wasn't that a line from a bad Rick Astley song?!?

Megan, watching with me while the soap opera began to unfold, rolled her eyes and mumbled something that sounded like "what bullshit."

I agreed. Matt was so ego-driven that he thrived for moments like this, when he could be the seemingly strong protector, the perfect guy. Granted, Charlie was a piece of work herself, but it was disgusting how he feigned sincerity to pad his own ego.

And worst of all, naïve Charlie was playing right into his hands. Looking up at Matt when he grabbed her hand, she wiped her tears with the back of her hand and smiled softly.

"Oh Matt," Charlie cried. "I can't imagine my life without you!"

Just like that, in mere seconds, Charlie's crush jumped from Mr. Blond Barfly back to Matt. I wasn't too shocked. Charlie probably fell in love as often as most people changed their underwear.

Still, it was all getting too much for me to watch. We tried playing Uno with our dwindling group once we ate dinner but that remained next to impossible—even with the brighter lights of the bar overhead, it was still very hard to tell the blue cards from the green.

Bored, I retreated to our tent to read a little in the tent by flashlight and to escape the loud, reverberating music that pounded throughout the campsite. I noticed some movement near Dominick's tent as I approached and spotted Rutger, zipping it closed from the outside.

"He's in quite bad shape," said Rutger, turning towards me as I approached. "Terrible fever."

When your champion eater doesn't show up for dinner, you just know something is wrong.

Rutger's droopy eyes hung even heavier and he stood frozen in time, seemingly paralyzed with frustration. He was drained himself. Even as experienced as Rutger was in navigating through the wild African bush, even he had to be feeling the strain of doing so much day after day while the others, Skonky and Charlie, did so little. Poor Rutger was doing the best he could, and he knew as well as we did that he deserved to lead this tour.

"Well," Rutger sighed. "Hopefully tomorrow will be a better day for him. For all of us."

I realized for the first time that night that Megan and I weren't the only ones stuck in survival mode. Rutger needed to survive long enough to get to Victoria Falls with us, where he'd probably return to Cape Town and lead a new group of tourists, hopefully.

Others, like Dominick, just needed to survive.

BULLETS FOR BREAKFAST

I never did get back to sleep that night. Damn Lariam. Something about being scared nearly half to death does that to a person.

I didn't remember any wild dreams or nightmares—just waking up at some point with the intense sensation that the tent was closing in on me and that I needed to get out. And I thought taking Lariam would be cool—sort of a legal LSD.

I tried to calm myself down after charging to the closed flap and thrusting my head into the night for some air. It was no use. My heart pounded hard. The commotion woke Megan long enough for her to ask if I was okay, but she managed to get back to sleep fairly easily. I knew she was right when she said I should see a doctor to change my prescription. If these night terrors became a nightly occurrence, I knew I'd be in trouble.

I lay quietly, drifting between that state of almost falling asleep and just being awake enough, until I heard the sound of someone leaping down from the truck. It had to be Rutger—the early riser himself. Both he and Skonky never slept in tents, instead they hunkered down on the back benches of the truck, with the windows shut tight and a large mosquito net over both of them.

If Rutger was stirring that meant him waking us wasn't too far off. And with a rushed morning since we had to catch the convoy through the Caprivi Strip, I decided to get a jump on everyone and shower.

By the time I had returned, invigorated by the almost scalding water of the shower, the entire group had been wakened and tents had begun collapsing. Megan still looked asleep, crawling from the tent on all fours and yawning like a slumbering lion.

"Not much time, guys," warned Rutger, surveying the toppling tents like a field commander. "If we miss the convoy, we lose a day and have to spend another one here."

Rutger wanted to move on as badly as we did.

While Megan and I brought down the tent, I noticed Rutger racing over to Dominick, who rigidly emerged from the tent with a blank, pained expression on his face. Dominick didn't appear to say much when Rutger approached him, though even a blind man could detect how he was feeling. As Dominick pointed to his stomach, Helen, in the middle of folding the tent she shared with Abe, jogged over and placed her hand across his forehead, then joined the discussion.

"Let's take his temperature," Helen suggested which prompted Rutger to go and fetch the first aid kit.

After a few minutes, they got their reading.

"104," Helen announced. "That's high but he should be okay."

104?!? Didn't people die at 106 or 107?

Waiting it out sounded risky to Megan and I. I mean I know Helen is a nurse and all but this exchange made me start to question her competence.

But Rutger was satisfied with her assessment and soon after Dominick boarded the truck with the rest of us.

"We're not eating here," boomed Skonky as he looked at his watch. "We have to queue up when we join the convoy so we'll just set up in the middle of the road there while we wait."

Waiting another hour for breakfast didn't bother me, but I had my apprehensions about breaking bread surrounded by an African militia, as I guess most people would. It just seemed kind of disrespectful. I mean, here we are, arrogantly having a picnic in the middle of the road, while a militia armed with AK-47s is watching the perimeter for the enemy. To me, that image just screamed 'disrespectful white foreigners.'

As we boarded, I caught a glimpse of Charlie, wearing a long green T-shirt that covered her knees and with her arms wrapped around Matt, she whispered something softly into his shoulder.

"We all need love, Charlie..."Matt whispered back. "Remember that."

"I think I'm going to be sick, too!" Megan joked.

Even with Mary gone, I knew it wouldn't take long at all for another one of my fine, fellow travelers to fill that vacated role of annoying the shit out of me. Megan and I actually made a game out of it, checking in with one another almost every night for our latest 'pick,' that is, the one person who annoyed us so much that we'd ditch them in the middle of the

African bush if we had our way. With Mary gone, Matt topped Megan's list quite a few times, but he was more pathetic to me than annoying. For my money, you still couldn't beat Travel Snob Stacey, who increasingly imagined herself as a sultry sex kitten, and Abe, who had all the mobility and pleasantness of a giant tortoise flipped on its back.

After releasing Charlie from his embrace, Matt, with his head tilted slightly back and with a wry smile, arrogantly swaggered up the steps of truck, nodding towards Bill in the rear of the truck.

"Not bad, Matty," said Bill, leaning over to the window to inspect Charlie, who was discussing something outside with Skonky. The billowing clouds of exhaust spewing from Ella had to be killing her.

"She's a lovely girl, Bill," Matt stated. He sat with his arms spread wide across his seat, basking in the consuming crush of one, naïve girl. Cocky guys like him lived for moments like this. Maybe he wasn't so far from the top of my list after all.

With a little help from Rutger, Dominick was the last one to board Ella that morning. The entire truck watched in virtual silence as he dragged himself to his seat, eventually dropping down into it with a thud. The poor devil looked like he was still asleep—his eyes slightly glazed and heavy from fever—so it was no surprise that he pulled the hood of his sweatshirt over his eyes and slouched against the window in a futile attempt for more rest.

"I don't know what he has," Stacey whispered into Megan's ear as she leaned forward in the seat behind us. "But it better not be contagious!"

My stomach rumbled slightly from hunger as Rutger, behind the wheel for the first time, put the truck into gear after Skonky took the passenger's seat. Under the rising sun of a new morning, Ella roared out of Ngepi as I struggled not to think of how hungry I was. My mind raced as I thought of all the bad diners and truck stops I had frequented at one time or another, either for breakfast or for a drunken meal, and wished for the shittiest meal I ever had from any of them right now. Fuck cereal. The thought of devouring a fat, ham and cheese omelet was heaven.

It didn't take long at all before we reached the checkpoint area for the military convoy, which resembled more of a parking lot due to the number of cars and trucks of all shapes and sizes parked in uniform rows one right after another. The curious eyes of many people met us as we approached, as most decided to wait outside of their cars and trucks until the convoy began.

Most of the battered cars that had lined up looked like they'd be more at home in a junkyard than on a major road. One truck, wrapped completely in wire, held dozens of live chickens.

Three serious-looking soldiers, decked out in immaculate, brown uniforms and each holding a long rifle, talked amongst themselves. All three cautiously watched as Rutger halted Ella right behind a small gray pick-up truck. They were headed our way.

"What do we do, Charlie?" Megan asked our surly cook, now filling the seat in the rear of the truck that Rutger had vacated.

Charlie shrugged.

"I don't know, man," Charlie laughed. "I don't even know where we're going today!"

Why was Charlie on this trip again?

Before the soldiers reached the rear of the truck, Skonky jumped from the cab and greeted the men, handing one of them a fistful of white and yellow papers. The sullen looking soldier glanced at the papers without reading them and then handed them to another, electing to walk slowly around the rear of the truck as his eyes darted up and down Ella's entire body. When he rounded towards the main door, Aubrey bounced up from his seat and slowly creaked it open, giving a short, respectful wave.

The intimidation was so thick you could feel it. We were in a situation where things could go horribly wrong, where a cross word or impolite behavior could very well find you in a third world jail.

Clutching the handrail, the stern-looking soldier ascended the steps in fashion, embracing his power with each pronounced movement. Coming to a full stop when he reached the landing, he smiled reassuringly and slightly cleared his throat.

"Good morning and welcome," boomed the soldier, studying our faces. Pacing slowly up the aisle with his hands clasped behind his back, the soldier stopped when he reached Connor.

"Passport, please."

Without blinking, Connor reached into his back pocket and picked his passport out from a pile of folded bills and other small papers, handing the small blue booklet over to the soldier. I was glad Rutger had the sense to pass them out before we had arrived.

The soldier, flipping right to Connor's photo, examined it before turning his attention to the rest of us. Shutting the passport, the uniformed man then squeezed the passport between his fingers and slapped it repeatedly into his open palm. This guy had intimidation down to a science.

Handing the passport back to Connor, the solider methodically paced back up the aisle and spun on his heels in one fluid movement, stopping when he arrived near the front once again.

"I hope you enjoy Africa," announced the soldier, who then slowly descended the steps.

I watched out the window as the soldier returned to his colleagues and Skonky, who took the papers back from the other soldier and then signed off on a clipboard. A few minutes later, Skonky climbed back into the cab and the soldiers walked off.

"Good job, guys," Skonky whispered. "I heard of entire trucks being unpacked if the military got suspicious!"

Suspicious? Maybe it wasn't suspicious, but what would you call setting up our little picnic table, amid all of the military personnel and weapons of warfare, to eat our little breakfast?

I wasn't disappointed in the least when Skonky, after returning to the cab to talk to Rutger about something, announced that breakfast would be served from inside the truck rather than outside as initially planned. If there was any possibility of pissing off an African militia, I wanted no part of it.

Of all the truly unique African experiences, there was nothing quite like driving in a military-escorted convoy. There we were, in a long, parading line of vehicles and with several armored vehicles crammed with soldiers on either side of us. It was another one of those experiences, like when we boarded that military-style truck to get into the Delta that made me feel like I was going off to war myself.

The convoy continued for about an hour before the lead vehicles began to slow down and stop, forcing all of the others to do the same. A thin soldier with a pistol sprinted from the start of the convoy to the back, sending me into a slight panic at first as I thought we might be under attack. Then, I heard what he was shouting.

"Rest stop," the soldier bellowed in a deep voice. "Men on one side, women on the other."

One by one, we climbed down from Ella. Bill wisely left his camera behind and buried it beneath a pile of clothes under his seat in case the jeep-load of soldiers came after him. Every vehicle in the convoy threw its door wide-open, as men and women alike trudged towards the shoulders of the road. They took their rest stops very seriously in Africa.

I stood against the truck as I watched Megan, along with several local women, disappear into the bush. The perfect opportunity, I thought, for a rebel group to raise hell, when there'd be so much confusion and disorder that they could really do some damage. The soldiers, though, looked the least bit concerned, telling jokes to one another and smoking cigarettes, leading me to believe that although there had been incidents in the past, the military escort was more a show of force than anything else.

Minutes later, Megan emerged from the bush looking over her shoulder, and then shaking her head as she approached.

"This place..." she said, nervously laughing.

"The woman next to me," Megan continued, "told me it wasn't the rebels you needed to look out for—it was the lions. They see them in the bush here all of the time!"

****

The convoy uneventfully concluded a little over an hour later, signified by the military vehicles first slowing down and then pulling to one side while a lone soldier hopped out of the jeep and waved everyone on through the billowing dust. He must have been the new hire.

A roving herd of dogs galloped behind the truck as we pulled in to Chobe that afternoon, a nice-looking, if unspectacular campground that at least had its own pool. Another popular overland truck destination, it didn't take terribly long for Bill and Connor to go exploring for familiar female faces. I hoped I wouldn't have to witness the continuing soap opera of Matt and Charlie so soon, if ever again.

Megan, myself, and most of the others checked out the frigidly cold pool while Dominick retreated to his tent as quickly as we helped him assemble it, he didn't even appear at dinner that evening. Putting together a small plate of dinner, Rutger made his way to Dominick's tent, unzipping the main door and tunneling in after not getting a response. I could hear the two talking briefly, and then Rutger emerged from the tent without the plate, biting his lower lip and shaking his head.

"How's Dominick?" asked Megan as Rutger approached.

"Not good, I'm afraid," he sighed. "I'm thinking we can let him keep going like this without medical attention."

I saw Rutger glance over at Skonky as he spoke, but there was no acknowledgement that I could see. With a brown bottle of beer in his hand, it was becoming all too obvious that looking after anyone was not Skonky's forte. I mean, the guy was oblivious.

Hopefully, I told myself, Dominick would get better and Megan and I would survive this last week with Skonky. It was a simple plan: at Victoria Falls, we'd get new guides, hopefully as responsible and knowledgeable as Rutger, and they'd take us the rest of the way to Nairobi. For all we heard, that was the most dangerous part of the trip—highly unpredictable in every way.

When dinner winded down that evening, my world fell apart.

"I just spoke to the office," said Skonky, rising to his feet after polishing off his beer. He looked more and more like an evil troll every day, especially as he stood barefoot in front of the roaring fire.

"Two guys named Mark and Seth were originally going to take over in Vic Falls and guide those of you going on to Kenya."

I didn't like where I thought this was going.

"Thing is, they've been running a lot of tours lately, so they won't be taking you."

NO!!!!!

"I will."

Skonky?!? Three more weeks of Skonky?!?

"Cool," Bill declared, breaking several moments of long silence.

"Sounds good."

An awkward silence followed.

To say there wasn't a great deal of excitement over Skonky's announcement was an understatement. Our ever-growing sick ward, combined with Skonky's reckless partying and the high degree of additional dangers I anticipated on the second leg of the trip, had all the makings of an accident waiting to happen. Could we even trust Skonky anymore? And what about Charlie? She wasn't going too, was she?

"This is all too much," I told Megan as we left the smoldering fire ring.

"Three more weeks of Skonky?!?"

Megan said very little, she was probably in too much shock after hearing the news. The early morning Chobe game drive we signed up for would prove a nice distraction but wouldn't hide the major obstacle we now faced, an obstacle formidable enough to break the little spirit we had left to continue the tour. Megan didn't have to tell me that night, but we both realized that if we needed another reason to pull the plug on our Africa trip once we got to Victoria Falls, we had a huge one.

ITALY CALLING

The nice thing about early morning game drives was that they still got you back to camp in plenty of time to relax. The game drive through Chobe, scheduled to last until 10 a.m. or so, would return us in time for a breakfast of bacon and eggs back at the truck and a day of leisure, since we were staying put the entire day.

I grabbed a box of crackers I had been saving and my binoculars and Megan grabbed her camera from the tent. The crackers would stave off the hunger only temporarily. I knew I'd return from the game drive starving, even if the waiting frying pan was barely detectable beneath the customary pool of grease.

While waiting for our driver, Megan made small talk with Helen and Abe. I sat silently, reflecting on the entire African experience and still trying to embrace the concept of having to deal with Skonky and his give-a-damn attitude for the next three weeks. And then there was Dominick—would the poor guy even be alive? Who knew what he picked up, but those filthy utensils and supposedly clean dishes with food stuck to them couldn't be helping.

The very moment I began questioning just how much fun I was having on the tour, a noisy, military-style jeep rattled up slowly and stopped abruptly. After scanning the surrounding scattered tents, the driver waved for us to climb aboard.

"Should be a good day for viewing," the driver said with a smile as I handed him the fee of $10 for Megan and myself.

"A nice, cool morning."

Climbing aboard, Megan and I chose the row directly behind the driver, while Helen and Abe sat behind us. The morning air was extremely chilly—too cold to be wearing my pair of khaki shorts, as the brisk, early morning air blasted our open-air vehicle as we raced towards the game park. I knew I should have worn those pants Megan bought me with the zip-away legs.

We arrived at the entrance to the game park a short while later, joining a short queue of similar-looking trucks and jeeps crammed with tourists. As far as game parks went, Chobe's entrance gate was the most impressive yet, protected with a towering, chicken-wire fence that made the surrounding grassland appear more like a prison than a nature preserve. Decorated with signboards related to the regulations of the park and poaching laws, the intimidating fence combined with the two, no-nonsense looking guards armed with scope rifles stationed at the gate, quickly conveyed that Chobe took its wildlife very seriously.

When we reached the front of the queue, our driver handed over a small stack of bills and a folded piece of paper to one of the guards, which he glanced at quickly before returning it. Once the guard stepped back, we began down the solitary dirt road that led into the park and caught up to the small convoy of jeeps already in front us. Payoff was immediate.

"They're stopped for something," I said aloud, nodding towards the small caravan of stopped vehicles housed around a large watering hole.

"Hippos," the driver answered, speeding us to the circle of vehicles.

"Hippos!" shrieked Megan, clutching the camera resting in her lap.

Our driver took off in the jeep as if he spotted an elusive metered parking space in the city—gunning the engine while weaving between the parked vehicles to get us close. By the time we stopped, we were directly parallel and about twenty five feet away from one of the most memorable images of the entire tour, a family of eight hippos of various sizes on an early-morning swim.

Wisely, our driver had deftly maneuvered the vehicle to allow enough room in front if we needed to make a quick escape.

"They look fun," the driver stated seriously. "But never underestimate the hippo!"

The leader of the hippo gang clearly was the enormous, hulking male that we watched ease himself into the dark blue water from a tiny sand bar. You could just sense it, the entire herd giving way as the massive hippo slowly bobbed forward, sinking down into the depths just low enough to keep his eyes fixed squarely on the gathering fleet of vehicles.

The male watched us with increasing interest, spraying water while letting loose the occasional guttural, pig-like grunt. Only after the male grunted did the rest of the herd respond in kind, some disappearing beneath the water only to rise up as their leader had a short time later. Easily, the show stealer through all of this was the tiny baby hippo that had been following its mother on another sand bar a short distance away. The baby, its wet, slick skin resembling rubber, stayed so close to its mother that it sometimes bumped into her hind legs, lifting its bowed head up only to follow mom into the water and join the rest of the herd.

Maybe that was my fascination with hippos: like most wild animals, the danger could be deceiving, cloaked behind the sheer wonder of being so close. As much as the hippos resembled large, almost cute (in an ugly-sort-of-way) pigs, the danger and sheer power of the creatures was undeniable. By all outward appearances, the hippos looked completely benign, seemingly content just floating through the water with one another and oblivious to everything else.

That is, except for the massive male, who not only continued to train his steely eyes on the steadily growing group of vehicles but also had managed to stealthily creep to within fifteen feet of us, though still hunkered down in the receding waters. Megan's tender handhold had quickly become a death grip.

With a loud, growl emanating from the pit of his stomach, the hippo parted his massive jaws, revealing a jagged collection of pointed yellow teeth. Megan squeezed even harder.

"Um...don't you think we should be going?" she asked, trailing off at the end of her sentence. Though we were still relatively safe, it was still rather frightening to see a pissed off hippo. Our guide wasn't breaking a sweat; if anything, he was looking to move in even closer.

Moments later, we had another example of the treasures of Chobe. This time in the form of a gray, massive shape that materialized from the thick greenery on the left, snapping and rustling whatever branch happened to be in its wake.

"My gosh!" exclaimed Helen. "It's an elephant!"

The massive elephant, at least twice as big as Ella, slammed through the tangled vegetation and charged across the road no more than twenty feet in front of us, heading straight for the same watering hole we spotted the hippo herd in.

"It's a male," stated the driver, carefully watching the creature as he passed. "It's musting."

'Musting' we had learned from Rutger, took place when a young male elephant was in heat. Musting elephants were easy to spot, as the eyes of the elephant were darkened from thick, watery tears. Not to mention the aggressiveness.

Rutger's advice when encountering animals always veered on the side of being extremely cautious—which always made sense to me. So when he had mentioned to leave an area at once if you even spotted a musting elephant, I made it a point to take note and remember.

Though cautious, our driver was not Rutger, understanding that good photo opportunities were not something to pass up despite the inherent dangers. We didn't rush towards the elephant as we did with the hippos but quietly stayed put. And what we saw was nothing short of amazing.

The huge creature, completely oblivious to the convoy as it stamped across the road in front of us, stopped once it reached the muddy shore of the watering hole, pausing momentarily as it sniffed the air with its trunk. Then, lowering itself to one bent knee at a time, the mammoth elephant collapsed to the ground in one swift motion, rolling back and forth until the mud from the bank had almost completely covered its back, trumpeting joyfully the entire time.

"You're very lucky to see this!" exclaimed the driver. "Musting elephants usually aren't this social!"

After several minutes of muddy frolicking that left it nearly covered in black mud, the elephant slowly rose to his feet with surprising grace, letting loose a final, low-pitched trumpet. Then, after raising his trunk high into the air one last time, he strode with authority back into the bush from where he had emerged, amid a chorus of snapping tree branches.

Continuing on, we reached a small crowded intersection that rivaled only Michigan Avenue during rush hour in sheer madness, where vehicles dashed to a small clearing further ahead. Something big was going on—you didn't need to be an experienced guide to figure that out.

Picking up on the panic, our driver grabbed the walkie talkie lying on the seat next to him and began speaking into it excitedly, receiving acknowledgement from a noisy, static-covered voice on the other end. It had to be another driver, maybe at the scene further up the road already, and though I didn't speak the language, I just had a feeling the reward would be huge once we navigated through the traffic and got there.

Following the other vehicles, our driver sped beneath the low, drooping branches that tried to grab us from above, skipping over the tiny bumps of earth scattered throughout. I grabbed my water bottle off the floor when it rolled back to me, tucking it safely between my legs.

The reckless drive ended when we could go no further through the caravan of nearly a dozen vehicles, which formed a semi-circle around a small area of scattered shrubs. Inching closer, we were the jackals, trying to sneak through for that tiny, leftover crumb that our driver managed to find as he maneuvered carefully between two behemoth trucks. Picking up my binoculars, I could see what the fuss was about. Across the field were two female, lions basking in the sun with a pair of tiny cubs in tow.

Our driver was all smiles. Guides were funny—they'd repeat over and over again how game drives were completely chance and luck, but each one would proudly puff their chests out if you happened to be along for one of those lucky and chance-filled days.

The lions themselves were still quite a ways away. Without good binoculars or a zoom lens, they looked like nothing more than tawny-colored objects. With the binoculars, though, you could see that the lions were hunkering down for another warm day as the afternoon approached, the two adult females reclining beneath the shade of a squatty tree as the cubs frolicked a few feet away, never venturing far.

****

Back at camp later that morning, I didn't use any of my 'alone' time to attempt to come to terms with having to endure Africa for another three-plus weeks—I was still undecided about what I really wanted, and thinking about it without discussing things with Megan didn't make much sense. I guess I needed a push, one way or another, to help me make the decision. On one side, I knew that the second-half of the trip sounded way more interesting than the first, which included Zanzibar Island, added opportunities to actually mingle with locals more than we had, and the famed Serengeti, almost a guarantee of spectacular game sightings. Conversely, dealing with Skonky's inept leadership, weeks of being on a truck most of the day and sleeping in a tent nearly every night, and eating crap food in between almost assured that I would lose my sanity and regret going on. It was just way too daunting for one man to think about by himself.

When Megan and I excused ourselves later that night to do our 'chores,' specifically, the tired, tedious routine of filtering our water for the umpteenth time. It was funny—while I battled with the plunger to force the water through the filter, I thought about how neither Megan nor myself still hadn't discussed our pivotal arrival into Victoria Falls the following day— that magical point where the first leg of the trip ended and the new leg began. In other words, the ideal spot to pull the plug on the whole damn thing. If we needed that proverbial straw to break the camel's back, the thankless task of filtering our water for the hundredth time was it.

"Y'know," started Megan, counting the drops of pink chemical as they splashed into the container of recently filtered water. "I just don't know how much more I can do this."

Eureka! A breakthrough!

"Yeah," I said, dismembering the hoses from the filter and shaking them loose. "We really need to talk about what we want to do. About Nairobi."

After brushing our teeth, we climbed into our tent and just let everything fly, in probably one of the most therapeutic talks I've ever had in my life.

"I guess I'm on the fence," I said. "Three more weeks is a long time left, especially if Skonky is running things like he has been."

"And without Rutger," reminded Megan. "He's the one who cares about if we're enjoying ourselves—not Skonky."

"And what about Charlie? She's wouldn't be coming too, would she?"

"I hope not," Megan sighed. "If she's not complaining, she's loafing!"

"Besides, Nairobi's supposed to be pretty unpredictable. It all is, the further north you go."

And then there was Skonky. The guy told us he contracted malaria half a dozen times. Looking after someone's well being, let along his own, was not his best suit.

"The thing that gets me," I said, reclining to the floor of the tent. "Is the complete lack of fun."

"I mean, can you honestly tell me this is 'fun'?!? This is vacation, right?"

Megan paused thoughtfully, and then nodded.

"You're right," she laughed. "Driving all day isn't fun. Staying in a tent worrying about not getting mauled isn't fun."

"This is vacation," Megan added. "I guess maybe we didn't think how tough things would be. It's exhausting."

"And these people," I sighed, fumbling with the flashlight next to me. "Abe just annoys me all the time without really doing anything, and then there's Stacey. And Mary..."

We laughed a little while longer as we continued going down our laundry list of bitches—great therapy for three weeks of misery and aggravation. The good memories of Africa were absent, game drives and desert walks tucked beneath Abe slurping his cereal out of the bowl and me struggling to sleep on those nights when Megan sat up vigilantly with the flashlight. Finally, Megan offered what we had both been considering: getting out.

"What would you say," asked Megan, stroking my hand, "if we ended the trip and flew to Europe instead?"

"...Only if you really want to."

Megan's eyes looked so tired.

"I guess I'm undecided. Some days I wish we would leave."

I paused.

"You sound like you're ready to quit. Like I am."

Even through the dim light, I could see wet tears welling in her eyes.

"It's so hard some times," Megan sobbed.

"There's just too much to worry about. I can't even enjoy myself!"

We sat quietly for what seemed like several minutes. Then, clearing her throat, Megan spoke.

"If I had a say, I wouldn't go on. But I don't want you to not go on because of me."

My mind was already in Italy that evening—imagining colorful, peaceful beaches, huge plates of pasta, and grocery stores filled with all sorts of breads and cheeses. Maybe it was a rash decision we came to that night. I had a notorious history of changing my mind suddenly and then completely falling in love with a new idea, like when I changed my major four times in junior college during one semester. Leaving the danger and misery of Africa for Italy just sounded so right, and I could just feel the waves of relief and happiness wash over the both of us as we entertained the idea. Maybe Africa wasn't for us—we were okay with that. So after a little more discussion, it was decided. Come tomorrow, we'd confidentially ask Rutger, who we knew we could trust, what the refund policy was if we chose to leave the tour once we reached Victoria Falls.

Though I buzzed with nervousness and excitement, it was time to get some sleep. Tomorrow, we'd be in the 'The Las Vegas of Africa,' as Skonky referred to Victoria Falls for reasons he hadn't made clear to us.

Or, as Megan and I saw it, our last stop in Africa.

DOMINICK, WE HARDLY KNEW YOU

My unparalleled excitement of ending our trip was tempered with a great deal of nervousness when I woke that morning. I wasn't looking forward to telling Rutger what Megan and I had decided last night. How could you tell a rugged guy who probably encountered every calamity imaginable throughout Africa that my girlfriend and I were quitting because we were miserable and exhausted?

As I stirred from my sleeping bag, I heard Megan's heavy breathing pause for a second, then saw her open her eyes slowly. Not wanting to draw too much attention to ourselves that morning, I thought it best that we get to Rutger early, before everyone else managed to crowd around the breakfast table.

"Ready?" I asked Megan, reassuringly grasping her leg with my hand.

She sat up quickly and nodded, wiping remnants of sleep from her eyes.

With as much confidence as we could muster, we emerged from the tent and made a determined walk towards Rutger, who we spotted in the cab of the truck inspecting something below the steering wheel. With Skonky nowhere in sight, the timing was perfect.

Using his long, sinewy fingers, Rutger was halfway through unscrewing a greasy, exposed nut before greeting us with a smile.

"Rutger?" I asked sheepishly. "Can we talk to you?"

"Sure," Rutger answered, clapping the imagined dirt off his fingers and swinging his legs around and over the edge of the seat.

"What's on your mind?"

I took a deep breath. You're a nice place to visit, Africa, but three weeks is plenty for me.

"Well, we talked about it last night and Megan and I don't think we want to continue on to Nairobi after all."

Rutger's smile diminished slightly into a serious expression as he scanned both of our faces, then lowered his head a bit.

"I suppose you've thought a lot about this, yes?"

Megan stepped forward.

"We've been thinking about it for a while, yes," Megan replied. "It's just too stressful—for me, in particular. It's just too much."

"And you guys have been great," I interrupted, "but it's just harder than we thought."

Rutger bit his lip slightly.

"If that's your choice and you've thought about it, then you shouldn't go on," he stated quietly. "But give it a little more thought. We're in Victoria Falls for a few days in real beds, so you have a couple of days before deciding anything for sure."

"Besides," Rutger whispered like he was revealing a huge secret. "You've made it this far already, and there's so much more to see!"

Megan and I both knew Rutger was right about that. The Serengeti, Mt. Kilimanjaro, Zanzibar and the Spice Islands.

"We're going to think about it some more, then," I volunteered, actually meaning it. What Rutger said mattered—even if he didn't always say that much.

"But what about a refund?" Megan asked, swatting a bug away from her ear. "Y'know, if we decide not to?"

Rutger grimaced as if in pain.

"Gee guys," Rutger offered regrettably. "I really don't know if you can even get one at this point, since everything gets booked from Cape Town."

"What did Skonky say?"

Megan and I stood silently while we looked at one another, searching for the diplomatic way of saying he just didn't seem approachable.

"Skonky doesn't know," I said. Saying less was the right way.

"Then let me ask him for you," assured Rutger. "And I'll tell him to get back to you on it, okay?"

Thanking Rutger, Megan and I walked back to the tent holding hands as we always did, both embracing the relief that always came after doing something difficult. Only a few more days, I told myself. We'd have our freedom back in Italy, doing what we wanted to do and when we wanted to do it. No more bad food, no more tents, no more disease around every corner. It's been fun, Africa, but it's time to move on. You understand.

I rode that high wave of excitement for the remainder of what seemed like one of the most perfect mornings in Africa—one of the best I could remember now that the whole burden of feeling trapped had been conveniently lifted off my shoulders.

I think Skonky found out that Megan and I were thinking about jumping ship sometime before boarding for Victoria Falls. It was during breakfast, actually, that I caught him staring at us a couple of times, and then looking away when I looked in his direction. He was unusually quiet that morning, rarely looking at anyone except when he briefly rose from his seat to mention that we'd have another opportunity to bungee jump and skydive if we were interested in Victoria Falls. Oh yeah—and another optional booze cruise was planned for the evening, too.

Finishing his little briefing, Skonky returned to the bent metal chair he had been sitting on with a sour look on his face, staring mostly at the ground or the cigarette lighter he had begun twirling between his fingers. If he took Megan and I deciding to depart the tour personally, he was giving himself way too much credit. Granted, hearing that Skonky had been selected to guide us on the second half at the last minute didn't exactly make my decision to continue a difficult one, but there was so much more at play than just him.

Of course, you could always count on someone who looked like death warmed over to deflect any speck of attention flashed your way. That particular morning, Dominick appeared in his worst shape yet, somehow managing to outdo himself on a daily basis. The entire breakfast area fell completely silent when Dominick, with all of the drama of a Broadway opening night, unzipped the door flap of his tent and stiffly crawled several feet on his hands and knees towards the table, until Rutger raced to his side in disbelief and helped him to his feet. With Dominick's arm draped over his shoulder, Rutger literally dragged him to an empty folding chair and dropped him into it, holding him steady momentarily until Dominick's balance kicked in. Even his long-time nemesis Charlie, who criticized him often for eating so much food, looked sympathetic at the pathetic sight before us.

In a word, Dominick looked horrible. Save for his red, swollen eyes that seemed to barely open, Dominick's skin was bleach white.

His arms hung low at his side, looking extremely heavy in relation to his weakened frame.

This had gone on several days too long.

While Dominick sat silently, trying to muster what little strength he had left to maintain his sloped posture, Rutger, darted over to a still-sulking Skonky, whispering something Afrikaans in his ear that sparked a tiny, impassioned debate. Abruptly, a determined Skonky sprung from his seat and raced down the dirt path to the camp office before returning a short time later. Giving Rutger a quick 'thumbs up,' Skonky slumped back into his metal chair, looking a little nervous. Something was going on. You could just feel it.

Studying poor Dominick as I hoisted my backpack onto the truck, I spied Skonky strolling over behind him and crouching down low as he spoke.

"Hey Bill!" Skonky called out. "Bring down Dominick's bag. The black one."

"This is it, yeah?" Bill shouted from the top step. Dominick nodded his head, prompting Bill to toss the misshapen bag into the high grass below.

"Sleeping bag's down there already, right?"

After Dominick nodded his head a second time, Bill hopped down from the steel steps and pulled the bag forward, resting it at Dominick's feet. Watching the whole exchange from the truck window, little did I know it'd be one the last time I'd ever see Dominick.

What happened next happened very quickly, almost as if it was standard African Wanderer procedure. Dominick, with help from Skonky and Bill, rose to his feet, though he was basically dragged and dropped to the shady spot beneath a nearby tree. As Bill dragged Dominick's gear over to him, Skonky slapped the oblivious shell of a man on the back before climbing into the cab and starting the engine.

"Um—I think we're forgetting Dominick," Stacey told Rutger, now stationed at his usual spot near front of the truck. "Aren't we going to wait?"

Dominick had looked up at us when he heard the engine kick on, forcing a light smile and straining himself to extend his hand just enough to slightly wave. As sick as Dominick was, I honestly believe that he was happy to be left behind.

"Dominick's not going on," Rutger stated calmly. "He's pretty sick—too sick to even try to get to Victoria Falls."

"The people here are going to look after him and get him the help he needs. He'll eventually be lifted out of here. Probably."

Probably, if he didn't need to be just embalmed and buried.

At least for Mary's case, there existed a possibility that she may become well enough to join up with us again in Victoria Falls. But Dominick? Judging by Rutger's brief diagnosis, all doubt had been removed that he'd meet up with us later on and continue to Nairobi. I could only guess how sick the poor guy was, but if he needed medical attention that urgently, I figured things had to be pretty grim.

Fending off panic before it set in, Rutger assured us a doctor lived at the campsite who'd take care of Dominick immediately, that Dominick would be safe, and that there was really no alternative since his condition was getting progressively worse.

In spite of the situation with Dominick, I was shocked to find myself seriously thinking about continuing to go on to Nairobi anyway, as Rutger's words to Megan and myself played over and over in my head that entire morning on the truck. Like a wise sage, maybe his words did ring true. And the more I thought of it, the more I discovered that leaving the tour was not the black and white decision I had hoped it would be. After months of planning, Megan and I had made it to Africa, after meticulously arranging for the time away and putting up with all the hassle that goes with it. Maybe we had gotten through the really dull parts already, with the promises of a little more flexibility, like in Zanzibar, when we'd have entire days on our own, and opportunities to upgrade into real beds in our future.

"I've been thinking," I said, gently squeezing her tiny hand in mine. "Maybe we should go on, just because I don't know if we'll get the chance again."

Her eyes lit up a little and a wry smile came to her face.

"I was kind of thinking the same thing today...isn't that funny?"

"Skonky's a concern, but we handle him alright," I reasoned.

"Yeah," Megan sighed. "We probably won't get back here, and it's silly to get this far and quit, being so close to the Serengeti and all."

"Think we can handle three more weeks in the tent, though?"

"We can always upgrade," I said. "Someone told us that we'll be staying in places that let you stay in rooms with beds for only a few bucks more."

"I think we'll be okay."

Megan looked me in the eyes and then threw her arms around my neck, pulling me close. She kissed me on the cheek to seal the deal. From that point on, it was decided—we were on our way to Nairobi.

I napped on the truck for most of the morning, thinking a lot about Dominick and how weird it was that we'd left him in such an awful state in the middle of Africa underneath a tree. I woke at some point and noticed Megan had left my side, then looked towards the back of the truck and saw her in an involved conversation with Stacey.

This couldn't be good.

Spotting me looking for her, Megan emphatically motioned for me to join in their conservation Stacey had one of her classic, smug looks on her face. If she wanted to inspect my passport so she could brag about the many places she had visited around the world, I was going to scream.

"I was telling Megan that we aren't going to have to worry about Skonky much longer," Stacey said in a hushed voice.

"Not if I have my way."

Megan nodded approvingly as I moved in closer.

"I've called the office as soon as Skonky told us he was taking us all the way through to Nairobi," Stacey declared firmly.

"No way. That's what this letter's for."

I glanced at the neatly-written letter Stacey gripped in her hand, spotting a few words that stood out in my quick scan like "gross misconduct" and "lack of leadership and discipline."

"The way I see it," Stacey continued, "I'm a paying customer and the customer's always right. And if the office wants to see my complaints written up to document them, so be it. As long as it means we'll get rid of him!"

I believed Stacey. She was just bitchy, tenacious, and whiny enough to see something like this through. In other words, she was a good ally.

Leaning over Stacey's shoulder, Megan eyed the letter quickly before gazing back at me.

"If it helps," Megan offered, "we'd be willing to sign the letter. Maybe some of the others would, too,"

My beautiful justice fighter, once again, was dead on. If we managed to get even half of the group to sign it, African Wanderer would have to listen.

"Maybe we can all get together some time in Vic Falls and make sure we're all on the same page," I volunteered.

"We probably all have our own things we want to bring up."

Smiling approvingly, Stacey agreed with the suggestion and the three of us promised we'd meet some time the next day to put it all together. Instantly, I felt better with our decision to go on to Nairobi, knowing that if African Wanderer knew about our dissatisfaction with Skonky, they'd have to remove him, or at the very least reprimand him enough so he wouldn't turn the second leg of the tour into another beer romp marred with illness and danger. At least that's what I hoped for.

I didn't feel sorry for Skonky. As I watched him smoke a dark, cherry pipe from the rear window of the cab, I realized that it had to be this way. For once, Stacey was right—we deserved to have an enjoyable experience, not having to be consumed with worrying about our individual personal safety due to a total breakdown in leadership. Skonky was a huge liability. Though I didn't plan on telling anything but the truth to African Wanderer, I knew damn well that it would be more than enough to get them to take action.

Of course Skonky would know that someone ratted him out to African Wanderer, especially if he didn't get the news that he wasn't going on to Nairobi with us until the last minute. Only then did it hit me that Megan and I would probably stand out as his logical guess as to who turned him in. It seemed all too obvious: we didn't give in when he shook us down for the money he claimed we owed him for the Okavango Delta; we approached Rutger about backing out of the tour yet Skonky seemed too upset to even bring it up; and we backed out of countless booze cruises and other optional activities. In short, all signs incorrectly pointed to the 'prudish' American couple of Paul Duprey and Megan Brown being the instigators.

The days leading up to Nairobi wouldn't be easy. I prayed that Victoria Falls, the so-called 'Las Vegas of Africa,' would offer enough to take my mind off things. As my mind wandered off in multiple directions, Rutger's booming exclamation brought me back to the present.

"Here we are guys!" proclaimed Rutger, pointing out the window. "What you've all been waiting for!"

We were met with the usual stares from locals as Ella rammed through the bustling city of Victoria Falls, Zimbabwe, which to my surprise did appear cleaner and more 'Western' than the other African cities we had been through. As we roared past the densely forested entrance to the actual Falls, the city pleasantly reminded me of Cape Town—a beautiful blend of nature and commerce.

"Over there!" screamed Megan as she pointed out the window. "Look!"

Standing motionless, a small herd of nearly a dozen buffalo vigilantly stared at the roadway ahead amid a section of thinning and fallen trees.

"Elephants, too," said Rutger, acknowledging the buffalo. "You'll see their droppings all over the place."

I think that impressed me the most about Victoria Falls—how man and nature proved it was possible to coexist in such close proximity to one another within a perfectly-planned community. The outskirts of town were left as wild as any spot in the African bush, an area of dense, wild vegetation that provided a beautiful contrast to the more urban center of town. And it was urbane, in every sense of the word, with shopping malls, souvenir stores, craft villages—even a casino.

"And a Subway!" exclaimed Megan, with her index finger stuck on a page in her Lonely Planet guide.

"Subway? You mean, the sandwich shop?" I asked.

"Yup," Megan replied, slamming the guidebook shut. "I know what's for lunch!"

Though we didn't spot our proposed lunch destination as we departed what amounted to the main street through Victoria Falls and headed to Savanna Lodge, we did take note of some of the more humorous-sounding dining options available to the hungry tourist, namely Wimpy Burger, Supa Chicken and Supa Pies. My personal favorite, though, was McDonuts, its arch-scribed name emblazed in all-too familiar gold characters across a red background. Cheezy enough for a photo, that's for sure.

As anxious as I was to start exploring Victoria Falls, Megan had other ideas—namely, napping for a little bit in a real bed at a real lodge. I read a little about Victoria Falls in the guidebook, then left the room to track down Rutger, who I spotted helping another man unload the back of the truck. Beneath the strain of heavy weight, Rutger looked almost frail, his lanky arms overburdened as he struggled to gently ease a large, blue plastic container to the ground, lowering himself gently to his knees before sliding it to the earth.

"The whole truck, huh?" I asked, as I ran to help Rutger push the blue container further away.

Rutger didn't say anything until the blue container came to a rest on a small grassy area behind the truck. Then, taking a deep breath while holding his hand to his chest, he flashed an appreciative smile.

"It's a lot of work," Rutger gasped.

"So what's on your mind?"

"Megan and I have talked things over, and we've decided that we're going on to Nairobi after all."

Rutger looked pleased, his eyes dancing slightly at the news.

"I'm glad to hear it," Rutger replied, grabbing and shaking my hand in an exaggerated manner. "I'm sure you'll find you made the right decision!"

"I'm just glad we weren't shut out," I explained. "Skonky never even mentioned it, so I didn't know if he contacted the office on it or not."

"Don't know anything about that," Rutger said woodenly, seeming slightly standoffish as he headed back towards the truck.

With Megan awake from her nap when I returned to our room, we grabbed her camera and started making our way into town. Waiting by the gated entrance of the Lodge was Stacey, hair wetted and clinging to her neck but with a noticeable smile on her face as we approached.

"So what did you two do this afternoon?" Stacey chided.

"Not much," Megan said, stifling a yawn. "Just rested a little before we headed into town."

Exploding with news, Stacey stood with her arms folded across her chest to contain herself.

"Well, I had a great afternoon," Stacey proclaimed merrily. "Aubrey and I slept together."

"You did?!?"

Megan loved gossip. Though this was a far cry from Entertainment Tonight, it was the best we had.

Stacey stood smiling with a twinkle in her eye, like the housecat who just lapped up the bowl of cream.

"Aubrey's an animal," she purred. "And it just totally loosened up my back."

Observing a moment of awkward silence, I figured Stacey's perchance for exaggeration would make the lamest thirty-second brother into a Casanova.

"I'm waiting for Aubrey—we're going into town, too."

"Oh," Megan stated. "We can wait and go together...."

Stacey flashed a frustrated look as she nodded towards the hostel.

"Don't bother. Who knows how long he'll be."

Promising Stacey we'd catch up with her tomorrow regarding the letter, we started down the road into town. Just turning the corner in front of us, already on their way back to the Lodge, was Matt, Bill, and Connor, being hotly pursued by two thin men in ragged clothes, each hawking small, wooden carvings of animals.

"My friends," bellowed the taller of the two, hand clutched around a wooden piece. "This hippo for $400—buy one get one."

"Okay, okay," his associate countered as he grabbed Matt by the shoulder. "The mask carving for 300, because I like you."

The Aussie guys laughed a little and probably felt a little embarrassed by all the attention. Connor had a small bag of souvenirs with him already, so you couldn't blame the hawkers for being so persistent—they smelled blood.

The pursuit ended just outside of the gates to the Lodge, the hawkers relentlessly chasing and grabbing the three guys for some kind of response. Unexpectedly, the one hawker got through to Connor, who plunked down 300—the amount the hawker eventually dropped his price to—for a crude, dark wood carving of a hippo. Megan and I quickened our pace as the dealing went down behind us, glancing back at the action rather than stopping and giving the hawkers new prey to pursue.

The path into town was pretty straightforward—a left at the corner, and then a right at a small park would take you right in. The housing area we were staying in, to my surprise, appeared quite modern, and we passed many homes on our walk that would fit right in to any American suburb, complete with picket-fenced yards, patios and such.

We began discussing the weirdness with the Stacey and Aubrey situation when we saw a dark shape scurry up a tree about twenty feet away, then heard the excited yapping of an angry dog. Slowing our pace as we approached, the unmistakable hissing of a baboon filled the air.

"Baboons?!? Here!?!" Megan shrieked.

Before I could answer Megan, an entire herd of several adults scurried along the branches of an older tree encompassing an entire lawn, all staying well outside of the dog's reach. The baboons looked even meaner and more unpredictable up close, and part of me just expected a shower of the angry, hissing bastards to rain down and tear the mutt apart.

Before we turned at the park to head into town, we noticed a tiny, white building that stood isolated amid a gravel-covered parking lot. Very nondescript—except for the sign that read "Doctor's Office" atop the door.

"Look!" exclaimed Megan as she tugged on my arm. "You can switch your malaria medication here!"

And here I thought—and hoped—she had forgotten about it. Granted, Lariam and I were not the best of friends, and if I had to do it all over again, I probably would take a medication with less potential side effects. The weird Lariam dreams still came almost nightly, though I was getting a better grip on them once I realized where they came from and that cracking the tent window to bring a little light in usually helped. Was the Lariam mind-fucking me? Yes, it was. But to me, going to a third world doctor's office, unless I was gravely ill, scared me more than the occasional bad dream because the image I had in my mind, as unfair as it may have been, was one of unsanitary conditions, a long wait, and an impossible language barrier, three things I did not need while trying to unwind in Victoria Falls. I returned Megan's enthusiasm with a typical "I'll think about it." That was usually enough to buy me some time. We kept walking, and she let it go.

I knew we were on the cusp of downtown Victoria Falls when souvenir dealers and illicit money changer alike took quick notice of us.

"For you, my friend," bellowed a hawker as held up a shiny, wooden walking stick. "Last one I have, and yours for 400."

The money changers were by far the worst, though—relentless and intimidating at the same time. Rutger made it a point to tell us, under no circumstances, to change money with anyone who approached us directly on the streets. In some cases, you'd be taken to a remote place and robbed. In other cases, you'd be ripped off and given a stack of newspaper with misleading real bills placed on top. And in the rarest of cases, undercover cops would arrest you since changing money on the streets is illegal. According to Rutger because Zimbabwe currency had become so devalued and U.S. dollars were at a premium, the best rates could still be had at a legitimate currency exchange, which surprisingly also offered unadvertised black market rates if you knew to ask for them. That was the catch—you had to be aware that you could get a black market rate at such a place—they wouldn't volunteer it.

"Even if the post rated is around seventy per U.S. dollar," warned Rutger. "Don't settle for anything less than 350."

"They'll give it you if you let them know."

I couldn't help but think what kind of a nutty country Zimbabwe was, when legitimate businesses would give you an under-the-table exchange rate just to get your money, but I was eager to find out once we located the office. I didn't know as much about the embattled leader of the country Mogabi, as Megan did, but from what I could ascertain, he wasn't the shrewdest.

The best cure against the aggressive street 'businessmen,' as they liked to call themselves, was to duck in any one of the shops that lined main street, as they'd never follow you inside. To gain reprieve from the onslaught we briefly stopped inside the Livingstone Adventure Office to get directions to the currency exchange and thought about booking a helicopter ride over the Falls. On the way to the exchange it became clear that nearly everything in Victoria Falls is named after Livingstone. If only he would have trademarked the name....

A small, well-dressed woman behind a desk at the currency exchange greeted Megan and myself as we entered the currency office, then rose forcefully from her desk to shoo away a small contingent of hawkers who loitered outside while waiting for our return. Her demeanor was warm towards us, but she didn't put up with nonsense. I liked that.

"And what can I do for you today?" asked the woman, who glanced over our shoulders towards the door to make sure we were alone.

"We have some money we'd like to change—$80 U.S.," Megan said coolly.

"...And we want the black market rate."

A lot of things always went into play when you changed money in Africa—you never wanted to change too much and be left with worthless currency, since each country used its own. On the other hand, too little might mean you'd have to go without the usual cache of snacks if we made a surprise stop at a grocer on the way out of town. This scene, however, topped everything, as we were in a reputable, well-respected international business attempting to bargain for black market currency rates in an unstable African country. This was the stuff of spy novels.

Unfazed, the woman demonstrated little emotion with Megan's request.

"I'll give you 350 per U.S. dollar. Best rate you'll find."

Thanks to Rutger's briefing, we knew she was telling the truth, and Megan handed over the $80 and received a thick stack of tattered, brightly colored bills. It was a lot of money, but we planned on doing some major souvenir shopping. The most unbelievable part of the entire exchange, though, was still to come.

"And what rate would you like me to write on the official receipt?" asked the helpful woman. "The official rate of seventy or the black market rate?"

How accommodating could you get? Not only did we get the black market rate—we also had found someone willing to fudge the numbers for us!

We chose the official rate because Rutger had warned us that some businesses and agents, like the park entrance to Victoria Falls, demanded to see an official exchange receipt from visitors to verify the 'legitimate' rate of seventy. It seemed like everyone was in on the game, but no one saw the point to put a stop to it. But with my fistful of Zim dollars, I wasn't complaining.

ET TU, ABE?

"...So after these numerous indiscretions, which include repeated intoxication, lack of concern for the health of his passengers, and sexual harassment, we demand that Van be removed from the tour."

Stacey was all smiles, beaming like a proud parent as she read the last word of her freshly scribed letter aloud from her bunk bed. Mentioning that she began writing as soon as she spoke to the director at the head office early that morning, everything was already in motion by the time Megan and I grabbed breakfast and made our way into her room. We kept the drapes pulled—our act of conspiracy had to remain a secret.

"It's...good," stammered Megan. "But what exactly do you mean when you say sexual harassment?"

Megan's question was a valid one. I knew Skonky could be an irresponsible, reckless drunk, but I took exception with labeling him a pervert.

"Like, all the time," sniped Stacey, curling her hair around her finger.

"He'd say the most obscene things to me," Stacey added. "Y'know, like innuendos about having his way with me. He even slapped my butt once!"

As she related her claims of 'mental anguish and cruelty' to Megan and myself, I wasn't hearing a woman shaken by trauma. That's not to say she was making it all up, but we both had seen Stacey in action enough to witness her instigating exchanges like the one she was now complaining about, all in an effort to get the sexual attention she seemed to be craving. That was exactly Stacey's style. And to me, as much as I wanted to see Skonky get the boot, it seemed almost hypocritical to put it in that Skonky initiated sexual harassment towards her, especially since we had a pretty strong case without it.

"If we're all signing it," I reasoned, "maybe we should just include instances that affected all of us."

"I mean, you could always include your own, personal experiences in another letter."

Taking a deep breath, Stacey huffed as she sprung to her feet and paced towards the door.

"Well, whatever," she replied, flustered and crossed that phrase out.

"Let's just all sign this so I can fax it to the office."

Megan briefly shot me a glance before taking the pen from Stacey and adding her name at the bottom. I always had a funny feeling in the pit of my stomach whenever I went out on a limb and signed letters like this. There was something about having written documentation of unhappiness versus just chewing someone's ass out. Nevertheless, I signed the document, too, making sure not to sign too large on the cramped piece of paper. That was three of us—and the more signatures we had, the better.

Matt and Connor were removed from consideration—they weren't going on to Nairobi so it didn't matter if they signed or not. Bill wasn't an option, either—he seemed like a hip guy, but we knew we risked our plot getting back to Matt if we approached him, whom I never really did trust. Dominick had been dumped God knows where, Mary hadn't returned from Johannesburg, if she was returning at all, so that really just left Aubrey, Helen and Abe. It'd be nice to get them on board too.

Aubrey didn't take much convincing to sign the letter.

"I'm still pissed about my air mattress!" Aubrey spat angrily as he stabbed the pen into the paper.

"Damn Skonky!"

After Aubrey, Stacey left her room to fetch Helen and Abe, who she claimed were both interested in signing. To our surprise, Abe signed but Helen didn't.

"He never really did anything to me," Helen stated casually. "I'd be fine with him the rest of the way."

I should have expected as much. Life with Abe had made her accustomed to putting up with jerks.

Tucking the signed letter into her handbag, Stacey flashed a final look at the roomful of co-conspirators and headed to the Lodge's business office in search of a fax machine. With the shit about to hit the fan, the best thing to do was to get as far away as possible from the whirling blades.

****

For me, there was no better place to escape than back in town, where the bright daylight sun assuredly chased away the demons of the night, making downtown Victoria Falls a reasonably-safe place to trek through. Besides, we still had to find that Subway restaurant!

Once downtown, we detoured into a large, maddening grocery store and stocked up on chips, crackers and the like while we had the chance. It was Megan who recalled, as we battled through the crammed aisles, that not only did the grocer receive a write-up in the guidebook we had with us, but it also made mention of the elusive Subway shop as being in the same area. The excitement passed, however, when a quick inspection outside revealed only long-abandoned storefronts flanking the grocer on either side. Just our luck—the one type of Western meal virtually impossible to screw up and we had to do without.

The runner-up that day was Wimpy Burger, more towards the center of town and home of probably one of the greasiest burgers I had ever eaten.

"This is just bad," said a disappointed Megan, nibbling on the soggy bun. She didn't have the same capacity for greasy food that I did, though later that afternoon my stomach reprimanded me in its own way for scarfing the entire thing down.

Our last stop in town that day was the open-air craft market. If you ever travel to Victoria Falls, don't worry about having to seek it out—I guarantee that someone will lead you right to it, escorting you directly past the dozens and dozens of stalls of craftsmen selling identical wood carvings until you reach their own personal 'store' which is their stall space selling the same wood carvings.

"Welcome to my store, my friend," the thin, crooked-toothed man who led us into the market offered when we stopped in front of his booth.

"Looking is free."

Animal carvings, tribal masks, drums—all carved from shiny wood and all waiting to be sold, lined several deep across a bold red blanket on the dirt ground. Politely, Megan and I looked over his wares, both of us being careful not to stare at one object too long so it wouldn't be interpreted as interest. If I was looking for anything that afternoon, I was looking for something unique, so before long, we thanked the man for his hospitality and turned to leave before being cut off by an approaching teen.

"My stuff is much better," he proclaimed as he beat his hand on his chest. "Come—it's right over here!"

It probably didn't help that Megan and I were the only tourists visiting the craft market at that time. Sharks waited hungrily for their turn to move in for the kill. The teen's stand offered a little more variety in different sizes of carved hippos.

The whole craft market experience turned into sort of a game for us.

The funniest was hearing what I coined as the 'official line of the craft market' from each and every merchant without fail at your initial approach of the tiny, crammed stall they had set up shop in:

"Welcome to my store! Looking is free, my friend!"

That afternoon, I began feeling pretty good about Victoria Falls, Africa, and continuing on to Nairobi, despite the realization that the letter we signed could still could come back and bite us in the ass. The past two days were pretty relaxing, and we still had another whole day to do whatever we pleased before heading out again, hopefully with a new guide and without Charlie, who I figured would be surly no matter who she was teamed with. Scary moments aside, exploring Victoria Falls was very enjoyable, although we'd decided against a helicopter ride over the Falls.

And best of all, if things stood the way they were now, we'd be starting the journey to Nairobi without the people who annoyed me the most, Matt and Mary, in particular. I'd miss Connor, who turned out to be a friendly, happy-go lucky guy.

When our taxi dropped us off back at the lodge, we noticed immediately that Connor and Bill were hanging out with two unfamiliar guys on a bench.

"They're back!" cried Connor sarcastically in a whiny voice. "We were worried sick about you two!"

"You know how couples are, Bill," chimed Connor. "Needing their alone time and all."

One of the guys, pale but with striking, dark hair and blue eyes, slid to one side of the bench.

"Here," he said, motioning for us to sit on the empty space. "My name is Vernor."

"And I'm Thom," said the other guy with an Australian accent. Thom looked even thinner than Dominick, very lean and with sandy brown hair.

The cheap pair of pink flip-flops on his feet stood out like a neon sign against his otherwise preppy look of a polo-type shirt and khaki shorts.

"Oh yeah," piped in Bill, as if he just remembered something. "These two guys are coming along with us to Nairobi."

Nairobi?!? Two more?!?

After Megan and I took turns introducing ourselves to our new travel partners, I couldn't help but drift back into territorial mode—much like I did when I saw the gang return from the Delta excursion and invade Megan and mine's tropical paradise. After losing Dominick, probably Mary, and Connor and Matt, that meant four less people–specifically, more room on the truck, more food, less luggage, and less of a hassle.

But two more people? Even if Vernor and Thom were nice guys, I couldn't say I was ready to really welcome anyone else along on the trip. I mean, as much as I hated the routine of overland life, I had in a way, resigned myself to the very comfort that the routine brought with it. Just the mere presence of these two new guys could screw everything up—especially if one managed to annoy me as much as the dearly departed Mary.

The look on Megan's face told me that she was thinking the same thing I was, though the fact that she could practice her German on Vernor would help in her case. She loved breaking out the German whenever she could, her eyes lighting up in excitement as they conversed about life back in the Rhineland. Vernor, instantly looking more comfortable, seemed to appreciate that she made the effort, smiling as the two chatted back and forth.

At least Bill and Connor didn't bring up anything about Skonky—either they hadn't heard anything or did and agreed with the rest of us that he had to go. I tended to believe they just didn't know about the plot to get rid of him. It was hard to tell what side of the fence Bill was on—he was pretty easy-going himself, and I think he was at that early-twenties age where he was willing to just go with the flow and not make too many waves. Connor, also, was hard to read, though as much as I liked Connor, his close friendship with Matt still made the subject one that had to remain secret.

It became apparent at dinner later that night, however, that something was afoot, as Skonky seemed even more withdrawn than usual, sitting by himself and looking towards the ground most of the night as he puffed away on cigarettes. He must have known, or at least been told by the office, that he wasn't taking us through to Nairobi. But what did they tell him? That we voted to have him removed because we didn't care for his brand of leadership? I hoped they were a little more guarded than that until he returned in a few days to Cape Town, but given the professionalism we had already experienced from African Wanderer, that was anyone's guess.

I didn't much feel like eating that evening, picking mostly at the couple of barbecued ribs on my plate and a piece of dry bread. Part of me wondered if we had been too sensitive about Skonky and taken too drastic a measure. We survived three weeks with him, what were three more? And it wasn't like we had to hang out with him all the time, either.

I went back and forth on the whole issue, deciding ultimately that I wasn't so much fearful that we were too harsh than I was fearful of what he might do if he knew the way everything went down. I had no problem standing behind my signature, but I knew it could get pretty ugly if Skonky decided to take it out on us.

Aside from Thom and Vernor, who had officially joined our ranks and broke up the long stretches of silence during the meal with the occasional query about the sites we'd seen on the first half, the only sound heard was the slight clink of fork against plate—nothing more. Deathly quiet.

We were as guilty as hell and we knew it.

Thank god for the native tribal dancers, who stalked up the dark driveway that evening until finally assaulting the entire outdoor dining area with an explosion of drums and song.

"Welcome to Victoria Falls," yelled one, at the top of his voice above a low drum rhythm.

"Sit back and listen—to the songs of the warrior!"

The six men, dressed only in leopard loin-cloths, boots and ornamental headdresses, attacked each song with pure athleticism that would rival the National Basketball Association. They sprang themselves high into the air before coming back down in a tucked position, rolling themselves across the lawn like balls. How the dancers managed to maintain the same, steady drum rhythms, not to mention their own flowing, melodious interpretations, was purely amazing.

The men were extremely polished. The more I began practicing guitar, the more I realized the amount of sheer effort and talent it took to reach a point of fluidity. Maybe they were Africa's equivalent to the pan flutists from South America who seemed to infiltrate every street corner in every American city with their own brand of cover songs and stylings. You couldn't argue with their effort, and the sheer pride that each man seemed to resonate as they sung energetically about their heritage.

I threw a brightly colored bill into their tip jar when they finished, passing on the CD they were hawking that Helen bought after bumming some money from Abe. Helen bought everything. With Mary gone, she was now the sole target of every hustler in Africa.

"So what do you want to do...now?" I whispered to Megan, as the men packed up their drums and the group began milling from their seats. Maybe seeing half-naked dudes dancing around would at least give me a shot at love, I thought.

Megan smiled one of her wry little smiles, one that said "I know exactly what you want, but you're going to have to convince me." I never minded that—I always thought I could be very convincing if I put my mind to it.

BIG MOUTH STRIKES AGAIN

I sprung up surrounded by darkness and completely out of breath. My heart raced rapidly, pounding through my chest. Air—I needed air!

Fumbling through the black and towards what I suspected was the foot of the bed, I braced the wobbly wood ladder that hung from the top bunk and eased myself to the floor, the ladder letting out a slight whine. Unlatching the chain from the front door, I threw it wide open and sucked in the sticky, night air. Relief.

Taking deep, steady breaths, I spied the tiny and slightly busted alarm clock resting alone on the nightstand. 3:15. I wiped the sweat from my brow with the back of my arm, heartbeat steadily returning to normal. Sometimes I really wondered if a bout with malaria could really be any worse than the Lariam they give you to prevent it.

After finally managing to fall back asleep, I awoke later that morning suddenly, after being shook by a heavy thud from directly above. Something was on the roof—the dark, sun-cast shadow of the morning visitor stretched across most of the room, proving to me that I wasn't hearing things. Neither was Megan.

"What is that?" she mumbled into her pillow, looking at me through eyes yet to open.

"I think it's a monkey," I said. "Like the ones we saw in the Delta."

The shadow became a little more elongated beneath the sun and then began running, disappearing from our roof in a short leap and landing with a familiar thud, presumably on the next roof over. Was it breakfast time already?

Savanna Lodge was used to the little pests, made clear to me after hearing a concert of human voices excitedly trail the sound of the leaping monkeys.

"Do you ever worry about your dreams," Megan asked carefully, sliding into her shorts.

"I mean, you can't die from a bad one, can you?"

Slightly annoyed and crabby from lack of sleepy, I answered abruptly.

"What did you dream about now?"

"Well since you asked," Megan began softly, lowering herself to the bottom bunk.

"You and I were in the middle of the African bush somewhere—it kind of looked like the Delta. Anyway, something spooked us and we started running—I don't even know what it was."

Megan swallowed hard.

"I just woke up and my heart was pounding so fast—I couldn't breathe. I should have brought an inhaler, I guess."

"An inhaler?"

"For asthma. Just in case."

"But honey," I began, attempting to muster as much compassion as I could through my growing annoyance. "A bad dream won't give you asthma!"

"Well, I'd still feel better with one!" snapped Megan, placing her hand over her heart as she rose to her feet.

"Sometimes I swear you just don't understand what I'm going through!"

Oh, I understood all right. I understood that she had to be as miserable as I was being jostled all day on a truck and then having to sleep on the hard ground or worn-out beds every night. But what I didn't understand was how she could convince herself from one day to the next that she had contracted some life-threatening illness. If it wasn't her heart, it was asthma. If it wasn't asthma, it was some exotic jungle affliction she read in that damn medical guide. And my patience was becoming threadbare over the whole thing.

"Look, I hear what you're saying," I told Megan as I embraced her. "We can talk about it some more after breakfast."

"Today has to be the day, you know," Megan stated ominously, stepping away from me as she adjusted her belt.

"With Skonky."

"Oughta be interesting, if nothing else," I joked, kneeling to tie my shoes.

We nearly barreled into Rutger as we flung the door open and hurried outside, in the midst of one of his famous, door-to-door wake-up knocks.

"Someone's in a hurry this morning," he said, clinging to the wall in amusement as we marched into the hallway.

To our surprise, we turned the corner and saw a nearly full breakfast table already, minus ourselves, Aubrey and Stacey. Even the new guys,

Thom and Vernor were there, Thom speaking more to Matt and Bill about cricket while Vernor shared his ballroom dancing resume with Helen, who gushed over his achievements like a schoolgirl. Skonky, seated at the far head of the table, looked up briefly as we sat down before looking away. He didn't look as moody as we'd seen him the past couple of days, but you could just sense something was on his mind. Something big.

Stacey arrived just as a glum-looking waitress carted in a big, bright bowl of fruit salad, her black hair sopping wet and tightly clinging to the back of her neck. Taking an empty seat neck to Abe, Aubrey conspicuously showed up moments later, greeted by a knowing wink and a playful elbow in the side from Bill as he lowered himself to the table.

Rutger nodded to Skonky as he jumped into his wicker chair and hopped towards the other head of the table. Finally, everyone had arrived. And it was all about to go down right now.

All eyes were fixed on Skonky as he slowly rose from his chair, just after the waitresses returned with a wide plate of toast she centered on the table. Clearing his throat slightly, he looked as serious as I've ever seen.

"Before we begin," Skonky stated solemnly, "I have some news on the second leg of the tour and Nairobi." He folded his arms across his chest.

"There's been a change of plans," Skonky began. His words were stripped of all emotion.

"...And I won't be going on with you."

As tempted as I was to catch everyone's reaction from around the table, I didn't dare. Does that look less guilty, to maintain eye contact, or should one look away?

The table was quiet—deathly quiet—as we all waited for Skonky to continue. A lone fly danced around our breakfast, noisily buzzing around the lip of the fruit bowl.

"Seth'll be your guide," he continued as he looked down at the table. "He's supposed to be here tonight. He's actually on his way back from Nairobi driving right now."

To everyone's surprise, Skonky had decided he was done speaking and slumped back into his chair, looking away from all of us and fumbling with the familiar lighter he had left on the table. Rutger didn't miss a beat, springing to his feet quickly.

"Of course," Rutger added. "Skonky, Charlie and I will be going back to Cape Town tomorrow morning, after Seth arrives."

"So keep in mind, all of you, that you're all on your own the rest of the today for your meals," Rutger lectured.

"There's lot of good stuff in town, so feel free to splurge."

With a smile, Rutger sat back down and passed the fruit bowl to Helen, seated on his left. I almost felt sorry for Skonky, seeing him so alone in his self-exile at the end of the table, rarely looking up as the weight of the world seemingly came down on him.

Try as I might, I just couldn't muster any pity.

If Skonky's little speech before breakfast was the worst of it, it really wasn't that bad, all things considered. Breakfast remained a little on the awkwardly quiet side, but only until Rutger enthusiastically interrupted.

"I almost forget about the shirts!" he said excitedly, setting his mug of coffee onto a coaster.

"You guys didn't design your shirts!"

Rutger pulled at the dark green African Wanderer shirt he was wearing, one that commemorated an African overland tour made earlier in the year. One sleeve listed the first names, I assumed of everyone who made the trip, while the other showed the corresponding country flags where the tourists hailed from. The back was completely filled with assorted quotes and other noteworthy tidbits, like the four flat tires they had to overcome.

"They're $12 U.S. each," Skonky said glumly.

"If you can design it as a group by afternoon, you'll get them tomorrow."

"Awesome!" Matt yelled enthusiastically, rising from his seat.

"Let's go—Bill, Connor!"

As the three Australian guys moved to an empty corner of table, Stacey followed with a pencil and a piece of scrap paper. Matt's body language said it all—this was going to be THEIR shirt, not the groups, designed completely the way the Aussies wanted it. That was the problem with having all of those Australians—they were cocky and didn't seem to care if you knew it.

Aubrey and Stacey looked over Matt's shoulder once the group began cackling over the quotes they wanted to include on the shirt but said nothing.

"Hey!" exclaimed Megan, just as I reached across to stab into a chunk of overripe honeydew.

"We never did our laundry!"

"But I think they'll do it here for us," chimed Megan, leaning over the breakfast table as she peeked into the kitchen. I imagined she and I, covered in dust, sadly watching Ella speed away as we stood with all of our stinky gear on the side of the road.

"At least, I think Rutger told us that."

I jogged to our room to retrieve the laundry bag, stuffed snugly into my backpack, while Megan asked the waitress, who disappeared into the kitchen and returned a short moment later with a somber, heavy-set woman next to her.

"I can get it done tomorrow, yes," I caught the woman telling Megan as I arrived with the heavy sack. She took it from my hands by the drawstring and twirled it slightly.

"Washed and ironed by 8 a.m. tomorrow, Missus."

We may have to stall Seth if he wanted us on the road by then, but I doubted we'd be leaving that early. Especially on his first day.

Matt, still seated with Connor, sprung to his feet as Megan and I retreated back to the room.

"We finished with the shirt," he announced proudly. "Check it out!"

One glance at the scrap paper with the design scrawled across it confirmed my suspicions—the shirt was completely and exclusively designed by the Australians, specifically Matt. Even every 'clever' quote on the back was a quote by Matt.

"I don't think I'm interested, are you?" Megan asked, turning towards me. She couldn't have sounded more disinterested.

"No, I don't think so, Matt. Probably get one for the second half."

"Oh," Matt replied, sounding a little surprised. "Okay, then."

I wasn't about to lose any sleep if I offended Matt by not wanting his shirt. As much as I was looking forward to losing Skonky and Charlie, Matt wasn't too far down on that list, either.

With as many water containers as we could carry piled neatly into my daypack, we finally set out for downtown Victoria Falls later that afternoon. It seemed so familiar now—the tiny doctor's office, the thatch Coke kiosk right off the main road, the angry, adventurous clan of baboons taunting the same aggravated dog. Just like home.

Even the constant barrage of hustlers wasn't getting to us like it did, thanks to an insight Aubrey mentioned the previous night over dinner.

"Just wave them off," he lectured, motioning with his hand like he was refusing dessert. "If they're not sure you can speak English, they'll give up."

And would you believe it worked? It wasn't perfect, but after the initial wave of hustling, only the heartiest and most persistent trailed you for a little while longer, before resigning themselves to defeat a short time later. Leave it to Charlie Brown to come up with something so simple it seemed absolutely brilliant.

That afternoon felt like one of the steamiest yet—humid, tiring and miserable—as we trudged through downtown past the usual array of personal money changers. At Megan's request, we made a slight side-trip before the cooling mists of Victoria Falls. Our destination? A visit to the "Authentic African Craft Village" on the outskirts of town. In retrospect it was about as authentic as Disney World's spin on global ethnicity at Epcot Center.

Looking like a frontier fort from the outside due to the towering, dark logs that vertically surrounded it, the inside of the village told a different story through recreations and models of typical life within a tribal African village, complete with assorted huts sculpted from Earth, food caches cleverly constructed to keep animal raiders at bay, and tools designed to make a seemingly primitive life that much more manageable.

Most entertaining was our guide, a slightly kooky African in his twenties, who was decked out in a bright lavender shirt and white sneakers. His smile and innocence was very endearing, and he even offered to pose in various photographs for us and utilized some of the more unusual tools to "give life," as he said. A very cool guy, though I figured he was hoping we'd buy something in the gift shop at the end of the tour so he'd see a little commission.

Vapors climbed from the steaming asphalt at our feet as we marched towards the Falls, greeting us as Megan and I began our ascent up a the pothole-ridden road that initially brought us into town and over a bridge, cars occasionally whizzing dangerously close. The word 'oppressive' comes to mind—shirts clinging with sweat, throat dry and parched. The filthiest swimming pool would be paradise.

Megan wasn't faring much better than I was, especially since she was now on her asthma kick and had convinced herself she had somehow contracted it since we left for Africa three weeks ago. I noticed her taking pronounced, deep breaths from time to time since she decided that this was her affliction a few short days ago. The humid air did nothing to allay her fears.

"Water," she gasped, just as we crossed over the bridge. "Stop!"

With her face flushed red, Megan handed me the now-empty plastic tankard she had been carrying between exaggerated breaths—for a second I thought she was practicing Lamaze. Fishing a sweaty, slightly-warmed two-liter of water from my backpack, she guzzled a quick swallow.

"I don't know, Duprey," she whined, wiping her brow with the back of her arm. When she called me by my last name, I knew I had to tread lightly.

We continued on our death march after our quick rest, cautiously passing the grassy area where we spotted the herd of buffalo previously. Locals passed us, along with the occasional tourist, as we approached the entrance, along with a few scattered beggars and an umbrella salesman, who warned us to buy one or be soaked. Promises, promises. The most unusual sight was the local, a middle-aged guy who was decked out in an all-too-familiar Subway uniform shirt, unbeknownst to him that the mere sight of the famed sandwich-makers logo was enough to make both Megan and I long for a foot-long stacked high. Passing us, Megan did a double take, half-tempted to run after him and ask him to make us a sandwich, half convinced he was a mirage, a figment of our imagination and stomachs.

"Do you think...?" she trailed off, keeping her eye on him as he disappeared over the bridge behind us.

"I really doubt it," I countered. "I mean, the guidebook told us where it was, and we've seen the whole city. I don't think it's around anymore."

"What would Jared say?"

Our grinding walk continued until our second wind kicked in, when we finally spotted the gated entrance to the Falls area. Joining a single line of more than ten people, a surly-looking man hunched over in a darkened booth with a tinny, noisy fan as his only company presided over it all, looking to be about as miserable from the weather as we were.

"I need your receipt," he barked over the fan to the white couple at the window. "An official one—from the change bureau."

"Look," whispered Megan, tugging my arm with one hand as she pointed to plaque posted outside of the booth. The plaque read that the entrance fee to the Falls for tourists was a little over $6 U.S.—only if you could produce an official receipt from the change bureau stating that you exchanged at the 'official' rate. Otherwise, the price was almost $20 U.S.

Megan was well-prepared by the time it was our turn at the window, handing the attendant the receipt, which she wisely saved in her wallet, before he even asked for it. After his quiet inspection, we were sent through and charged the lower price.

Mounds of elephant droppings littered the main hiking path that ascended slightly higher, a not-so-subtle reminder that yes, we were still in Africa. As we climbed higher and higher up the steep, gradual incline, neither one of us stopped glancing over our shoulders, making sure we were alone except for the steady stream of tourists joining us. Alone except for the building, thunderous roar of Victoria Falls, growing louder and more boisterous with every step forward.

"I can smell the water!" Megan exclaimed. "Can you?"

Smell the water? My sense of smell wasn't the greatest, but sometimes I thought Megan smelled too well. To this day, she still argues with me that the inside of my tool chest smells of vomit, though I have no idea what she's talking about.

Turning a sharp corner blazoned through the thin, grassy underbrush, I was taken back instantly to how I imagined Livingstone felt when he first laid eyes upon the beauty and unequalled might of Victoria Falls. Like Livingstone, it was finally right in front of our eyes, powerful, rushing waters in a continuous downpour from 200 feet above us, bashing against the rocks below while spraying a steady, soothing mist in its wake.

With excitement, Megan clutched my hand with hers, and then wrapped her arms around my waist.

"I'm so glad I'm here with you," she cooed, resting her head on my shoulder. Breaking free and taking a step back, she looked into my eyes and I could see her joy.

"I never dreamed I'd ever be here. With you."

I pulled Megan close. She was right, and I was having one of those moments myself when I didn't believe all of this was happening. Not only was I on the adventure of a lifetime, but I had a beautiful woman on my arm that just meant everything to me. Life was good.

We traipsed around the entire circumference of the Falls, following the main hiking path, mostly, but sometimes ducking down a smaller footpath or two for a better view and a cooling blast of mist. The mists were refreshingly cool, though at certain lookout points closest to the mightiest sections of the Falls, barrages of the cold water rained down heavily.

No longer worried about elephants, since an encounter seemed increasingly unlikely the closer we got to the Falls, my worries instead shifted to lions. The smaller footpaths tended to be more secluded and flanked by low-lying bushes and shrub—the perfect shade for the King of the Jungle, I thought.

It wasn't the fear of being stalked by wild animals that did us in, however—just our aching, tired legs. The time was right to start heading back—the sun had diminished somewhat, and we still had a sizeable journey back to Savanna. After a few gulps of water, we left the park and started back the way we came.

We grabbed a cab back to the lodge, anticipating cooling off at the frigid swimming pool. Except for us, the pool was surprisingly empty.

Climbing out of the pool and onto the deck while Megan continued dunking herself, I shut my eyes tight and lay in the grass, attempting to bring myself into a total state of relaxation. The light breeze tickled my face. Birds carried their late afternoon song from high above. My bed is soft grass. A car door slams.

My eyes remained shut. Just someone coming back from town who won't even think about disturbing us by the pool.

"Hey guys! Yoo-hoo!"

Mary?!?

My stomach sank to the very pit of my being. That voice. That screeching, annoying, all-too-familiar voice. Just when I thought it was safe to go back into the water, it had returned. I needed an aspirin.

Hell, I needed a gun.

Sitting up, I peered open my eyes ever so slightly, hoping on the off-chance that maybe it was some sick and twisted daydream, that maybe my eyes wouldn't reveal the absolute last person I wanted to see for the rest of my life.

"I'm back!" cackled Mary, with her bulky, dark-green backpack hoisted high over her shoulder. "Didja miss me?!?"

"Of course we missed you!" I yelled to Mary as she approached, crushed straw hat tilted back on her head. "You look well."

"I am," she said, looking at Megan and myself. "They fixed me up in Jo'burg and I knew I had to get back here in a hurry if I wanted to join you!"

Yeah, thank God for that.

At least she wasn't too graphic as she re-counted her experiences in the Johannesburg hospital. She was refreshingly brief, actually, mentioning only that she had some procedure done to clear the blockage (YUCK!) and that was that.

"...And my doctor said he might consider not going on the rest of the trip," Mary declared, "but I decided to, anyway. I missed you guys."

Right.

Megan and I caught her up on some of the recent highlights—Skonky not taking us to Nairobi (though we never shared with the big-mouth how that came about), Dominick getting ditched, and the unusual little quirks of Victoria Falls like money changing and the like.

"Oh, I know all about the good rates you can get here," Mary proudly squawked. "My cab driver was such a nice man."

"You changed money with the cabbie?" Megan asked suspiciously. It had 'scam' written all over it.

"He was just beautiful," Mary continued. "He told me all about a charity he started for his ill son that he was collecting for. Naturally, I just had to help him out with a donation of my own."

Maybe I was just a little too jaded having lived in a major city, but that didn't sound like the brightest way to spend your money to me.

Mary reached into the silly, little change purse that dangled from her neck, pulling out a fat stack of bills.

"Then, when he told me he'd exchange money with me, he gave me a really good rate," she bragged. "Three-hundred of theirs for every one of mine."

Clutching the pile in a fist, she began flipping through the enormous stack of ten-note Zimbabwean dollars that dominated her pile, mixed with the occasional five-note. A confused look fell over her face.

"I don't understand…" Mary said softly as she dug through the pile. "All I see here are tens!."

"Where are the hundreds?!?"

And I always thought something like cricket or soccer must have been the most popular sport in Africa. In short time, it had quickly become ripping off Mary.

HELLOS AND GOODBYES

"Y'know, we really have to get going...."

"Will you calm down already?" snapped Megan.

"They aren't going to leave without us!"

When Megan crawled out from beneath the bed covers and stood on her own two feet, I decided it best to back off. I knew I could be an impatient pain-in-the-ass when it came to harping on her, though by her own admittance, she'd never be mistaken for a morning person.

I glanced at my watch. Ten minutes after eight. We needed to hurry if we wanted to pick up our laundry and eat that morning before heading out, assuming Seth had arrived and was ready to lead us to Nairobi.

When Megan had finished slipping into her clothes from the previous night, we marched in the kitchen, to the spot where we met the woman the previous day that we handed our laundry to. I didn't recognize the young, thin woman with light skin at the counter, but she smiled politely and waved us into the back when Megan mentioned the laundry.

"She's right in back," the woman said sweetly. "Come!"

With care, we walked through the loud kitchen, a sea of tense, hurried voices and clanging cookware. Rounding a corner with a small, dirty sink hanging precariously from the wall, we spotted the laundress, seated next to an opened ironing board and surrounded by several piles of clothes. Our clothes appeared to be in two piles—one crisply folded, the other half grouped in a wicker basket.

"Good morning," the seated woman greeted. "I should have the rest of your things ironed for you later this morning."

"How much longer?" I asked, looking back around the corner to see if a new African Wanderer truck had appeared in the driveway.

"I mean, we're supposed to leave early this morning."

"I've been tired," the woman offered apologetically, stifling a yawn. "Maybe an hour or so."

Sighing, I looked at Megan, who also tried to sneak a peek at the driveway and any sign of Seth.

"We don't really need them ironed, do we?"

"I don't think so," Megan agreed, before turning to the woman.

"Can we just take them now?"

Nodding her head, the woman rose and started slowly towards the wicker basket, prompting me to grab the freshly washed laundry bag from atop the pile. With Megan's aid, we piled everything back into the white stuff-sack, and then paid the woman before returning to our room.

"I didn't see another truck out there, did you?"

"Nope," I answered. "Maybe Seth's here anyway, though."

Opening the door to our room just wide enough to toss the bag of cleaned clothes in, we raced to breakfast hoping for any news on when we'd be leaving Victoria Falls. Spotting Stacey, seated with a plate of two, slightly-runny eggs, Megan motioned me over as she plopped down next to her.

"Any news on when we're leaving yet?"

"It won't be any time soon," Stacey replied, pulling her wet, clinging hair off the back of her neck.

"Wait, you mean we're here for another day?" Megan asked.

"Not officially," Stacey stated dryly.

"Rutger said something about Seth meeting us a few days from now. I think someone else is going to guide us until then."

"Not Skonky though, right?" Megan nervously questioned.

Stacey smirked.

"I doubt it," answered Stacey. "There's no way African Wanderer would send him back out with us. Not after that letter."

Yeah. The letter. The letter that Skonky probably figures Megan and I crafted all by ourselves.

"See," Megan offered, swiveling on the bench towards me.

"We didn't have to hurry this morning for our laundry after all."

"Yeah, I guess not. I'll bet it still wouldn't have gotten ironed, though."

"Well you'd better make sure that it does!" Stacey commanded in that dramatic tone of hers.

"They weren't going to iron mine until Rutger overhead and told me about the flies."

"Flies?" Megan asked, slightly disgusted. "What flies?"

"You know," Stacey explained, in a condescending tone like she'd know even if Rutger hadn't told her.

"The ones that lay eggs in drying laundry. You need the heat from an iron to kill the eggs."

"The Tumbu fly?" I asked, remembering something I had read in the guide book. "The one that burrows into your skin and you have to use a piece of raw meat to lure it out?"

"Yuck! He didn't say anything about that!"

As the waitress headed towards us to take our breakfast order, Megan sprung to her feet.

"We have to iron those clothes. All of them!"

Racing back to our room, we grabbed the sack of laundry and hurried back to the kitchen with it, dumping the entire contents onto the now-vacant chair adjacent to the free ironing board. Throwing everything back into the bag made it impossible to tell what had been ironed and what still needed to be. The only way both of us would be satisfied was to iron every single thing—just in case the Tumbu fly or any other pest had made the rounds through camp the previous day.

The woman we had handed our laundry off to never did return while we scrambled. Would we be stuck in Victoria Falls for yet another full day? It seemed likely, especially after remembering that Rutger, Skonky and Charlie all had to be heading back to Cape Town the following day for another tour in Ella, the lone truck anchored in the driveway.

It became obvious around the Lodge that we were all waiting for some kind of word when we'd be leaving. As much as I had seen of downtown Victoria Falls the past several days, leaving the Lodge to travel back to the city wasn't allowed, with the possibility that our replacement guide could show up at any moment, ready to take us back out on the road.

Mary hung out in the bar area with Helen and Abe, rehashing some boring story I thought I once heard her tell about some camping trip she went on in the Australian outback. I didn't know where Stacey and Aubrey were—I didn't want to know, either. Matt and Connor enjoying their last, few hours in Africa before flying back to Australia later that afternoon, sat in the grass with Charlie, playfully wrestling one another when Charlie, still looking enamored with Matt, wasn't pulling on his arm. Vernor, one of the newest additions, nervously glanced up from the book he was reading whenever a car motored past, probably just wanting to get started. Bill and Thom smacked a weathered cricket bat around, one time launching the ball into the pool.

I found myself dozing off next to Megan after we moved poolside, wondering if perhaps having an extra day in Victoria Falls before heading off to Nairobi was by design. What if this was some sort of sign, that extra day our one last chance to come to our senses and abandon the tour before we committed ourselves to another three weeks? Could the second leg really be that much more miserable?

Lying on my back in the short, prickly grass, I shut my eyes for only a few minutes when the rumbling of slow, heavy tires over the gravel driveway got my attention. A truck, nearly identical to Ella but more compact and appearing slightly beaten up, barreled down the drive, stopping just short of our idle ride. A tall, skeletal man, tanned bronze and with a scraggly, brown beard, leaped from her cab. Seth?

"Woody!" yelled Rutger, who seemed to materialize in thin air.

"It's about time you got here!"

Woody?

"Apologies, Rutger," Woody replied happily, shaking Rutger's outstretched hand.

"I just got word that you needed me here a few days ago. Where is Van?"

"Skonky? He's around here somewhere, I'm sure. Let me show you around."

With a small duffel bag tossed over his shoulder, Woody, smiling brightly, followed Rutger down the long hallway that housed the rooms they were occupying. Lightly rapping on one, Rutger motioned Woody inside with him once it creaked open.

"Skonky's probably telling him everything!" Megan whispered.

"He doesn't look like a bad guy," I replied.

"Maybe he knows what Skonky's like...I hope."

Whatever that secret meeting was about, it couldn't have been about too much, because Woody, Rutger and Skonky all emerged together a short time later.

"Everyone over here, guys!" Rutger called out to the group.

"Everyone to the bar!"

Once everyone had grabbed an empty seat, Rutger, standing between Skonky and a smiling Woody, stepped forward. Skonky still looked pissed as he stared at his feet.

"If you don't already know, this is Woody," Rutger said, stepping aside briefly as Woody, saluted with his right hand and stepped forward.

"Woody's been with African Wanderer for a while now, so I know you'll be in good hands. Woody?"

Like all of the guides we had encountered in Africa, Woody looked the part: a rugged, no-frills type who carried himself with confidence. Like Skonky and Rutger, Woody didn't believe in wearing footwear either, and a small, faint tattoo of a Tasmanian devil sporting a huge erection rested on his left shoulder.

"Seth, your lead guide, is going to meet up with us in a few days," Woody explained, moving his eyes over the assembled crowd.

"I have to tell you, this is just as exciting for me as it must be for you, since I've never made it all the way to Nairobi myself!"

My stomach sank, and if I didn't know any better, Skonky cracked a telling smile. Sure, Skonky must have thought, you got rid of me...but at least I had experience!

"...But it's going to be a lot of fun for everyone," Woody continued. "And I'm told we're going to end it all in Nairobi with a big game dinner featuring antelope, crocodile...you name it!"

As much as I welcomed Woody's genuine enthusiasm, I couldn't help but feel slightly defeated after learning we'd be traveling with an inexperienced guide. I shrugged my shoulders when Megan flashed me a similarly discouraging look.

"Maybe the second's half not so bad after all," I mumbled.

"Let's hope it's not," Megan added.

"The plan is for everyone to get a good night's sleep and head out in the morning," chimed Rutger. "So you're staying here tonight."

"What time?"

"Let's plan for eight, since we have lots of driving," Woody responded. Everyone groaned. Great. Driving.

"Don't whine, because if you weren't going on to Nairobi, you'd be driving back with us!" grumbled Skonky.

"We're leaving at six in the morning."

Skonky's interruption was met with silence before Rutger, clearing his throat slightly, continued.

"You also may be happy to know that Ella will be taking you the rest of the way to Nairobi," Rutger announced.

"This other truck is far too small for all of you."

After Woody mentioned again how excited he was to be joining us, Rutger adjourned the little gathering and we all went our separate ways once again.

"We'd better start getting ready, Matty," Connor told his partner.

"In a minute, Connor," Matt snapped back.

"I want to talk to Charlie."

I started heading back towards my section by the swimming pool until Megan tugged at my arm.

"Hey! Maybe we should say goodbye to Rutger now. While he's away from Skonky."

Turning my head, I spotted Rutger at the bar, sipping on a glass bottle of Coke.

"You mean we aren't going to say goodbye to Skonky?" I teased.

"I think he's really going to miss us!"

"C'mon, you!"

Grabbing hold of my hand, Megan and I walked through the emptying lounge area and stopped just next to Rutger, who smiled as he looked up from his half-empty bottle.

"We just wanted to thank you, Rutger," Megan said sweetly.

"Y'know, in case we don't get to say goodbye later."

"Well, we've had a lot of fun together," Rutger replied in a low yet strong voice as he set his bottle down onto a thatch coaster.

"I am glad that you two have decided to go on."

"Me too," I answered half-truthfully. "I mean, who knows when we'll get back here."

"It's important that you look at life that way," Rutger agreed.

"Sometimes it's very scary. But you always have to follow your heart."

"Well, I think you were a big part of making the first leg," Megan interrupted. "I mean, we learned so much from you."

Rutger smiled sheepishly as he spun the bottle halfway around.

"Thank you. And enjoy yourself the rest of the way."

After we exchanged a few handshakes and snapped some photos, I was glad we had made the effort to let Rutger know what a great job he did of holding things together under the strain of Skonky. With Rutger, the trip to Victoria Falls was barely tolerable, marked mostly with expectations that were never met, miles and miles of boredom and drunken binges.

So after wishing Rutger well, I made the decision not to spend the rest of my rare day of leisure worrying about being led to Nairobi, at least temporarily, by a guy as much as a virgin as we were.

I'm not certain how much time had passed before Matt and Connor, with a wet-eyed Charlie in tow, dropped the several, overstuffed bags they had been dragging on the patch of lawn closest to the driveway. Charlie, weeping like she was attending a funeral, might have gotten a little pity from me if she wasn't such a bitch.

"Well," announced Matt, throwing his hands defiantly on his hips as he scanned the grounds one final time.

"This is it, I guess."

Connor said nothing, squinting as he adjusted the brim of the weathered gray cap resting atop his head.

"It's been a lot of fun, people," Matt added.

One by one, the entire, scattered group walked over to wish the pair of Aussies well and exchange goodbyes.

"You're the best Matt!" Mary squeaked.

"Maybe we can all get together in Perth some time, y'know? Exchange photos and all that."

"Uhh...yeah, Mary. I'll write you."

"Take care, Matt," I said, with the same gusto one uses when they order a pizza over the telephone.

"Yeah...you and Megan take care, too."

Perhaps feeling just as uncomfortable as we were, Matt turned his attention back to Charlie, embracing her as she sniffled and choked back tears.

"There's love out there for everyone, Charlie...that's just the way it worked out between us."

"Oh, Matt!" Charlie gasped.

"I can't imagine being without you!"

I can. Paradise.

Rolling his eyes, Connor turned his back slightly to the couple and extended his hand to me.

"Take care you two!" Connor chided. "Good luck with the marriage and all that good stuff!"

Marriage?!?

"Come now, Megan," Connor replied, gripping my hand tightly. "You guys are practically married now!"

"We're going to miss you, man," I interrupted, steering things away from that always-awkward topic.

"I'm not looking forward to going back," Connor added, just as a brown, station wagon pulled up the driveway.

"I really should have taken a few more vacation days so I could rest more."

"Yeah," inserted Megan, putting her hands into her pockets.

"Some restful vacation."

The chirp of the cab horn made Charlie pull Matt even closer.

"Can I go with you, Matt?" Charlie whined.

"With US?!?"

"To the airport. Please, Matt?!?"

Looking more than a little shocked, Matt stood paralyzed as Connor, grabbing his bags, marched to the cab.

"Bye, everyone," Connor called out from over his shoulder.

"Bye, Connor."

I could safely wager that Matt wasn't the only one shocked with Charlie's needy, almost pathetic behavior. I mean, this was Charlie—gruff, lazy and always angry Charlie. The Charlie who bickered with Dominick over how much food he should eat, the Charlie who snapped at me for wanting a drink of water in the desert, and the Charlie who seemed mad at the world when asked to do anything related to her assigned job on the tour, like cleaning camp and cooking. Yet here she was, somehow dying of heartbreak as shallow Matt, of all people, prepared to leave.

The blank expression drifted from Matt's face as he released Charlie from his weak embrace and bent down to grab his sack.

"Come on, then," Matt told Charlie. "We have a plane to catch, you know."

Like a scolded puppy dog, Charlie sheepishly followed Matt as he dragged his gear to the cab, climbing into the open back seat next to

Connor. Once the cabbie, stationed at the trunk, aided Matt in squeezing the luggage into the now-crowded trunk, Matt slid into the open seat next to Charlie, smiling through more tears.

"This is really bizarre," Megan deadpanned.

"Maybe she'll be a bridesmaid at his wedding," I returned.

"She may have to wear shoes, though."

With an audible grind, the cabbie pulled the car forward just short of Woody's truck before backing it up, then slowed momentarily for a final round of goodbyes.

"Behave, all of you!" shouted Matt through the open window.

"Love one another!"

"Oh God," I quipped. "I think I'm going to be sick."

And just like that, the cab sped off to the airport, returning nearly an hour later with a dour-looking Charlie as its only passenger. Though she looked like she had just buried her best friend, I still couldn't muster up any sympathy for her. She deserved a pompous ass like Matt.

Megan seemed pretty thoughtful after that, keeping relatively to herself the rest of the night except for when we wrestled to force our jug full of tap water through our temperamental filter. If this kept up all the way to Nairobi three weeks later, I knew I didn't have to worry about missing my strength training.

"Y'know, I'm really glad we got to say goodbye to Rutger," Megan declared suddenly, just as my final force of the plunger went down.

"Without him, I really don't think we could have done it."

I nodded.

"Let's get some sleep, huh? There may not be too many more nights on mattresses."

Spinning towards me, Megan lovingly clutched my hand and gazed into my eyes as she bit her lower lip.

"I just know things are going to get better on this trip," Megan stated confidently through her smile.

"...And I just know we can get through this together."

Holding Megan close, I knew that our dream was still alive. Our dream for that Africa we both still hoped to find.

Fumbling Through the Dark

"Once we get on the truck this morning, you know there's no going back."

I swung my backpack hard into the overhead compartment for dramatic effect. Megan wasn't impressed.

"Yeah, I know," she replied.

"But I have a feeling—this time—things'll be good."

I'd settle for 'alright.' Lately, things seemed like they couldn't get worse.

As Megan slumped down into our familiar seat on Ella, I hoped she was right. Since leaving with the group from Cape Town nearly three weeks ago, it was difficult to imagine how the stretch from Victoria Falls to Nairobi could be any more miserable. Vacation? It was downright laughable to have considered this trip to Africa a vacation the way Megan and I had planned it, as it resembled more of a grueling endurance test.

But change was in the air—I could just feel it. As soon as we left the familiar outskirts of Victoria Falls, our first good omen appeared in the form of the Bob Dylan cassette Woody popped into the sound system. "Highway 61 Revisited"—a very good sign. Though I knew little about our driver, Woody, aside from his gaunt appearance, it was a definite plus he was into Dylan. Plus, he couldn't possibly be any worse than Skonky.

Though I didn't know if Skonky was the worst thing about the first three weeks through Africa, his recklessness and lack of passion certainly didn't help. I mean, how can you have confidence in a guide, entrusted with guarding your personal safety in the harsh, African bush, who bullies a tourist into a puke-filled drinking contest? Skonky was definitely a lightning rod for what made things miserable for me in Africa. Toss in very few wildlife sightings, days filled with driving across barren and boring landscapes, and the turmoil my nightmare-inducing malaria medication was causing me for the complete picture of misery. Things had to get better. They couldn't get any worse.

Our reunion with Ella that first day had been a quiet one. Most of the travelers also aboard the truck had to be just as road-weary as I was and slowly assimilating themselves back to the trademark routines of overland travel. Mary surprised me the most with her silence, as she did nothing more than stare out the window.

I probably envied the elderly couple from Canada, Helen and Abe, the most, if only because they never appeared bored sitting on the truck, even if it encompassed the better part of the day. Abe could spend hours tracing the truck's route on his tattered, fold-out map while Helen would only be interrupted from her book on African vegetation to wait on her crotchety, partially immobile husband.

The romance between Stacey, the annoying, ugly American, and Aubrey, the Dutch guy who bore a striking resemblance to Charlie Brown, had thankfully cooled again, and the two were sitting apart from one another. Was Aubrey really that naïve when it came to sex? How could he not see that Stacey really only gave him the time of day when she had that longing?

The two Aussie guys, Thom and Bill, slept silently in the back of the truck, stirring occasionally whenever it hit a rough patch. Thom seemed like a good guy, not like that arrogant jerk, Matt, we finally got rid of in Victoria Falls. By default, he was a shoe-in to become Bill's new wingman and Thom was good-looking enough to at least provide Bill with a better chance of finding romance.

The other guy who joined the tour in Victoria Falls, Vernor, rested his chin on his hand as he gazed thoughtfully out the window.

The hours slowly mounted as we drove through a particularly barren and sparsely-populated patch of Zimbabwe to reach our accommodations for the night, Bwagi Lodge, which we were told rested right on the border Zimbabwe shared with Zambia. Aside from the occasional tiny villages of half-a-dozen thatch homes and the random roadside kiosk, there was little else to see besides patches of wilted trees or dried, sandy earth. I had looked out the window for signs of life, initially, mostly to compensate for Rutger not being around anymore, but that got old in a hurry.

As the sun began to set, the urgency of it all hit Woody, who realized pretty quickly it would be difficult to find Bwagi Lodge, known to be hidden pretty well off the main road, with daylight, let alone wrapped in the pitch darkness of night. Speeding up every time he hit a straight-away,

Woody would always markedly slow down at every approaching intersection or landmark, frantically craning his head in either direction for several moments before picking which way to continue.

"I'll bet he's lost," Bill said nonchalantly from his seat in the rear. A dark, long shadow crawled forward from the front of the truck, baring its teeth and ready to pounce.

"I don't even see how he knows where to go, period," added Megan, glaring out the window with a distressed look on her face.

"Even if there are signs out here, he won't be able to see them that much longer."

Darkness continued its stealthy creep as our journey into shadow continued, the now-black night making the battered roads before us even more treacherous. Even with high-beam headlights blasting forward, I couldn't fathom Woody being able to see more than ten feet in front of him. All around us, things took spooky, eerie shapes, from the now-foreboding wilderness.

Then, without warning, Woody pulled over to the right shoulder and came to a sudden stop. We had to be lost.

"What?" Megan whispered anxiously.

I looked up towards Woody, who had stuck his entire arm outside of the window and pointed to a patch of earth below.

"Bill you lookit that!" yelled Thom, following Woody's pointed finger. "It's huge!"

Scurrying out of our seats and rushing to the windows, we spied the source of all the excitement: a long, stretched-out puff adder, lying completely exposed just off the main road. Brazenly lying in wait—that was the way of the puff adder. And always in a foul mood.

We pressed on, Woody pushing Ella even faster as time passed and anxiety continued to rise. The entire crew on the truck was now completely silent, starving and bathed in darkness, all eyes on Woody expecting a sign—any sign—that we'd soon be where we needed to be.

Then, the awakening revelation we'd anxiously been waiting for came to be, as Woody raised his left hand from the steering wheel and pointed deliberately toward a narrow, dirt road on the left.

"We're here...I think!" exclaimed Aubrey.

His hunch was dead on, as the unmarked dirt road somehow led us straight to the campsite, where we were greeted by a hooded, mysterious-looking night watchman. Speaking briefly to Woody while we fumbled through the dark, the guard retreated to a shack several yards back, keeping a vigilant eye on us the entire time.

Even with the high beams of the truck for illumination, putting up the tents was rarely more difficult, as poles disappeared into the high, disheveled grass and grommets became tiny, vanishing pinholes.

It was well past ten in the evening before Woody had found the time to prepare dinner for us—a plate of beans and rice for Vernor, who, to my surprise, had declared himself a vegetarian, and that old standby, greasy sausage and some sort of sticky rice for us carnivores. And it wasn't until over dinner, when we were all equally exhausted and tired, that Woody shared some of the words the watchman had offered when we first pulled up.

"In that river," Woody began, stabbing at a chunk of meat with his fork. "Just over the ridge from your tents, are a mess of crocs."

I swallowed hard; we all did.

"Oh, don't worry, guys. They never come up this far on land," Woody reassured the group.

THE MAN WHO CRIED HIPPO

Another canoe trip had arrived. My body hadn't exactly welcomed the first night back in the tent with open arms and my neck was smarting from lack of pillow, since the laundry bag, except for a few pairs of clean underwear, was completely empty. Another canoe trip? This was going to be hell.

The grumbling Megan and I made after the last trip earned us quite the reputation, so the teasing naturally followed once Woody casually mentioned over a quick and chilly breakfast this journey would be slightly over thirteen kilometers—the longest yet.

"Maybe we shouldn't give you two paddles," joked Bill. "You may start beating each other with them."

With the usual precision, camp was broken down quickly before heading out to our rendezvous point on the Zambezi River—the same river we were warned about the previous night because of the crocodiles. Between my general surliness about canoeing and Megan's fear of all things moving, I figured we'd have one hell of an afternoon ahead of us. And I was right.

Several men of all shapes and sizes were busy already by the time we arrived at our spot, gathered around a small caravan of trucks with several canoes neatly stacked on top of each one. One particularly muscular man leaped from truck to truck with the dexterity of a ballet dancer, scaling the stack of vessels effortlessly to unlatch the top one from the thick, white rope that secured it tightly. With the help of another, the man gently lowered each metallic canoe one at a time, always straining slightly but only until a few other men on the ground shouldered the weight. All the while, another faction unpacked what we knew as 'wet bags'—those heavy, green plastic bags designed to keep gear dry.

"We are bush-camping tonight," Woody reminded us, after he had stopped the truck and climbed into the rear of the vehicle where we were sitting. "Take only what you need, and only what will fit."

"It will be hot on the river, and hours of it can lead to dehydration," lectured a pot-bellied man with a dark complexion. "Keep drinking water, but don't drink directly from the river unless you treat it."

That man was Eddington, one of our guides on our canoe trip up the Zambezi. Through enormous, dark sunglasses that rested high on his nose, he was all business as he thoroughly explained every rule we were expected to abide to, all of which, he explained, were for our own safety.

"These waters can be dangerous if you get too far ahead and don't listen to us," he warned, as he rested on a paddle stuck into the ground. "Always let the guides go first when there's wildlife in the area!"

"That's exactly right," chimed in the other guide, a smaller, thin man dressed in khaki shorts and a dark T-shirt who introduced himself later as Biggie.

"Hippos, especially, get very nervous, so you'll need to do exactly as we say when you see them. We mustn't panic them!"

After the guides, as all guides always did, assured us they 'never lost anyone' and that 'we'd have a great time,' we split off into pairs to finish readying our wet bags. The pairings weren't as obvious this time—Aubrey and Vernor were a team, mostly because Aubrey still wanted to pretend nothing was going on between him and Stacey while Vernor seemed kind of put-off by Mary's renewed blabbering; Eddington and the highly sinkable Abe; Bill and Thom, the two Aussies making a fast friendship; Woody and Mary; and Biggie, Stacey and Helen all packed into one canoe slightly longer than the rest. Of course, Megan and I remained a team as always, but this time, I'd be trying my hand at steering for the first time—at least until lunch.

Once everything was strapped down tightly inside the canoes and everyone had returned from a final restroom break in the bushes, the canoes headed out into the water after receiving a gentle push from the guys on shore. Wobbling slightly and headed toward the center of the river, I battled her through the splashing whitecaps, paddling in vain.

"I thought this river was calm!" Megan whined, just as a gush of cold water splashed into our laps. "I don't even think we're moving!"

"Just keep paddling!" I urged Megan while muscling my paddle as we bobbed forward. "We can catch up!"

"Tell them to wait for us!" she screamed back. "Tell them!"

The incoming waves punished our craft as we tried with all our might to catch up to the rest of the group, well ahead of us somehow. So much for paddling with the current like our guides had claimed we would be.

"Hey!" I yelled to Eddington, manning the canoe closest to us, yet at least thirty feet ahead. "We're way back here—can you wait?"

Eddington, the guide who lectured us about keeping our canoe between his and Biggie's at all times, stuck both of his oversized paddles into the water and pushed back in a short, deliberate motion, watching silently while Megan and I battled the choppy current. All the while, Abe, Eddington's shipmate, sat motionless, arms folded across his chest.

"Thanks, man," I told Eddington as we floated past. "We didn't want to get left behind."

Megan and I continued downstream on the Zambezi. If I didn't know any better, I would have sworn we had been battling an upstream current.

"Dammit!" I cursed, trying to muscle the tiny craft through the choppy waves. The chilly water beneath us roughly bounced against the sides as we struggled forward, occasionally dancing over and soaking everything. Our water bottles were mired in a mini-lake on the floor of the canoe, a buoy amid a rocky treacherous storm.

"You know," started Megan, angrily fighting her paddle ahead of her. "I really didn't need to canoe again!"

I couldn't tell what was frustrating Megan more—my blind determination to climb past the others while battling to keep the craft straight or our constant struggle through the harsh waters as we kept moving down the river.

"We need to stop!" she gasped. "Water!"

I looked at her—her face was red and flushed. Wisely, even though it killed me to watch Aubrey and Vernor keep pushing ahead at the front of the pack effortlessly, we stopped a minute or so while we both took a long gulp. Then we pushed on, speaking little to one another but still shouting the occasional curse word or bemoaning agonizingly long canoes trips. To keep my sanity and anger under control, I envisioned myself as a sort of machine as I dug my paddle deep into the water and kicked it back out hard, repeating the process with the same, constant precision.

"You don't need to paddle that hard!" Megan nagged. "You're just going to tire yourself out!"

I kept on, though—not necessarily to catch up with everyone else as much as I hoped paddling harder would magically make our lunch stop appear that much sooner. Through it all, my steering also improved, as Megan and I always kept parallel to Biggie's canoe and we steadily gained ground on the tightening group, until we finally found ourselves within shouting distance of everyone.

"We thought the crocs got ya back there!" Thom yelled from his canoe, maybe ten feet away.

"Yeah," added Bill. "But since we heard you two bitching the whole time, we figured you were still alive!"

"I just hate this," I said softly, leaning forwarding in the canoe.

"On your right!" Stacey bellowed as her canoe gently struck the side of ours, pushing ours slightly to the left. Biggie, in the rear, smiled warmly.

"How are you kids doing?" Helen asked from the middle of her canoe. "I have to say, this trip is much easier than last time."

Stacey rolled her eyes and looked away at this statement of the obvious. The trip was a lot easier for Helen this time because she wasn't paddling.

"I'll bet there aren't even hippos here," I whined to Megan.

"This is just the worst," Megan agreed, sighing as she lazily dipped her paddle back into the dark water. "I hated it last time and I still hate it. And I'm hungry," she added.

Eventually, after about another hour of endless, uneventful paddling, Biggie shouted to all of us to head to the shore after sighting a large, barren area surrounding a big tree.

"Over there!" he bellowed, rising slightly in his slow-moving canoe as he pointed. "That's the spot."

Suddenly, the mad dash was on, as canoe after canoe starting speeding for the tiny bank of dirt nestled below the tree. What was once a makeshift docking area quickly transformed into a bumper car track, with reckless, uncontrolled canoes creating a tinny 'thud' on impact with one another.

It wasn't until after we beached the canoes on the dirt mound and scrambled up the hill did I realize the folly of it all: hurrying to the lunch spot would accomplish nothing since the food hadn't even arrived. Naturally, it was all being carted in Eddington and Abe's canoe, still a few minutes behind the rest of us.

"That figures," huffed Megan, throwing her hand on her hip as she watched the canoe wriggle toward the dock. "I'd be tired too if I were Eddington and had to do all the paddling."

Watching the two pull slowly into the docking area was an amusing sight. The slightly-out-of-shape Eddington was soaked in sweat, huffing hard while Abe sat seemingly oblivious to it all, arms crossed over his chest like the angry child he resembled when we first boarded the canoes hours ago. Poor Eddington—if only he'd have spotted a hungry croc along a way to feed his miserable shipmate to.

We collectively huddled ourselves on the beach as the missing canoe finally came in for the landing, each one of us with the anticipation of food sharp in our minds. Forming a human chain, we quickly emptied the canoe of everything even resembling food and watched longingly as Woody carved up a few of the most ripe and luscious tomatoes I ever laid eyes on. Half expecting a breakout of the classic TLC sandwich, Woody threw us a pleasant surprise when it was, indeed, lunch meat that had been hiding in the dark blue cooler we carted with us.

"We're about half-way there," Eddington said softly as we devoured lunch.

When lunch ended, we continued downstream and the river became noticeably wider. Bill and Thom ventured out thirty feet in front of everyone, the threat of being the first to encounter wildlife enough to make Megan and me stop battling for the over-rated lead position. It didn't take very long after lunch for things to get exciting.

"Hey!" shouted Biggie, waving his paddle in the air. "Move to the middle and tighten up. Quickly!"

With his eyes trained on a few small dots I noticed close to the east end of the shore, Biggie, Stacey and Helen steered their canoe to the center of the river with amazing precision. All of the canoes behind Biggie fell in perfect line behind him, while those of us in the two canoes slightly ahead of the pack, Thom and Bill and Megan and myself, steered straight to the middle and paused until Biggie caught up.

"Hippos," Biggie stated calmly, eyes fixed on the gray specks ahead of us. "A small one and two larger ones—can you see?"

All eyes moved to the gray shapes on the shore, which slowly became larger as we continued paddling slowly downstream.

<HHHUUHHHH HHHHHHUHHHHHH HUUUUUUUHHHH>

"That's them grunting," Biggie commented, still watching the shapes that now clearly resembled hippos. "And you never, ever want to get too close to them because you'll threaten them, or cut one off from another."

"I heard," recited Mary in her usual chipper manner. "That hippos kill the most people in Africa."

"It's true," Biggie confirmed. "They're very aggressive in the water because that's where they feel safest. And if you threaten them on shore, they'll head right to it, taking out anything in their way."

The symphony of grunts became its loudest as we passed directly parallel to the small pod, all the while being followed by three sets of eyes that rose eerily from the waters below. Though several yards still separated us, I never felt entirely safe from the mammoth creatures until they were once again out of sight.

Breaking away from the group again after we passed, Megan and I resumed our position slightly ahead of Biggie, moving to one side as he instructed or dropping back behind him whenever he gave the word. Megan herself was on full alert now, glancing nervously back and forth and biting her lower lip in anticipation of the next surprise.

When the river began to narrow back down, Biggie herded all of us behind him to form a single, straight line.

"We need to stay together here," he warned. "Crocs."

With that, Biggie lifted his paddle out of the water and pointed with it at a large, angry-looking crocodile sunning itself on a small island no more than ten yards away from us. Probably ten feet in length and massively wide, seeing it reminded me of the many nature programs I had seen take place on rivers like this. You know the ones: unsuspecting animal drinks at shore, croc snatches with huge jaws and drags to miserable death. Still remaining motionless, even as we almost pulled parallel, the croc unexpectedly dived and disappeared into the water below, amid a few gasps and screams.

"Not to worry," Biggie reassured the group. "The canoe is too big—he'd never attack."

As much as Biggie knew his stuff, I almost half-expected to see the croc, seconds after it disappeared into the dark water below, its large, teeth-bared head rising up next to our canoe to take a chomp out of it.

Only until after our nerves calmed did I realize that what began as the 'Canoe Trip from Hell' had quickly morphed into one of our most exciting and exhilarating experiences in Africa.

It wasn't the only croc we passed as we proceeded down the river that afternoon, but certainly the largest and most intimidating, as few of the much smaller ones we spotted even noticed us as they continued sunning themselves along the shore. Still, the evil-looking grin etched across their long jaws said enough to me, their mouths agape while sunning themselves beneath the baking sun.

Remaining vigilant and on guard, we proceeded down the increasingly narrow expanse of river as a tight group and fairly silent, not wanting to startle anything else that may have been lurking around. Without warning, the river opened slightly wider and the current suddenly picked up. I grew a little nervous as we began uncontrollably speeding through the water, tiny splashes adding to the few inches already on the floor of the canoe.

The rush of strong current had inadvertently carried us right between a pod of nervous hippos.

"Alright guys," Biggie spoke softly with a trace of anxiety. "Let's go nice and slow."

On our right and about twenty yards away was a pod of at least five, large hippos, bouncing in the water like buoys while filling the air with a symphony of grunts and snorts. On the left, a huge, lone hippo, had his steely eyes fixed on our line of canoes as we trickled through the passage. Probably an additional ten yards farther from us than the pod, the solitary hippo grew increasingly vocal as we drew closer.

Biggie must have felt our levels of building anxiety—it was difficult to keep it contained. I glanced at Megan, who was nervously biting her lower lip. Biggie sharply banged his paddle against the top of his canoe, a tactic designed to frighten the hippos, I wondered if Biggie wished he hadn't mentioned to us that cutting off hippos from one another was the most dangerous situation found in African waters. To his credit, though, he remained calm, glancing back and forth at the hippos while ordering our canoes to a crawl. Then, after glancing back to Eddington briefly, we made our move.

"Listen to me," Biggie said with urgency over the orchestra of bellowing hippos. "Single file, as fast as you can, until I say otherwise. Go!"

With Biggie leading the way, we blazed our way in between and through the panicking hippos, a flurry of paddles striking the water with authority. I tried not to over think steering—luckily I had gotten the hang of it by, staying directly behind Bill and Thom's canoe the whole time, afraid to look back at the grunting hippos, who sounded even louder and more upset during our retreat. A few minutes later, when Biggie slowed down, we knew it was safe.

"Nice work, guys," he said, after taking a deep breath and turning to us. "Sometimes you get hippos hanging out behind that blind curve and you need to act fast."

The afterglow was unbelievable. A tremendous rush traveled over my body, a souvenir of another close, exciting call in the wilds of Africa. Still a little nervous on the outside, I wasn't nearly as bad as Megan, still chewing on her lip, and Helen, who I figured would probably jump off the canoe and swim to shore if only she knew how. I took a deep, long breath. With impending danger passed, it was time for some fun.

With our canoes still bunched together, I broke out what turned out to be one of my most able imitations of African wildlife: the hippo, down to the pig-like grunting we had all grown familiar with while on the canoe trip. Having never tried my impression before then, I didn't know if it was descent or not, yet Megan still requests it to this day when she shares her stories of life in Africa with her friends. And how my impression nearly gave our guide a heart attack.

"HHHUUUUUHHHH HHHHHHHUUUUUH HHHHUUUUHHHH!" I snorted from the rear of the canoe in a deep tone.

Bringing her paddle from the water and clutching it tightly, Megan instantly hunched low in the canoe.

"Where is it?!" she shrieked.

"HHHUUUUUHHHH HHHHHHHUUUUUH HHHHUUUUHHHH!"

Biggie, crouched low in the canoe in front of us and within earshot, hunched even lower and began listening. With eyes darting back and forth, he held up his hand and listened silently.

"HHHUUUUUHHHH HHHHHHHUUUUUH HHHHUUUUHHHH!"

"Cut it out!" laughed Megan, after turning to the rear of the canoe and busting me during my latest bellow.

"It's Paul, everyone!" Megan called out. "It's no hippo."

"You guys are trying to kill me!" Biggie said, holding his hand over his heart in between deep breaths.

As Megan and I became more comfortable with the canoe, we unknowingly drifted ahead of the others, believing Biggie when he stated, immediately after our narrow scrape, that we had passed all of the hippos we'd probably see that afternoon.

The landscape along the beach had become increasingly bare as we continued downstream and finally reached camp, a small section of dark, sandy beach that held a few scattered trees.

"This is it!" bellowed Biggie, first pointing with his paddle before leading his canoe to the shore.

After helping unpack all of the tents, latched tightly to the interior of Woody and Mary's canoe, Megan and I grabbed one that looked relatively dry and dragged it up the beach.

Darkness arrived quickly that evening, amid the occasional unseen hippo grunt and elephant trumpet. Large ripples danced across the water as a massive bull elephant, completely submerged save for its trunk, methodically stalked across the river. Much like our other bush-camping experience, thousands of magnificently bright stars blanketed the night sky above us in a dazzling array, stretching across the blackness overhead as far as the eye could see.

After dinner, with our bellies full, we spent the rest of the night, lying on our backs beneath the big sky. Megan and I watched for shooting stars, sporadically dancing through the night sometimes mere minutes apart.

I overheard someone mention Vernor had gone into his tent for the night because he wasn't feeling well but I hadn't noticed, though it did seem the vegetarian pot prepared for him had gone untouched.

For my money, Biggie and Eddington, were the most interesting members of the group. They were both friendly, very knowledgeable about their home, and full of advice, just the type of people Megan and I liked to grill about their experiences in the jungles of Africa.

"Never turn you back on the leopard!" whispered Biggie, with some urgency after we asked which animal they feared the most. "At least if you keep your eye on them, you have a chance."

Eddington nodded, then offered his opinion on which was Africa's most dangerous animal.

"The elephant, definitely," he said, stoically, biting down on his pipe. "Anger one and it'll chase you down and stomp you dead."

"Elephants?" Megan asked, sighing nervously as she glanced across the beach. "Like, the ones that hang around here?!?"

Eddington poked Biggie in the ribs and smile.

"You all better stay in your tents tonight," Eddington teased. "Unless you want to get trampled!"

"Yes," added Biggie, with a twinkle in his eye, following Eddington's lead. "But then again, an elephant may just trample you and your tent!"

I really enjoyed talking to the guides about all things Africa and life in their Zimbabwe homes, as it was one of the first and few opportunities we really had to get to chat at length to some locals. They told us how they had both gotten malaria in Harare, Zimbabwe's capital city, probably while out clubbing one night.

Megan, being the eternally curious person she is and unabashed about asking personal questions, set her sights on getting some dirt.

"So how conservative is Zimbabwe, culturally?" she asked innocently.

"Oh, Zimbabwe is a very modern, open society," Eddington replied. "Men and women can date and live together before marriage."

"Do you have strip clubs?" asked Megan seriously to a surprised Eddington. "I mean, can you buy adult entertainment in Africa, if you wanted to?"

Eddington and Biggie, along with the rest of us crowded onto the beach, erupted in laughter. Megan's question remained unanswered.

I couldn't speak for Megan, but I began to feel a lot more comfortable with the group as we sat up on the beach late into the night, exchanging jokes and anecdotes about our lives. Maybe it was Matt's absence, maybe it was seeing that Mary was learning that her place wasn't in the middle of everything, but it was very comforting, whatever it was. It wasn't until the fire began dying its customary, slow death for the night did Megan and I retreat to our tents, both listening restlessly to the foreign sounds around us before drifting off to sleep.

SETH

After an uneventful morning canoe to our pickup point and a bumpy ride on a dilapidated truck, Ella magically appeared in the bush. It was a beautiful sight, especially when I spotted the familiar breakfast table hanging from her side and filled with the standard assortment of cereals and breads.

We all crowded close to the breakfast table as we feasted, then Woody made an announcement.

"Listen up guys," he announced as he put his arm around the shoulders of a blond guy beside him. "This is the man we've all been waiting for—Seth!"

With his pale, blue eyes half-open, Seth, at first glance, appeared either half-asleep, half-bored, or both. Running his hand through the slightly receding patch of blond, matted hair atop his head, he cleared his throat as he stepped out from beneath Woody's arm.

"Yeah...I'm Seth," the man said meekly, looking mostly at the ground as he whispered his greeting. "After you guys finish, we'll head out."

With those few, anticlimactic words, Seth gave us a final look-over before retreating to the rear of the truck, taking a brief supply inventory with Woody at his side.

"That's Seth?" Stacey dramatically whispered into Megan's ear. "He seems a little too soft to take us to Nairobi—he doesn't even seem like he wants to be here."

Megan shrugged.

"He has experience, I guess," Stacey added. "He must. He's not wearing shoes, either."

Admittedly, I expected Seth to be a little more enthusiastic once he had arrived, but knowing the little I did about life as an African Wanderer guide from Rutger, the poor guy had must have been road weary and would need a few days to get into gear. Watching him as he slammed the rear door of the truck shut before moving to the cab and climbing in, I prayed Seth was at least a partial answer to some of our trials and tribulations in Africa. He wouldn't be our savior, but he couldn't be awful as Skonky...could he?

We headed out for the day once breakfast was packed up, with Seth now seated behind Ella's increasingly familiar steering wheel on the right with Woody to his left. One thing I noticed immediately about Seth was his driving—not as reckless as Skonky's, but every bit as fast, if not faster. Turns were more afterthoughts than anything else, leaned into hard without the slightest hesitation, and it took some getting used to.

The plan for the day was to drive through more of Zambia until we reached the city of Lusaka, where we could then expect several more hours of driving ahead of us until we reached camp.

The scenery was typical Africa for much of the journey—grassy landscapes dotted with the occasional villages—until we reached Lusaka, a fairly industrialized city highlighted by heavy traffic and an abundance of advertising placards that hawked cigarettes and liquor. Seth, familiar with the urban sprawl that was Lusaka, pulled off the main, congested road we had taken into the city and guided Ella into a completely gated, strip mall shopping center.

"A shopping mall?" a stunned Stacey exclaimed. "Here?"

"Alright!" Bill declared, gazing out the window. "Food!"

The mere sight of that shopping center in Lusaka provided me with that dose of much-needed western civilization I had been craving since Cape Town.

Oh yeah—and the Subway sandwich shop both Megan and I had been craving since Victoria Falls.

There is something both comforting and creepy about franchise restaurants like Subway. The comfort lies in knowing that no matter which restaurant you visit, you can always expect pretty much the same thing, right down to the humiliating uniforms and the disgruntled assistant manager who wished they had stayed in school. Yet, that's also what made the Subway experience in African so absolutely surreal to me, standing in that line of nearly a dozen people deep. The nondescript Subway could have been completely ripped from anywhere in America and dropped in Lusaka and you wouldn't even be able to tell the difference.

We enjoyed our sandwiches thoroughly, savoring every bite of the familiar food.

After finishing our meal, we checked out most of the stores in the strip mall and met up with the other group members in the grocery store.

By the time we got back to the truck, Woody and Seth had just completed loading it with groceries while everyone else was settling in for even more driving.

As we had been promised back in Cape Town, private chalets would become increasingly available for a small fee as we continued further along on our journey. To Megan and myself, the very thought of upgrading became increasingly tempting and our long drive rewarded us with just such a treat.

"Let's do it!" begged Megan, squeezing my arm as Seth lackadaisically pointed out the humble-looking, thatch-covered huts from across camp.

Though the chalets in camp didn't resemble the lap of luxury, they did translate into a night in a bed, something both Megan and I could definitely appreciate, a steal at a mere $7 U.S. for the two of us for one night. I secretly hoped our stay might raise the possibility of another night of passionate love-making in Africa, something that occurred a little less frequently than I had desired.

After plunking down our money at the bar and being handed a key by a burly, bearded man, Megan raced to the assigned cabin with great fervor, hopping up and down on the tiny porch while I made my way up more slowly with most of the gear in tow. Reaching the top stair, Megan wrestled briefly with the key until we heard the familiar 'click' of the lock and the front door creaked open.

"Here we are!" Megan exclaimed, still hopping. "This is so cool!"

My enthusiasm didn't match hers—it rarely did, when it came to sleeping in unfamiliar places—but the chalet would be serviceable, if nothing else. Two double beds, a la "I Love Lucy," sat high off a half-wood, half-dirt floor, probably left that way for lack of wood rather than rustic charm. Covered in stiff, white sheets, each bed had its own mosquito net suspended high above it, though one had been marred with a large and obvious tear.

To my dismay, that's all there was to the tiny, ten by fifteen foot chalet. Maybe I was being a little ridiculous expecting to find a large-screen television with digital satellite reception. Setting our gear down on the bed with the torn mosquito net, I averted my eyes from the cone-shaped thatch roof above, adorned in spiraling, intricate spider webs.

That evening, while the other group members embarked on a game drive, Seth and Woody built a fire for us as night slowly crept over. Dinner would be provided by our campground hosts and it would wait until the game drive was over. This provided us with the perfect opportunity to get to know Seth a little better, who really hadn't said much since we met him.

It didn't take long for Seth to open up. After cracking his second beer, I sensed he was more relaxed, becoming more animated and speaking louder as he sat Indian-style on the ground as he shared his tales of guiding in the African bush.

"Once this guy came out of his tent in the middle of the night and startled a lion," Seth began, recounting the scene with a slight glimmer in his eye. "...So he ducks behind this tree," he laughed. "And the lion started chasing him around and around this tree all night, until someone finally scared it off with a gun!"

Seth rolled on his back in laughter, holding his sides to contain himself. His low, hearty laugh was as infectious as we imagined the poor dope he told us about trying to outwit a lion from behind a skinny little tree.

We never did learn too much about Seth's personal life. What he did reveal to us that evening was that he was in his early twenties and had a girlfriend back home in South Africa.

Meanwhile, the remaining group members returned from their game drive sat around the fire, eagerly discussing that evening's dinner.

Vernor, with his back slumped against the tree, instantly perked up, his eyes growing wide with excitement and exclaimed, spinning enthusiastically towards Helen, "Game meat is quite delicious!"

Just when I thought things couldn't get any more bizarre on the tour, I find out we'd been teamed with probably the only vegetarian who eats game meat.

"Umm...Vernor?" Megan asked curiously, picking up on it like the rest of us. "I thought you were a vegetarian."

"Oh, I am," Vernor said, proudly puffing out his chest. "But game meat? It's delicious, and the animals aren't cruelly tortured like chickens and cows. Do you know chickens get their heads cut off with little guillotines?" Vernor added, disgustedly, squeezing his thumb and index finger together in a quick motion as if he was snapping something in two.

"So let me get this straight, Vernor," Megan insisted. "Instead of eating animals that have been raised to be eaten, like chickens and cows, you exclusively eat meat from animals that may be in short supply and slaughtered regardless?"

Vernor paused thoughtfully for a moment.

"Yes," he stated matter-of-factly, nodding his head. "Yes."

The more I got to know Vernor, the more I became intrigued with his slightly kooky take on life. To me, as bizarre as some of his ideas were, he stuck with them so passionately it was almost admirable.

Vernor's candidness, though blunt at times, was a refreshing change of pace, almost as if he had his mind made up from the first day that he was going to tell it like he saw it, speaking his mind and not worrying about who didn't like what he had to say. Megan claimed it was a very 'German' characteristic to be so blunt—all I knew was that I enjoyed the obvious eye rolling and bored expressions that wiped across his face whenever Mary's stories really got to him. After a while, even she seemed to recognize it, concentrating her tales and insights on the one or two people who continued to smile and listen out of courtesy, usually Helen and Abe.

Seth excused himself shortly after that exchange, though, and Megan and I approached him when we spotted him a short time later, shining a flashlight along the riverbank, looking like an usher at a theater trying to track down an empty seat. Startling him after Megan stepped on a small branch, Seth motioned us closer and handed me the flashlight.

"Over there," Seth ordered, pointing his finger towards the center of the river. "Lookit that big bastard!"

The lone beam of light danced up and down across the black water, a single spotlight against the dark night sky. Landing on a dark, massive shape, I slowly guided the light in either direction until I spotted it—probably the largest crocodile I'd ever seen.

To me, crocodiles always appeared the most menacing of all the creatures we'd seen in Africa. The one inhabiting the river, a mere twenty yards away, was no exception. Maybe it was the way you usually spotted them alone, solitary, stealthy predators eagerly awaiting opportunity with bared, grinning teeth.

The brute we watched from safely above lay deathly still, peering forward into the milky black of night. Those unblinking, trained eyes were the eeriest of all, glowing a brilliant, demonic red under the beam of our flashlight.

"He wouldn't come up on land...would he?" asked Megan, measuring the steep distance up from the riverbank as she peered over the side.

"No way," stated Seth, suddenly coming to life again. "You really only need to fear them if you wander too close to the river. Most animals here are like that—they're only going to give you problems if you invade their space or surprise them."

"So what about here?" I asked, growing a little nervous. "What do we need to be careful of around here?"

It was a question Megan and I had stopped asking early on, primarily because Skonky didn't know or never seemed to care. But Seth seemed different. Though he didn't possess the passion of Rutger, he enjoyed sharing his knowledge.

"The usual things are around here," Seth offered, as he traced the beam of his flashlight up the croc's entire body.

"Hippos, maybe an occasional elephant are all you need to worry about."

Megan, looking nervous, sought a little reassurance.

"So, tell us, because we heard lots of different things," she began, nervously biting her lip. "Animals won't come into a tent, will they?"

Seth smiled a knowing smile as he turned his back to the crocodile to face Megan.

"Usually, no," he said.

BROTHER, CAN YOU SPARE A KWACHA?

The group trickled into breakfast sporadically the following morning, some choosing to shower while others, like us, didn't get up until it was absolutely necessary. "It was twenty feet away from me, maybe," Stacey excitedly explained to us over my breakfast of bran flakes. "It was probably around five in the morning, and the hippo had its back to me when I opened my tent. I was like 'Okay, then' and zipped it shut."

Stacey. Leave it to her to have one of those totally cool and unique experiences. Even if Megan and I wouldn't have gotten back to sleep after such an encounter, I would have loved such a close brush with a hippo.

"So it must have been up there grazing, then," added Woody, looking up from a mug of dark brown coffee.

"I guess so," commented Stacey with a slight laugh. "I mean, I didn't want to stare or anything."

Thom, seated next to Bill and listening to the whole thing, gave his Aussie partner a playful jab in the side with his elbow.

"Aubrey?" Thom bellowed from across the fire ring. "That's a fine way to leave your girlfriend. You'd better have a good excuse!"

While Stacey giggled it off, you could almost see the red wave of embarrassment completely wash over Aubrey, uncomfortably fidgeting with his cereal spoon as he lunged it into his bowl of bran flakes.

"Very funny, buttie," mumbled Aubrey, pursing his lips before cracking a knowing smile.

Since the departure of Skonky, the group did seem a lot closer, sharing more good-natured fun and more openness. Though Seth had only been acting as tour leader for the past couple of days, the manner in which he ran things with Woody was much more precise and professional than Skonky could ever have managed with Rutger. The two worked extremely well together, spelling each other on long drives, cooking varied, tasty meals jointly, and maintaining a degree of cleanliness never seen before.

Those days of foul, putrid water left in the bus pan for us to wash our dishes in were long over. Woody always made sure of that. Instead, you'd be hard-pressed to find a food-encrusted fork or dirty plate mixed in with the clean ones, because like all good leaders, their own pride in getting a job done right seemingly trickled down to us.

Once we finished breakfast and boarded the truck with the last of our gear, Seth reminded us that our beach holiday would begin soon after we crossed the border from Zambia into Malawi.

"I'm telling you, guys," Seth promised, with a hint of excitement in his eyes. "The beaches of Malawi are just fantastic. Bright sun, beautiful water...the best!"

The beach. If Megan and I were back in Chicago, that's where we'd be spending most of our Saturday afternoons—me in search of an elusive tan and she hoping to sneak under the eyes of the Nazi-like lifeguards to feel the waters of Lake Michigan against her waist.

The Malawi border crossing wasn't as stressful as some of the others we had the pleasure of encountering. The standard entry and exit paperwork was pretty routine as we walked from one country's border post to the other, made even quicker by a stamp-happy guard who barely looked up as we shuffled by in front of him.

For whatever reason, the Malawi border crossing appeared to be popular with the scores of young children that lined the roadside along with us, though the cynic in me knew it was because they were smart enough to know where the money was. Looking a little more disheveled in appearance than I was used to seeing back home, the joys of childhood were still very apparent, even through the mismatched, tattered clothing and slightly hardened faces. Mary, who instantly befriended a small group of wide-eyed girls by giving them each a pencil for school, got a huge kick when she received a stirring rendition of a short, yet high-spirited dance routine in thanks.

One thin boy, wearing a stretched-out white shirt and a gray cap, gleefully raced up and down the broken curb pushing his 'car'—an intricate, wire metal frame with wheels propelled forward by an arm's length handle. Two small potatoes—its passengers, I presume—sat in the front seat.

"That's a great car!" praised Megan.

"No," corrected the boy, without missing a beat. "It's a Toyota!"

Most entertaining, though, was a small boy, about ten years old, whose appearance screamed an undeniable sense of attitude and flair. Maybe it was the outfit he wore—brown cowboy boots, purple corduroys, and a white, slightly soiled T-shirt—but somehow it all worked together. And walking with a slight swagger, the boy eyed all of us nonplussed as he coolly lowered himself to the ground next to Abe.

"Well hello, young man!" said Abe, hunching his frame down slightly.

Smiling slightly, the boy made a half-hearted wave with his right-hand, then looked away slightly.

"And how old are you?" continued Abe, undeterred, as he moved in even closer to the boy to get his attention.

With a quizzical look, the boy searched Abe's face as the question was repeated several more times. This went on for a little bit until a slightly older boy, settling next to the purple-clad cowboy, whispered something into his ear that made him laugh.

"He just started school," the older boy explained to Abe. "He knows his numbers."

"Oh," acknowledged Abe, now looking a little confused himself as he again moved in closer to the young boy.

"Then how old do you think I am?" Abe asked. "What number?"

Shooting a quick glance to his older friend, the boy smiled briefly, paused for a second and then spoke.

"Oh."

"Oh? Do you think I look twenty?"

Moving behind Abe, Megan and I shot our thumbs up and motioned to the sky, coaching the curious boy as he looked on. Way older.

"Thirty?" continued Abe. "Do I look thirty?"

Still no answer from the boy, who smiled as Megan and I made our antics more outrageous, both emphatically pointing with our index fingers straight into the air.

"How about fifty?"

Rising from the curb and then throwing his hand into his hip pocket, the boy drew a deep breath, looked at his friend and us one final time, and then spouted out one of the funniest things I ever heard in my life.

"Fifty? Oh!" exclaimed the boy, in a tone that read 'Don't bullshit me, old man!' You don't look a day under a hundred!" he exclaimed.

I doubt Abe found the entire exchange as funny as the rest of us did—through the mouth of babes, as the old saying goes. It was absolutely perfect—seeing an innocent kid put a sometimes-condescending ass like Abe in his place. Priceless.

When Ella did finally arrive up the dirt road with Woody and Seth at her helm, we were rounded up quickly and as we headed off, the flock of children surrounded the truck to wave their goodbyes. Megan tossed the little cowboy a light blue shirt of hers to replace his tattered one, a gesture that netted a bright smile and a hearty 'thumbs up' in return.

When we left the border crossing into Malawi, we didn't immediately enter the lush, pastoral beach paradise I was hoping for. Actually, we found ourselves right in the middle of one of the most urban areas we had come across yet in all of Africa—a bustling crowded town.

Over time, those congested and hurried streets became as much of an image of Africa to me as the sparse, Namibian landscape or a majestic herd of marching elephants. The acrid smells of automobile exhaust, the relentless shouts of hawkers from their rickety stalls, haphazardly lined in rows along the street, the small swarm of local people always seen milling near markets and looking surprisingly comfortable beneath the building mid-day heat. That was Africa, too.

We stopped in the city for a short time, just long enough to hunt for a reasonable exchange rate and move on.

JUST DO IT

The following morning, Seth hardly seemed like the sleepy, mildly interested guy we had met after the canoe trip on the Zambezi. Instead, he was noticeably pumped, bouncing with excitement as he helped Woody pack up the truck one final time before we entered Malawi.

"Malawi is going to be the best time," Seth promised as we finished our breakfast. "The sun, the sand, the people—you'll see why!"

Malawi roads were not terrible—in fact, they were probably some of the smoothest we had encountered over the hundreds of miles we had logged since leaving Cape Town. But take any road riddled with sharp, mountainous turns and mix in a speed that skimmed that magical point of total vehicle rollover and you're easily left with a precarious and unforgettable journey that would test anyone's courage. And it did.

"He's nuts!" exclaimed Megan, grabbing my shirt to steady herself on her bouncing seat. The springs holding our seat into the floor gave way beneath a hideous moan, teetering back and forth under the strain like an amusement park ride.

The lush, tropical Malawi landscape flew rapidly past our windows, and an immense beach appeared briefly from behind dense trees, then disappeared, peaking out in short bursts as we continued winding down the road ahead. We were close. So close.

Though the sun had given way in large part to overcast, almost rainy skies, I could see some of the appeal already as we continued making our way to the beach. All the ingredients for a truly tropical paradise were there—the lush, full, fruit trees, the mild, breezy air coming just off the water, the tranquil and inviting waters of Lake Malawi. I could feel the truck slowing down, and I looked up to see Aubrey slowly rise from his seat in front of me.

"Now what's this all about?!?" he whined, drawing our attention to the alarming site directly ahead: a small contingent of armed, uniform people stationed behind a long stick fashioned across the road.

"This must be the welcoming committee," mumbled Thom, initially reaching for his camera but then thinking better of it.

Slowing Ella to a halt, Seth stuck his head out of the cab and spoke briefly to one of the uniformed men, who spoke into a small radio. Then another man showed up. The boss, I assume, though he looked more like a picture out of a bad trailer park.

Clad from head to toe in a cheaply made, white tracksuit, he looked more like a Wal-Mart cover model than the picture of authority, a higher-ranking member of either the police or military. Even worse, the bad tracksuit the guy was wearing was a Nike knock-off, right down to the inverted 'swoosh' symbol that wasn't fooling anyone and the name 'Nice' decorated across the front of it in silver letters. After watching the man in white say a few words to Seth, who climbed down from the cab to meet him, we heard a light rap at the door, which Aubrey promptly threw open.

"This man is with the police, guys," explained Seth in a quiet voice as he poked his head through the door. Seth, too, saw the weirdness in all of it—the seriousness of an unexpected and random police search mixed with a walking sight gag. "Please cooperate, okay?"

Nodding in unison, Seth then turned back to the man, who thanked him and slowly scaled the three steel steps into the back of the truck. Then, after stumbling slightly after reaching the top, the 'Nice' spokesmodel stood straight.

"Good afternoon!" he said, voice booming as he walked up the aisle. "Are you enjoying Africa?"

With authority, we answered with a loud 'yes,' though the officer seemed primarily interested in checking beneath our seats as he paced to the rear of the vehicle, slowing down and crouching while scanning the floor. Then, walking back up to the front of the truck, the man stopped in mid-stride.

"Sir!" he addressed Thom, who looked a little taken aback. "Your passport, please."

With cool assurance, Thom reached slowly into his hip pocket and produced the red booklet, which the man flipped through quickly before looking deep into his eyes and returning it with a smile.

He did the same routine on Stacey, who was not nearly as intimidated, flipping through the first few pages before sincerely smiling and returning it.

Once back at the front of the truck, the man gave a short wave and slowly climbed back down to the steel steps. Then, when the inspection officer motioned for one of the uniformed men to remove the man-made stick border, we were back on way to Khande Beach—our first destination in Malawi.

"I never heard of 'Nice' before!" cackled Thom as the checkpoint disappeared behind us. "I thought they only sold 'Reebox' here!"

Anticipation grew as we continued on to Khande Beach, reaching a crescendo when a battered yellow sign spun halfway around a wooden pole pointed down a narrow, dirt road heralding the way. The sea of tropical trees parted for Ella as she slowly crawled forward while we all sat on the edge of our seats, waiting for that beach holiday to finally arrive.

In minutes, it was within sight. As soon as I climbed off the truck with my backpack slung over my shoulder, I was instantly transported back to the Caribbean. It all seemed to be right there—the gentle, light breeze pushing gently off the water, the sweeping foam off the lake as it rolled against the beach. The thatch huts and lilting palm trees everywhere, lazily swaying beneath the afternoon sky completed the scene. It couldn't look anymore peaceful. The water looked gloriously refreshing as the sun crawled across it, though the possibility of it being rife with bilharzia, the same, parasitic strain we feared becoming infected with during the Orange River canoe trip, was the only deterrent I needed from dipping a toe in it.

Thom, well aware of the risks, didn't seem to mind, and swam all the way to a small island about a kilometer away. Vernor, too, joined him in the lake. And then there was Mary.

"So you aren't going in the lake, eh?" Mary asked me, squinting beneath the bright sun with her hands on her hips.

"Yeah," I explained. "It's just something I don't want to risk."

"But," Mary argued, "if we shower here, aren't we also showering with that same water? I think we should all just go in!"

For a second, Mary's logic almost made sense—until I remembered how that same logic led her to get ripped off by changing money with a cab driver, sick to her stomach after eating a native root, and left her with a broken wristwatch that still couldn't keep time.

"Like I said," my voice getting a little louder. "It's a personal choice."

Then, plopping down on my beach towel, I shut my eyes and hoped she'd go away.

As nice as it was to finally relax on the beach, though, my wallet and I grew a little restless after a while. I was always a sucker for buying souvenirs. Dusting the sand off me as I rose to my feet, I told Megan, sunning herself by my side with eyes shut tightly, where I was headed—through the locked gate and into what I imagined to be Victoria Falls Part Two.

"Have fun checking it out," Megan mocked, curling up even more into the sand.

I think I was the first of the group brave enough to venture out to that land beyond the gates. Not that there was anything to be afraid of, but that gate had to be there for a reason, possibly the only thing capable of keeping aggressive hawkers at bay.

Since my trip to the Bahamas a few years ago, I enjoyed haggling. I tried not to draw too much attention to myself, but as one set of eyes, partially obscured behind a stall selling drums, met mine, I knew I was in trouble.

At full speed, the young, short teenager behind the eyes stormed towards me, waving his arms and shouting.

"So good to see you, my friend," he exclaimed, grabbing my elbow. "Come, let's look at my drums!"

"No, that's okay," I explained, now noticing that the entire road was quickly becoming filled with hawkers, emerging from their thatch cocoons. "I'm really just kind of looking...."

"Then look with me!" the youth shouted, tightening his already firm grip. "Come!"

Grudgingly, I followed him from the middle of the street to his stall, decorated with a cardboard sign with the words 'The African Arts Museum' burned in red paint. It was the usual fare we had seen in Victoria Falls, for the most part: the same hippo carvings, a few drums, some jewelry, and some canvas drawings.

"You like the hippos," he said, smiling. "Make me an offer."

"No, really," I said. "Thanks for showing me, but I'm not buying anything today. I'm just looking."

"Here!" he ordered, after picking up the rough hippo statue. "Take a look!"

"Sorry," I replied firmly. "Maybe I'll be back."

I left the dejected shopkeeper behind me as I spun around and made my way back to the street. Then the true bombardment began—dozens of hawkers swarming me like locust from all directions, each trying to tempt me to visit their shop next.

"The best of Africa," one proclaimed. "Follow me!"

"Visit mine next!" another commanded. "I will look for you!"

I always did have a hard time saying no, so I ended spending much more time than I really wanted to, checking out practically each hawker's stall, though very few offered anything unique. If nothing else, though, at least most of the hawkers had a great sense of humor, young guys who had adopted well-known or sometimes downright humorous aliases that made nearly every introduction memorable. I mean, who wouldn't want to get their hair braided by someone named 'Dr. Love'?

My personal favorite was the dude who introduced himself to me as 'David Jones,' which I discovered later was the name of an Australian department store chain. Never too pushy, David had me pegged from the very moment, promising with laughing eyes to show me something 'very special' for sale in his shop. I was intrigued, to say the least, and was a little surprised to see a huge assortment of ceramic pipes.

"These look good, no?" he fished, standing straight and tall with his hands behind his back. "Something for you, maybe?"

Looking down at the pipes—some brightly colored, some in the shape of tiny, ornate skulls, I knew they weren't for me. I never could figure out how to pack weed into those tiny fuckers.

"Sorry," I explained, still looking through the pipes. "I'm really not a pipe guy."

Gliding behind a table and reaching deep down into a large, wooden box, David pulled out a short, tubular object wrapped in a red bandana.

"Then how about this?" he said softly, first glancing behind me before unrolling the cloth.

He unsheathed a six-inch long, fat rod of packed weed from the bandana, and I was completely speechless. It was right out of your favorite Cheech and Chong movie.

"Holy shit!" I mumbled.

"$6 for this one, $10 for a whole foot," David said through his smile.

"Ummmm...let me think about it," I said, staring at the fat stick. It was almost mesmerizing.

"You know where to find me," he said coolly. David knew I was coming back.

With a spring in my step, I fought through the army of clawing hawkers and made my way back to the beach and Megan.

"So how was it?" Megan asked.

I dug my feet into the sand next to her.

"Good. They have the usual stuff...statues, paintings...weed."

Megan moved her sunglasses down to the edge of her nose.

"Did you say weed?"

"It was nuts, Meg," I explained, trying to do justice to the firm, fat log of marijuana as I described it, using my hands like I had just seen the fish that got away.

"Are you going to get some?" she asked brightly.

"That depends," I said, inadvertently sounding like a drug pusher. "Would you smoke some with me?"

"No," she said, firmly, after taking a short sigh. "I...I just have too much else to worry about here." She paused. "But I don't mind if you do."

"I'll bet you," Megan said confidently, gesturing toward Bill. "If you ask him, he'll go in on it."

I thought about it as she laid back down on the blanket, then I looked at Bill and Thom, sitting on the beach watching a small flock of girls from another overland truck prancing in the tide. They'd be in. Of course they would.

Climbing slowly to my feet, I surprised Bill when I stopped just behind him.

"Dude," I said, crouching down to get in close. "They have weed in the market. Not just tiny joints. Like, Cheech and Chong size."

Again, I used my hands to articulate the massive bulk.

"So are we going to get some, then?" asked Thom, grinning slightly.

"We should," I said. "It's $6 for the small one, which is plenty. I don't have any papers, though, and I doubt they do."

"No worries," Bill stated coolly. "I do. In my backpack."

The guys handed me a few crumbled bills from their pockets and, after flashing Megan a quick 'thumbs up,' I made my way back through the gate, cutting through a sea of noisy hawkers and back over to 'David Jones.'

"You have returned," he said, nodding in delight. "Good."

Counting out the six singles after I handed them over, David then reached back into the chest and pulled it out—a thick, tightly packed log.

"Come back for more, if you wish," David stated, firmly handing the weed to me.

I fought my way back through the gate past shouting hawkers and returned to the beach and Bill, who pulled a small pack of rolling papers out of his pocket and handed it to me.

With a book of matches from the bar, we finally got the first, stubborn joint to light. Tasty—the sort of taste that brings you back for more.

"It's really smooth," said Thom, lovingly watching the tip of the burning joint as he exhaled.

"Mmm-hmmm," seconded Bill. "Very nice."

"Hey!" said a voice directly behind me. "What's that?"

Turning quickly, I saw Seth and Woody standing behind me and both smiling ear to ear.

"I see you visited the market," Seth said with a grin. "May I?"

"Oh yeah, man," I said, handing him the slightly wet joint. "It's cool."

Actually, it was sort of bizarre, seeing the two guides responsible for our complete well being, join us and match us drag for drag as we whittled through those couple of joints.

We finished smoking the three joints I rolled and that was it. The weed seemed to do wonders for Bill, who I saw actually initiate a conversation with one of the blond girls we had seen on the beach earlier, then subtly motion Thom over for backup.

I was feeling pretty good, myself, and chose to lie on the sandy beach and listen to the waves roll in while Megan and a bunch of the others went to inspect the village outside the gates. I always loved the steady and predictable roar of waves as they crashed against the beach—it was one of the few sounds I could count on to completely relax me. With my eyes shut, I drifted in and out of sleep, dozing lightly when Megan returned from her little excursion.

"Hey," she said, touching me lightly with her foot. "I'm back."

I opened my eyes slowly—the bright sky was intense at first.

"So what did you buy?"

"Nothing yet," she said excitedly. "But I saw a canvas print of a guy playing guitar and I thought of you."

"Really?" I said, moving to a sitting position.

"Yep," she continued. "The guy making them is named Banjo, and he had a print I liked, too. He said he'd put them on T-shirts for us if we wanted."

"C'mon!" she said, enthusiastically as she kicked a little sand on me. "Let's go look!"

I did love Megan's enthusiasm—it was always a great feeling to see her so excited about something. When we met Banjo, he proudly showed me the print Megan liked, all the while Megan beamed excitedly through those big brown eyes. I, too, became caught up in the excitement— which must have been why I agreed to pay $30 U.S. dollars for the shirts.

I ordered a large black shirt with the guitar player print for myself while Megan ordered a medium white with a colorful, dancing woman showcased on the front.

"No worries," Banjo promised in a low, raspy voice as he tucked our crumbled bills into his front pocket. "Tomorrow morning you will have your shirts."

AFRICA TRIP

The new morning brought dark, ominous clouds, and autumn-like, overcast skies—the type of day ideal for curling up on the sofa with a fistful of rented films. Yellow umbrellas near the bar swayed back and forth after being rocked by the sudden, strong wind gusts that tore fiercely across the beach. The sun-worshippers that lined the beach the day before were no more, instead covered in jeans and sweatshirts as they huddled beneath verandas to stay out of the cold, drizzling rain.

With a healthy amount of trepidation, Megan and I skipped over the puddle-strewn path leading into the craft village as soon as we devoured breakfast the next morning. We headed into the market to pick up our shirts. Banjo, seated on the dirt floor of his darkened 'Black History Museum' shop, wasn't as jolly and warm as he appeared when we first met, looking tired and frustrated as he cursed to himself after blasting the yellow shirt laid out in front of him with a stream of brown paint. When he did notice us standing at his counter, Banjo quickly sprung to his feet.

"I have them for you," Banjo said, in a voice completely stripped of emotion. "Just the way you wanted."

The small cabinet behind the counter creaked open slowly as Banjo reached deep inside, pulling out two wrinkled but folded T-shirts and handing them to Megan—one light blue, one white.

"Ummm...where's the black one?" I asked. Banjo didn't bat an eye, keeping his poker face.

"No black shirts, my friend, so I used a blue one."

Megan detected my disappointment, shooting me a quick, calming look.

"Well," Megan stated cheerfully, as she began to unfurl the blue shirt, draping it over the counter. "Let's take a look at least."

Before my eyes, I watched Megan's expression transform from reserved optimism to downright disappointment as she viewed the drab, pre-worn shirt being passed off to us as new. The image of the guitarist had been illustrated across the chest, but not in the same, sharp, reds, greens and blacks we were sold on. Painted slightly crooked in a lone, ugly, deep brown color, the design on the finished shirt Banjo had handed us was unrecognizable. I hated it.

"Look at this, Banjo!" demanded Megan, managing to sound angry and disappointed at the same time. "This design isn't even in the same colors!"

Banjo knew he was busted. At least he didn't try to lie.

"The paints," he said. "My school didn't have the ones I needed so I used a different color."

"And the black shirt?" I piped in. "The blue is just horrible!"

Banjo knew he was beaten, shaking his head slowly.

"I only had the blue in your size," he said, apologetically, keeping his eyes low to the ground.

I grabbed the other shirt, the one designed for Megan, and unfolded it.

"Here's yours," I said aloud, draping it across the counter where the blue one had been. Though the shirt was white as Megan had requested, the brightly painted dancers promised to her highlighted in that same, drab brown. And her shirt was in worse shape than mine, a well-worn Gap shirt with yellowed sweat stains beneath the arms.

"Banjo..." Megan intoned, sounding like a mother reprimanding her child as she moved over the shirt, tracing the dancers with her index finger.

"That shirt, too, I had to do without my paints," Banjo sincerely explained. "But it is still nice, no?"

Pulling Megan aside, we spoke in low tones about the shirts, immediately remembering the mistake we made by handing him half of the cash over first before seeing the finished products. We both knew that money was gone.

"I don't want mine," I said bluntly, loud enough for Banjo to hear. "It's ugly, it's not what I wanted, and I won't wear it."

"Mine's...okay," Megan countered in a whisper, glancing over her shoulder at the shirt, still draped over the counter stall. "I mean, it's not what I wanted either, but he won't give us our money back..."

I nodded that I understood, and then Megan turned to Banjo, standing silently and looking sullen next to a handcrafted African drum.

"We'll take that one," Megan said, as she pointed to the white shirt. "But not this other one...," she said, nodding toward my blue one.

Banjo didn't argue or even look surprised—I think he knew himself that he had been taking a risk that might not pay off.

We made our way back to camp and found for the most part everyone was off doing their own thing that morning. Mary, who declined leaving with some of the guys that morning for Livingstonia, the nearby town, was spotted briefly in the bar before seeming to completely disappear. Seth had mischief in his eyes, winking at me knowingly when I caught him reading the back of a pancake box he'd pulled from one of the plastic crates. I didn't know what Seth was up to as I glanced at the gray, overcast sky, but I knew I'd find out soon.

Malawi. After the first afternoon, it was hardly the sun-filled days of relaxing stretched out on the beach that I had hoped for. A thin, black dog with sad eyes brushed against my legs as it ran to the small hole in the sand that Seth dug out the previous night for our fire, plopping itself down on the slightly smoldering coals. I know exactly how you feel, boy.

Megan and I found Bill when we scaled Ella's ladder to retrieve our books. He was stretched out across the back seat with his book held over his face.

"Been getting a lot of reading done?" he asked, swiveling to his feet as I began digging through the daypack on my seat.

"Way more than I thought I would in Malawi," I grudgingly said. "I just hope Zanzibar isn't like this."

Megan, who was watching something out of the side of the window, giggled slightly.

"I don't think everyone minds reading. Look!"

With Megan at the window, I saw our old pal Abe, seated rigidly on a tiny, canvas chair just below our window and looking as guilty as a criminal as he slyly glanced back and forth.

"So what?", Bill said, unimpressed.

"Just wait," Megan baited. "He'll do it again!"

Seated with both hands on his lap, Abe was definitely guilty of something, glancing back and forth nervously as best as his stiff frame would allow while his one fist tightly clenched a rolled-up magazine. Then, deliberately unfurling the magazine, he revealed his reading material that morning: a 'Maxim' with a nearly-naked Brittany Spears on the cover and the headline 'Sex Moves to Make You a Master,' which Abe mechanically held open wide and up to his face like he was hiding behind it.

"Oh my God!", I screamed, "That's beautiful!"

The sight of Abe was priceless. Here you had a guy who could barely get out of a chair ogling a magazine that teased "Dozens of New Positions to Go from Dud to Stud." And the way he read the magazine, too—first suspiciously checking to make sure that his wife was nowhere around, and then holding it open like he was reading the Sunday paper.

My only regret was that I didn't snap a photo of it. I was too busy crying from laughing so hard with Megan and Bill to even think about it. When I finally did maintain my composure, Abe spotted Helen returning from her little walk into the village and hid the magazine beneath his chair and underneath his bulky 'Birds of Africa' volume, then nervously scratched at his face.

I climbed down from the truck with a Lonely Planet guide on East Africa to read through just in time to hear Abe taking Helen to task for opening up her purse again, this time for some hand-made postcards that she said some village boy sold her.

"You can't even mail these!" he sighed in disgust as he grabbed at one, a bright crayon drawing of a beach.

"This paper's too thin!"

I had heard enough of Mr. Sunshine, a crotchety prick to his wife when you considered just how much she did for him. Heading off to the gazebo to read a little, I left Megan back at our tent, wanting to sleep a little more while she had the chance.

"Who knows where we'll be tomorrow," she stated as she fluffed up her pillow. "If I can sleep, I'm going to!"

****

I left Megan and found a little spot beneath a tree, where I read a little more about Nairobi, or as the guidebook referred to it, "Nairobbery." When I headed back a short time later to see if Megan was awake, I heard the clang of metal as I walked past the truck. It was Seth, fishing a large, flat frying pan from the rear of the truck.

"Hey—uh," Seth started in a whisper, spying over his shoulder. "Thanks."

"For what?"

"Ya know!" whispered Seth, "The smokes."

"Oh, that!" I replied, making sure no one from the group was nearby. "It's really no big deal. I mean, you'd do the same, right?"

"And I am!" beamed Seth in an excited whisper. "Look, have you ever tried hash cakes?"

"Hash cakes? Oh sure," I lied. "Who hasn't?!?"

"Well, I'm making up a batch. This local stuff here? Crazy shit, man!"

"How crazy?" I replied, as I pictured myself running naked through the African bush while screaming at the top of my lungs.

"The craziest!" laughed Seth.

"About one hour," he squealed in a high voice, smiling as he looked into the pan. "Come back around then and we'll have some pancakes!"

Seth looked as excited as a schoolgirl, biting his lower lip excitedly as he eyes grew wide with excitement. I wanted to ask him what would happen if someone like Helen or Mary saw the pancakes and unknowingly wanted to taste them but I figured I'd let him handle the worrying for a change. This was clearly Seth's project, anyway—Woody wasn't even interested in trying them, from what I could tell, instead sitting and smoking his Marlboros as he stretched out his long, bird-like legs.

I made absolutely no effort to be quiet when I ripped the rusty zipper of the tent door down and climbed inside. I knew Megan loved to hear about this sort of stuff. Surprisingly, though, she was already awake, biting her bottom lip nervously as she intently studied the page of her African health guide on meningitis. Great.

"I'm glad you're back", she exclaimed excitedly as she raised her eyes from the book. "Do I feel warm to you?"

Grabbing my hand just as I completed zipping shut the tent flap, she slapped my palm against her forehead as she watched my face for any change in expression.

"No honey," I said slightly exasperated, bringing my hand down to my side. "Don't you feel okay?"

I knew I was on a slippery slope the moment I looked into those slightly teary brown eyes. She needed reassurance from me more than a recital of the entire laundry list of diseases she had convinced herself she had contracted since we been traveling through Africa.

Me? I just needed a break.

Megan lowered her eyes.

"I don't know how I feel," she said softly. "Sometimes I just feel so weak and tired…"

I grasped her hand tightly.

"Yeah, I know," I said, trying to sound as reassuring as I could. "We all do. But it's going to be OK. Trust me."

Maybe I wasn't such an impatient guy after all, though I suspected those limitations expanded once I started traveling with Megan. The poor kid. I could feel her fears trembling through her as she sobbed lightly into my shoulder before she finally pulled away and dried her eyes.

****

We needed to take our mind off of things, so I was thankful Megan and I had our travel chess game to pass the time. Though we played it with an intensity that was hardly relaxing, it was still a good, stimulation way to pass the time.

After almost an hour of play, our game of chess had crawled to a virtual standstill, with my rook free and mowing down pawn after pawn though I just knew she was plotting something with her queen, slowly creeping up the right side of the board. Like always, I was deep in concentration, studying the board in the hopes of uncovering her next move while planning my next three. The deepest of concentrations. Virtually impenetrable. Until I noticed light wisp of smoke rose from the grill next to 'Ella.' Pancakes.

Keeping one eye on the chess board in front of me while the other tracked the activity near the truck wasn't easy, especially since I couldn't see anything going on. I wanted some sort of invitation, rather than come across like a desperate stoner and hang around the pancake griddle until Seth had finished with a short stack. My curiosity was piqued, though—the few, nagging concerns I had about hash cakes teaming with my Lariam and really sending me over the edge during the night were put on hold, as being able to finally try something I had heard so much about from my friends who went away to college took precedent. I just had to know what I was missing, and I had passed on enough unique opportunities in my life to know that I had to grab this one.

"Hey!" Megan cried, taking note of my stare that carried over her shoulder. "What are you looking at?!"

As those few words were spoken, Seth, the Emeril Laagasi of Overland touring, stepped out from behind "Ella' with what looked like a small plateful of golden pancakes. Noticing me, he motioned with the spatula in his hand.

"Ummm...," I said in a low voice. "I think the pancakes are ready."

Megan chuckled after turning and noticing Seth, then sat back in her chair.

"Well I don't want any," she declared, "but have fun, okay?"

I smiled to her as I rose quickly from my chair. Megan was the hippest girlfriend a guy could ask for. When she told you it didn't bother her, it really didn't.

Kissing Megan on the forehead, I crept behind Bill, nursing a second beer at the bar, and tapped him lightly on the shoulder.

"Ready for some more breakfast?" I asked.

"I think the pancakes are ready!"

Bill licked his lips.

"Yeah," he cooed. "I'm feeling a little hungry!"

When Bill and I arrived at the truck, Seth had already thought of everything, down to the syrup and the three chairs arranged in a tight semi-circle. And, of course, the feature attraction—the one-dozen, innocent-looking pancakes, slightly larger than a silver dollar and resting in three stacks on a plastic plate. With a few more cooking on the grill, Seth briefly looked up.

"Help yourself guys," he urged. "While they're warm!"

I stepped back and decided to wait for Seth, expecting Bill to do the same but instead witnessed the stout Aussie grab two, slightly brown cakes with his meaty hand and plop them down on his plate like he was in a buffet line. After drowning them in syrup and take a small bite, that was all I needed to see.

Following Bill's lead, I grabbed the three pancakes remaining in the stack and slapped them onto the clean plate next to me, then poured a small stream of syrup on the center. If I didn't know any better, I'd swear they were straight from mom's kitchen.

"So how are they, guys?" Seth asked expectantly.

Cutting off a small piece from the bottom cake with the edge of my fork, I sniffed at it briefly as I tried not to think of how awful it probably tasted. Then, with a sudden movement, I opened my mouth and chewed. Not bad. Not bad at all.

"Quite nice," Bill declared, looking down at his plate with approval. "Very nice indeed!"

"I guess you could say I perfected things over the years," Seth said, dropping the last pancake from the griddle onto the plate. "You really only taste the pancake."

I didn't know if I'd go that far—there was a sort of gritty, hard aftertaste that a lot of syrup helped hide, but they were far tastier than I thought they'd be. I downed the three on my plate quickly, expecting to experience some sort of intense high during mid-bite. And I waited.

Disappointed, I grabbed another pancake from the tiny plate and rolled it through the small puddle of syrup that remained on my plate. And even after devouring that, still nothing.

"Hey Paul," mumbled Seth through a mouthful of pancake. "Take more—there's plenty."

I politely declined. I wasn't a huge fan of pancakes to begin with, so if I wasn't getting a buzz, I didn't want to bother. Knowing Seth, four had to be plenty.

"I'm good Seth. Thanks a lot".

As Bill forked at another small stack of pancakes, Vernor and Aubrey suddenly appeared from their trip to Livingstonia, marching hastily up the main road and looking surprisingly energetic for a couple of guys who spent the better part of the day hiking.

I panicked, dropping my empty plate on the table like it was on fire. The paranoia was kicking in, at least. Seth, the old, casual pro, remained sharp, keeping his wits as he inhaled the last few bites that remained on his plate after covering the few cakes left on with a handy dish towel. You knew he found himself in this situation before. A lot.

"You guys made it back pretty good," declared Bill nervously, placing his now-empty plate on top of mine.

Aubrey and Vernor flashed a curious look to one another, the type of look you flash when you know you busted somebody. They knew they caught us in the middle of something—they just didn't know what.

"Eh...," Vernor stated, craning his neck towards the incriminating table. "It was alright. A nice hike, but nothing really up there."

Vernor moved towards the table and stopped in front of the small bowl of batter, eyeing it curiously. He looked as if he was about to pick it up until the sound of someone else approaching distracted all of us. It was Thom, limping slightly and looking completely exhausted.

"Look who finally made it," chided Aubrey, watching Thom hobble forward on his tired legs. I didn't expect Aubrey to show much sympathy for Thom, showing the hurt of hiking to Livingstonia wearing his beat-up pair of flip-flops.

"What happened, man?" Seth asked, quickly moving the bowl of batter that Vernor had been eying to the fresh bin of soapy dishwater.

Thom looked horrible. From the waist down, he was completely covered in a coat of dark, caked-on dirt.

"These shoes of mine aren't the best," Thom offered in a low voice, managing a tired smile.

"At least not for hiking."

Aubrey and Vernor took off while Thom, after throwing back a healthy belt of water, relayed the hardships of navigating up, down and up again along rock-encrusted ridges in a pair of well-worn pink flip-flops.

"I probably wouldn't have gone at all, had I known Livingstonia was so empty and all." Thom stated, putting his hands in his pockets.

"Oh well."

Darting a quick glance around camp to ensure that is was just the four of us around, Bill moved in close next to Thom.

"We've got some 'special' pancakes left, Thom," he whispered. "If you're interested."

"That does sound interesting!" Thom said with a smile.

Pulling the dish towel off like a magician, Seth grabbed the plate and thrust it toward Thom, who pulled a single cake off the last remaining stack and tore it apart with his fingers.

"Much obliged," Thom said, dropping a piece into his mouth. "Thanks for thinking of me."

Thanking Seth, I retreated back to the chess game I had abandoned, hoping that Megan wouldn't be too pissed at me for leaving her for those several minutes. I nodded to Woody when I passed him along the way, who smiled and nodded back. He just wasn't into the pancakes, though I hoped the older and wiser Woody didn't already know something I was about to find out.

"And?" whispered Megan when I sat down in front of the chess game.

"I might be a little light-headed," I offered, "but I can't really tell yet. Maybe that's it."

At that moment, for the first time since we hung out at the gazebo earlier that morning, I spotted Mary, slowing headed our way. She looked a little shy on her approach, arms folded across her chest and headed pointed towards the sand.

"Uh oh," offered Megan. "Here comes trouble!"

"Just play it cool." I reminded her, nodding towards the chess board. "It's my move."

I stared down at the chessboard, taking a deep breath to clear my mind and get myself locked back into the trance of deep concentration I found earlier.

Clear your mind. Focus.

I could hear Mary's nasally breathing behind me.

"You two are the best of friends, aren't you?" she said with melancholy.

Megan smiled at me lovingly, and then looked to Mary.

"Yeah, I'd say so," Megan offered. "I mean, you have to be."

Mary sighed loudly.

"I'll bet it's a lot of work, though, huh?"

I grabbed hold of the table with my left hand to steady it.

Easy.

"It's work, sure," countered Megan. "But it's worth it."

Inexplicably, I trained my eyes on a tiny, free black square on the board. 'Black' was really black, the darkest black I had ever seen. Cool.

****

With dinner expected soon and the setting sun making it difficult to see, Megan suggested we quit the game until later that evening and I readily agreed. We never did finish that chess game—anything resembling concentration later on that night proved impossible.

A dizzy sensation flooded my mind once I rose to my feet for the short walk to the fire ring. Stopping in mid-stride, I tried to right myself. I always prided myself on covering up my inebriations pretty well—I was not about to compromise. Friends always told me that I carried myself so well when I drank that it was virtually undetectable. I hoped I could pull it off again, though I was beginning to feel completely overwhelmed, praying that my slow, deliberate gait wouldn't give me away.

I felt only slightly better after I dropped myself into a chair next to Megan, though still clinging to the belief that I should still be able to maintain a grasp on things as long as I could stay seated. Now that's a formula for success. Truly brilliant.

"So do you feel any different yet?" whispered Megan as she threw her arm around me.

"Nope." I said, playing it straight as best I could. "A little buzz, but that's it."

In truth, I thought it best to keep the change coming over me to myself and attempt to be as chill as I possibly could. A couple of things were in play, the main one being that I ate the hash cakes voluntarily and didn't want any sympathy or concern if I made a terrible, mind-altering mistake in doing so. If the hash cakes were my ticket to my own, private hell, then I didn't want to worry Megan by taking her along for the ride. I could only imagine how much she'd panic if she had me to worry about, on top of her meningitis scare, the wild animals she was convinced were waiting to feed on her, world hunger, and the threat of nuclear war, among other things.

Most importantly, I knew I was in for a bumpy ride and I didn't want her to see me scared.

There. I said it. My being scared wasn't the manliest emotion I could exhibit, but that was the reality. No night of drinking that lasted until the sun greeted me the following morning or smoking enough weed to feel the fresh-cut lawn beneath my shoes could have possibly prepared me for the bad shit headed my way. From the very pit of my stomach, I knew I was in way over my head.

All it took were a few bites of dinner—of what I can't even remember—to send the rest of the night into one, spiraling blur. Maybe that aftershock, that intense, almost crippling high that crept over my entire body, was all part of the hash cake experience—I had no idea. As incoherent voices and blurred, shiny lights swirled past my eyes, I remember wishing that Seth would have shared that information before snacking on four of those damn things.

I was beyond high. I was completely wiped out, a limp, husk of a man propped precariously on a chair and struggling to concentrate just enough to keep himself steady. I could hear Megan's voice next to me but couldn't decipher what was being said, her words lost among the other buzzing, amplified tones filling my head. My body uncontrollably teetered back and forth against the back of my chair, my head swimming in an ocean of confused thought and nonsensical ideas. And I couldn't have been the only one.

Thom disappeared almost as soon as dinner started, saying nothing as he climbed inside the dark truck and hunkered down on his usual spot in the rear. Fellow Aussie Bill looked completely maniacal, gritting his teeth in an eerie smile while sitting frozen, completely still except for his eyes, which darted back and forth in utter paranoia. Looking stark mad, Bill at least maintained enough sense to just chill out and deal with it, rather than run his mouth about something stupid. You could have pulled the chair out from beneath him and Bill would still be locked in that same, freakish, pose—a living reminder to keep pancakes a staple of breakfast only.

And Seth. He was probably the worst of all of us, his eyes mere, puffy slits as he swaggered on his tiny steel chair next to Woody, trying to blend in as best he could with his sober assistant at his side but failing miserably. Whereas Thom, Bill, and myself knew that the best remedy included not drawing attention to ourselves, Seth didn't mind being the spectacle, singing some off-key song as he clanged away with his fork against the side of his chair to a chorus of giggles and murmurs.

Once Aubrey got under Seth's skin, though, I expected the whole Skonky debacle to resemble a children's birthday party.

"So tell us where we are going tomorrow," Aubrey said bluntly to Seth as he picked up a forkful of rice of his plate.

The look on Seth's face as he tried to locate where the voice was coming from was priceless, one I hadn't seen since the time I woke up that old, grizzled drunk who had fallen asleep at the bar in my restaurant days. Like that pickled alcoholic, Seth flashed one of those 'what the fuck?' faces for the audacious attempt at killing his buzz.

"Hey man," warbled Seth, who nearly spilled out of his chair as he struggled to grab the crumpled packages of smokes under his chair.

"You'll know tomorrow, 'kay?"

Clenching a pack of cigarettes with a tight fist, Seth then sat back in his chair hard and cursed to himself until he managed to free one of the slightly mangled cigarettes. His body was a display of contortions, arms flailing as he removed the lighter from his front pants pocket while his legs kicked high into the air, doing their best to keep him steady. Even a blind man could see something was up. But I still don't think Aubrey did.

"No, I want to know where we are going now," Aubrey demanded behind a nervous chuckle. "I think you have to tell us these things so we know."

The transformation in Seth's eyes was instant—from melancholy cool to seething, inexplicable anger in a split-second, the intensity magnified by the flick of the campfire light being pushed by the billowing ocean breeze. Dropping his lit cigarette to his side, Seth's steely gaze aimed right at Aubrey, who stared back while awaiting our leader's answer. We all did. Silently.

"He's going to hit him!" Megan whispered.

Breaking his stare, Seth sat back, smiled and took a deep breath, then lifted the cigarette to his lips and inhaled deeply.

"Tomorrow," Woody said, leaning forward in his chair and looking gravely serious.

"Trust me. Bright and early tomorrow."

The silence only persisted for a little while longer, until Woody and Seth both got up and went off to bed, I suppose. My paranoia raged. I heard the voices around me start, conspiracy-filled whispers and murmurs that swirled throughout camp. They knew. Everyone knew. I was with Seth when he ate the hash cakes, they said angrily. And I was the one who bought the big stick of weed and shared it with everyone, brazenly smoking it on the beach.

My mind raced as I sat silently, trying to decipher the voices that seemed to grow louder and louder, filled with malice. Anger. Conspiracy. Then, when they unexpectedly fell silent and Stacy approached, I expected the worst.

"Hey guys," she said solemnly to Megan and myself.

"You guys are on clean-up tonight."

I took a deep, calming breath and exhaled slowly. It was all in my mind. They didn't want to lynch me. Only my sanity was quickly spiraling out of control.

I don't remember much about doing dish duty that night, only dumping the huge pot filled with soapy water right where Helen and Abe had been sitting, who chuckled and thought little of it as they moved to drier seats on the other side of the semi-circle. Megan still had no idea what I was going through. Though I was taking things slower than I usually did. I remained committed to keeping myself steady and as quiet as possible. If I started running my mouth, letting some of that madness out that was trapped inside, it'd be a dead giveaway.

The only thought that remained constant in my mind was the notion of making it to the tent and sleeping off whatever was mind-fucking me. I struggled to keep my mind a clear, black slate, battling the intrusive, random images that fired through my brain to deceive me. Sleep was the answer, I convinced myself. It always worked on those 5 a.m. drinking binges and it would work now, too.

The skewed sensations ravaging my mind reached a peak just as I stumbled into the tent with designs on sleeping it off. I was floating now, drifting between numbing euphoria and maddening alertness, neither one being a very desirable spot. Laying my head down on my laundry bag pillow, I forced myself to reach out and touch the tent wall, making sure that it remained those few inches from my head instead of the immeasurable number of feet away it appeared to be.

I don't remember Megan falling asleep next to me, though I'm sure she did. Shutting my eyes to the dizzying, spinning shapes in front of me, the darkness offered little comfort, my mind an electrical storm of stark, confused imagery that fired one after another while burning deep within me, each more hideous than the last.

Praying silently to myself, just like anyone who's ever lived through a night of regret, I eventually fell asleep.

SHOVE OFF

"We're way ahead of schedule," Woody boasted as we entered the small shack with our passports in hand. Though no one would ever admit to it, each of us still tried to be first. "Getting to camp this afternoon will not be a problem."

As superstitious as I can be, I suspected, instantly, those very words would come back to bite us in the ass. But at least I had gotten through my night of hash cake-induced delirium relatively unscathed. Three hours later, sitting with the rest of the group beneath a tiny, barren tree outside of the Tanzanian border patrol office while a frustrated-yet-smiling Woody and a numb Seth watched as the three stoic uniformed officials flipped through Ella's registry binder once again, I remembered how much I hated being right.

"I'll be glad when this day is over," huffed Stacey, kicking at a small gray rock. "This is ridiculous."

As expected, she and Aubrey had cooled off considerably since their fling in the chalet at Khande Beach. I don't think I even saw the two of them speak to one another since then.

The mood was glum and especially depressing as we waited. When Woody and Seth, finally having produced enough documentation to satisfy the border officials, emerged from the office, the rush for camp was on.

"Well, guys," remarked Woody, ringing his hands and craned his neck towards the cab. "I guess it's time to hit the road!"

With that, we began our long descent into the mountainous highlands of Tanzania. It would take us two days to cross Tanzania and reach the coast.

Throughout the course of the next two days, Seth simply appeared awful, looking completely and utterly weak. Sitting slumped forward over lunch, his eyes looked dead and lifeless while his skin took on a sickly, lightly yellow hue. It appeared, Dominick, our long departed (and hopefully not dead) fellow traveller had nothing on Seth.

"I need to see a doctor, you know?" Seth weakly offered, coughing into his hand. "There's gotta be something wrong with me."

The yellowing skin made this armchair physician initially suspect hepatitis, which I believed would explain his weakness, too. I remembered receiving a vaccination for that contagious disease just before leaving for Africa, providing some relief when I recalled sharing several joints with him back in Malawi.

"Why not malaria, though?" Megan argued, after I told her my theory once we climbed in the truck that morning.

"Malaria," I said dismissively. "The guy's yellow, isn't he?"

"Yeah, but remember Skonky?" Megan asked, reaching for the medical guide conveniently tucked beneath her seat. "He caught malaria, like, five or six times, and you know the guides aren't taking any medication for it!"

We debated a little more on the topic, each of us referencing the battered Lonely Planet guide to support our respective argument, before letting it drop entirely. Megan suspected Seth had hepatitis, too, but still held out that there could be a touch of malaria in the mix. I did see her point. Aside from Rutger, I still hadn't witnessed another of the guides even applying mosquito repellent despite their penchant for walking around shirtless and barefoot most of the time.

I slumped back in my seat and prepared myself for probably one of the most uncomfortable and boring drives to date, a day Woody warned would be spent almost exclusively in the truck to reach camp with a brief stop in Dar es Salaam. I was looking forward to our stop in Dar—after several days of remote, rainy weather, it'd be nice to at least see a bustling city again, even if the scorching late-morning sun persisted. Then we'd take a short ferry ride, camp overnight and then a longer ferry ride to Zanzibar tomorrow. Zanzibar. The name just conjured remote and exotic beauty. I still held out hope that we'd hit a glorious, sun-filled beach before long. We had to.

I grabbed a short story collection from the backpack beneath my seat and got through a couple of them to help pass the time. The incessant rattling of the cab and the unexpected jolts had become routine, but, like a confined prisoner, I had learned to adapt.

Nothing could be done about the funky smell, though. I didn't think I could ever grow used to the foul-smelling chemistry of the stale exhaust from the truck mixed with the sheer stink of ten, sweaty people cramped together. The yellow, sweat-stained shirt that always found its way to Aubrey's back had remained the worst, though Abe, decked out in a sleeveless shirt on especially warm days, could be pretty damn ripe himself. At the very least, I always soaked my blue shirt and rung it out every night, leaving it to dry across some seats in the truck overnight so it would be ready to wear the following morning. There is nothing more upsetting than seeing black water spill out of your clothes while you are ringing them.

By late morning, I felt like I was baking inside the truck, with the hot, searing rays of the sun driving unfettered into every window available. My arm, resting against the window, glowed with a deep, red color, reminding me once again of the horror stories African Wanderer related at orientation about people falling asleep in the truck and waking up scorched. I spread a large dollop of suntan lotion on both my arms and then my face to prevent myself from living that fate.

The sweltering heat reached a crescendo by the time Woody pulled us over to stop for lunch on the outskirts of Dar, amid scores of people on bicycles and on foot who glanced at us curiously the moment we began descending the truck. Even sickly Seth looked warm, finally ditching his quilt on the front seat as he slowly followed Woody to the rear of the truck to retrieve lunch.

Dar was filthy—a swirling, polluted sea of congestion. Dilapidated vans spewed black exhaust while swaggering down the pothole-ridden road. I could just feel the heavy thickness of the putrid air as it filled my lungs and my stomach slowly turned sour.

Quickly, I put my sunglasses on. Though cracked on one handle, the broken pair would at least shield my eyes from the onslaught of swirling debris that filled the street. If there was something grosser than eating sardines for lunch on a hot and humid day in the middle of such urban filth, I couldn't think of it. The mere sight of watching Woody meticulously open the warm can and then dump the brown, smelly contents of it onto a plate was just about enough for me. My stomach jumped momentarily out of rebellion, as if to say there was no way it would allow those foul and fishy creatures to enter it. I obliged, fishing out the obligatory jar of peanut butter I had grown to rely on for so long.

"Come now, Paul," Woody urged, fishing out a fat hunk from the bottom of the pile and plopping it down on some bread. "There's plenty here, you know."

I had to turn away from the plate, my eyes locked on what looked like a small bone or spine protruding from one of the brown hunks of flesh. I suddenly remembered why I tried sardines once, years ago swimming in hot sauce, and had never attempted it again.

With my peanut butter sandwich in hand, I made my way over to Megan, leaning against a small patch of cyclone fence. She attacked the bulky sandwich wrapped tightly in her fist relentlessly, those two over-flowing bowls of cereal I saw her with early in the morning a distant memory.

"Peanut butter," I told her, when she put her sandwich down for a drink of water. "Those sardines are nasty, right?"

As she held the bottle to her lips, I glanced down briefly on her plate and spotted the incriminating evidence—a small fleck of sardine, fallen from between the bread and stuck to her plate. My stomach jumped again, this time the heaviest yet.

"You're eating those?!" I exclaimed, backing away from her plate as if the sandwich would attack. "I thought you hated those...like I do."

Calmly, she lowered the bottle and grabbed hold of the soggy and messy sandwich in front of her.

"I'm too hungry, man," Megan apologized. "I'm just too hungry."

I let her finish her sandwich in peace, hoping that was the last I'd ever see of sardines, anywhere.

Our adventure within the city limits of Dar es Salaam was brief, and we soon found ourselves back in the truck, heading toward the ferry. I knew we had to be close once the streets of some small, urban area we entered resembled a crowd departing from a Rolling Stones concert. The sun had just begun to droop down past the horizon while we found ourselves in a storm of humanity that barely seemed to take notice of our truck as it boldly inched forward along the swarming street. Plodding slowly along, the rush of people shuttling past us was a true mix: women with children in tow, doing their best to pull wandering children along quickly; men who, despite the humid night air, remained sharply dressed in their button-down suits as they retreated from work; and scores of young people arm and arm, laughing with friends as they jogged past slower-moving pockets to commandeer their place in line.

We walked on foot with the rest of the crowd as one ferry departed without us. Everyone, that is, except Woody and Seth, stationed behind the wheel of Ella and ready to lurch the truck forward through the crowd once the ferry pulled back into port. We became a mild spectacle once again, but as always, it never got too uncomfortable. As the only Caucasian sect of people I saw even near the ferry, I would have been compelled to stare myself.

Watching the fully-crammed ferry that departed before my eyes, I estimated the full, round-trip journey to be slightly less than ten, efficient minutes, not including the mess of tangled, weaving bodies that struggled to free themselves of one another once the gates flew open wide. At the same time, I remained vigilant as the bodies in queue behind me pushed forward as more and more people milled around us in anticipation, each jockeying for an enviable spot for the next departure. I never could shake the apprehension I had about being pick-pocketed. At the other extreme, Mary, the poster child of naivety herself, looked out across the water with a goofy grin on her face and her thin-strapped money pouch dangling from her neck.

"Mary better hope what they say is true," I told Megan. "That God really does look out for children and fools."

The building anxiousness of the crowd was palpable as the empty ferry, a flat, island of steel, slowly drew nearer to us. Women clutched their children fast, ready to pull them off their feet as they sprung forward, while Woody, manning the lead vehicle in a small procession of three, held his iron grip over the wheel, ready to roll forward in the idling vehicle before being buried by the mob.

All eyes remained locked on the arriving. Finally, when it carefully eased into the dock in front of us, we knew it was time. No sooner did the ferry come to a complete stop did the obnoxiously loud wail of an air horn fill the air, the signal for the gates to drop.

And then the rush began.

Exhibiting the same, steely boldness he aired out weaving us through the highlands, Woody let up on Ella's brake and eased her forward immediately, tapping his horn briefly only once, when an older man stopped with his bicycle in the middle of Woody's designated parking space. The rest of us became swallowed by the rushing crowd, carried across it until breaking free right behind the truck. The swarm seemed relentless, with people spreading out in all directions, mindful of only one thing—finding a spot on the ferry.

I had pictured something completely different when I first learned we would be taking a ferry, yet, as crowded as the ferry ride was, it never became uncomfortable. With all of us spreading ourselves out around the truck, we had managed to secure a small, yet relatively spacious area to ourselves. A space that Vernor, of all people, shared a small moment of bliss with Mary, as the two showcased the mutual skill of ballroom dancing by grabbing hold of one another and traipsing around the deck, amid many pairs of curious and questioning eyes. Even for Vernor, it ranked as a pretty bizarre spectacle, seeing him glide across the deck with a gleeful Mary in tow.

When we reached the other side of the dock a short time later, the mass of confined humanity spilled out as soon as the familiar horn sounded, lifting the gate. Slightly more orderly than an evacuation of a toppling highrise, there was little Woody could do with Ella than inch forward slowly through the streets until he found enough clearance to anchor her to a curb to give us enough time to climb back aboard. In that sense, it was a plus we stood out in the crowd, helping identifying the white heads bobbing up and down.

Helen and Abe brought up the rear as usual, with Helen being badgered by a gaunt woman with a small child held tight to her bosom. The woman was definitely one of the most persistent we had seen yet, thrusting her small daughter at Helen while she pleaded for food, keeping pace with Helen's quickening steps. It wasn't until Helen finally landed her foot on the bottom of Ella's step, after politely saying 'No,' did the woman finally back down, throwing her free hand up into the air in frustration while cursing under her breath.

Thankfully, that was the single minor accident that marked our first ferry trip—rather uneventful when you consider how the slow-moving truck, before we managed to climb aboard and secure it, would have made an easy target for crime. The worst scenario I had in mind consisted of a small, yet stealthy, group of bandits leaping aboard while the door swung open and grabbing anything they could get their hands on before disappearing into the still mob-like crowd.

Night had fallen upon us by the time the road had opened up enough for Woody to pick up some speed, all but guaranteeing it'd be another one of those dreadful situations that required fumbling through the darkness in order to set up camp. I held out a little hope for something better when I discovered the place we were staying at was known as 'Makquena Lodge,' but that was all dashed when I learned 'Lodge' translated into 'tired and barren patch of dirt for your tent.'

That night at Makquena Lodge was easily one of the steamiest we had spent in Africa, extremely humid with no breeze to speak of. Listening to Woody explain the itinerary to us for the following day, it seemed like sheer madness, a schedule so tight it just sounded like a disaster waiting to happen.

"The first ferry you need to catch is at seven," he said, his voice booming despite having his head lowered into the large kettle of dinner he methodically stirred. "The one we just took, right? After that, back in the truck. We need to make good time—about an hour into Dar, at most."

Woody removed the wooden spoon from the pot, now covered in a reddish sauce, and then plunked it back in, stirring it again while continuing to recount the plan as if he were thinking aloud instead of communicating to us.

"The ferry from Dar to Zanzibar leaves only once a day. We miss that and we're done for." I understood Woody's apparent nervousness a little better once Seth mentioned he'd be staying behind instead of Woody to look after the truck—and to visit a physician to find out what was causing his weakness and yellow coloring.

"It'll be Woody's first time there, just like yours, but we have a contact there that's gonna take care of everything," Seth mumbled as he sat in his chair with a bottle of water. "If things get really bad, I may have to leave the tour, but if I see a doctor and get fixed right up, I should be fine."

Looking at him close-up for probably the first time all day, his skin clearly had a more-yellow tinge to it than it had previously, while his face appeared even more drawn-out and tired than usual. It was hepatitis. It had to be.

If that was the last we saw of Seth, it had been a hell of a ride, though I had a feeling, based on the whole ruggedness factor of all of these overland guides, he'd be right where we left him when we returned from Zanzibar. And as far as Woody taking us over to the island, I welcomed the idea, not only because Seth was in no shape to lead us, but because Woody, providing he relaxed once he got there, deserved a bit of a beach break for carrying the load by himself for the past several days. In Zanzibar, Woody wouldn't have to worry about driving for several days straight, or slaving over a boiling pot of food every night. All of that nonsense would be left back on the mainland. Based on how he handled the tour after Seth went down, Woody had managed to win my complete confidence.

Woody continued stirring the large, cast-iron pot a few minutes longer until placing the lid careful on top and slinking back into his chair. I knew what that meant: we had hours to kill before dinner.

The best way for me to kill time on the trip had always been to shower—not only to shake off the truck stink, but it became especially vital on the hot, humid evenings when every piece of clothing on you just seems to stick from sweat. Makqena Lodge, though, with its outdoor showers, really put my modesty to the test.

Grouped together on a tiny, plaza-like platform near the beach, the five showers, to a particularly curious eye, left little to the imagination. When showering, the only thing that separated you from the outside world was the thin, splitting thatch walls of your individual unit and the soap bubbles on your body.

Still, despite their design, the showers did retain enough privacy, confirmed when Stacey, Aubrey and Thom each headed straight for them after a campground guide pointed them out. Waiting back until an older, European guy from another tour company departed his shower, Megan and I made our move.

Despite the pitfalls I mentioned earlier, I still clung to every opportunity for Megan and I to shower together throughout Africa. It was no substitute for the lack of intimacy, but showering with a woman was a special privilege. And I still noticed that wry, knowing look in Megan's eyes as she surveyed my body while laying out our fresh clothes and towels on the small bench inside the stall.

The most flawed aspect of the shower design was the changing area, where the thatch walls only seemed to elevate waist-high and the floor actually seemed to rise, further fueling my skepticism that some aspects of the shower design weren't there for ambience. It all seemed too convenient to me.

As I fidgeted with the slightly busted lock, trying to force the black, metal bar into the cracked wooden hole, Mary nervously approached the empty shower next to us. Pausing momentarily as she looked back and forth across the beach, she slowly stepped inside.

"I don't like this at all!" she said aloud, directed to no one in particular. "Not one bit."

I said nothing to encourage her, instead helping Megan finish laying out our soaps and shampoos when I completed my wrestling match with the lock. I suspected it'd bother Mary, knowing a man was in the adjacent stall, so I decided it best to go about my business and ignore her. Like I usually did.

With everything in place, I turned the faucet handle slowly and adjusted the temperature before we rushed into the water. Then, compensating for the low thatch wall, Megan hunched herself low, leaving her shirt for last, before pulling it off over her head while leaping into the shower. I saved my pants for last before joining her, fearing the same lower walls and elevated floor made my manhood available for the entire world to gaze at.

The water felt nice—not too hot, but warm enough to be refreshing. Each shower head rose from the stone floor and crooked back down to resemble a shepherd's cane. And once you were beneath the pulsating jets, you could just faintly make out who was in the showers adjacent to you, though only from the neck up as expected. Aubrey must have finished just as we jumped in, because only Stacey and Thom remained, Stacey singing some disco song from the 1970s to herself as she ducked her long hair beneath the spraying water.

I forgot all about Mary until I felt the water pressure hiccup briefly and heard a steady trickle coming from the directly adjacent thatch wall. Letting Megan do a final rinse while I shampooed my hair, I ducked beneath the shower to rinse and heard a cry as soon as I came back up.

"Can you see me?" I heard a voice shriek with horror as I wiped the soap out of my eyes. "Can you?"

I turned my attention to the voice. Mary, of course, nervously laughingly as she fumbled for something.

"What's going on?" Megan whispered to me, crouched low as she pulled her panties up to her waist.

"It's Mary," I said disgustedly. "Miss Modesty herself."

"You can't see anything, Mary!" Megan shouted toward the wall in Mary's direction.

We giggled as we headed back to the truck to drop our dirty laundry off, where Seth still sat, looking exhausted.

"So how are you doing, anyway?" I asked.

Looking up at my through his heavy, slightly puffy eyelids, Seth didn't even appear to have the energy to speak.

"Just tired, man," he mumbled. "Just so unbelievably tired."

I glanced around camp quickly and spotted only Woody, sitting with his hands on his lap.

"So it wasn't the weed, was it,? You didn't smoke it all...?" I asked Seth softly, watching Megan out of the corner of my eye as she fumbled with a backpack on the truck. He smiled lightly.

"No way, man," he stated. "It's more than that."

Megan and I plodded over to the bar once she finished cinching up the backpack and returned just as Woody put the finishing touches on dinner. That night, it consisted of a whole mess of pap, that white flavorless paste I had mistaken for mashed potatoes once before, and some red sauce to pour over it. I don't think there's enough red sauce in the world to make pap tasty enough for my palate.

Woody used dinner as a sort of mini-debriefing, again going over the fine points of the next day while stressing to us the importance of being ready to leave on time.

"If we miss just one ferry," he warned. "You'll lose an entire day in Zanzibar, so we really need to hurry tomorrow, guys."

A nervous excitement was building inside me, as I imagined five days of complete freedom as Megan and I wandered across the exotic, tropical island, eating fresh seafood, finally stocking up on souvenirs, and sprawled out on a gloriously sunny beach. We were due.

As dinner wound down, a young man sharply dressed in a crisp, black suit with a flashlight in his hand strode by camp, stopping once

Woody waved heartily to him. "How's everything, my friends?" the man asked merrily as he scanned the group.

"Well," Woody replied. "Very well."

Spinning around to get a better glimpse at our guest, Mary listened momentarily as Woody and he exchanged pleasantries. Then, when a break in the conversation occurred, Mary jumped in.

"Let me ask you," she chirped to the well-dressed man. "Can I leave my laundry here with someone to do for me while we're at Zanzibar? We're coming back here, right Woody?"

Woody nodded silently before the man replied.

"I'm sorry, miss," he explained sympathetically. "We don't do that here."

Mary stared at the man briefly then bit her bottom lip. "Do you have a girlfriend or wife who will?"

Chuckling the ignorance off in a low voice, the man backed up a few feet from us as he turned to walk away.

"No, no, no," he replied. "That's something you're going to have to do."

Mary shrugged her shoulders as the man waved a final time and disappeared down a narrow footpath.

STONE TOWN

"Good job this morning, guys!" Woody beamed, inspecting our now-barren camp like a drill sergeant, hands clasped tightly behind his back as he marched through the sun-scorched grass.

"We can eat on the ferry too, right?" whined Megan, just as Woody walked past. "I mean, if we get hungry...."

Woody flashed a quick look at Seth, buried back underneath his familiar quilt. Then, dropping the makeshift hood as he answered Megan's question, Seth's countenance imparted why he'd be staying behind.

"There's food on the ferry, yes," Seth mumbled, revealing his puffy, dull eyes and pale, yellow skin. Seth couldn't look any more yellow. He was a human post-it-note.

"Tell 'em about the market at night, Woody," Seth said weakly, coughing harshly after completing his sentence.

Every single one of us watched Seth as he slowly rose to his feet from his chair and limped over to the fire, dragging his quilt behind through the dusty footpath. Looking at him weakly hold himself up as he stood, shivering, I stopped wondering if he'd continue along with us when we returned back from Zanzibar. Wondering if he'd still be alive was the question that needed answering.

Woody, picking up on our concern, came across as especially chipper when he described dinner for us that night.

"Like Seth was saying, there's a huge outdoor fish market right on the beach," Woody explained, gesturing slightly with his hands. "And from what I hear, it's great. You pick out what you want and they cook it right there on the beach for you, nice and fresh!"

Fresh fish. I could feel my taste buds awaken at the mere mention of it. An enormous tuna fillet or a hot, steamed lobster would go a long way towards helping me forget about those damned sardines. Sardines. They gave other, tasty fish a bad name.

When the pair of cabs arrived, Seth managed a slight wave, mumbling something about looking after the stuff we left behind and getting himself to a doctor. He looked bad, but I had a feeling he'd be fine if he really would get himself to a doctor instead of trying to pull a 'Skonky' and muddle through it.

The cabbies sped us to the first ferry, the one back to the mainland of Dar, quickly, leaving me to suspect Woody gave the drivers the same urgent plea he gave us a day earlier. The ferry ride was the same mixture of frantic, crowded chaos as the previous day, though our drivers were proficient at guiding us through the massive, departing crowds once we climbed back aboard the cabs when the ferry reached the other side. They weaved back and forth around people like they were bright orange cones on a driver's education course.

Woody appeared to have thought of everything to ensure everyone's inaugural visit to Zanzibar went as well as it could, right down to pointing out a competitive change bureau a few blocks from the gigantic ferry terminal we were scheduled to depart from in less than an hour. It was a great relief to actually have a pocket full of local currency for a change, especially with lunchtime quickly approaching and the long ferry ride to Zanzibar ahead of us.

After handing each of us a crème-colored ticket, Woody marched us down a congested main road clogged with exhaust-spewing vehicles and people on bicycles to the ferry terminal, where we politely side-stepped at least a half-dozen vendors selling everything from sunglasses to bagged cashews. Pausing briefly, I counted out a small handful of change and handed it to a teenage boy for a cold bottle of water. It had been ages since I actually tasted cold, bottled water.

As we approached the steel ramp that led up to the huge, white ship, Woody led us to one side for a final briefing.

"Look for me once we land in Zanzibar," he instructed. "If we stay together, it'll be easier for us to find Sharif, the guide who's supposed to take care of us in Stone Town."

"Sharif?" Stacey quizzed Woody. "What does he look like?"

Woody shrugged and gestured wildly. "I dunno," he said, flopping his arms back down to his side. "Hopefully, he'll find us."

"...And have your passports ready to pull out, too," he reminded us.

As I studied the sturdy ticket in my hand, I heard Abe, standing nearby, whisper something to Helen, who then dug through her small handbag before shrugging her shoulders after coming up empty. Abe's face turned very sour, then lightened slightly as he stepped forward and addressed Woody.

"Umm...I don't have my passport," Abe stated firmly, looking in Helen's direction. "I thought my wife was supposed to bring it, but she tells me she didn't."

****

Woody must have been thrown for a loop at the news but remained calm, moving in close to keep the conversation from reaching the ears of the white-uniformed crew members of the ferry waiting to set sail.

"You're sure, Abe?"

"Mmm-hmmm," Abe replied, removing his baseball cap to scratch his head. "It must be back in the safe. Inside the truck."

My stomach sank briefly inside me when Woody thoughtfully paused, an expression I interpreted as a sure sign we'd return for the old fart's passport. The suspense was palatable, with all of us glancing at one another while we observed our leader mulling things over thoughtfully. "We're not going back, guys," Woody firmly stated as he looked Abe in the eye. "We'll figure it out when we get to Zanzibar. If the island is as loose as I heard, it shouldn't be a problem."

It was a choice we could all live with and I was glad Woody had the guts to try it. With that crisis in check for the moment, we followed Woody and walked up the steel ramp to the ship, where we each handed our tickets to a portly woman who ripped off a small square from each before handing them back.

"Keep these," she urged. "Round-trip."

Aboard the large ship and with a 'standard passage' ticket in our hand, our only option was to follow the stairs down below deck. I never learned what perks—if any—'premium passage' ticket-holders received, other than being allowed to sit above deck in a small enclosure.

I expected the worst, but, instead, I followed the group through the stairwell and into the air-conditioned seating area, I couldn't help but crack a telling, wide smile like I had gotten away with something. Compared to the traveling I had grown accustomed to in Africa, where passengers were always stuffed into tight spaces, the ferry to Zanzibar was pure luxury. Rows of spacious, cushioned chairs dotted the entire floor, offering plenty of room to stretch out on the just over half-full ship. A bartender on the far end mixed a delicious-looking, bright yellow drink, dressing it with speared chunks of juicy pineapple. Crew members with bags of fresh macadamia nuts walked the aisles, smiling cheerfully. Two large-screen television sets in the front of the room, broadcasting some incomprehensible martial arts movie. I eased myself into a soft, black chair near the middle of an empty row.

If this were any indicator, Zanzibar would be a blast.

For the most part, the group sat on the ferry within a couple of rows of each other, though speeding across the ocean after leaving the dock proved too much at times for Woody, who disappeared on several occasions for fresh air from above. I didn't blame him after I began to feel a little queasy myself, with my stomach bouncing as I watched the waves slap hard against the ship from the window on our immediate right. We were flying, skipping across the Indian Ocean like a big, white stone.

With little fanfare, a suddenly chummy Aubrey and Stacey settled into the two seats directly in front of us. Stacey was so transparent it was comical, batting her eyes lovingly at Aubrey as she rested her head on his shoulder. When she started whispering in his ear, it was clear Aubrey was eating it up, who returned her overtures by holding her hand.

"I'll bet she knows who she wants to bunk with," I whispered to Megan, who watched the whole bizarre scene play out with me. Megan just shook her head.

The fairly relaxing ferry ride lasted just around three hours, marred slightly when I felt something crawling on me and discovered a big, black cockroach slowly ascending up my bare leg. Smacking it off me onto the floor, I kept a weary eye trained on the floor for the remainder of the ride.

When the first glimpses of land came rushing towards us through the window, seats immediately began to empty as people began milling around the stairwell, all anxiously awaiting that pending moment of freedom. Most of us hung back with Woody—why bother hurrying when you didn't even know where you were going? Minutes passed before the engine suddenly fell silent while the ship shook slightly as it softly bumped the dock. When the doors flew open and a steady stream of people began spilling out, I knew we had arrived.

Zanzibar.

Grabbing a firm hold of my backpack, I kept Woody and the others in sight as Megan and I followed them and hiked out onto the expansive, wooden pier, the entire foot of it enveloped with waiting people ready to whisk their loved ones away. Rows and rows of broken-down taxicabs crowded the street.

"There's more people here than I figured," Woody said, sheepishly as he scanned the crowd for some kind of acknowledgement from a friendly face.

"So what does he look like, then?" Bill inquired as he flipped his darkened sunglasses up. "This guide?"

"I dunno," Woody responded, sounding slightly annoyed as he flailed his arms in the air. "But hopefully he'll see this and find us." Woody tugged quickly at the green 'African Wanderer Adventure Tour' T-shirt he was wearing. Yep, that would do it. Or else maybe we'd be spotted since we were the only herd of lost-looking white people that had exited the ship.

Standing together in a small, vulnerable-looking circle just off the pier, we were approached by a few zealously misleading cabbies who claimed to be 'the ones we were looking for' until Woody politely refused them and sent them on their way. It wasn't until most of the cabs had departed, some full, some empty, did we notice a short, dark-complexioned man with a round belly approach us with a warm, genuine smile. Instantly, we all knew it was Sharif.

"Greetings!" the man said cheerily, spreading his arms wide above his head. "Greetings to everyone!"

Clad in billowy, white clothing and black sandals, his eyes sparkled with merriment as he suddenly grabbed Woody's hand and shook it firmly.

"Sharif!" Woody exclaimed, with a trace of relief in his voice as he slung his bag over his shoulder. "I was hoping you'd find us!"

"No worries," Sharif replied. "You were easier to pick out of the crowd than I would be!"

Like little, hatchling chicks, we stuck uncomfortably close to Sharif as he led us to the tiny immigration hut a few blocks away from the pier, my heel being stepped on by Abe, our illegal cargo, on more than one occasion, as if I needed a reminder that we should have left him behind.

Sharif beamed in delight the entire way, walking alongside Woody while reassuring him he'd take care of every single thing during our stay in Zanzibar. With his slight potbelly creeping up through his shirt and the coarse beard, Sharif was Africa's answer to Santa Claus, our jolly and capable protector.

The afternoon air was rife with humidity, made worse by the sight of the glorious blue ocean we walked parallel to. At some point during our walk, Woody must have clued Sharif in on the situation with Abe's passport, because Sharif pulled Abe to the side with him just as we approached the outside counter of the little hut.

"Just go on," Sharif ordered, motioning us towards the building while he positioned himself in front of Abe. "We'll be waiting for you right here."

As I anticipated, immigration was a non-event, with the lone, silent attendant too busy routinely checking the never-ending flow of papers from the arriving passengers to ever look up and notice Abe, hunched over even lower than usual and behind Sharif to hide from a detecting eye.

I stood with my daypack tightly clutched in my hand as we waited near the main intersection for the cabs Sharif had summoned to take us the hostel we'd be staying at. Meanwhile, we watched a parade of hawkers with fresh pineapples and locals with full, covered baskets shuffle past. As I waited, my eyes already revealed to me the uniqueness that was Zanzibar, a true melting pot when it came to the racial diversity of its people. The people who called Zanzibar home were a varied mix of native Africans and Middle-Eastern people, who I later learned, were descendants of the spice traders who settled on the island long ago and Indians.

The entire group was crowded into two, fairly clean cabs when they arrived a short time later and sped down a series of cramped, stone-covered streets laced with buildings, each stacked one on top of another and creating a somewhat closed-in sensation. The housing was very nondescript—dull, rock structures that appeared to have been standing for generations.

"Where we are now is called Stone Town," Sharif said from his seat at the front of our cab. "It's the oldest part of Zanzibar—some of these buildings you see are centuries old!"

Though I had never been to an urbanized area of the Middle East and only had images of television documentaries as a reference, I could clearly see that same influence in Stone Town. Its crowded market stalls, selling bright tapestries, linens and exotic spices lined one after another on its busy streets. A bell chimed in the distance—the call to prayer for practicing Muslims.

"This hardly seems like Africa, no?" queried Sharif, as we passed two men in traditional Middle-Eastern garb, disappearing into an adjacent doorway.

Our hostel, an ordinary, white stucco building, was only a few, long blocks from the busiest section of Stone Town, rife with storefronts, makeshift souvenir stands and people—lots of people. We'd be close enough to the action but not to close.

While Woody and Sharif worked out the arrangements with a thin, dodgy-looking manager, struggling to keep cool with a small, circular fan behind the counter, Megan and I went off with the key handed to us and found our way to our room, just off the stairway on the second, more humid floor. The windows that faced the hallway and the door were lined with thick, steel bars.

"That's a little unnerving, isn't it?" I asked Megan as I forced the key into the sticking lock.

"We should be pretty safe, though," reasoned Megan, watching my struggles. "I mean, we have a key and even we can't get in."

When I heard the tumbler finally click, I eased the shaky doorknob open and pushed forward until the door finally gave. At least it had a bed.

It wasn't the worst room I ever stayed in, but it left a little to be desired, though I don't think I could ever get used to sleeping under a mosquito net—especially like the old, weathered one that hung low above the double-bed. The screenless windows that overlooked the alley, also cloaked in bars, opened only slightly but we did have a large, industrial-sized fan to use as we pleased, which we immediately positioned toward the bed to cool down the room. The mini-fridge was an especially nice touch—I always appreciated cold water. Overall, the room was barren and a little rundown, but serviceable nonetheless.

Dropping our backpacks on the bed, we double-checked the lock on our door before heading down for a quick briefing. The one issue that needed to be agreed upon was how long we'd be staying in Stone Town—the three days originally planned on, or shorted to two so we could pick up another day at the beach resort we'd be staying at further north. The sticking point was how each of us wanted to spend our time in Stone Town, a choice made complicated because of an itinerary that actually consisted of interesting activities for once, like a tour of a spice plantation, an excursion to Prison Island, which boasted a tortoise habitat, and a speedboat trip in search of marine life on the Indian Ocean.

For me, the dilemma was trying to narrow down what I wanted to do. I figured taking the spice tour was a gimmee, but the tortoises also sounded pretty cool and could conceivably be scheduled on the same day, one right after another. While we discussed all of the options as a group, to determine if it was feasible to move on from Stone Town the day after next, Mary let her intentions be known. She wanted no part of Stone Town.

"Spice Tour, eh?" she said, glancing briefly at the brochure before tossing it on a table. "That's doesn't sound interesting to me—not when we could leave tomorrow and go to the beach."

Then Aubrey spoke up.

"I'm doing the spice plantation tour tomorrow," he said, firmly as he set his brochure aside.

"Let's do it, too," Megan stated, excitedly, turning towards me.

"Alright then," I told Sharif. "We'll go, too."

Mary's expression sank as the list of people interested in the spice tour continued to grow, then, surprisingly, she signed on herself after realizing exploring Stone Town by herself might be a little dull. Everyone except Bill and Thom, who planned to explore the nightlife later that evening and couldn't be bothered with the early wake-up time of 8 a.m. joined the tour group. Along with Aubrey, Helen and Abe, we also signed on to see the tortoises of Prison Island when we returned from the spice plantation late in the afternoon. Tomorrow would be a busy day, but since it would be our only one in Stone Town before moving on to the beach resort, we had to make the best of it.

With our agenda finally squared away, which included meeting back at the hostel around 7 p.m. so we could walk down as a group to the fish market for dinner, everyone split up and went their separate ways. As I watched Bill and Thom race out the front door, headed for the souvenir stalls, I realized Megan and I wouldn't be going anywhere until she laid down first for one of her infamous afternoon naps. Grudgingly, I lay down next to her—and fell asleep well before she did.

Waking almost an hour later, Megan and we grabbed a quick fast food lunch, a surprisingly good chicken sandwich, and followed the noise of people and cars until it led us to the middle of Stone Town. The heat of the day was stifling—we had brought both of our liter-and-a-half water bottles along and feared it wouldn't be enough.

The shopkeepers and the stall-owners were a fairly even mix of native Africans, people of Middle Eastern descent and Indians, yet the one thing they had most in common was their aggressiveness in hawking their wares.

"Put it on, sir!" pleaded an older black man managing a rickety stall when he saw me pick up a bright Rastafarian hat. "That hat was made for you!"

I politely declined when I remembered the cracker white woman I pointed out to Megan on the ferry to Zanzibar, dressed in a billowy African shirt and looking completely out of place. As a fellow cracker who knew enough about the Rastafarian movement to know it called for Africans to free themselves from the shackles of whitey and return to their motherland, not purchasing the hat was probably a good idea.

I halfheartedly examined the assorted chess sets everyone seemed to be selling. For Megan, her obsession quickly became the khanga—a brightly colored, versatile cloth local women used for everything from fastening around their waist as a makeshift skirt to knotting around their neck into a cradle for their baby. Instantly, I knew it was going to be a long day of shopping.

"What about this one?" Megan'd ask me, after racing into any store with khangas in the window and holding up every bright red one the clerk managed to find, each one of them looking nearly identical to me.

Megan stopped in her tracks when she saw it. The one.

"In here!" she cried excitedly. "That's what I'm looking for!"

The red and pink khanga, sandwiched in between a dark blue and a green one, didn't look too different from some of the other ones I thought I had examined with her already, but if it meant she would just buy one and we could move on, it was the most beautiful thing I ever laid eyes on.

Megan and I, after entering the shop, burrowed through a small opening in between several unopened boxes and approached the two African men behind the counter about the khanga. Flashing a quick look at one another, the shorter, slightly annoyed man hopped over, grabbed the metal pole the other man handed to him, and speared the khanga down from its place in the window.

"It's just beautiful!" remarked Megan, holding it against her as she looked down at the garment. Along its bottom, written in white, was a phrase in Swahili.

"Can you tell me what this says?" Megan asked the man politely, still admiring the khanga as she wrapped it around her waist.

"It's Swahili," the man replied, slightly bored.

"Yeah, but what does it mean?" Megan inquired.

The man paused and looked away, then placed his hands in his pockets.

"Ummm...'there is beauty all around us'....," the man mumbled, shrugging his shoulders as his voice trailed off.

Megan shot me a quick look and smiled, then turned back to the man.

"Are you sure?" she teased. "You sound like you made that up!"

"Yeah," I offered. "Tell us what it really says!"

The man's eyes grew smaller and a little harder as he started back at us.

"Do you think I don't know what I'm talking about?" he said accusingly, then turned to his partner at the counter and barked something in Swahili.

"He'll tell you what it says—exactly what I said it does!"

Megan suddenly looking very uncomfortable and a little scared, passing the khanga to one hand and holding it low. Sensing our humor may have been a little too subtle, I did what I could to avoid the train wreck I feared was coming.

"Hey, we're sorry," I said. "We we're just joking around."

Acting like he didn't hear me, the shopkeeper tiptoed back through the maze of fabrics and handed the pole to the man still behind the counter. His steely gaze appeared to lighten a little when he returned.

"So do you want it?" he asked Megan, still sounding annoyed. "400."

With sixty of their dollars equaling approximately one US dollar, it seemed like a great deal at just under $7 US. Bargaining was still necessary, however, an art form a virgin like Megan was still learning the finer points of.

"Three hundred," she replied calmly. "I'll take it for three hundred."

Judging by the shopkeeper's angered expression at Megan's response, we must have pissed him off far greater than I thought. He didn't want to play any more games—he didn't even look like he cared if he got the sale or not. He just wanted us out.

"400!" he stated, his voice rising angrily.

"And I said 300!" Megan replied, just as loudly.

With the speed of a striking snake, the man snatched the khanga from her hand. Megan stood stunned.

"Go buy it from an Indian, then," the shopkeeper threatened as he turned his back to us. "This is Africa! I will not sell it to you!"

We both watched silently as the man hopped back over the counter and disappeared into a small room in the back. The other man wouldn't even look our way.

"Let's get out of here," I said. "They won't sell it to us."

"But I like that one!" Megan begged. "I was just trying to bargain with him!"

Grabbing her hand, I led her out of the shop and back into the street, where we played all of the events back over to figure out what the hell happened in there. We settled on the following: the guy was a jerk and we pissed him off further with our jokes. I thought Megan could have been a little more flexible in her bargaining, especially given the guy's quickly deteriorating mood, but she disagreed.

"I go in low, he raises me, and then we agree on the price," she said, scanning additional storefronts for another red khanga. "That's the way it's done!"

We checked out a few more shops for khangas, with Megan lamenting the entire time about the perfectly unique red-and-pink that had slipped through her fingers.

"Look," I reasoned soon after, glancing at my watch. "It's been almost a half-hour. Why don't you go in there and try to buy it? He may not even remember you!"

The odds were slim, but enough for her to cling to for her one-of-a-kind khanga. Megan would tell you otherwise, but she was pretty gutsy when she needed to be. And for her, after she bit her lower lip and thought about it for a brief second, she decided it was worth it.

My advice to her, as I kept back in case the shopkeeper recognized us as a couple, was to walk in like she owned the place. She walked in all right—and quickly retreated as soon as the shopkeeper recognized her.

"Get out of my store!" he yelled angrily. "Out!"

"Can you believe that guy," Megan sneered angrily. "What a loser!"

"We'll find you another one," I reassured. "We have plenty of time."

Megan and I finished hitting the rest of the souvenir shops down the main road, while she remained focused on getting that elusive khanga. She came up empty-handed, however, looking sad as we loped back to the hostel carrying our only purchase of the day—a few postcards featuring the Indian Ocean.

"There's still plenty of time left in Zanzibar," I reassured her.

Deciding to cut our losses for the day, we headed back to the hostel to shower and change our clothes before dinner. The air was still muggy and humid, though our room at the hostel was surprisingly tolerable with the large, noisy fan standing tall in the corner.

****

We met up with our group in the lobby, and Woody led us all out the door, down the main street and into a short, round tunnel that we sidestepped through to avoid getting hit by legions of speeding cars. Aubrey, sporting a spiky, fresh haircut that left his blond hair cropped as close to his skull as possible, was the butt of a lot of jokes on our hike, with Thom rubbing the back of his head while Bill tormented Stacey.

"So what do you think of your lover-boy's new look?" Bill squawked, laughing harder when Aubrey tried to swipe at Thom from behind.

Stacey shook her head disgustedly.

"He looks like a silly boy," Stacey huffed. "I told him not to do it!"

The fish market and the swarms of people milling around it came into full view just as we exited the tunnel, stall after stall set right on the ocean and illuminated with strategically placed torches. A small gathering of people selling crafts sat in the grass across the way, with their canvas paintings and jewelry spread out around them.

"This is it," Woody said, stopping to survey the lay of the land as he placed his hands on his hips. "Let's dig in!"

With a little caution, Megan and I approached the first table we saw, where an older, African man, obscured behind rows and rows of kabobs, manned a small charcoal grill behind him filled with food. We leaned over to inspect the arrays of kabobs stacked high in front of us, some made with beef, some with chicken, and some with an indistinguishable seafood poked through them. Oh yeah—and every kabob had already been cooked.

"I don't get it," I asked Megan, stepping back from the table. "We don't even know when this was cooked."

The grill man turned toward the table and smiled to us as he grabbed a well-done beef kabob and threw it on his grill, then handed one off his grill, a chicken one, to a small child waiting at the table.

"Ready for something fresh?" the old man offered.

We smiled sheepishly.

"Still looking," Megan replied.

I hung back a little to watch what the others in the group were doing, and found each of them devouring some type of food.

I was starving. I knew I had to eat, especially since we had no snacks with us back at the hostel. After walking the entire breadth of the food stalls, pushing my way through the milling crowds when necessary, I found my way back at the stall where Woody ordered his food from, still extremely busy and at least offering the illusion everything had to be fairly fresh based on the number of people ordering. I selected two beef kabobs, two chicken and a plate of fries, hoping with each bite of the meat that I wouldn't regret my decision to break down and give in.

Megan managed to find probably the only freshly prepared item in the entire market—crepes with chocolate and bananas, made when you ordered.

The night ended with a walk back into town to check out what we heard was one of the hottest nightclubs in town, which was suspiciously empty and silent when the entire group arrived together.

"The CD player is broken," apologized the young male DJ. "We'll have it fixed next week."

The perfect end to a perfect evening.

A SENTENCE IN PARADISE

The humid, dry air of a new day rushed to greet me as Megan and I, electing to travel only with her camera and our two, tall water bottles, climbed down the short, front porch of the hostel and into the waiting hatchback cab. The two cabs that picked all of us up for the Spice Tour whisked us through the streets of Zanzibar quickly, taking us away from the increasingly familiar Stone Town and through a more contemporarily urban area. Nearly all of the traffic on the main roads consisted of matatus, short mini-buses resembling Volkswagen hippy vans and packed with as many people as they could hold plus a few extra, casually clinging to the rear of the vehicle by using the back bumper as a makeshift step. The decaying roads were hard enough to tolerate sitting down.

Both cabs eased us to a stop just outside of a large, white palatial building, with the one we had been following emptying of Helen, Abe, Mary and one African man, who motioned us forward. It was on the steps of that building, that the native African, who told us we could call him David, gave us our itinerary for the day. He was a real character—a bright, smiling man whose slightly off-center manner in speaking English made him that much more endearing.

"Welcome to Zaahn....Zi Baar!" David exclaimed, throwing his arms back into the air. "It's ..how you say...lovely cooountry!"

The day's events had been meticulously planned for us, according to David, beginning with a quick tour of historic sites, a journey to an actual plantation where assorted fruits and spices were harvested, and concluding with lunch at Sharif's home, where his wife would serve us a fine, home-cooked meal incorporating many of the native spices of Zanzibar.

"So juust enjoy Zaaahn Zi Baar!" David added. "And take sum looovely piktares!"

David retreated to the cab and handed us off to another guide, a thin, younger man with a mustache, as we explored an old fort and the House of

Wonders, its name earned centuries ago for being the first building in the area to feature electricity, running water and a working elevator.

Probably the most striking historical site we visited during the early morning was an old, dank slave dungeon, which our guide claimed typically housed one hundred slaves but appeared uncomfortably cramped with less than a dozen of us inside. Just being inside the room, essentially a cave carved into cold, gray rock, was a creepy experience, as the rustic, barbaric conditions in which the slaves had been kept was maintained, according to the guide, to remind everyone of a particularly dark period in the history of Zanzibar.

"Even after all these years," our guide solemnly related. "The tension that exists between native Africans and the Arabs—the ones who sold us into slavery—remains uneasy."

Megan felt a little vindicated hearing that, after the whole kanga debacle. Maybe it helped explain some of the shopkeeper's anger.

We met David back at the two taxis and headed across town for a glimpse of some palace ruins, now made part of some private land, we were told, but still close enough to the road to supposedly peek at without being charged admission. David, now occupying our cab in the previously-vacant front passenger seat, fielded scores of questions from Megan about kangas, culminating in her asking where she could find a quality, bright red one. "All around you," David said, pointing towards the many shops on the right side of the road. "But if you see one in the window you like, we will stop!"

No sooner did David say the word 'stop' did Megan, studying each shop window as we passed, beg him to do just that.

"Please please, please!" Megan begged, bumping her head slightly as she leaned over the front seat. "It's the exact one I want—the red one—right in that window!"

Glancing quickly at David, the cab driver pulled over to the right after David silently nodded his head and smiled.

"The red one in the window, you say?" he asked Megan, glancing back at the tiny shop.

"Here, let me give you money!" Megan shrieked excitedly, handing him a pair of $5000 bills. "Will this be enough?"

David smiled warmly.

"I will try to get the local discount!" he replied, jumping out of the vehicle and striding toward the shop.

Megan watched excitedly, his gaze locked on the broken screen door of the shop until David emerged from it a short time later with a medium-sized paper sack.

"He's got it!" she shrieked as she pulled on my arm. "He's got it!"

Not waiting until he climbed back into the cab, David handed the parcel to Megan through the open window with a fistful of assorted change and dollar bills.

"You are awesome!" Megan gushed. "And...it was even cheaper than the other one I saw!"

"You are much welcome," David said, humbly as he buckled his seat belt. "Much welcome."

****

It didn't take me long to remember why visiting ruins never impressed me much when our driver stopped in front of a large field where a few columns dotted the expansive, green earth.

"You need to imagine friends," David said as he pointed at the columns. "That this was once a great castle!"

Aside from the few, small columns that jutted up through the grass, nothing more than a few busted pieces of rock, which I assumed was part of the exhibit, littered the ground. Nearby, a man dressed in a long-flowing traditional robe sat on a small stool nearby, eyeing our two stopped vehicles.

"If you want a closer look," David began. "You can get out...But you need to pay him."

Shrugging at one another silently, the ruins didn't leave make much of an impression on anyone. Vernor, still seated in the rear of the cab and almost sneering at the ruins as he shook his head disgustedly, summed it up best.

"I've seen much more interesting things in my life!"

****

Leaving the swirl of the urban chaos around us, our cab headed slightly north in the direction of lush, green fields I had spotted earlier on the horizon. It amazed me how these two worlds—one of congested, urban life, the other of tranquil, natural beauty—managed to exist so close to one another yet seemed so far removed.

The road became dirt, marred with fresh tractor indentations as the taxi veered off the main road and down a narrow, bumpy path. We didn't pass a single person or sign of any sort as we drove for what must have been several miles, a mysterious journey through sprawling miles of trees, vines, and rows and rows of plants. Turning a wide corner, we finally spotted a filthy, red jeep, parked with a lone, thin man sitting on its hood. I noticed the handle of what looked like a large knife rising up near his belt. I hoped David knew him.

Stopping adjacent to the red Jeep, we piled out of the two cabs and were introduced to Michael, our guide to the plantations of Zanzibar. He and David looked very close, exchange warm laughs and assorted handshakes before both men led us through a nondescript green field.

"What surprises people the most about the tour," Michael said, snatching at an overhanging vine as he walked past. "Is how there are so many good things to eat all around you, sometimes looking nothing like they do in the market."

Michael stopped just short of a large tree with some orangish-green fruit hanging off it. The golden skin glistened against the sun.

"Dr. Papaya," he said, snatching a drooping fruit from a branch. In a swift motion, Michael pulled the black handle near his belt I spotted earlier and revealed a long, shiny machete, then carved into the fruit with the deft precision of a surgeon as its juices dripped from the blade.

"Come," he smiled. "Taste Dr. Papaya."

One by one, each of us floated past Michael and his machete, dropping a hand below the fruit to catch a freshly-cut chunk as it slid off the knife. It was juicy and delicious—prefect for a hot, stifling day.

"It is good, yes?" Michael stated after tossing what remained of the fruit beneath the tree where it came from. "I call it Dr. Papaya, though, because it is such good medicine, too."

According to Michael, papaya was one of the strongest natural medicines in all of Zanzibar, perfect for the treatment of any sort of skin irritation.

"Sea urchin," Michael claimed. "Put Dr. Papaya on a sea urchin bite and you'll be fine."

The alternate uses of naturally grown foods and herbs were the theme throughout the plantation tour. In many cases, the sometimes-odd appearances of everyday supermarket finds growing in the world was a revelation all its own, looking nothing like how I expected to find them. And we saw—and tasted—a lot, with some flavors so delectable I would have rather munched on an entire fruit myself rather than share. Overall, perhaps the best-tasting was something referred to by Michael as a 'custard-apple.' A fat bulbous fruit that hung high off a tree and with juicy, white flesh that softly gave way when you bit into it. The fresh pineapple had to be a close second, though, which, to my surprise, didn't grow from a tree but from a spiky, low-lying bush and was typically planted in straight rows, one following another. Watching the juice squirt out from the fruit as Michael hacked into it was nearly enough to make my mouth water—tasting the slightly acidic but refreshing flesh was even better.

I expected more from the freshly cut coconut than the almost chewy, flavorless meat inside it. The milk was good, but I couldn't get into pressing my lips against the lone coconut being passed around to drink from after I was one of the last ones it got passed to. Retrieving the coconut, which hung at least twenty five feet-high from a long, narrow tree remained the most impressive feat of the day—sheer athleticism with a healthy dose of courage. I didn't blame Michael for not attempting the climb, instead handing his blade to a slightly muscular man standing by who shimmied up the tree in quick fashion with the machete loosely strapped to his waist. The blade dangled precariously next to his leg without slipping or puncturing his skin.

Reaching the top of the tree, which was as thin as a palm tree and appeared barely strong enough to support his weight, the man grabbed the machete and began hacking away, not stopping until a lone coconut fell heavy onto the dirt below. It was amazing, with the man scaling back down with the same, calculated grace.

When we weren't devouring fruits like pineapples and avocados, Michael revealed to us herbs, beans and roots that also grew at the plantation. Ginger root, which elicited a wry smile from Stacey once Michael mentioned it was a sex stimulant, grew almost buried beneath the soil, requiring Michael's able handle to pry a small piece up from the cracked, brittle earth. As before, simply turning a corner or walking to an adjacent field almost always introduced something completely different, whether it was coffee beans, nutmeg, or pepper growing on the vine, still at its mildest, we were told, as indicated by its dull green color.

By the time the tour of the spice plantation was complete, I was feeling very hungry. All of the sampling I had done just woke my usually dormant stomach and made me yearn for more, especially when I remembered our next and final destination—lunch at Sharif's place.

Though I wasn't skeptical at the time, I do question today whether or not we were really at Sharif's place and if that was his wife who prepared us dinner, or some local woman or distant relation making a buck. It just seemed odd to me that, after being told we would be eating lunch at Sharif's place with his family, he was nowhere to be found by the time we had stopped in front of the small, sandy-colored stone house we were told was his.

Before entering, we removed our shoes, noticing the several pairs that lined the front porch already. A thin, dark-complexioned woman with slightly wild, curly hair led us to a large, round table, where I sipped on a glass of cold water and made small talk with some of the others, more to distract my ravenous hunger than out of courtesy.

Minutes passed before the woman appeared with two large bowls of steaming, dark perfumed rice, filling the air with a slightly spicy and fragrant smell. After setting them down in the middle of the table on the slightly wrinkled, white tablecloth, she made two more trips back and forth, once arriving with a yellow-green fruit punch and once more with silverware, before disappearing back into the rear of the house.

Instead of lunch with Sharif and his family, we instead found ourselves alone in the middle of someone's dining room with several bowls of food in front of us. Aside from Megan, I never learned if it bothered anyone else that we didn't get to meet up with Sharif that afternoon for a leisurely lunch and an opportunity to get to know our smiling guide a little bit better.

Lunch was very tasty, with the rice being an interesting mélange of tangy, sometimes hot spices that settled down nicely after a long sip of the yellow-green papaya juice. While the flavorful dish didn't stuff me, it made my mouth feel alive without making me feel to heavy for the day's next event—the excursion to Prison Island.

For a moment, I felt like a rock star being whisked away to the airport to some far-off venue as the squealing cab stopped short of the front door, preparing to whisk us all back to the hostel. The cab driver was insistent, first getting us outside with short toots of the horn and then ushering us into the stuffy vehicle.

"We must hurry and get all of you back!" he explained, glancing at the cheap, metal wristwatch on his arm. "There's so little time!"

Whipping us through the cramped, stone-paved roads, the driver proceeded with the skill of an Indy Car champion, tilting and weaving us through small crowds of slow-moving crowds and the occasional wandering chicken. I closed my eyes only once, when our driver appeared unlikely to give way to another taxi coming from the opposite direction. As both stubborn vehicles sped forward, I just couldn't look, bracing myself for an impact I imagined would send me straight through the already-cracked windshield in front of me. Only after I heard a car horn in the distance and realized we were still moving did I open my eyes again. This man was determined.

When we pulled up to the hostel, the few of us making the trip to Prison Island—Aubrey, Helen, Abe, Megan and myself—all hurried inside to grab what we needed. We had to be quick—it was nearly 2 p.m., the time of our scheduled departure. Fortunately, the speedboat that would take us out was only a few hundred feet away, tied up near the shore. We changed into our swimsuits, refilled our water bottles with what remained from filtering the previous night, and checked to make sure our camera and sun block was still inside the daypack.

Sharif was downstairs in the lobby when we came back down, looking a little perturbed and preoccupied. I was curious why we hadn't see him for lunch, but he didn't appear to be in any mood to discuss anything. Sharif looked strictly business, maybe growing impatient with babysitting us.

When the last member of the Prison Island group, Abe, finally made it downstairs, Sharif led the five of us down the sandy beach, stopping as soon as we reached a white and blue speedboat. Bouncing and bobbing in the low waters of the Indian Ocean, I could hear the bottom of the boat scrape the sand when the tide rolled in.

"Just wait here!" Sharif ordered. "I will get the captain."

I kept an eye on Sharif as he hurried down a short section of beach toward a small but muscular man in a white T-shirt and a small, black cap on his head. After the two shook hands, Sharif headed off and the captain, with a thick, braided rope in his hand, approached.

"So you are my crew to Prison Island, yes?" he joked, tossing the rope into the back of the boat. The entire rear of the vessel was filled with assorted nets, poles, cages and snorkeling equipment. That was for Aubrey and Megan—lying on the beach would be just fine with me.

"You have to excuse the mess," the captain told us as he began to untie the boat.

'I do a lot of fishing when I'm not taking people out."

While the captain, knee deep in the water, tugged the boat forward, Aubrey and I pushed it from the rear.

"Prison Island is just over there," the captain said, pointing to a small, fairly close patch of land that basked beneath the bright afternoon sun.

"It's a little further than it looks—about twenty minutes away or so."

We pushed the boat a little bit further ahead into the Ocean, up until the captain's hand shot up into the air telling us to stop. We were just about waist deep—the water felt perfect.

"Carefully climb aboard, please," he said, slowly boarding the craft himself and held himself tight to the stern.

One by one, each of made our attempt to board the steadily bouncing ship, which at times seemed to buck the way a wild horse would that didn't want any riders. With each receiving a boost from Aubrey, Helen and Abe made it aboard easier than I expected. For Aubrey, Megan and myself, boarding was not a problem, either, though I did always expect any small boat to tip whenever I tried to climb aboard.

Once aboard, the captain, whose real name I never did find out, looked back and nodded in approval.

"Hold on before I start the motor," he warned. "And if you don't like things bumpy, come up front."

I staked out a spot for Megan and myself in the rear of the ship. I wasn't so much worried about getting sick sea as I was about falling overboard, imagining myself tumbling backwards into the Ocean as the boat sped off completely unaware. The front and the rear of the boat were sectioned off with a large beam that extended the entire width of the ship—that would be my anchor.

Of course, poor Abe never made things easy. I wasn't surprised when the man with all of the grace and mobility of a turtle decided that he needed to position himself near the front of the boat, requiring him to somehow navigate past the same large beam I intended to hold on to. I couldn't decide if it was more comical or sad, watching Abe negotiate his rigid frame underneath the stationary bar like he was trying to limbo below it. Arching his back as far as he could, which wasn't far at all, he made a few pathetic attempts at sneaking underneath until Aubrey and I did our good dead for the day and hoisted him over the top. It was better than Abe leaning on me the whole trip for something to hold on to or puking.

As we all held tight to a part of the boat, the captain kicked a small plastic crate away from the motor and crouched low next to it. Then, quickly ripping the weathered pull cord, the engine responded which a low whirling sound.

"Hold on tight!" he yelled.

I glanced down at my white-knuckled grip on the beam. If I'd fall in the water, I'd probably leave my arm behind.

The motor squelched slightly as we slowly headed out, bouncing hard over the high, incoming waves until we caught speed. The initial take-off was the worst—very jarring on the stomach and requiring some clever footwork to keep yourself properly balanced. When we did level off at a smooth speed, we started skipping across the once-mountainous waves like a smooth stone.

"This is going to be so cool!" Megan yelled over the throaty motor behind us.

"I mean, how often do you see huge tortoises?"

The captain nodded his head.

"Prison Island is beautiful," he agreed. "The tortoises, the beach...it is very beautiful."

Aubrey, standing to the left of me, moved slightly towards the driver and spoke up.

"So these big turtles, then," Aubrey began seriously.

"Can we ride them?"

As we flashed incredulous looks in Aubrey's direction, the captain laughed heartily.

"Aubrey!" exclaimed Megan. "Why would you want to crush a turtle?"

Aubrey bit his lip.

"I'm just asking," Aubrey blurted defensively.

I saw some picture in a book once, I think, of a girl riding a turtle.'

"Yeah, a kid," I reasoned. "Not a grown man!"

The captain smiled and shook his head.

"No, my friend," he said, stifling laughter. "No turtle riding allowed!"

As we drifted closer and closer to Prison Island, the more and more convinced I became that I had finally managed to find my elusive beach paradise, if only for a few, precious hours. Completely mesmerized by the sheer beauty of the approaching land, I was staring at a scene ripped from a vacation commercial, complete with a few sun-worshipers laying on a small sandbank, just out of the reach of the foaming surf on pristine white sand.

Paradise.

Cutting the motor as we drifted slowly near the dock on the small island, the captain then leaped from the boat onto the small pier and lashed the heavy rope around a pole.

"You can grab the snorkeling equipment and toss it onto the pier," he said, looking over back into the boat. "No one will take it here."

Hopping firmly onto the dock, I checked my watch as I started to race up the small, grassy hill, following the small, wooden sign that pointed toward the tortoise habitat, almost forgetting to wait for Megan as she slowly climbed from the boat. We climbed the short hill together, turning an abrupt corner where we spotted the habitat, a small section of land completely surrounded by a tall, yet thin, metal fence, and absolutely filled with dozens and dozens of large tortoises.

The caretaker smiled warmly as Megan and I entered, making a point to carefully close the chicken wire gate behind us.

"Just watch your fingers," the caretaker warned. "They're very curious and like fingers and toes!"

With scores and scores of large tortoises laid out at our feet, it was a completely surreal scene. The average size from head to tail appeared approximately three feet long, though some of the older ones, estimated to be well over 100 years old, were slightly larger and carried a bulkier shell.

Despite the isolation created by the fence, in place to keep poachers from ravaging the island of its tortoises as they had in the past, the habitat still offered a glimpse of tortoises doing what tortoises did best. Most lay motionless, heads tucked almost completely within their shells as they basked in the sun, while others watched intruders like us, carefully, through narrow, curious eyes. A pair of medium-sized tortoises shared a large leaf of lettuce, each munching on one end until it completely disappeared. Perhaps the largest tortoise in the entire compound sat alone, with a corner of its shell near its tail completely missing after an injury from an errant tree branch, the caretaker explained.

The most interesting tortoises were the brave ones, the ones that crept slowly toward us like they were invulnerable, little tanks, not stopping until they found something to snap at with their tiny, yet powerful jaws. The strap on Megan's camera bag was a favorite taste treat, as a few turtles attempted to take a bite out of the curious-looking item. With both of us wearing sandals, our main concern became keeping our toes away from those same, hungry mouths.

A small placard posted within the compound, mostly detailing the history of the island and preservation information, also provided us with one of the wildest moments on the trip. According to the placard, tortoises most enjoyed being stroked on the rear of their front leg. Tortoises enjoyed the sensation so much, the sign read, they would lift themselves up as high off the ground as they could as a sign of appreciation. Picking out a large, somewhat calm-looking tortoise, we had to put it to the test.

Eyeing us first rather suspiciously as Megan and I each knelt down next to the tortoise, one on either side, we went for the little patch of exposed rubbery skin near the back of the front leg. Instantly, as a glazed look spread across its face as we began stroking, the reptile slowly rose higher and higher on its hind legs. The tortoise was in complete ecstasy, and it appeared we made a friend for life.

"No one's every going to believe this!" Megan laughed as the tortoise continued climbing. "It's unreal!"

Though it took mere seconds to send the tortoise to his orgasmic plane of existence, its appreciation was obvious, as it stood high, almost appearing to smile as the tickling continued.

"Now watch!" I said when we finally stopped out stroking. "This'll probably be the best part."

Almost instantly after moving our hands away from the tortoise, the reptile slowly eased back down to the ground, like an automobile coming down from a hydraulic lift at a garage. In a single, completely fluid movement that lasted almost an entire minute, the large tortoise's expression appeared stoic as it came back down to meet the ground.

I would have offered it a cigarette if I had one.

After snapping scores of photos of us surrounded by tortoises and thanking the caretaker, we headed back down to the beach, where Megan grabbed her snorkeling gear and raced down the beach to catch up with Aubrey.

"You'll be fine, right?" she called out to me as she looked back, halfway between Aubrey and myself.

"Trust me," I said, all smiles. "It's all good."

With the sunbathers I had spotted earlier now departed from the small patch of beach, I moved in, positioning myself in just enough sand to catch the steady flow of bubbling surf as it slowly trickled in. I tuned out Helen and Abe, who were scouring the beach for some vacant hermit crab shells, and truly lost myself in the paradise that was Prison Island: the perfectly warm sun; the clear, pale-blue sky; the warm ocean water and the sand that crumbled beneath my feet like it was a dry mixture of white dough. It didn't get any better than this.

Megan returned from snorkeling nearly a half-hour later, disappointed with struggling against the current and barely seeing a thing through the grit of the ocean. We spent the rest of our time on Prison Island together, frolicking in and riding the waves as they slapped up against the beach.

"You know, I've never seen you look so relaxed," Megan said happily as she splashed around in an incoming wave.

"This," I replied as I spread my hand in front of me. "This is why we're going to the Caribbean next year!"

A SLICE OVER DINNER

After returning to our room to pack up our belongings the following morning, we said our goodbyes to Sharif while we all waited beneath the shade of the narrow street for the cab to take us north. He looked a lot more at ease today, just as jolly as that first day off the ferry.

"It was a pleasure meeting all of you," Sharif beamed, traveling from person to person to shake hands. "Enjoy the rest of your stay in Africa!"

Just as he grabbed Woody's hand firmly, a large, gray van spun around the corner and stopped quickly in front of the hostel door, its brakes squealing softly.

"Take care of my friends," Sharif bellowed to the driver as he emerged from the front seat. "These are good friends."

Returning a slight wave to Sharif, the driver smiled as he raced around the vehicle and opened every door, finishing with the large, slightly rusted doors in the rear.

"Throw everything back there," he instructed us, blocking the lone path inside the van with his body. "And make yourself comfortable—it's a couple hours drive to the beach!"

****

I noticed the Indian Ocean on our left nearly two hours into the drive, revealing itself only when the dense, green hugging the road parted just enough before disappearing again. My anticipation built. The weather was holding. The glimpse of the blue water was beautiful. And best of all, our resort was close.

Our driver signaled for a left turn in what appeared to be the middle of nowhere until a well-hidden path through some trees revealed itself, winding us through a patch of small shrubs. In the immediate distance were several, long buildings, all seemingly interconnected and flanked around the ocean like silent guards. Dozens of young, white vacationers milled around, some with towels in hand, heading to the beach, some enjoying an early morning beer while talking with friends.

It wasn't Africa. It was Daytona Beach.

"We're staying here?" Megan asked, grabbing hard on my knee. "This looks awesome!"

My only response was an ear-to-ear smile, one of the largest ones I had flashed during the entire trip.

A small, middle-aged man emerged from the small office the van stopped in front of, smiling slightly through a somewhat stern exterior.

"Asante sana," he announced, shaking Woody's hand.

"Asante sana," Woody replied. "Are the rooms ready?"

The man nodded harshly.

"Oh yes," he replied as he motioned to Woody. "Follow me."

Woody followed the man briefly into his office, where the two stared momentarily at a clipboard. They emerged a few minutes later, each with a couple of large, old keys in their hands.

"Here, Megan," Woody said, handing her a worn black one. "He'll take you to your room first."

The manager nodded approvingly as he handed Woody the keys from his hand.

"I'll be back," he told him. "Please...follow me!"

The three of us marched up the three, short steps of the porch, stopping when the manager signaled in front of a door marked '23.' Fishing around with the dark key inside the loose lock, the manager gave a slight push upon hearing a 'click' and the door whined open. Reaching around the open doorway, he flipped a hidden light switch on the right wall.

"Here you are, my friends," the manager said coolly. "Please enjoy."

At first glance alone, our accommodations appeared a lot nicer then I had expected, not the sparse, flea-infested, hole-in-the-wall I had expected. Adorned in festive, bright-red bed linens, the double-sized bunk beds waited seductively on the far right of the room, while a small wicker table and two chairs offered an appealing comfort we had yet to see in any place we had stayed at previously.

"It looks really nice," I told the manager as he backed out of our room. "Thanks."

Looking the door behind him, I excitedly dug through my daypack and pulled out the orange-and-white swimsuit I had packed while Megan ducked into the bathroom.

I could feel my heart race slightly quicker when Megan emerged in her just-right dark blue bikini, the one that seemed to hug everything in just the right places. Mesmerized as I stared, like a famished dog eying a bone, Megan smiled sweetly.

"C'mon , you," she said, lightly pecking me on the cheek. "Let's go!"

****

Once outside, part of me wanted to sprint the couple hundred feet to the water, stopping only after the steadily bubbling incoming tide washed over me. Instead, letting the anticipation build, Megan and I proceeded at a casual pace, letting all of the anxiety from the past five weeks melt away with every step. There weren't any lions, black mambas, or leopards here. Only paradise.

We dropped our towels near the center of the beach, far enough away from everyone else, and kicked off our sandals.

"This is beautiful!" Megan exclaimed, admiring the beach as she rotated her head, taking in the scenery. "It almost doesn't seem like Africa!"

A brief blast of wind pelted gritty sand, clinging fast to the back of my legs. It wasn't the soft, sinking type at Prison Island, but it would do just fine. A few sailboats in the far distance raced across the horizon, charging ahead beneath the crisp force of the billowing winds.

"This is just like the Caribbean," I told Megan. "You'll see!"

The tide pulled back just as we approached the lip of the ocean, revealing a floor completely lined with assorted shapes of rocks, some looking particularly sharp. With my big toe extended, I cautiously dipped it forward into the chilly waters, just as the tide had finished completely rolling out.

Megan's approach was never as subtle. Wading out ankle-deep while I stood motionless, she tightened her body as she moved further and further out. Then, just as the returning tide licked her waist, she plunged herself completely, resurfacing several feet ahead from where she started.

"Woooooo!" she screamed, slapping her wet hair back over the top of her head. "Now you go!"

With the water line now hovering just above my knee, I couldn't even think about immersing myself as suddenly into the frigid water as Megan had. My toes actually felt numb as I moved carefully over the slick rocks in search of a sandy bottom.

"C'mon, you wimp!" Megan chided as she extended her arms. "Come to me!"

Gritting my teeth, I marched forward toward Megan, one slow step at a time until my waist slowly disappeared beneath me. "I'm coming to get you!" Megan teased, pinching the air with her two hands. "Here I come!"

With less than fifteen feet between us, I resigned myself to dunking in quickly before Megan arrived. Those cold, wet hands of hers would be merciless.

"Wooo-hooo!" screamed Megan as she slapped the surface of the water. The breezy air chilled my wet shoulders.

"A little cold, though, don't you think?" I added, dropping back down to keep my shoulders beneath the water.

We only spent a few more minutes splashing in the ocean before retreating back to our beach towels for some afternoon sun. It was too cold for me to stay in for any length of time, but I was sure once I dried off and the heat got to me the chilly waters would seem perfect.

It didn't take long for the hawkers patrolling the beach to start making the rounds, possibly identifying us as the new meat, so to speak, to barrage with their sales pitches for snorkeling, massage, and the usual corral trinkets.

"Sail with me...Captain Jim!" a man with dreadlocks exclaimed as he pounded his chest proudly. "We give you food, four hours on the boat, and the best time in Africa!"

Captain Jim, Dr. Cousteau, and several others all took turns offering us what they each promised were the best scuba experiences available.

"We'll have to talk it over with Aubrey," Megan told me after she sent the last guide away. "I know he wanted to go, so maybe we can get some kind of discount."

Most of the people from our overland truck were spread out across the beach in little bunches. Aubrey, Vernor and Stacey were sharing a single beach blanket about thirty feet down from us, with Stacey laughing about something as she pointed towards a perplexed-looking Vernor. Mary had settled next to Bill and Thom, her conquering heroes who had arrived late yesterday in their rental scooters. I didn't know where Woody was, but someone had said Helen and Abe were trying to find someone to wash the large bag of laundry they had brought on the ferry with them.

Megan and I didn't move from our entrenched spot on the beach until late afternoon, when we began checking out the long row of restaurants that began near the hotel and lined a large portion of beach. Though most offered the same choice of grilled burgers and hot dogs, one particular place, complete with a huge chalk sign heralding its menu, stood out above all the rest. Ocean Seafood.

"Look at these prices!" Megan squealed as she scanned the menu. "Large lobster tails for $12 U.S.! King-size for $15!"

Seafood sounded awesome, especially fresh from the ocean and unusually affordable.

"I guess I know where we'll be eating dinner tonight!"

We each grabbed a decent burger at a nearly grill before heading back down to the beach, stopping first by Aubrey and Vernor, seated on the same beach towel but without Stacey.

"I wanted to talk to you two," Aubrey said as we approached. Vernor smiled lightly, rising to his feet to stretch.

"Snorkeling tomorrow, yes?"

Megan glanced quickly at me.

"I want to, yeah," she told Aubrey. "But I don't think Paul does."

"No," I said firmly. "I don't. But go ahead."

"Well, okay then," Aubrey said as he looked at Megan. "We need to tell everyone and get a group together so we can save money."

Megan nodded.

"We can do that tomorrow," she replied. "They don't look too busy."

Megan's eyes landed on the mammoth-sized Nelson Mandela autobiography, Long Walk to Freedom, lying facedown on the corner of the beach towel. Aubrey hadn't been seen without it since we left Cape Town.

"Are you almost done?" Megan asked Aubrey as she pointed toward the book with her foot.

"I am done," Aubrey stated, as he rose to his feet. "It's just helping hold down the towel."

"Can I read it, then?" Megan asked eagerly.

Aubrey paused thoughtfully, hands on his hips.

"I don't know," he replied cautiously. "I have bad experiences with the books I loan. No one ever returns them."

"Please, please, please!" begged Megan. "I promise you'll get it back!"

Aubrey studied Megan's eager face briefly, and then stared at the slightly battered book, covered in a handful of sand.

"I guess so," Aubrey agreed, cautiously. "But be careful with it. And I need it back before we finish the tour next week, too!"

Aubrey reached down, grabbing the book off the blanket and placing a water bottle in the same spot.

"Just don't forget," he warned Megan as he handed her the book.

"I promise," she replied.

With her book in hand, Megan and I dropped our beach towels and dug ourselves into another small section of sand on the increasingly crowded beach. Aubrey and Vernor had decided to check out the ocean for themselves, though the exploration proved to be short-lived when Aubrey emerged from the water limping back to shore, claiming his foot had been scraped badly by something he brushed up against.

"You need papaya," Megan told Aubrey, after inspecting the two-inch long gash on the top of his left foot. "Y'know...Dr. Papaya."

Vernor, standing nearby with a sour look on his face, shook his head adamantly.

"No, no, no," he countered. "You don't need the fruit!"

While Aubrey and Vernor argued about treating his injury, Megan and I, quickly losing interest, returned to our room to relax before dinner. Though the early evening sun danced off the whitecaps beautifully, certain to create a beautiful sunset, I was just too tired to witness it. We both napped soundly until the sounds outside our door of people headed to dinner woke us. Dinner. And lobster.

After quickly showering, we left and room and headed to the seafood beachside restaurant we had spotted earlier in the day.

"This is the place," Megan said smiling as we walked through the bamboo-clad doorway of the restaurant we had scoped out earlier. "I'd know that smell anywhere!"

I spotted Aubrey, Vernor and Stacey all seated together as the host showed us to our table but I pretended not to. That didn't last long.

"Yoo-hoo!" Stacey called out, just as Megan slid her chair out from underneath the table. "Don't you want to sit with us?"

Megan looked at me for an answer, getting only a shrug. With most of my enthusiasm sucked out of me, I followed Megan to the conveniently large table the three were seated at. Stacey sat smiling between her two male suitors, like a cat and her cream.

"So how's the foot, Aubrey?"

"Much better now, thanks," he answered. "Woody said the swelling should go down in a day or so on its own."

Vernor mumbled something about 'the fruit' but I couldn't make it out.

"I haven't even seen Woody all day," commented Megan. "Or Helen and Abe, for that matter."

Stacey grinned devilishly, moving forward in her throne-like wicker chair.

"Well, you heard about Helen and Abe's laundry, right?"

We both shook our heads, prompting Stacey to continue.

"Nearly all of the money they brought to Zanzibar is gone!" Stacey exclaimed before lowering her voice. "Helen left the money in a pocket when she turned in the laundry and no one claims to have seen it."

"I'll bet Abe's really pissed now," I said, taking a sip from the sweating water glass in front of me.

Stacey rolled her eyes.

"I don't see why she bothers, personally."

A frazzled waiter arrived at our table to take our order a short time later, looking like he was in no mood for questions of any kind. I settled on the barracuda. As usual, despite Megan claiming she would order a large lobster tail, she waffled, biting her lower lip as she scanned the menu repeatedly.

"I just don't know...," she muttered. "Lobster tail or scallops...."

"Get it," Stacey commanded. "I just finished one. Trust me."

After a final glance at the menu, Megan relayed her order of one lobster tail to the waiter, tapping her foot impatiently as he firmly gripped a metal tray at his side.

I watched the waiter hand the paper order slip to a sweaty-looking chef in the open grill area at the rear of the restaurant, who mouthed it out for a second before spinning to the freezer behind him. Digging around inside the mammoth cooler, he pulled out to objects loosely wrapped in plastic and set them down. Megan noticed, too.

"This is fresh, right?"

"I don't know," I said, straining to look from my seat as I saw steam gush up from what must have been the grill. "It looked like they pulled the seafood out of the freezer."

"So what difference does it make?" Aubrey asked as he leaned forward, picking up a straw from the table. "Fresh...frozen...it's still a good deal."

Megan shook her head angrily.

"Look where we are, Aubrey," she said, waving her arm behind her. "We're on the Indian Ocean and we can't even get fresh seafood?"

The irony seemed to be lost on Aubrey, who took a sip from the beer resting near his elbow. Like Megan, I was starting to believe that, despite the abundance all around, the entire concept of fresh food was lost on the people of Zanzibar: first at the fish market and now at the beach.

Soon, the waiter arrived with two steaming-hot plates, met with 'oohs' and 'ahhs' from the group.

"Well," Megan grudgingly stated as she leaned over her plate. "The lobster smells good, at least."

The waiter, empty tray in hand, started heading back to the kitchen until Megan called out.

"Excuse me," she said in a low but sweet voice. "But may I have some butter?"

The waiter returned a puzzled look.

"Butter?"

"Yeah," Megan said. "Drawn butter. It usually comes with lobster."

The waiter's puzzled gaze extended over the rest of the table.

"Let me see," he replied. "I'll be back."

What ensued next reminded me of a 'Three Stooges' episode. With a look of complete bewilderment still etched across his face, the waiter huddled the three cooks in the kitchen together as he told them of this unusual request. The sweaty one occasionally peered over towards our table, obviously befuddled himself.

"I thought everyone served butter," Megan said, picking at the rubbery flesh of the lobster tail.

Before long, the waiter sheepishly returned to our table and managed a polite smile.

"There's no butter, miss. Sorry."

Thanking the waiter, a slightly distraught Megan began picking at the dry lobster tail in front of her, breaking off a small wedge with her fork and tasting it.

"So how is it?" I asked, in between bites of my barracuda. Mine was very fishy but wasn't bad.

"The lobster's okay, though it's a little dry without butter," Megan replied before turning to Stacey.

"Did you really think this was that great? You can tell it's been frozen!"

Surprised, Stacey recovered quickly.

"Hey," Stacey laughed smugly. "I said it was good—not the best."

****

Aubrey and Vernor remained at the table drinking with us once we finished dinner—Stacey excused herself but didn't return while we were there. As the liquor flowed, inhibitions relaxed, and the conversation drifted into a really weird territory, and I was glad Stacey wasn't around.

"I've seen a lot of circumcised penises on this trip," Aubrey said casually, like he was discussing seeing a lot of red Ford Taurus' on the highway.

I suddenly felt warm. Uncomfortably warm.

"Yes," Vernor agreed, looking thoughtful as he lowered a pint of beer from his mouth. "That is very unusual to me as well."

I didn't want to look at anyone—not even Megan—as I secretly hoped this embarrassing conversation topic would die a quick, painless death.

I was wrong.

"It's a cleanliness issue, isn't it?" Megan said, looking towards me.

"I think American society does it because the foreskin traps a lot of germs, right?"

At the moment, I wished I was anywhere else but at that table. The table sat silently, awaiting my answer. As an American with a circumcised penis, I guess that made me an expert.

"From what I heard, yes," I said, stifling a nervous laugh. "Nearly everyone in America is circumcised, I think."

Vernor's eyes grew wide.

"So you are then, yes?"

I laughed nervously.

"Yep," I said, briefly averting eye contact. "I certainly am."

Megan found my embarrassment cute, squeezing my knee firmly while she leaned over and pecked me on the cheek.

"Izz eet?" Aubrey asked, inching forward in his chair. "Then how do you masturbate?"

My jaw dropped wide open and I looked at Megan, who didn't know if she should be stunned to hear such to-the-point questions or amused to see my reaction. Aubrey asked the intrusive question with the same comfort he would if he had been inquiring about my recipe for barbecued ribs.

Before I could find any words at all, Vernor chimed in immediately.

"The foreskin feels good—it's not dry!" he argued excitedly as he turned to Megan.

"So do you shake or rub, then?" Aubrey asked eagerly as he inched even closer.

"What?" I was growing increasingly uncomfortable.

"I shake and rub," Aubrey replied matter-of-factly.

"Shake or rub?" Megan commented. "That sounds like it hurts!"

I didn't believe this conversation. I had heard Europeans were open-minded and a little more liberal when it came to sex, but this was ridiculous. As uncomfortable as I initially felt, though, it was almost funny to look back at Vernor and Aubrey and see them listening for my take on things with such anticipation, as if they were attending a lecture series on the American penis and prepared to take notes. I couldn't disappoint.

"It's all good," I replied. "I mean, I guess as men, we all do the same things...y'know, grabbing it and all that."

Vernor knowingly nodded his head, his eyes still wide with acceptance, while Aubrey didn't do much of anything, still trying to get a grip on life with a circumcised penis.

A NOVEL IS BORN

When our room service waiter greeted us the following morning, he said, cheerfully, "Mambo Jambo!" as he quickly wiped our tabletop with a wet rag.

"Jambo!" returned Megan. "We'd like some breakfast, please."

"Two breakfasts," the man replied. We shook our heads when he pointed to the steaming coffee pitcher in his hand. "And no coffee."

The waiter disappeared behind a small wooden wall across the courtyard, where I also spotted a few female waiters dressed in the same-type floral shirt hurriedly emerge with several stacked trays. The sun was buried beneath a cloud-laden sky—invisible but still very warm.

With two trays, one stacked on top of the other, our waiter emerged from behind the wall a short time later, glancing down as he climbed the steps before setting down our breakfast.

"Jambo again!" the waiter said, grabbing hold of the top tray and placing it in front of Megan: one soft-boiled egg, a large slice of cantaloupe, a banana, and a piece of toast. "I have a question," Megan began, as she unfolded her napkin and then dropped it into her lap. "If 'Jambo' is hello, what's 'Mambo Jambo?'"

Unfazed as he moved my tray in front of me, the waiter smiled.

"'Mambo Jambo' is 'Hello, how are you,'" the waiter explained.

"And 'thank-you?'" Megan queried, picking up her fork to attack her egg. "How do you say 'thank-you?'"

"Asante sana," the waiter replied.

"In that case," Megan said cheerfully. "Asante sana!"

"Asante sana, banana," the waiter replied, spreading his hand wide over the breakfast tray. His way of thanking us while telling us to eat, I guess.

I walked with Megan to the beach after we ate breakfast. There Stacey, Aubrey, Mary and Vernor sat together and appeared to be waiting. Aubrey, looking annoyed, glanced deliberately at his wristwatch as we approached.

"We were going to leave without you," Aubrey warned as he rose to his feet and dusted the sand off his swimsuit. He threw his hands high on his hips, still looking stern.

"I made arrangements already with that man over there," Aubrey stated, nodding his head towards a short, mustached man wearing a green T-shirt. The man, bent over on one knee, tied a dirty white sneaker.

"Who's that?" Megan whispered, squinting through the hazy light towards the man.

"Captain Morgan," Stacey answered with a smile as she rubbed sun block onto her nose.

Megan turned quickly, facing Stacey.

"Captain Morgan? Whose his first mate—Jack Daniels?"

Megan's crack elicited a toothy smile from Vernor, but Aubrey pretended not to hear it.

"We get four hours and lunch for $10 U.S. each," Aubrey said dryly as he pulled his yellow Charlie Brown shirt off from over his head. "He said it's the best deal on the beach."

****

I excused myself and made my way to an empty spot I had eyed on the far end of the beach once I saw 'Captain Morgan' approach, who had tossed a heavy coiled rope near Vernor's feet. Dragging a large paddle behind him, I watched 'Morgan' as he gestured to Aubrey for help with the tiny blue cooler of food resting against a docked sailboat. Megan looked almost sad to see me go, but that was the way it had to be, because I knew I would only be miserable if I had gone along.

Using a great deal of care, the snorkelers and 'Captain Morgan' waded toward a dilapidated speedboat, anchored nearly thirty feet from the shore. Aubrey, with his sore foot still surely on his mind, moved particularly gingerly as he and Vernor each held tightly to the cooler handles.

Maybe twenty or so people, including myself, had spread ourselves across the entire length of the beach, witnessing 'Captain Morgan' and his crew disappear on their puttering vessel behind a large, rock wall. Shutting my eyes as I stretched myself off across my beach towel, I grew more and more relaxed as I listened to the ocean. I slipped into one of my trance-like states once again, absolutely perfect for sorting through, recycling and discarding thoughts and ideas like I usually did during such moments of solitude. Feeling the hot, searing sun against my skin reminded me of a seemingly distant memory, specifically of that moment when Megan and I were so ready to pull the plug and end it all back in Victoria Falls.

It all seemed so long ago to me, those late, anxiety-filled nights where we each thought we wanted nothing more than to hop on the next plane back home and beg for our jobs back. African Wanderer was right—the second half of the trip is completely different than the first leg. It's better. We hadn't even been to the Serengeti and it was so very clear to me. The second half didn't seem to require nearly as much driving, though I think it was really just planned a little better to create that illusion. Plus there was the canoe trip down the Zambezi, more interaction with native people, and a lot more freedom, like we had in Stone Town. When I thought of those early days in Africa, I remember the boredom more than anything else.

****

I fell asleep for a little while, growing sleepy beneath the basking glow of the sun. When Megan did return from snorkeling, hours later, she didn't give a very glowing review of her experience.

"It's way cold out there with that wind," she complained, looking annoyed. "And it was too windy to really stay in one spot if you saw something, anyway!"

"I would have liked to have seen more lunch," she snapped. "Cheese and crackers, and Aubrey scarfed most of them down like he'd been lost at sea for two weeks!"

Throwing my arm around Megan as I lifted myself off my cozy spot on the beach, we walked together to the burger grill, while she continued to vent every step of the way.

"...And Mary! If that woman could only hear how annoying she was, maybe she'd do us all a favor and shut up!"

Megan and I grabbed a quick sandwich lunch and then hiked the quarter-mile or so to "town," which consisted of a small school and a grocery store. Though the chocolate candy bars on the grocery store counter were a little melted from the humidity, it was still a nice change of pace to sink my teeth into something with coconut in it. I thought I had been going through withdrawal.

"Hey!" Megan exclaimed as she grabbed her snack of choice, a package of grape-flavored 'supa-gorilla' gum. "There's something else here for you."

I traced her pointed finger to a small section of school supplies, where it landed on a pile of thin, shiny notebooks.

"Y'know...for the book!"

Yeah, the book. The book about our trip through Africa that was destined to forge a path for me into the world of publishing. The book idea that was so original it would only be a matter of time before Hollywood types engaged in a bidding war to lock up the rights for a big-budget feature film. The one that would let me break free of the nine-to-five life, exchanging my cubicle for a densely-wooded cottage in northern Michigan where the ideas would keep pouring in.

The mere thought of even starting a book about our experiences in Africa was completely intimidating. To me, a comical look at overland travel through Africa with strangers just seemed so perfectly entertaining—a can't- miss idea, yet that was also the very thing that intimidated me the most about starting it.

If the book sucked, it wouldn't be because the idea wasn't entertaining—it would be because of me. And that's not even acknowledging the dozen or so other ideas I had previously formulated for the 'Great American Novel'—not one allowed me ever to work past page three.

I took a deep breath and then stared down my opponent, the hunter-green, book-sized tablet positioned on the bottom shelf between a crate of pencils on the left and breakfast cereal on the right. It didn't look so tough, not next to a box of Frosted Flakes.

"Let's do it, I guess," I said to Megan, stepping back as she reached down below and grabbed the top notebook. It was no 'Rocky' moment of triumph, but at the very least, I figured I could flesh some things out and maybe even attempt journaling again with some down time—all without applying too much pressure on myself.

When we returned to the beach, three of the young, native black men who I had seen hustling anything they could over the past few days milled around the lone volleyball net, occasionally scooping the white weathered ball off the sand to hit it back and forth to one another. Before long, Aubrey and Vernor, sitting in the sand just west of the court, were enthusiastically recruited by a slightly chubby man to join them.

As the small group playfully knocked the ball around among themselves, I grew increasingly interested in joining in myself

"I think I'm going to go play, too," I told Megan as she quietly lay still under her large sunglasses.

"That's great sweetie," she exclaimed, sitting up slightly on her elbows. "You really should."

After a quick peck, I was on my way, jogging toward Aubrey, Vernor and the couple of other guys on the side of the net closest to me. Getting a little exercise would be good for me.

In total, seven men, including myself, were spread out across the one side of the net, all looking for an opportunity to volley the ball back over the other side to the three native men. I had managed to touch the ball only once before a group of six, muscular black men, silently watching the volleyball action, stepped onto the opposite side of the court.

"Let's play a game!" yelled the man who I figured was the self-appointed leader, a lean-muscled figure with thick glasses.

"Alright," Vernor replied, after most of us nodded with approval.

The man in the glasses mustered a slight smile, then shouted, "Black versus white!"

Instantly, I felt a weird sensation in the pit of my stomach. I froze, remembering the racial overtones of the attempted kanga purchase. Glancing behind me at the motley crew of the other white dudes I shared the court with—primarily a collection of short, out-of-shape middle-aged guys—no one could really find any words.

While my teammates and I stood dumb-founded, the leader on the other side of the net aggressively paced in front of his team. Making a tight fist, he shook it hard while he mumbled something to himself. Then, as his teammates sorted out their positions, he turned his attention back on his opponents.

"Where are you from?" the man in glasses yelled as he pointed to Aubrey.

"Netherlands," Aubrey answered, sheepishly.

"And you?" the man yelled as he cupped the ball resting at his feet with one hand and pointed to me with the other.

"U.S.," I said.

The man smiled.

"We're going to beat the U.S.!" he yelled, tossing the ball high into the air above him, letting it land hard into the sand below.

I knew I didn't like the way things were shaking out—there was way more in play than simple volleyball game. Before the first serve was even fired into the air, I knew if I were a betting man I'd bet it all on our opponents. An intimidating collection of young, athletic beach-combers, they practiced with precision while they waited for us to move into position, deftly launching the ball at will so it hovered just above their side of the net, eagerly awaiting a well-placed fist to spike it deep into the sand.

Anxiously awaiting the first serve on the other side of the net was my team, the anointed representatives of the entire white race, a collection of middle-aged, pasty and questionably athletic men.

We were in big trouble.

I took my position in the first row on the left, believing that if the game did go that long, we'd at least have our biggest guy rotate across the entire net during that time. I played my best volleyball up against the net, and the looks of intimidation I was spotting from most of my teammates told me very few would be willing to go up and spike it back down if they had to.

When everyone appeared ready, the man in the glasses, now standing in the middle position of the front row, held the ball high into the air.

"Volley for serve, okay?"

"Alright," I said. "Let's play."

Tossing the ball to a man behind him, the leader crouched down as the volleyed ball lazily sailed over his head and into our section of court. The bald, hairy guy on our team, calling out for it from his spot in the back row, charged full-speed but managed to hit it with a weak, low fist. As I watched the dead ball roll a few feet across the sand before stopping, our opponents gave a loud, deep, shout into the air. We were in for a beating. A big one.

"We won the serve, Mazungas," the leader taunted as he backed up from the net, awaiting the serve.

Great. 'Mazunga.' Think African for 'Cracker.'

As much as I'd like to paint a grand picture of the underdogs that no one counted on charging ahead to a win in dramatic fashion, it just didn't happen. Oh, we had our moments—our bald dude made a couple really good dives to save the volley; Vernor and I set each other up for some solid, well-placed spikes for score—but that can't be confused in any way of our team being even remotely competitive throughout the entire fifteen-point match. Aside from the fluke volley we did manage to return back to our opponents, our play was littered with miscommunication and overall poor execution, nothing like the smooth, selfless play of our opponents, who continued to howl after scoring every point while still interjecting the occasional 'Mazunga' comment.

When match point did arrive, it lacked all traces of drama because we were trailing so badly, our opponents at fourteen while we had managed only six. So when they notched the final point they needed for victory, off an errant smack by Aubrey that sent the ball sailing well out of bounds, it was no surprise.

"We beat the Mazungas!" yelled the leader as his teammates shouted their jubilation into the air. "We beat the U.S.!"

Strutting with joy as they kicked the volleyball around, I shrugged my shoulders and walked off the court, able to hold my head high for playing well but a little pissed off at how classless our opponents were by making it a racial issue.

Megan slapped my back in support as I sat in the sand next to her.

"You played really well, sweetie," she said compassionately as she glanced towards the volleyball court. "It looks like they might play again."

I shook my head defiantly.

"I'm not interested in that again," I said firmly. "All that racial shit just isn't right. You know they wouldn't dig it!"

We spent the little that remained of the humid afternoon riding in the strong waves that slapped against the beach.

Tomorrow we'd depart Zanzibar, boarding a late morning ferry back to the coast and spending the night in that same, humid campground we left poor, miserable Seth in. As I listened to the darkness while I rested my head on my pillow, I wondered if we'd even see the guy again.

LAZARUS RISEN

Repeating in reverse the sequence of events that landed us in Zanzibar, we made our lengthy journey back to the campground. After hours of weary travel, I sighed deeply when, through a brief clearing of large trees branches, I recognized the unmistakable shape of Ella, more beautiful that I could even imagine as she eagerly waited to attack the roads. A pair of bare feet hung out from the open cab door—either Seth was making a slight repair or he never made it to the doctor, joining that big safari in the sky.

Our answer came soon enough, as the pair of legs, tipped off with the sound of our tires scraping over the road of broken gravel, briefly flopped like a fish out of water on the cushioned seats before slowly emerging from the cab. It was Seth, and he looked much like the Seth of old.

Standing and waving as the cab slowed down, the yellow pigment that had crept over his countenance had disappeared, leaving a slightly sunburned glow in its place. With his eyes no longer drooping, Seth was a new person, widely grinning as we emerged from the vehicle.

"I didn't think you guys were coming back to get me," he teased, dropping his waving hand to his side.

"You look much better, man," Bill returned, shaking our returning leader's hand. "What was it, then?"

"Just like I thought, Woody," Seth called out to our other guide just as he dropped his pack onto a small patch of grass.

"Malaria, then?"

"Yeah, Woody," Seth continued as Woody slapped him on the back. "And hepatitis."

Megan shot me a knowing glance and smiled, one of those 'I told you so' glances.

"The doc said I should go back to Cape Town, but if I keep taking these, I'll be fine."

Reaching into his pocket, Seth pulled out a small vial and tossed it to Woody, who quickly scanned the label.

After a brief meeting together, Seth and Woody addressed the group.

"I hate to cut this reunion short," Seth began. "But if we don't get on the road now, we'll never make it to our campground in Arusha tonight!"

****

Back on the road once again, my thoughts drifted to the beautiful girl sitting beside me. I never cared about anyone as deeply as I cared about her, and everything we had just felt so right. That was probably why I still had my doubts—after having been through my share of failed relationships, I sometimes still slipped into that 'waiting for the other shoe to drop' mode. Since I first met her, she told me confidently how she'd travel across the reaches of the globe, possibly for up to two years as she explored Asia, Europe and parts of Australia. Not only did she put her trip on hold so I could save enough money and join her a year later, but our trip looked nothing like the one she had planned. Africa wasn't even on the radar for her. And if she saw Africa as a disappointment she blamed me for, then maybe that was the other shoe I was waiting for.

****

Worrying—that's how I passed my time. Some people read, others sang along to music, but not me. Thankfully, I enjoyed a brief respite from that tremendous weight in the late afternoon, as I was so locked into my own thoughts that I hadn't even noticed the more populated, almost touristy portion of road we sojourned through, a true sign the Serengeti and some of the more popular destinations in all of Africa were nearby. Looking up toward the front of the truck when I heard Woody rap quickly on the window with his knuckles, I followed his outstretched finger as it pointed to our immediate right.

"There it is!" Megan wailed, reaching for her camera bag beneath her seat. "It's Kilimanjaro!"

Straining to see through the thick patch of trees as we motored past, a large clearing finally revealed her in all of her splendor. Wrapped in white, billowy clouds, the peak appeared almost ghost-like, an apparition that hovered alone and high above us. Before long, a vast portion of the earth-colored base of Kilimanjaro finally did reveal itself to us, an expansive, harsh table that looked every bit as inhospitable as I had heard.

As we all left our seats and crowded around the windows on our right, with those holding cameras receiving precedence, Seth charged onward, almost seeming oblivious to the natural wonder in our presence. Kilimanjaro was completely mesmerizing—even if you tried to look away from her magnificence, it wouldn't be an easy task.

"I just can't believe it!" Bill kept repeating. "Fuckin' Kilimanjaro!"

"That would be a nice climb," Aubrey added, holding on outstretched hand above his eyes to minimize the glare.

I think Seth surprised all of us by pulling Ella over to a sizeable patch of clearing minutes later, affording probably the most open and picturesque view of mighty Kilimanjaro around.

"I should have let you know I planned on stopping for pictures," he explained sheepishly as we jumped off the truck. "I knew of this spot—one of the best around here."

Hanging back, Seth stood patiently while we gazed at mighty Kilimanjaro, her peak still cloaked in heavy cloud, but looking even more massive from the ground. I didn't get as geeked out as Megan, who persists that one day she will get me to base camp at Mt. Everest with her, but even I could appreciate the striking beauty and sheer size of Kilimanjaro, undaunting as she stood proudly across the Africa horizon.

Megan was truly geeked, though, snapping photo after photo as she tilted her camera from side to side. In total, including the photos she snapped from the truck, she spent nearly two entire rolls on Kilimanjaro. Back on the truck, Megan immediately grabbed her Nelson Mandela book and delved right back into it, moving her lips as she read in the cute manner I always teased her about. Helen and Abe sat silently next to each other, Helen occasionally glancing out the window while Abe stared forward, arms crossed. Vernor, reading some tiny, torn paperback, combated the heat by wrapping a white T-shirt up and around his head into something resembling a turban.

Stacey slept, still seated behind us and still nowhere near Aubrey, who had begun reading some spiritual book with 'God' in its title. As usual,

Bill's headset was turned up way too high, and watching him pound along on imaginary drums to the Red Hot Chili Peppers even made me feel awkward. Mary, meanwhile, looked out the window in boredom, occasionally glancing back towards the rear of the truck in Bill's direction but never leaving her seat.

We found ourselves in total darkness by the time we drove through Arusha, what looked to be a fairly sizable city by Africa standards but whose streets were now largely deserted, save for the occasional straggler. At night, especially from the truck, Africa did take on an almost eerie quality, especially as we moved past Arusha and into the more forested regions. Our destination for the night was the charmingly named Mesarani Snake Park, just outside of Arusha. Scores of plywood billboards, decorated with all types of snakes and plastered throughout the campground, pointed in the direction of a long row of buildings on the other side of the park.

"They must keep snakes here, then," I told Megan, straining to see something from the truck window as Seth rounded the campground.

"As long as they're not crawling around us when we sleep," she added.

Through the few, rather dim electric lights that hung near our campsite, I noticed two men sitting casually beneath a tree across the way. As Seth stopped the truck, the men stepped forward, ominous-looking figures who each carried what looked like a long, thick pole. The shapes, disappearing in and out of the dark shadows of the African night as they approached, moved silently across the dirt ground, their free-flowing dress rustling slightly in the wind. Gathered around Ella once we scrambled off her, we curiously waited for the men to reveal themselves.

"Jambo!" Seth called out into the night.

The shapes continued striding forward, stopping just inside the weak beam of light that cast against the back bumper of the truck. The campground caretakers were members of the Maasai tribe, men with shaved heads and dressed in the traditional garb of a red, flowing cloak and sandals. It was our first encounter with the Maasai tribe—a proud group of people, rich in tradition, that spread themselves over a great portion of northern Tanzania.

Seth appeared quietly respectful as he worked out the arrangements with the two men, listening to them as they instructed him on the law of the land. Using the heavy, wooden walking stick held fast in his hand, the taller of the two men, who also did most of the speaking, pointed out the important amenities, notably the showers, the bar and the actual snake park, also boasting a few crocodiles. I had heard each male member of the Maasai tribe needed to slay a lion by himself to be recognized as an adult and as I watched the effortless way our caretaker twirled their heavy clubs around, I believed it.

****

Megan and I rested that late evening, emerging only to eat our dinner of greasy sausage and some flavorless rice. Over dinner, Seth shared with us some great news regarding the Serengeti—specifically that we could 'upgrade' both nights we would spend near the game reserve by staying in posh African lodges. The price was a mere $7 U.S. each.

"It's really a good deal, guys," Seth urged us. "These same places charge up to $100 U.S. a night during peak, so you really luck out."

It was too good to pass up—even I knew that. And best of all, it signaled the virtual end to camping, aside from the night when we returned to Mesarani two days from now when the Serengeti excursion had concluded. Nothing else drove home the fact that our tour was coming to a close than hearing that, which translated to two nights in lodges, one night in the youth hostel in Nairobi, and then the crown jewel—the five-star hotel I had booked for us at the tour's end in Nairobi.

PAYOFF

The slightly crisp, mid-morning air was a welcome change from the steamy, stickiness of Zanzibar—there was nothing quite like snuggling deep inside a well-cushioned sleeping bag. Despite my comfort and my best efforts, though, I couldn't force myself back to sleep after yet another bout of vertigo. What the attacks now lacked in frequency, they made up for in sheer terror, though at least I was able to keep this latest fit—one that culminated in my usual, perceived life-or-death struggle to break free from the spinning tent for some fresh air—from Megan. I knew she was right. I should have gotten off the Lariam.

The night terrors aside, I figured my building excitement for our excursion into the Serengeti would still make sleep non-existent. Just venturing into that magical land, one teaming with all types of wildlife, just seemed overwhelming, with lion, zebra, giraffe and leopard all coexisting in their struggle for survival. I knew I should have guarded myself about expecting too much but I couldn't. Seeing the Serengeti, as well as sprinting even closer to the Africa tour finish line, just made me feel so damn good inside.

I climbed out of the tent as soon as I heard the familiar, squeaky creak of Ella's rear door being swung wide open. It was Woody, scanning neatly stacked crates of food through eyes that still looked as if they would prefer to be closed. Seth, wrapped tightly in his blue quilt so only his nose remained visible, shuffled to his side.

****

"Both Woody and I are staying back with Ella, Seth announced over breakfast as he rose from his seat with his empty coffee mug in hand. "You'll be in good hands in the Serengeti, though—we use these guides all the time. What that means is, take only your daypack, because you aren't coming back for two days."

"They'll take you to the lodges you'll be staying at after each game drive today and tomorrow," Seth continued with little emotion. "Two days from today, you return then off to Nairobi."

Whenever I heard our tour through Africa discussed in terms of finality, I couldn't get over how close we were to finishing what once seemed like such an insurmountable task.

The breakfast area emptied quickly after Seth's speech, with everyone pushing their way through the now-littered and overflowing aisle of the truck to grab their belongings. Knowing that we would be stuck in a Jeep with the same people for two days, Megan and I quickly made our way to the two four-by-fours and anxiously waited until we saw which one Mary would likely go in—and then promptly chose the other one.

Within short notice, our Jeep became the most popular one with people battling over the few remaining spots...backpacks were removed, seats taken and tempers flared. There was after all a lot at stake—two eight hour days with Mary.

The driver, who introduced himself as Humphrey, smiled as he grabbed hold of our daypacks and tossed them into the trunk. Woody flashed a hearty wave to us as we took off in the two four-by-fours, smiling like a parent sending his kids off to camp for the summer.

Taking a deep breath as Snake Park disappeared into our trailing dust cloud, I took a deep sigh as I grabbed Megan's knee.

"This is it," I told her, just as she loaded a fresh roll of Fuji into her camera.

"The Serengeti, baby!" she replied, merrily, squeezing my hand.

Our driver, Humphrey, tore down the red clay road mercilessly, a tank commander powering us through the pairs and pairs of dug-in tire tracks that littered the ground below.

"We'll get there just after noon, if we hurry," Humphrey shouted to us from over his shoulder. "Just hold on!"

After a short and uneventful lunch break a few hours later, the drive continued and my anticipation continued to grow, further fueled when Marcus, the driver of the other truck, nimbly weaving his vehicle around the ripped-up road in front of us, tooted his horn and pointed out the window to the valley below, where a young, male elephant lazily trudged along through the forest. I hoped Megan had brought a lot of film.

The mountainous chasms and valleys almost instantly gave way to the typical, tall grasslands of Africa—the type that always seemed to teem with lions, giraffes and hyenas in nearly every nature documentary ever filmed. The warm afternoon sun felt nice—not hot but surprisingly temperate.

After our drivers stopped for a gratuitous photo opportunity in front of the gates of the Serengeti game preserve, I knew it'd be the last time I set foot off the truck, short of a guarded restroom break or arrival at the Lodge. After all, the tall grasses could hide anything.

With his dark black binoculars dangling from his neck, Humphrey threw himself full-fledge into 'game drive' mode as soon as our truck cleared the entrance gates, stealthily peering over his steering wheel a full 180 degrees as we slowly moved ahead. We probably weren't in the preserve for more than five minutes before Humphrey, after first shooting a quick glance through his binoculars, hit the gas pedal hard, forging a makeshift path of tire tracks through a long patch of short grass. He didn't say a word as we anxiously sat back, glancing momentarily at one another before trying to decipher what Humphrey spotted from so far away.

I fumbled for my binoculars, trying to hold them steady as we bumped along, before dropping them back around my neck. A few brownish objects, lying far ahead in the grass, slowly came into view while Marcus, following Humphrey's mad dash, pulled up along side of us in a dead heat. There was something out there, alright. Something big.

My heart jumped briefly when we came up close enough to identify our quarry—by far our most impressive sighting to date: three of the largest male lions I had ever seen, lying lazily in the short patch of grass. I was far closer than I had ever been to one at the zoo—maybe fifteen feet away from the closest one after Humphrey had finished circling the beasts and slowed to a halt.

Just being in their presence made me appreciate their sheer power—I could do nothing but respect their might. Their heads were massive, their bodies a compact collection of lean muscle.

For the most part, the three lions looked unimpressed with us as they panted heavily beneath the mid-afternoon sun, with the one in the rear dropping its head occasionally, seeking rest. Inching us a little closer after noticing another truck in the distance headed our way, Humphrey downplayed the low growl that emanated from the middle lion, even though it did make our driver cautiously stop more than once.

"He's just staking out his territory," Humphrey whispered to us as he clutched the steering wheel tightly. "That's okay. We're staying here."

I still couldn't believe that only a short, steel door and a several yards were all that separated me from the most feared predator in all of Africa, if not the world. Yet they seemed so disinterested, barely noticing the flash from the array of cameras pointed in their direction that ceaselessly snapped. "Three lions," Bill stated with awe. "We're here five minutes, Humphrey, and you show us three lions!"

Humphrey smiled.

"I do what I can," he replied modestly. "Hopefully I can show you much more, too!"

Finding the main road after following his own tire tracks back, Humphrey and Marcus stuck close to each other as we continued along at a fairly brisk pace.

"Up there!" Humphrey said over his shoulder, pointing to a stopped four-by-four nestled inside a grassy shoulder in front of us. "They see something!"

Hitting the gas even harder, Humphrey and Marcus sped their vehicles forward, slowing them gradually as they quietly pulled up alongside the green and black truck on the shoulder. An older woman on the other truck, unsuccessfully trying to hide her gray hair beneath an over-sized pith helmet, shushed us to be quiet as Humphrey jockeyed into position, inching only until we could see what the truck parked in front of us was blocking from sight.

Finally, after rolling just enough forward, we managed to catch a glimpse of what was so captivating—a male and female lion sleeping side-by-side, just off the road.

"They must be mating!" Megan whispered as she removed the lens cap from her camera.

Humphrey, hearing her, nodded. "They stay with each other for weeks, mating several times a day," he added with a smile. "Maybe that's why they look so tired."

The dozing couple wasn't exactly the picture of excitement—and I didn't see how they could manage to even rest where they had chosen to lie down, with the steady stream of gawkers like us stopping all day. And the flies were horrible, too, with dozens climbing over their snouts as they hopped from beast to beast. I'd never seen so many flies, not to mention all of the scars that crisscrossed the animals' faces.

Despite their slumbering, the lion couple did provide a pretty unique photo opportunity, one that everyone with a camera readily grabbed. After barely a half-hour in the park, I already felt like I had seen the best game viewing of the entire trip.

And best of all, we were just getting started.

When the lone road branched off into several different forks a short time later, Marcus, after tipping the brim of his cap to Humphrey, sped off with his crew down the path headed straight east. Humphrey, not selecting one of the nearly half-dozen offshoots, gave the truck a little more gas as he continued straight.

"This is why we have these radios," he called to us from the front seat as he grabbed the heavy, black receiver resting on his lap. "You can cover way more ground that way."

The rough, gravel roads made the ride especially bumpy. My knees, already crammed behind the seat in front of me, bore the brunt as they hit back and forth with every bounce.

****

Our wildlife viewing that afternoon had peaked with spotting the lions and slowly trailed off after that. After about forty-five minutes and driving down innumerable, tight roadways, our persistence paid off with one of the more infrequent sightings in all of Africa—the leopard. Humphrey, forcing our vehicle through the caravan of seven vehicles already tightly packed nearest to the tree that housed the leopard, stopped as close as he could, still about 200 yards away. Even my strong binoculars made identification a challenge.

"This truly is a unique sighting," Humphrey stated glowingly as he glanced through his binoculars at the creature.

I wondered if he could see the leopard, well hidden on a shaded, full branch, any better than I could. In the right light, the dark black, partially dangling object nearly did look like a leopard.

To anyone with a camera in hand, the distance didn't matter, as flash after flash fired off in the direction of the shady tree, all in the hopes of capturing the elusive predator on film. And Megan was right there with everyone else, firing shot after shot.

"I need to stop myself," Megan told me, lifting the camera strap up over her neck as she pushed the Minolta into my hands. "Don't give it back to me until we leave here!"

Continuing to dart across the huge Serengeti Game Reserve, we spotted the usual assortment of African animals that I, admittedly, had begun to tire off, particularly zebra, wildebeest, and any member of the antelope/gazelle family. We surprised an enormous yet gentle-looking giraffe at one point, munching on a leafy tree just off the road, and later spotted a ravenous yet nervous herd of hyena, munching on a small collection of bones.

"Probably from last night," Humphrey stated, nodding toward the bones. One of the hyenas paused only briefly as it noticed us, then returned to its snacking.

As the sun began to wane and drop over the horizon, a call came over the radio from Marcus, who said something about getting us to the lodge for the night, and no sooner did Humphrey place the radio back into his lap than we catch up with Marcus, who had stopped his vehicle on the main road so we could catch up and leave together. I was exhausted. When we finally reached our lodge, a sprawling, modern marvel that seemed to spring up from the green, tangled growth around it, a mix of weariness and euphoria set in. Sure, after six weeks of living out of a backpack, I was running on fumes. But the immense lodge, every bit as beautiful and accommodating as any nice hotel, was exactly what I needed to help me through it.

"Only $10 a night?" Megan shrieked into my ear after jumping up and down with excitement. "I hope they have a tub in the room!"

With a tray of complimentary fruit juice poured into crystal glasses waiting for us at the marble-clad front desk, I felt slightly out of place, not to mention smelly from sitting on a truck all day. The lobby was beautiful, decorated with vase after vase of bright, freshly-cut flowers, set atop rich, dark end-tables. Though the style was traditional comfort, the artwork was all African, with rich, colorful tapestries that draped the wall behind the front desk and a small collection of museum-quality, traditional tribal masks. Even during peak, $100 a night seemed a good deal.

Admittedly, I felt a little sheepish as I approached the desk with my weathered backpack tossed over my shoulder, but the hostess's warm smile quickly put me at ease. Welcoming everyone warmly, she mentioned that dinner would be served at 7 p.m. in the main restaurant as she passed out the room keys, one to a pair. With key in hand, Megan and I referenced a tiny, plastic map in the lobby to find our room, number 351, situated on almost the completely other side of the hotel. "Hurry, hurry, hurry!" Megan said excitedly as I fished the key into the lock before our room door. When the door swung open, I couldn't hide my smile. The smile of seeing a comfortable, cozy room with a cushiony queen bed.

"I can't believe this!" I said, throwing my backpack into a chair in the corner. "$10 a night!"

Beneath the drapes on the far end of the room was an entire wall of plate glass, which looked over a green, densely forested patch just off lodge grounds.

"Now that's cool!" Megan said as she skipped over the window. "We may even see something out there tonight!"

With a few hours before dinner, we took a brief nap on the cozy bed without even bothering to pull back the sheets.

I slipped into the lone pair of slacks I had brought with and a clean white T-shirt for dinner, hoping I wouldn't look too out of place in the restaurant. We headed to the restaurant right at 7 p.m., assuming everyone else, as famished as we were, would empty the buffet if we didn't. After enjoying a lovely buffet feast for dinner, we headed to our rooms early in preparation for the excitement we hoped tomorrow would bring.

THE RACE ALMOST RUN

We were all smiles when our four-by-four followed Marcus' away from the Lodge and back into the game preserve, each of us anticipating another day as thrilling as the one before. I only hoped the lodge we'd be staying at that night was comparable to the one we had just left.

Both vehicles slowly trekked through the now-familiar entrance to the Serengeti Game Reserve, merging onto a main road already cluttered with nearly a dozen assorted Jeeps and four-by-four vehicles. This time, instead of sticking to the main road as he had the previous day, Humphrey selected a fork that sprouted to the west, a narrow, nondescript path that appeared pretty isolated. Marcus still appeared to be deciding on his route as I watched his vehicle slowly disappeared from sight behind us.

Unlike the game drive from the previous day, this one began relatively calmly, with the occasional antelope sighting and little else. We spotted a lone hippo wallowing in a distant lake but, somehow, it just lacked the impact of canoeing next to an entire herd in the Zambezi River.

****

Things became much more interesting in the late morning, just as the radiant heat emanating from the bright red sun made me question why I had worn a long-sleeved shirt. The best sightings always seemed to occur just when I least expected them, just after the initial excitement of starting the game drive began to wane and I doubted we'd spot anything.

It was during those late morning hours, though, that we spotted a lion couple, male and female, mating beneath a large, dark tree. Within seconds, Humphrey excitedly whispered into his walkie-talkie to inform Marcus of his find—this was a big deal.

"This is the time of year when you have the best chance of seeing this," Humphrey explained as he reached for his binoculars.

There was something a little intrusive about watching the scene play out—spying on two animals mating must have stirred my guilt-riddled, Catholic sensibilities in some weird way. Still, there was something fascinating about watching the two beasts carry on as if we weren't even there. The female lion, looking the part of the tired and bored concubine, lay still on the ground with her back to us. If the female could wear a wristwatch, she most definitely would be glancing at it.

The male lion was all business, barely glancing at us as Marcus' noisy four-by-four arrived. He stood tall and proud in the high grass next to his waiting partner, seemingly oblivious to everything. Then, after some foreplay of growling and nipping , the male moved in quickly and mounted his partner, thrusting hard.

"I feel kinda dirty," Bill joked as he watched the action through his digital camera. "Like I'm filming some kind of porno!"

Humphrey later explained to us that it's typical for a lion couple to mate for an entire day to the point of complete exhaustion. Though I never knew lions had it so good, it did explain the frequent breaks between thrusting, when the large male would dismount his partner for minutes at a time before moving back in.

When the large male collapsed from exhaustion next to the female, we figured the show was virtually over and it was time to move on through the park. A few more trucks squealed onto the scene just as Humphrey carted us back down the road.

"I think they're staying back," Thom said, referring to Marcus' still-parked truck that quickly disappeared when we passed a tall patch of dry, golden grass.

"Remember, Humphrey," I joked. "Yesterday was awesome, but you still owe us a cheetah sighting!"

Humphrey, taking a quick sip of water, smiled as he swallowed.

"I will do my best," he said, chuckling. "I will do my best."

Bill, still sitting between Helen and Thom, moved forward in his seat.

"Let's screw with them anyway," he said with a twinkle in his eye. "When we see them next, we'll tell 'em we saw a cheetah, anyway."

"How about a cheetah giving birth?" Megan chimed in. "That'll drive Mary nuts!"

We spent the rest of the afternoon darting back and forth down innumerable, unremarkable roads. As sightings go, things died down considerable after the mating lions, aside from mass sightings of wildebeest and zebra herds, sometimes easily numbering well over a hundred. Our chance to mess with the other truck finally arrived in the late afternoon, just as Humphrey, after checking his wristwatch, told us we'd start heading back to the main road. As if on cue, Marcus' truck suddenly darted alongside, with his crew starting to exhibit some of the same signs of boredom we did, but Bill didn't miss a beat.

Springing to his feet, he climbed atop the rear seat and waved excitedly.

"Didja see the cheetah, then?" he said with a huge grin as he clutched the camera dangling from around his neck. "It's all right here, baby!"

Mary, standing tall in her truck with her arms tightly wrapped in front of her, failed to glance back at the rest of her group, to a person frowning in disbelief and shaking their heads at Bill's claim.

"Cheetah?" she quizzed Bill. "How far away was it, would you say?"

"Oh, back there, a little," Thom replied as he waved his arms wildly. "She was giving birth just as we pulled up."

For a moment, albeit briefly, Mary bought it, turning to Marcus in a serious manner before noticing that he was laughing to himself that she would take Bill's claim so seriously. Then, after glancing back at Stacey, who hadn't stopped shaking her head in disbelief, Mary finally got the joke.

"Oh, Bill!" she exclaimed. "You're such a kidder!"

Stacey, who had been sitting, then climbed aboard her seat and jumped in the conversation.

"Even if you saw the cheetahs," Stacey remarked. "We still probably saw more than you did!"

****

Bill bickered a little with Mary and Stacey about who saw more, a contest that ended with all parties admitting that no one saw much of anything after the mating lions. Humphrey, only half-listening to the argument, rose from his seat and scanned the surrounding area with binoculars before bouncing suddenly back down. After quickly barking something to Marcus,

Humphrey threw the truck into gear hard and we sped off, headed toward a large, open field of green grass just off the main road.

"He must see something," I told Megan as she grappled to hold onto the breakfast bagel she had just unwrapped. Humphrey just tore across the rock-strewn road, sending us bouncing and flying in every direction as we held on tightly, with Marcus keeping up every step of the way.

Though I knew we were within sight of our quarry as Humphrey slowly rolled to a stop amid the tall grass, I still couldn't see what the rushing was about. Then I trained my eyes at a particularly high patch of grass we were headed straight for, and spotted what looked like a dark, furry tail peeking just over the top.

Somehow, some way Humphrey had delivered. We had our cheetahs.

Even with binoculars, I'll never know how Humphrey spotted the animals, a mother and her male cub, from so far away. Crouched low, the mother was a collection of sinewy, lean muscle, almost resembling a track athlete wrapped in fur. Though Humphrey stayed back about twenty feet, the mother appeared unusually vigilant as she eyed the fluffy cub carefully.

"You did it, Humphrey!" Bill congratulated our guide, who went back to peering through his binoculars as soon as we stopped, with the lenses trained in a small patch just to the right of the mother and cub.

"There's one more!" Humphrey said in a serious tone, binoculars fixed on the patch behind the mother. "A male!"

We didn't have to strain to see the male—within seconds, the muscular animal stealthily approached the mother and cub, growling a low, guttural growl.

"He's trying to mate with the mother," Humphrey explained as he dropped his binoculars. "But the mother is more concerned with protecting her cub and won't let him get close."

It was a classic confrontation, with the female leopard angrily snarling at the male's every attempt to move in. The male, jumping back suddenly at times, persisted, though nothing he did riled up the female more than when he fiercely feigned towards the cub.

"There are times when the male cheetah has killed a new cub, just so he can mate," Humphrey added. "But I don't see that happening here. The mother is too watchful—she won't let him get close enough."

The back-and-forth between male and female continued, with even the tiny cub, echoing his mother's anger, barking at the assailant while he held fast to her side. The male, growing increasingly frustrated, seemed to grow weary of it all before long, waiting longer and longer between each approach before finally retreating back into the tall grass behind him.

"I hope you guys know how lucky you are," Humphrey smiled as we left the cheetahs and headed back to the main road. It was moments like this when I was glad Megan and I didn't bail out after Victoria Falls.

We left the Serengeti just around 4 p.m. that day, heading out earlier than usual so we could tour an authentic Maasai village on the way to the lodge if we chose to. Stopping just outside of the game preserve boundary, Humphrey fastened the black canvas top back over our vehicle, leaving a small, three-by-five section of the roof open for air.

"Bees!" Humphrey yelled suddenly as we sped down the two-lane highway. "Roll up the windows! Now!"

The huge swarm, consisting of at least one hundred, fat, black bees, buzzed angrily over the middle of the road in front of us, maybe 30 yards away. And with the small, open gap in the roof of our vehicle, I nervously realized we were speeding right through the mass. Hard.

Within agonizing seconds, Humphrey charged straight into the defiant swarm, which surprisingly appeared to buckle forward upon impact. Then, the sky appeared to rain black bees down upon us, and all I could think about was that roof.

"Close the windows!" Humphrey yelled as he hit the gas pedal hard. "Now. Hurry!"

I'm not sure if any bees found their way inside—I was way too busy cranking the stubborn handle of my window to make sure any particularly bold ones got sucked right out of our speeding vehicle. We made it through the firestorm uninjured but I'll never lose the image of that angry swarm, almost daring us to drive through it.

The roads around the Serengeti had quickly become familiar to me, as I recognized passing the narrow finger that led to our lodge from the previous night.

After driving an additional twenty minutes, I suddenly smelled that strong and wet, smoky odor I had encountered consistently throughout

Africa, always present when villages were near. This time, from atop a winding road, I spotted several dark clouds of smoke rising high into the air. We had reached the Maasai village.

Following the circular drive all the way down, Humphrey, with Marcus close behind, carefully pulled the truck through a rough, makeshift drive, intentionally parking well away from the high wooden entrance gate to the village.

"It's 400 per person for a tour of the village," Humphrey said, glancing through the rearview mirror as he backed the truck up against a rock wall. "And if you don't want to pay, you have to wait here."

Bill and Thom were the only two who decided to stay back, both claiming they'd be more content napping in the rear of the truck instead. The rest of us, with Mary racing ahead, as usual, cautiously approached the foreboding wooden gate, not exactly sure what to expect.

An older, gaunt man, dressed in the traditional Maasai robes of dark red and with a heavy, wooden pole gripped tightly in his right hand, smiled through his nearly toothless mouth as he beckoned us closer.

"You are here for the tour, yes?" he asked, and then stood back as he quickly counted our number. "That's 400 each for the tour and as many pictures as you wish."

I couldn't see where he kept it, but, somehow, the older man was able to make change for all of us, reaching into a deep pocket somewhere on his person and pulling out a fat roll of weathered bills.

Obviously, the village made some nice cash being in the tourist racket.

Stuffing the bills back into the mysterious pocket, the man directed us to move back to a slight incline overlooking the gate entrance. Then, ducking through a narrow opening in the gate, the man disappeared amid a din of excited, sometimes terse voices.

A few minutes passed before the old man appeared again, this time pulling the front gates wide open as he slowly slipped past them. Behind him, an entire village of men, women and children watched as a procession of maybe a dozen male warriors, each dressed in Maasai tribal costume, marched forward to a chorus of chanting voices and deep drum rhythms.

With a raw, unbridled energy, the warriors marched and danced until they stopped directly in front of us, all the while moving to the beat of the hollow-sounding drums. After a brief interlude of mock combat using their wooden poles, the warriors broke apart from one another and, after crouching low to the ground, used their muscular legs to catapult themselves high into the air. And they managed to leap pretty high, with one man in particular getting at least four feet of the ground.

"You try," one told me, thrusting his wooden pole into my hand.

"Uh, no...," I said, politely declining. "That's okay."

"Oh, go on," Megan urged. "It'll be fun!"

Never much of a jumper, I caved in anyway, using the pole I was offered to spring off the ground while a few of the men jumped along with me, whooping and hollering the entire time. I could only imagine how ridiculous looked, but I'm sure it didn't compare to how ridiculous I felt.

To my satisfaction, no sooner did I finish my weak attempts at leaping did a number of women from the village, without saying a word, cover the females in our group with traditional, collar-type necklaces.

"Come," urged one woman with her head shaved clean, as she grabbed Stacey and Megan as she led them to the center of the group. "We dance!"

Before long, every woman from our group had been ushered into the dance circle by the tribal women, all shuffling to the tireless, rhythmic pounding of the drums. Megan, with her face a blazing red, looked as if she might die of embarrassment, trying to keep up with the fluid hip swinging of the Maasai women.

When the dance concluded, a teenage boy with a coarse-looking beard led us through the gates and into the village, which basically consisted of one, straw-roofed hut after another, about two dozen, at least, laid out in a semi-circle. The center of the village, left completely open, remained that way, reserved for tribal assemblies. Not too surprising, souvenir stalls, manned by aggressive residents of the village, lined the path our tour guide led us down.

"Come, m'lady," one woman missing several teeth urged Megan as we walked by. "Try something on and see how good you look!"

Neither Megan nor myself were too interested in the assortment of hand-made bracelets and necklaces every village appeared to be hawking. She was much more successful with Mary and Helen, however. In the blink of an eye, they were both weighed down by strand after strand of brightly-colored necklaces, thrown over each of their hands like they were the targets in a game of ring toss.

"That's my wife," Abe muttered to me as we marched to the rear of the village. "She's always buying some crap she doesn't need!"

Our teenage guide stopped when we reached a small, dark hut with a small trickle of smoke wafting out of it, exactly opposite from the cave-like doorway. The tiny, narrow opening looked to be a tight fit, and I could feel myself starting to panic with claustrophobic thoughts.

"Please step inside," he directed. "We will show you how we live."

I hung back with Megan as the rest of the group piled into the hut through the small hole, watching the ground and noticing how people began piling up uncomfortably near the opening. I couldn't even think about climbing inside.

"Why don't you go," I told Megan, who, with Abe and myself, remained outside. "I can't make myself do it."

"You're sure?" she said, grabbing my hand.

"Oh yeah. It's way too cramped for me."

Like a rabbit retreating to its hole, Megan scurried through the small opening just as a male voice from inside the hut began speaking.

Suddenly, a tribal elder, noticing Abe and myself as we stood outside of the hut, approached with a concerned look on his face. He, too, was very thin.

"You are not interested?" he asked, studying my face.

"Oh, I am," I reassured him, motioning to the hut. "It's just too crowded in there."

The elder rested his eyes on Abe, who nodded in reply.

"Then you will see mine! Come!" he exclaimed.

Stepping aside, the man pointed with his wooden pole to the small hut directly behind us. It, too, had a small trickle of smoke escaping through a tiny opening in the roof. If it were possible, his hut appeared even smaller.

Personally, I didn't really care if I saw the inside of a hut or not, but the last thing I wanted to do was offend this man. So, taking a deep breath to calm myself, I followed the elder as he stooped down low and waddled through the narrow opening into the side of the dark hut.

A short, unhappy-looking woman, who had been kneeling over what appeared to be some sort of grain in the far corner, rose quickly to her feet when we entered before kneeling back down. Unable to stand upright because of the low ceiling, I searched through the darkness for a stool, finding one directly adjacent to the fierce fire in the center of the tiny hut.

Abe stumbled his way inside just as I sat back in the tiny stool, with the woman's scowling eyes fixed on me the entire time. The heat from the fire was brutally intense, unleashing a fury of dark smoke that hung low in the hut.

"This is entirely made of cow manure," the elder began once Abe settled into the stool next to me.

"Cow manure and straw."

The elder graciously shared with us the way tribal families lived, confirming that men did, indeed, need to slay a lion, as well as possess a herd of at least twenty cattle, before they were allowed to marry. The cattle were very important to the Maasai, the elder said, explaining that all of their nourishment came from the animal, including its blood.

As fascinating as the elder was, I was no match for the woody smoke that billowed right in front of me on its way through the roof. My eyes wouldn't stop watering, and the scent of burning manure did little to alleviate my misery. Hanging in for as long as I could, I bowed out just as Abe began opening his bag of questions.

"Sorry, but I'll be outside," I said, retreating back through the hole.

Abe emerged from the hut opening a few minutes later, just as the rest of our group had concluded their tour.

Megan quickly ran over to tell me how clumsy Aubrey had cracked one of the Masaai's beds made of trees branches when he sat on it.

"Can you image how long it takes to repair that?" she mused out loud.

By the time we returned to the truck after the tour, both Bill and Thom were racked out with sleep, obviously non-plussed that they had missed the cultural tour. With his mouth wide open, Bill lay across a majority of the back seat, drooling on the very spot he had sat in earlier. Thom, cramped as usual, clung close to the window he was seated against, almost looking like he was trying to escape.

The lodge we stayed in that night was probably even more opulent than the previous one, majestically resting high atop the edge of a green, rugged cliff. Rich, finished wood was everywhere, accenting the spacious lobby as well as the stairways of the multi-level hotel. Perhaps the best feature was the expansive outdoor deck, well over a hundred feet in length and hugging the mountainous edge of the lodge that overlooked a great deal of the forested area below.

As much as I enjoyed the game drives and spotting cheetah, leopards and lions, I was coming very close to getting my fill. I never even considered how exhausting it would be, sitting on a four-by-four truck for hours on end while we raced back and forth, looking for any signs of life in the vast Serengeti. Like anything, the truly exciting moments, like spying the cheetah family or three male lions, came less frequent than the moments you just wished you could end the drive for the game and just retreat to a lodge for the night. As much as I was looking forward to our last day in the Serengeti tomorrow, when we would tour the famous Ngorongoro Crater, I looked ahead even further ahead. To returning home.

For its part, the lodge featured every cozy comfort you could have wished for after a long day of driving. Our unspectacular yet cozy room on the ground floor, to Megan's enjoyment, featured a large, stately bathtub, instantly requiring her to strip down and soak. I rested on the double bed closest to the window, reading up a little more of the Maasai people and our next stop, Kenya, in the guidebook. I always found it a little weird to be in a room with Megan that housed two double beds. The whole Lucy and Desi thing just seemed so 1950s.

With dinner, again scheduled for 7 p.m. and nearly an hour away, I eventually stretched out across the entire length of the bed in relaxation. Just as Megan, clad in a white, terrycloth towel, emerged from the tub, an angry sound of something being pounded on rung out from outside.

THUMP THUMP THUMP

"What's that?!?" Megan whispered excitedly, clutching at her towel.

THUMP THUMP THUMP

I shot Megan a quick look, noticing a slightly anxious expression. The drapes were pulled shut over our window facing the small courtyard, but we were still in Africa, where I was convinced anything could wander anywhere. Maybe the lodge only created the illusion of safety, I thought. Maybe that thump was a large, bull elephant, angrily butting against the side of the building. What else could be making that hard, angry pounding?

The heavy pounding echoed again from outside, this time accompanied by a familiar voice.

"Aubrey!" Vernor's voice screamed loudly between a series of angry fists against the outside glass of what I assumed was their shared room.

"Aubrey!"

Admittedly, I felt a little silly for mistaking Vernor for an out-of-control elephant, but what I suspected was going on between Vernor and his roommate Aubrey would at least be a little more interesting. When the pounding stopped, Megan and I rushed to our door when we heard Vernor's exasperated voice next, back inside the lodge and shouting at Bill, whose shared room with Thom sat between ours and the feuding pair.

"I have no idea, Vernor," I heard Bill groggily say.

"I mean, I saw him with Stacey earlier, but I don't know where he is. I figured he was in the room."

"So did I!" Vernor boomed, his voice suddenly filled with rage.

"And now, since he has the only key, I can't get into the room to shower!"

Megan turned to smile knowingly at me. Stacey got her way after all.

"Where is her room?" stormed Vernor, his voice sounded more upset.

"Oh man, I don't know."

"Aubrey has to answer to this!" Vernor shouted.

I heard a door shut just after some hurried footsteps past our room. Vernor skulked away on his mission to find his roommate.

That was truly a dick move, Aubrey.

Judging by the palatable tension I sensed between Vernor and Aubrey over dinner, I suspected that Vernor did eventually find Aubrey and lay into him. Aubrey, seated on the far end of the group's shared, lone table with Stacey, spoke very little throughout the meal, usually only to her. And if I didn't know any better, Stacey, sporting her usual spackle job of make-up, loved every bit of the attention, flashing a cocky smile as she savored the moment of bedding Aubrey perhaps one, final time while the third point in their weird triangle, Vernor, boiled over with rage.

And they say women aren't evil.

If Vernor was still pissed, though, you wouldn't know by the way he laughed it up over our buffet dinner with Bill, Thom, Megan and me. That dinner was actually one of the most memorable during my entire stay in Africa, not because of the passable buffet food but because, for once, of how truly candid we all were about the tour. In other words, dinner that night became a mini-bitch session we managed to keep light and humorous, discussing everything from Seth's death-warmed-over-appearance every morning ("I got this picture of this thin, ghastly vulture he looks just like!" Bill laughed) to the meals ("If I see another sausage," Megan quipped. "I think I'm going to be sick") to living with the same, sometimes annoying people for weeks at a time. How could you discuss that topic without involving Vernor somehow?

"I heard what you told Mary today," I whispered to Vernor before breaking into my best Vernor impression.

"It does not matter what you say! It's measurable!"

Mary, seated on the opposite end of the table with Helen and Abe, flashed me an angry look while the rest of us cackled.

"Yes, but she was trying to tell me she was taller than me," Vernor said in a surprised voice as he shook his head. "Then she told me I was mean and that she wouldn't talk to me anymore."

"She just talks too much!" whined Vernor.

Bill nodded.

"Dealing with everyone here isn't easy," Thom added. "It's going to be weird not seeing everyone together in a few days."

As I finished my mandatory desert plate, filled with two coconut macaroons and a small scoop of vanilla ice cream, Thom's words rang through my head, well above the din of the African drum troop that had just begun performing in the lobby. The prospect of breaking free from most of these people, almost sounded too good to believe, like coming home to a new, exciting job that paid twice as much as the one I left behind.

LAST SUPPER

It's impossible to find that right set of words that can even possibly come close to capturing that unbridled sense of euphoria I was experiencing that morning over breakfast. As I dug the side of my fork into my stack of pancakes, all I could think about was spending the night in comfort at the posh, five-star Nairobi hotel I had booked online earlier before finally flying home.

For me, there was no better way to wrap up the pain of traveling through Africa than spending a night in unbridled luxury, and the room at the New Stanley hotel in downtown Nairobi would provide us with just that. I had been so long since I felt such excitement—not since Megan and I left the airport for Cape Town so many weeks ago, when I still had a sort of romanticized notion that six weeks of touring would just fly by.

I wasn't sure whether I was enthused to leave Africa because I was so disappointed with the tour, or if merely homesick. As mixed a bag as Africa proved to be, it did, ultimately, deliver everything it had promised, with plenty of wildlife sightings, unique experiences and long-lasting memories. The Serengeti game drives alone, though tiring, proved awesome, arguably allowing us to see more wildlife in a two days than during the entire six-week trip. The only thing I could be certain of after all that time on the road was that I was tired—more tired than I had ever been during my entire life. Returning home to my own place and to a warm bed would be a godsend.

Even knowing we'd soon be free of the overland tour, our personal prisons still couldn't shake neither Megan nor myself out of starvation mode. I think we both figured we'd go out with a bang, with pockets full of muffins and bagels stashed away in every pocket imaginable just in case. Megan and I didn't even need to speak about Nairobi that morning. The finish line, appearing just around the proverbial bend, appeared simply beautiful without words.

Like the day before, large patches of fog hung over the chilly morning air, like a depressing, rainy day in Chicago. Humphrey, as polite as always, smiled as we each returned to our now-familiar seats inside his truck.

There wouldn't be any final game drives before we heading back to Mesarani Snake Park, no final loops through the Serengeti where the chance always appeared very good we'd spot something. That morning, Humphrey was all business, speeding us back through the sometimes spooky mountainous roads, made spookier blanketed in thick, rolling fog, and red dirt roads to return us to camp. The deadline had been put in place—Nairobi by nightfall.

When we arrived back at Mesarani, Woody and Seth were finishing up their inventory of the few remaining goods in the rear of the truck, which amounted to nothing more than a smattering of brightly-labeled cans and some boxes of milk. In total, the inventory couldn't have taken very long at all. I suspected Seth had grabbed his clipboard just as he heard Humphrey's truck hit the small patch of gravel road leading into camp.

"Just finishing up here, guys!" Woody called out from inside the rear compartment as Humphrey halted his truck behind Ella. Woody, holding up two fingers after inspecting a small, hidden nook in the corner, returned to his exploring after Seth marked the clipboard in his hand with a half-eaten pencil.

Climbing down from the four-by-four for the last time felt liberating, too—they were fine in small doses but not as comfortable as Ella, especially after two days of rough driving. I felt a little guilty because I didn't realize that Humphrey and Marcus had waited around a little in camp hoping for a tip. Humphrey deserved one, and I wished I had thrown him a twenty for the effort, in retrospect.

"You guys are back earlier than I thought...good," Seth said, barely looking up from the clipboard. "'So how was it?"

"Quite nice, really!" Mary chirped.

"Yeah," Megan chimed in. "It just seems like the perfect way to end things here."

"Speaking of which," Woody said. "Things are going to be a little rushed today, since it is the last day."

Seth, dropping the clipboard to his side, walked to the cab of the truck and tossed it on the seat.

"Here's the plan, guys," Seth stated in mid-stride as he returned to the rear of the truck. "We'll leave in a half-hour, eat lunch just outside of Kenya, get through customs, check in at the hostel, and then go out tonight for the game dinner. After that, you're on your own."

Though the very thought of finally being free just seemed too impossible to get a firm grip on, the day was finally here. Today would be the last day we'd pull over onto the shoulder to eat our cold, crappy lunch. No more sleeping in tents on the rock-hard ground, no more endless hours on the truck, racing from one nondescript campground to the next, and no more having to tolerate some of these people that I'd usually rather kill than sit down and eat dinner with. Nairobi...five-star hotel...Nairobi...five-star hotel. It became my mantra.

It was due to all of those reasons that the drive that final day was very tolerable, as Seth raced us through the drizzling rain down that long, rugged road to Nairobi. As Megan's eyes darted across page after page of Aubrey's Nelson Mandela biography, I had become quite melancholy, with my relief-filled feelings of leaving the tour tempered with the hard reality of what awaited me at home. The economy still sucked, particularly for people in the computer industry like me. My savings had been completely wiped out. We'd stay with my parents since we had no place to live after giving up our lease.

Yep, things were looking pretty good.

Beyond that, I actually did feel a slight sadness as I looked around the truck from my familiar seat near the front. I think it was more respect than sadness, actually—respect for those with me who, despite the fronts that everyone liked to put over on one another about how easy the tour was, managed to make it through such a difficult, surprisingly grueling trip. And it was a shared adventure; we shared the same, collective fears of not sleeping safely through the night or contracting some weird disease, we shared the same desires for comfort after spending so much of the tour in misery, and we shared the same spirit for adventure, to do something that garnered us more than our share of puzzled, confused looks. No, I'll never write to Abe, invite Stacey to stay with us if she comes through Chicago, or look up Mary if I make it to Australia, but I couldn't take anything away from anyone that made it through six weeks later, all fellow inmates held captive through Africa.

We pulled over for lunch just as the sky filled with dark, ominous clouds. I couldn't think of a more fitting way to celebrate one of our last meals together, with the truck parked halfway down a man-made path through forest as the threat of a torrential downpour hung over head.

Lunch that day resembled more of a canned food drive, a bad one where everyone only donated food they had forgotten about and left to rot in the rear of the kitchen cupboard. Though there were no beets, Spam or the usual assortment of canned losers, Seth did manage to discover a few cans of sardines to compliment the fruit cocktail, tuna and the usual sandwich fixings. Sometimes starvation didn't seem like such a bad idea.

"This is it, guys," Woody chirped, squinting as he lined the rusty opener up against the can of tuna. "The few treasures we found left in the truck."

Treasures. Some treasures were better left buried.

Except for Aubrey and Vernor, everyone pretty much appeared sardined out, opting for anything but the smelly, gray creatures left bobbing in their can. When I felt compelled to tell Megan that the fruit cocktail was the best I ever tasted, I knew I had been away from descent food for far too long.

The sardines apparently didn't bother Aubrey, who attacked the can with fervor as he piled at least two sandwiches high with the foul fish. I still couldn't look at him without imagining him being tailed by hundreds of cutthroats as he wandered aimlessly like a tourist through the streets of Nairobi with his baby blue, metal suitcase tucked beneath his arm—the same suitcase that he insisted could never be stolen from him since it was locked and only he had the key.

Despite how he carried on with Stacey for most of the trip, he was most sensitive about that blue suitcase, biting his lip hard while staring angrily at anyone who dared tease him about it. He hated when any of the guides chided him about it, with Seth recently picking up where Skonky had left off teasing him about it. It probably helped Aubrey that his suitcase was largely forgotten about, well hidden from sight after being tucked away in Ella's rear compartment. With the days waning, though, and with each of us growing bold as our time together grew to a close, anything was fair game. Including Aubrey's suitcase.

"Hey, Aubrey!" Thom called out after swallowing a bite of his tuna sandwich. "I'm still waiting for that photo of you hitch-hiking with your suitcase!"

Seated alone, Aubrey pretended not to here, catching another mouthful of his limp sandwich while a few of us chuckled.

"Yeah, c'mon Aubrey!" Bill repeated. "You told us you would!"

Looking up at Bill to scowl, Aubrey turned his attention back quickly to his sandwich, not saying a word.

I knew Bill and Thom were up to something, as the two whispered among themselves before Thom, walking away with a smile, darted towards the rear of the truck. After hearing a heavy, metallic thud, Thom reappeared seconds later, with both hands clenched around the handle of Aubrey's suitcase. Not saying a word, Thom marched quickly towards the main road amid our laughter as he struggled with the bulky blue behemoth, placing it gently on the gravel shoulder before racing back.

"It's all ready for you, Aubrey!" Thom huffed, swallowing hard to catch his breath. "Just walk over there like you're hitchhiking so we can take a picture."

Aubrey's eyes grew hard as his gaze met Thom, full of angry venom. Half-expecting him to race to the road to grab his suitcase, I was completely surprised when Aubrey settled back even further into his chair, still without saying as much as a single word but chewing more deliberately.

"C'mon, Aubrey!" I urged, in an attempt to pry him out of his chair. "Just one quick photo."

I kept my eyes on blue suitcase, solitary waiting a good couple hundred feet from us. We hadn't managed to eat lunch yet without an audience, and who knew what kind of attention an unmanned suitcase would attract. If someone came by to grab it, it might save Aubrey the trouble of getting robbed in Nairobi.

Aubrey smacked his lips slowly as he considered the request, and then took a long sip of juice from his plastic mug.

"I want a dollar from everyone."

I didn't know what was crazier—that this man-child demanded payment for some good-nature humor or that it his price was only a few bucks. Either way, pretty sad.

"Fine, a dollar," Bill said. "Let's go."

Nodding his head as he looked around, Aubrey finally slowly rose from his chair.

"That's a dollar from everyone," he said again.

"Yeah, whatever," Megan said as she climbed back aboard the truck for the camera.

Naturally, Aubrey totally hammed it up once he met back up with his waiting suitcase on the side of the road, awkwardly sticking his thumb out hard as he bent over and grabbed at the bag like he was hitchhiking. I guess that was what got to me the most about Aubrey—he liked teasing people as much as anyone, but couldn't take a joke. That is, unless you paid him a dollar, which somehow made it better.

As we returned from the photo shoot with Aubrey's suitcase in tow, our lunchtime visitors finally wandered into camp, this time a couple of middle-aged Maasai men who grinned as they watched Seth clean up after lunch.

"You hungry?" Seth asked the men as he packed away the bread.

I don't think the men spoke English, or if they did, they weren't speaking it to us. Instead, they turned to one another and whispered in a language I wasn't familiar with.

"Here," Seth stated, handing the man closest to him, the thinner of the two, an opened but full can. "Sardines."

Sardines? Even I knew the Maasai's diet consisted only of cow. That's like giving a fat man a Speedo.

Grasping the can, silver with a photo of a sardine on it, the man lifted it chest high as he showed it to his partner, who immediately pointed to the fish swimming across the label. Then, after more whispering, the two men laughed heartily.

"What the fuck?" Seth mumbled angrily, as he slammed the crate filled with the little food that remained into the rear of the truck.

Seth didn't get it at all. He really didn't, becoming insulted when the thin man placed the can of sardines at his feet while he stood still next to his partner. I couldn't see how you could lead a tour through Africa and be completely ignorant of some of the common customs yet here it was, with our guide growing more pissed by the moment act this act of defiance.

"This is really starting to piss me off!" Seth mumbled to Woody, who came to his side to assist with the breakdown of lunch. "If they don't leave soon...."

I had never seen Seth—a level-headed, if not overly laid-back guy—so upset before, cursing to himself as the anger readily flowed inside him.

With the two Maasai men, seemingly oblivious, patiently waiting for a second choice, I could just sense things could get out of hand soon if someone didn't step in.

"Uh...Seth..." Megan said gently as she stepped in between our embattled guide and Woody. "The Maasai people only eat cow. That's it."

Briefly searching Megan's face, Seth froze his packing in mid-stream, placing the loaf of bread in his hand firmly down on the table.

"Cow?" he softly replied. "You sure?"

"Yes, Seth," Stacey responded. "They told us that on the tour."

Seth glanced over at the waiting Maasai, standing quietly as they probably tried to figure out what the hell we were talking about. I think they knew.

"Cow?" Seth mumbled sheepishly. "I don't have any fuckin' cow...."

We fell silent as Seth, jogging to the rear of the truck, rooted through the one plastic container already in storage. Returning empty-handed, he grabbed the half-loaf of bread he had left on the table and handed it to the thin Maasai man.

"Here," Seth said. "Take it."

Whether the men accepted the bread because he planned to eat it or because they just didn't want another scene was anyone's guess, though at least they held onto it this time and didn't place it next to the can of sardines left at their feet. We left the two men minutes later, wandering through our now-empty forested lunchroom with the can of sardines still waiting patiently for the next lucky visitor.

It seemed too fitting that bright beams of afternoon sun showered down upon as just as we arrived at the border crossing into Kenya, like finding that pot of gold at the end of the rainbow. Aside from that sunlight, though, there was little near the border crossing to be cheery about: shanty-like huts that appeared a slight nudge away from collapse; a main boulevard reeking of stale pollution and strewn with piles and piles of trash; and disheveled, sad-eyed children.

Naturally, my senses were on an all-time high alert by the time Ella grinded to a halt just outside of the immigration office. After all, we were just outside 'Nairobbery', our guidebook's not-so-clever way of referring to one of the most crime-ridden cities in the world. The irony wasn't lost on me—Chicago led all cities in the United States in homicides, yet I was convinced that every single local was secretly a thief with the singular goal of stealing my wallet, which I had adeptly moved to my front pocket the instant I headed outside.

I would guess at least thirty vendors had begun assaulting poor Woody, hanging back to keep an eye on things, as he stood leaning against the door to the truck with his arms crossed in front of him. The women actually seemed pushier than the men, waving everything from canvas paintings to kangas in his face while vainly trying to shout over one another. Woody could be one cool customer.

I hid my budding enthusiasm well when I handed my passport to the magistrate in the blue uniform, appearing serious even though I bubbled over inside with excitement. I remembered what we had heard from all the African Wanderer people at orientation about how unpredictable and crazy the second-leg to Nairobi typically was, specifically how you could easily waste an entire day at a border crossing if the immigration officer wanted to be a jerk about things. Several seconds and one, ink-soaked stamp later, I headed back outside to the truck with Megan, experiencing a slight sense of relief that our last border crossing was complete.

Woody was no longer watching the truck, ducking inside the immigration office himself when Vernor and Thom had returned. The very sight of our two guys locked inside the truck reminded me of one of those old frontier movies, where the small party of settlers could only keep the angry Indians at bay by staying behind the walls of their fort. I mean, the vendors were that ruthless, crowded several persons-deep around the single entrance door while the more resourceful ones opted for the windows, stretching just high enough to stick their wares through the open window.

Thom humored some of them, studying the rolls and rolls of wound canvas being tossed through his window by several sets of flailing arms. Vernor just chilled, looking away and barely acknowledging the frustrated hawkers outside.

"They're pretty bad here, huh?" asked Megan, as we silently stood watching the mob stake out the truck door.

"Mmm hmmm," I said, grabbing her hand tightly. "Watch your wallet and follow me!"

Maybe it was our bold thrust forward that seemed to catch the pile of vendors off guard, which quickly parted as we fought our way through.

"Miss!" a woman called out to Megan as she raced up the stairs. "For you, miss! Take it!"

The gray-haired, shifty-eyed woman reached as far as she could into the stairwell, waving a silky, orange scarf in her right hand, perfectly in the way of me being able to close the door of the truck behind us.

"You have to move," I said firmly, grabbing the handle of the steel truck door. "I'm closing it."

The woman frowned.

"Missus!" she called to Megan, who had resumed reading her book after plopping down into her seat. "She really does want this, sir. Missus!"

Deliberately, I pulled the door towards me until it butted up next to the aggressive woman. "On three, I'm closing it."

"One...."

The woman, not looking at me, struggled on her tiptoes to spot Megan.

"Two...."

"Missus!"

"Three. Bye."

Cursing under her breath, the woman pulled her arm away quickly and shot me an evil look as I slammed the door shut and locked it. Credit to her, though, for not giving up, as she parked herself beneath Megan's open window while she continued pestering her.

Each person making their way though the formidable crowd in order to get back on the truck must have felt like a rock star swimming in a sea of rabid fans, pulled in every direction until they reached the sanctuary of Ella once again. Mary and Helen thought the attention was cute, stopping just as I threw the door open to let them inside to admire the same, cheap souvenirs the hawkers surrounded them with—the very same we had seen since Victoria Falls.

****

I half-expected us to bounce over a large, person-sized bump on our way through the sea of persistent hawkers as we left immigration but it never did happen. My excitement was now at a fever pitch. Nairobi, here we come.

In what seemed like minutes after we left the border crossing, I could see what appeared to be a considerably sized chunk of urban sprawl on the horizon. I could smell it, too—specifically, the choking exhaust of less-than-roadworthy vehicles that occasional sputtered past us on the three-lane highway we sped down.

With the end clearly in sight, Aubrey sprung up from his seat in front of us and started heading down the aisle. Just when I thought he was heading over to Stacey, either to declare a weird, unyielding love or to tell her he was through being played like a fool, he stopped just in front of us. In front of Megan, actually, who didn't spot our guest until he cleared his throat just loud enough for her to take her eyes out of her book.

"Good book, eh?" he said smiling, struggling to view the page number she had been reading from upside-down.

"Almost done," Megan said, slamming the book shut. "Maybe a hundred pages or so."

Aubrey bit his lip in thought before sighing slightly.

"I'll let you finish it," Aubrey paused. "But only if you send it back to me. In Amsterdam."

Megan sat still for a moment before nodding her head in accord.

"Okay," she replied, still nodding. "Let me get you a pen and you can write down your address."

Before Megan started fumbling for one, I handed Aubrey the pencil I had brought along for journaling—it wasn't like I was using it or anything. In fat, puffy letters that resembled a child's, Aubrey scrawled out his address in the inside-cover of the book before handing it back to Megan.

"Thanks," Megan told Aubrey once he handed it back. "You'll get it as soon as I'm done."

Aubrey smiled before heading back up the aisle to his seat. There wouldn't be any emoting to Stacey after all.

Merging Ella into the traffic flow of reckless city drivers couldn't have been easy, but Seth did a capable job as always, nimbly guiding her through the congested and sometimes decaying streets of downtown Nairobi. Driving away again from the center of town, we found ourselves in a surprisingly quiet, mostly residential area just west of the city. With great care, Seth pulled the truck through a tight driveway that carried us right up to a single-level brown building. The entire grounds, almost completely bare of all vegetation, were surrounded by a towering metal fence. At that moment, with thoughts of getting to Italy flooding my mind, our accommodations couldn't have been more beautiful.

"This is it, guys," Seth mumbled with little emotion as we climbed down from the truck. "You don't have rooms here, since we're camping on the hostel grounds tonight, but we're welcome use the showers out back and everything else."

The campground, with mounded small stones scattered throughout the dried, yellow grass, wouldn't be mistaken for a Sealy mattress anytime soon. Even our sleeping pads wouldn't make much a difference on the hard ground, I feared. But one more night? With the assurance that the following night would be spent in a luxurious, five-star hotel?

I could do one night standing on my head.

I had just climbed back down from the truck after grabbing our backpacks when I heard the rest of the story.

"One more thing, guys," Woody said as he dragged his tent bag across the parking lot—I mean, 'campground.' "Seth and I start driving back at 5 a.m. tomorrow, so if you're sleeping out here, you're going to have to wake up so we can get your tents back."

"So like," Stacey snapped. "What are we supposed to do?"

Woody smiled and shrugged.

"Sorry, guys, but we need to start heading back all the way to Cape Town, so we can't really wait around."

The excitement that we all had to be feeling at the very end of the trip had suddenly been dashed—the mere suggestion of waking up early could do that sometimes, especially when there's no payoff. We stood paralyzed with blank expressions, mumbling disappointedly to one another over the news.

"What the hell are we supposed to do here at 5 a.m.?" Bill whispered to Thom. "There's nothing here!"

A quick glance around the hostel from where I was standing quickly confirmed that. Despite noticing several people hanging out in an open-air meeting area watching television, looking a lot like the hostel Megan and I stayed at in Cape Town before joining the tour, there appeared little else going on, let alone at five o'clock in the morning. Still a descent cab ride away from the city, 5 a.m. would be awfully lonely. And I doubted we could check in at our hotel that early, anyway.

Seth picked up on the disappointment right away, which was probably why he waited to lay that little bit of information on us until we arrived at the hostel and could no longer mutiny.

"Don't forget the game dinner tonight, guys!" he said in his best upbeat tone, which still sounded sleepy. "Meet here at seven, okay?"

Then Megan had one of her brainstorms. I loved her brainstorms.

"What about here, at the hostel," she whispered to Seth after slyly walking up to him. "I mean, can we stay in the hostel instead of camping?"

Her subtlety had been completely lost on Seth.

"Guys," Seth called out, dropping his sleeping bag to the ground. "You can always upgrade to a room here, if you want to."

My feet started moving me towards the hostel before I even made eye contact with Megan, who quickly followed behind me. I knew her well enough to know she wanted to sleep in, too—and hostels notoriously offered few private rooms so we'd need to hurry.

Somehow, Mary snuck past us and forced her way to the front desk first, where a twenty-something guy retreating to his room with bad, dark sideburns flashed a puzzled look as he saw the lot of us charging towards him. I was ready to steamroll anyone if it meant not sleeping in that parking lot.

Megan rolled her eyes as Mary cleared her throat before addressing the woman seated behind the desk. Just one more day, I told myself. One more day.

"May I use your telephone, please?" Mary unexpectedly announced. "I have a friend I may be able to stay with in the city."

I stood stunned as the woman, rising up briefly from her seat, pointed out an old, black telephone hanging against the far wall.

I let Megan speak to the clerk when it was our turn at the window—it was always hard to say 'no' to a woman, even by another woman.

"The private room is available, yes," the slender woman stated as her finger moved over the ledger. "The last one, too."

"Then we'll take it," I blurted out from behind Megan, who turned back to me and smiled.

Mary was still on the telephone talking to someone when Megan and I returned, dragging our weighted-down backpacks through the lobby and down the hallway to the private room. The worst part about the tour ending was probably having to carry all of our own crap again, which included not only my forty-plus pound backpack but also my smaller daypack, and my large, awkward bag of souvenirs. I still protected that abstract painting I picked up in Cape Town like it was my child—I'd be damned if I brought it this far to let it get destroyed.

We forced the old, metal key handed to us through the lock and opened the door just enough to throw our belongings inside, securing it again while we took a short walk to get some fresh air outside. With his blue suitcase tightly gripped in his hand, Aubrey waved to us from the hallway just before stepping inside an open door.

"I got one of the last spaces," he declared proudly as he wrestled his suitcase to the lower bunk. "Five a.m. is too early!"

I didn't make it my business to find out who was staying where for the night—part of me didn't really care, while the other part didn't want any flack for snagging the last private room, larger than most of the private rooms I had seen in a hostel and with four separate beds. Mary's glum expression told me she wouldn't be meeting with her friend a day earlier like she had hoped, Thom would probably sleep on the truck and risk contracting malaria like he had been for the past several weeks. I felt a little guilty watching Helen drag the tent she and Abe had planned on sharing through the tough, little rocks before stopping on a little patch behind the truck. If Megan and I hadn't secured the room, someone else would have. And I was too far along on the trip to worry about anyone else.

I didn't bother showering before dinner. The small shack in the backyard that housed the showers looked way too public for my liking. When I spotted two soapy dudes from our window, I knew it wasn't happening, and I was past the point of caring if the group knew I hadn't, anyway. Wetting my fluffed-up hair back down to my head, I slipped into my pair of dark slacks and put on my last, clean shirt—a black, collared shirt I hadn't even worn since packing it away within the furthest recesses of my backpack.

With everyone dressed as well as we could for our final night together, it was almost humorous when two of the shittiest taxi cabs I ever saw—a pair of brown, rusted-through station wagons belching black, acidic exhaust—arrived to take us to dinner at one of the better spots in Nairobi. The rear door of the wagon we hopped in wouldn't even lock, long busted open and rendered useless after years of countless rust. Seth, the lone passenger stuffed into the rear of the vehicle, took it in stride as he struggled to keep the door shut as we chugged and bounced our way to dinner.

"It's not so bad," he offered, bracing himself against the walls of the vehicle as grasped the door handle tightly. "It's nice to get a little air back here every now and then."

When I first heard the game dinner on the final night of the trip talked up, the idea was very exciting to me. Maybe I imagined sitting with local tribesmen around animal-skinned huts and a roaring fire as we dined together on exotic African game, a truly memorable way to come full-circle while being left with a type of experience unique to the continent. I didn't mind when Seth revealed that we were headed to a restaurant for our game dinner—that was cool with me. But when the cabs dropped us off where we'd be dining that night, a mammoth, neon-clad airport carrier with all of the authenticity of Olive Garden, I couldn't help but feel a little disappointed. Rain Forest Café was subdued by comparison.

Not since that cheesy American West restaurant in Cape Town, complete with its walls of dopey cowboy hats and plastic cow print seat covers, did I see such a forced attempt to embrace a theme. I almost felt embarrassed as the shy waiter led us to our table, noticing the several mounted animal heads that almost appeared to watch over you as you dined and the menus, written as if pulled out from Livingstone's diary.

I found the group's individual seat selection perhaps the most interesting aspect of the entire night. I wouldn't say we were ever one, big happy family, but I think being in a restaurant of the last night allowed most everyone to find themselves at that magical point of seeking the path of least resistance, of avoiding those persons who just had that special way of annoying us. And after six weeks in Africa, Mary was clearly the winner of that contest, seated on the far end of the table by herself until Helen and Abe took the empty seats parked next to her.

Mary looked completely pathetic—humorless and fidgeting uncomfortably as she adjusted her blue blouse while studying the menu. Try as I could, though, I just couldn't feel sorry for this woman. I enjoyed her silence; I cherished it. And with Thom, Bill, and Vernor sitting on the same end of the table as us, it only confirmed my suspicion that her game had gotten pretty old for all of us.

After our waiter returned with a water pitcher, he received only silence when he asked if we were ready to order, prompting him to recommending what he called 'the house special.'

"A plate of game meat," he said, sounding bored from reciting it several times a night, I was certain. "Some crocodile, antelope, zebra and hartebeest. And a potato."

When you're a game meat virgin like I was, ordering is pretty easy. As long as one tasted like chicken, I figured I'd be okay.

I believe everyone sprung for a game meat plate of their own, though I thought Abe might have ordered some chicken instead. Vernor, our vegetarian who made an exception for game meat, was hilarious, studying the menu like he was unraveling the puzzle behind the Rosetta stone as he rested his chin in his hand and spoke softly to himself.

"The hartebeest," Vernor said aloud as he kept his gaze fixed on the menu. "Is it good tonight?"

The waiter, caught slightly off-guard, rocked back and forth on his heels.

"Uhh...yes," he answered, shrugging his shoulders. "It's all very good."

Satisfied, Vernor slammed the menu shut and handed it to the waiter.

"One for me as well."

Seated beneath a rather large, mounted zebra head that looked fierce enough to tear you to shreds, I suddenly felt very much at peace. Spending six weeks in Africa like we did, though hardly a tour in the Peace Corps, was an accomplishment in its own right, a physical, mental and emotional test of endurance, more so than I ever imagined. Seeing it through to Nairobi, instead of bowing out back in Victoria Falls like Megan and I had considered, was one of the best decisions I ever made, and that had so much to do with so many factors. It was the game viewing in the Serengeti, my main reason for traveling to Africa. It was the canoe trip on the Zambezi, long and tiring but worth it in the end. And, believe it or not, it was also the people, specifically the absence of Skonky, our drunken, embattled guide and Matt, the self-appointed leader of his Aussie posse.

We joked around a lot with Woody and Seth, seated near us, as we waited for our dinner to arrive, with Bill teasing the two about their early drive back until they reminded him that he'd be getting up almost as early.

"If you plan on sleeping in that truck with Thom," Woody warned. "You might wake up in Cape Town, if you're not careful!"

Megan laughed.

"Now that'd be a good quote for the T-shirt."

"T-shirt?" Thom asked quizzically as he placed his glass of water down.

"That's right—he wasn't here," Bill stated, turning to Thom. "We made a T-shirt with our route on it and some funny quotes that were said over the first three weeks in Victoria Falls."

Yeah, we. More like Matt and the rest of the Aussies designed it and just asked us if we wanted to shell out the money to buy one.

"I'll bet we could make a really good one from Victoria Falls to Nairobi!" Megan said excitedly.

"Yeah," Woody said, disappointedly. "But unless you also ordered those shirts in Victoria Falls without quotes, you'd never get them back in time. There's just no other place to do it."

It was a shame, not only because the creation process would surely be a little more democratic but also because there were some funny quotes. Damn funny quotes.

"We'd have to put Vernor on there!" Thom shouted, bringing the rest of the table in on the conversation. "We could make an entire shirt of Vernor quotes."

"I've seen much more interesting things in my life!" I said, in my best Vernor voice.

Vernor, blushing, laughed along with us, probably not realizing just how quotable he truly was.

Probably a half-hour passed before our waiter, accompanied by another, older-looking man, carted out our meals on two, silver-clad dining carts. The restaurant was still pretty empty.

At least when everyone orders the same thing, it keeps you from glancing at your neighbor's plate and wishing you ordered what they did.

The oval-shaped plate waiting in front of me resembled everyone else's, with a small mound of white rice and a medium-sized potatoes on one side, and four tiny, toppled stacks of reddish meat chunks on the other. Hardly a feast fit for a king, but anything was better than another helping of any of Woody's campfire specialties.

"Enjoy!" said the waiter, turning on his heels to walk back to the kitchen.

"Excuse me!" I called to the waiter. "Which is which, so I know what I'm eating?"

I was pretty sure it was a question the waiter hated hearing, but should have grown used to by now. Leaning over to examine my plate, even he didn't appear certain which stack was which.

"That," he said pointing to the first stack. "Is most definitely antelope. I think. And that second stack is croco....no, that's antelope. And that first one is zebra. That third one? It looks like some more zebra on top, maybe some hartebeest is below it. I think that's hartebeest...."

I gave up after a while, nodding my head politely while I let the puzzled waiter decipher my plate until he thought I had heard enough. I mean, it was game meat—it'd probably be another thirty years before I ever ate it again, anyway.

All of the meat could have been mistaken for small steak shavings if I didn't know any better, cooked until just pink in the middle. Briefly catching a glimpse of Vernor, snacking on a chunk dangling from his fork as if to savor every bite, I cut a small piece off a hunk resting in one of my stacks and tasted it. A little dry, but not bad.

I tasted a little from each stack first, discovering that the only meat really containing a good, juicy flavor was the zebra...I thought. It tasted almost like steak—a little chewy, but pretty good. The others—hartebeest, crocodile, and antelope—pretty much possessed that same, drier taste. Maybe there was a reason why people didn't consume game meat in great quantities.

I guess I wasn't destined to be a game meat connoisseur, like Vernor was, though I had to admit I couldn't see why he'd compromise being a vegetarian for this meal in front of me.

Vernor was impressed with his meal, though, not only cleaning his plate but also ordering an additional side plate of zebra.

"This is some of the best game I've eaten," he said, seriously, wiping his mouth vigorously with his napkin. "Probably one of the highlights of the whole trip."

"And the worst?" I asked.

"I don't know," he said thoughtfully, glancing at the ceiling briefly before returning my gaze. "The people, maybe."

Overall, dinner was a nice, relaxing experience, complete with much-needed laughter and some sentiment that always accompanies a parting of the ways. I felt about Seth and Woody the same way I felt about Rutger—a couple of cool guys who did a very capable job of leading us.

When the bill arrived, Mary suggested we all throw in to treat Woody and Seth and I totally agreed—we all did.

The same shitty cabs, waiting for us out front, presumably, to drive us back to the hostel after dinner, shrouded in pitch darkness save for a lone lamp in the front window. Megan and I felt compelled to mill around Ella, just as Bill and Thom climbed aboard her for one final night of sleep, before turning ourselves to head to our beds.

"Have a safe trip back, guys," Megan called up to the truck as Thom unfurled his sleeping bag across the back seat.

"You too, now," called out Thom.

"Yeah," I replied. "It was nice getting to know you guys. We had some good times."

I didn't notice both Woody and Seth had been digging through the glove box for something until both men climbed down from the cab. They were the only two left I really cared about saying goodbye to.

"Thanks for dinner, you two," Woody said, resting his hands on his hips.

"We just wanted to thank the two of you for everything," Megan said, before extending her hand towards Seth. "It was a lot of fun."

Seth smiled sheepishly.

"We had a lot of fun, didn't we?" he answered, heartily shaking Megan's hand and then mine.

"I mean, you guys really made the second half cool. More so than the first half," I added.

Woody smiled.

"That's very nice to hear," Woody replied. "We try, you know."

Noticing Mary approaching in the distance with her toothbrush in her hand, I thought it best to cut things short.

"Well," I began. "You two have a long day tomorrow, so we'll let you get some rest. Drive safely."

"Thanks, guys," Seth said, giving a final wave. "We will."

Megan and I walked a few steps, heading back towards the hostel and just far enough so no one could hear us. Mary walked by quietly.

"Is there anyone else?" Megan whispered.

"Vernor, maybe, but I have no idea where he is. You?" I asked.

"Nope," she said with a deep sigh. "That's it, I guess."

We both glanced briefly at the few, quiet tents spread across the hard ground, then back at Ella, stoically resting for her final drive all the way back to Cape Town. Like a prized fighter who had just gone the distance and won, I was the happiest I had ever felt being so utterly exhausted. As we made our slow walk back to our room, it sunk in that our African Wanderer tour through Africa had officially ended. Tomorrow was a new day, one where we wouldn't be herded onto the truck for hours of non-stop driving. One where we would be free to go where we wanted to, eat when we wanted to, do whatever we wanted to, even if it was nothing at all. I knew I'd sleep well tonight.

"I TOLD HIM, DHL!"

Either I was too excited to sleep very late that morning or I was subconsciously expecting someone to bang on our door and wake us as had been the routine for the past six weeks. I fumbled across the nightstand for my wristwatch, knocking off the registration confirmation for our hotel, the posh-sounding and historic five-star New Stanley in downtown Nairobi.

8 a.m. I listened to the birds merrily chirping in the trees outside, then keyed in on a few voices I heard briefly outside in the hallway, a man and a woman, I guessed. The excitement of finally being free of the tour still resonated deep within me, and I looked forward to doing nothing much; a little shopping, and then shipping some of our bulky souvenirs back home, and enjoying a casual day with Megan.

After lying on my back with eyes open, I rolled over to snatch the hotel registration papers off the floor, rustling them just enough to stir Megan from her sleep as I re-read the terms over to myself. We had gotten a great deal for a five-star hotel, one of those that seemed too good to be true, at $100 a night.

"It's all there, right, honey?" Megan said softly through a smile as she supported herself on her elbows. "You must have gone through that half-a-dozen times since you pulled it out last night."

"I just want to make sure," I replied, setting the papers back down on the nightstand. "I'm not going to carry all of our crap around the streets of downtown Nairobi looking for a hotel."

"That's just going to be so nice!" Megan squealed. "I never stayed in a five-star hotel before! I wonder where everyone else is staying."

I slight chill ran down my spine, one brought on by imagining meeting Abe and Aubrey in the sauna at the Stanley's renowned health club.

"Let's just hope they aren't at the Stanley," I remarked. "Who even knows if they're still here."

We didn't bother showering that morning—in a matter of a few short hours, we figured we'd finally have the luxury of our private bathroom for a change. I was starving, though, and readily jumped at Megan's suggestion we eat breakfast at the hostel before heading to the Stanley, which would hopefully be closer to check-in time by then.

"Just imaging how it's going to look," Megan remarked, as we walked into the cozy dining area near the front desk and parked ourselves at a small, tilted table. "With all of our backpacks walking through the front lobby of a five-star hotel. It'll be priceless."

"It's the best way to end this," I said, grabbing a menu from the wire rack in the middle of the table. "Style all the way."

A husky waitress with her hair tied back, arriving swiftly with two glasses of ice water, took our orders quickly: two eggs, bacon and toast. Aside from a young guy at the desk and a woman reading a book with the help of the bright morning sunlight by the rear picture window, things were very quiet.

"We may be the only ones still here," Megan said, rising halfway from her chair as she peered around. "That's too bad, sort of...."

I shrugged.

"I don't know...who else did you want to see?" I asked.

"I don't know," Megan replied after taking a long sip of water. "Things just ended so quickly, you know. Like, once we got here, everyone was in such a hurry to bail."

"Well, I said 'goodbye' to who I wanted to," I stated as I moved in closer. "After all the shit Mary's pulled, I'm glad she's not here. Or Stacey."

Megan nodded.

"Stacey's not so bad, but you're right about Mary," she agreed. "I think we were all just ready to get back out on our own."

Megan was right—the tour ended more with a thud than anything else, with what little remained of the group dynamic completely eroded as every single one of us scrambled like rats looking for a way out. It was a little weird—to go from spending every waking minute with a group of people to being thrust out on your own once again literally overnight.

Breakfast, arriving piping-hot a few short minutes later, tasted great, with the salty bacon particularly flavorful.

"Well, we'll be at the airport tomorrow," Megan commented. "A few weeks in Europe, then back home to Chicago."

Yeah. With no money, no job, and no place to live. Sweet home, Chicago.

Once we finished breakfast and returned from the room, we looked over all our gear and realized we definitely needed to ship some things home. With my large backpack, a smaller daypack, and a large duffel bag full of heavy souvenirs, I'd be about as mobile in Italy as a flipped-over turtle.

I checked my Cape Town painting, making sure nothing had crushed it, and asked the smiling woman behind the front desk to call us a cab.

"A few minutes, sir," she stated over a ringing phone. "Right out front."

Thanking her, Megan and I dragged our gear to a small bench outside. A few more guests were grouped around a small television set broadcasting a soccer match.

"Look!" exclaimed Megan. "It's Vernor!"

Vernor, studying the screen intently with a glass of orange juice resting in his hand, looked lost in another world. I never got soccer—how could you invest hours into watching a sport that sometimes ended with a score of 1-0?

Keeping an eye on the driveway for any approaching cabs, I followed Megan as she approached Vernor, stopping directly adjacent to his chair before he finally noticed us.

"Hey you guys!" Vernor said "I thought you were gone!"

"A few minutes more," I said. "We have a cab coming. You?"

"A flight...a few hours later," he replied, his eyes darting between the television screen and us.

"Hey, it's been nice meeting you," Megan said.

"Yeah," I added. "You're a pretty funny guy."

Vernor smiled politely. I still wonder if he ever realized how funny his off-the-cuff remarks were.

"I had a good time," he said, sitting back in his chair.

A rusty, beaten-down cab, the same, shitty one with the broken rear-door lock that took us to dinner the previous night, slowly pulled up the hostel. Our cab had arrived, I guessed. After a final wave to Vernor, we tossed our gear into the trunk, which the driver then fastened shut with a heavy, wire cord, and we were off. Off to the New Stanley Hotel.

"I told him DHL!"

As we headed back into the people-clogged streets of downtown Nairobi, I felt as if the day had finally begun. From this point on, it was official: we were finally on our own again in Africa.

"So how long will you be at the Stanley?" the driver, a thin man wearing a soiled, white dress shirt asked.

"Only one day," I replied, as I studied the urban bustle outside the window. "Then we fly out."

"I will take you to the airport. Cheap," the driver replied. "What time will you be leaving?"

I shot Megan a look, who then discretely pointed to our pile of gear bouncing around in the decaying truck, kept inside the vehicle only by the grace of the loosely tied wire cord.

Before I knew it, the driver had pulled off Kenyatta Avenue, which had taken us through the heart of downtown, and into the circular drive of the New Stanley, where a pair of white-gloved men in long, dark cloaks quickly ascended on the cab and stacked our gear neatly on a single luggage cart. I could only imagine how this must have looked—two backpackers pulling up to the Stanley in a cab so shitty you had to tie the trunk shut.

Quickly, one man hustled the luggage cart in through a set of wide, opening doors, the handles accented with gold. The driver, hopping out of the cab, waited for an answer.

"I don't know," I said, remembering that our flight was around 10 a.m. the following morning. "We need a ride at noon."

I was always horrible at telling people 'no.' I was a much better liar.

"I will be here, then," he answered. "Just look for my cab."

After tipping the driver, I wandered with Megan through the stately lobby of the Stanley, a magnificent blend of black marble trimmed with deep, wooden accents. Black-and-white photographs of a bygone era lined the walls, featuring serious-looking men in dark suits posed side-by-side. The Stanley reveled in a long history as being the place to stay in Nairobi, a safe house of posh luxury in an uncertain land.

I instructed Megan to seat herself on the ledge of a dancing fountain in the center of the lobby as I cautiously approached the front desk, wishing I would have bothered shaving once the thin, tall man behind the counter waved me forward. I was convinced he had to think I was in the wrong place, that maybe I just needed to find a public restroom or something.

"Will you be staying with us today, sir?" the attendant inquired, standing perfectly straight.

"Yes—the name's Duprey."

As the man bent over slightly to type into the computer screen, I noticed several darkened photographs of Ernest Hemingway on the wall behind him.

"Did Hemingway stay here?"

"Yes, sir," responded the attendant, not looking up as he typed away at the keyboard. "He wrote many of his more famous novels here—'The Green Hills of Africa,' 'The Snows of Kilimanjaro'...."

I grew nervous after what felt like minutes passed but was probably only a few seconds. What if he didn't have the reservation? The website I made it on—what was it called again? I knew there was no way we could walk in anywhere in downtown Nairobi and get such a great deal.

"It should be around $100 a night!" I blurted out, just as the printer resting on the back counter began spitting something out.

"I have it right here, sir," he said with a slight smile. "It's all taken care of."

My hand shook nervously as I placed my signature on the dotted line, almost overwhelmed that I'd actually be spending the night in a five-star hotel. I turned and flashed a quick smile to Megan, who returned one of her own before rising to her feet and approaching. I heard a woman's voice behind me.

"If you will follow me, Mr. Duprey, I will show you to your room."

The woman, probably in her middle-thirties and very slim and with shoulder-length hair, led us to the long bank of ornate, glass elevators just around the corner from the front desk, offering the usual, courteous questions about what brought us to Nairobi along the way. Even she chuckled after hearing about our sometimes-agonizing plight with African Wanderer.

"If I was camping for nearly six weeks straight," she offered. "I'd pick the New Stanley, too!"

The elevator, stopping at the fifth floor, opened up to area where a gruff-looking security guard sat bored behind a shiny, oak desk. Two hallways then split off, with the woman leading us down the one headed just behind the desk.

"We have security on every floor," the woman explained as she made hurried steps across the carpeted floor. "You should feel quite safe."

On our left, the absolute picture of opulence, a teardrop-shaped rooftop swimming pool, where several guests with tropical looking drinks milled around. Even with a surprisingly strong, cool breeze whipping across and no sun to speak of, the pool still offered a huge temptation.

The woman pulled the magnetic swipe card out of a front pocket just as we reached room 540, the room at the end of the hall. Pushing forward on the handle once the green light by the lock had illuminated, we followed the woman inside one of the most luxurious places I had ever seen. Our room.

"Take a moment to look things over," the woman urged, stepping back towards the door.

The only question I had was why we couldn't stay here another night. The room had everything—a large, marble bathtub with double vanity; a king-sized bed wrapped in the finest Egyptian cotton; double glass doors that opened out to a large, stately balcony. Completely stunned, I tried to put on my best poker face but couldn't help but crack a smile. Just like Megan.

"It's beautiful!" she told the woman. "We're very happy!"

The woman then excused herself, but not before leaving us a small pamphlet regarding hotel services that included not only the health club I had heard about, but massage therapy, a business office for Internet access, and scores of bars and restaurants. I could easily spend an entire day at the hotel alone.

"You really did a nice job here, baby!" Megan shrieked as she threw her arms around me and pecked me on the cheek. "Woo-hoo!"

After our luggage arrived a few minutes later, I couldn't help but break into practical mode. Specifically, that meant shipping off as much as we could back home to my parents in Chicago to make life a little bit easier once we hit Europe. I couldn't imagine—I didn't want to imagine—trekking through the summer heat of Italy with all of the crap I had strapped to my back. It was impossible. The one problem we had, though, was getting our hands on some boxes to ship everything back in.

"If we can just take care of this, I promise I'm through for the day," I told Megan, who wanted to do nothing more than relax. I spotted the post office on the map in the guidebook—it didn't look far at all.

"I know you're right," she said in a tired voice. "But where are we going to get boxes?"

Leaving the comfort of our room, we ventured into downtown Nairobi, where, across the street from our hotel, I spotted a small row of grocery stores. Splitting up made the most sense, with each of us after at least two, good-sized boxes to ship our excess belongings home. I managed to score a few right away by asking a clerk, who explained they'd need to charge me something nominal for them. They weren't huge, but they'd be better than nothing. And though it meant my Cape Town artwork stayed with me, so be it—I knew I could tuck it neatly into one of the straps that hung from the side of my backpack and I wasn't about to let it out of my sight.

Returning to the hotel, Megan went up to the room with the boxes while I asked the concierge, a wide-eyed man with a haunting stare, for directions to the post office.

"Post office?" he asked in a surprised voice. "Only use DHL, my friend. You will get it in a few days. Guaranteed."

"That sounds expensive," I said.

The man glanced quickly at a ringing phone behind him before returning his gaze to me.

"They are expensive, but good," he replied, glancing back at the phone until it became silent.

"I do not trust the post office," he said ominously. "And neither should you!"

Thanking the attendant, I waited until I stepped inside the elevator to check my ever-dwindling supply of cash. I was running pretty low, down to my last few traveler's checks and not much else. Remembering the price of nearly eighty U.S. dollars I was quoted by UPS in Victoria Falls to sending my painting to Chicago, I knew that sending two, heavy boxes of our gear home wouldn't come cheap. If it even was an option.

Seated on the bed when I arrived back at the room, Megan appeared only mildly interested as she viewed CNN's international feed from the television perched atop an intricate dresser.

"Sometimes you think six weeks is such a long time," she said, clicking the television off with the remote control resting on the bed. "Then you see how little actually changes."

Spread across the other half of the bed was a big, bulky pile of her clothes—a pair of jeans, a few long-sleeved shirts, and maybe three or four T-shirts. Like myself, she packed way too much.

"This is what I came up with," she said, nodding towards the pile. "Maybe we can pack our souvenirs in with our extra clothes in one box and then send our sleeping bags and pads in the other. Did you get directions?"

I laughed.

"All I really got," I began. "Was a warning by the guy downstairs to use DHL or someone other than the post office. I think they lost his mail once or something."

Grabbing one of the slightly beaten but sturdy boxes from the far end of the room, Megan began stuffing her clothes in on one side.

"DHL?" she said, slightly disgusted. "We don't have money for that!"

"That's what I said," I replied. "I mean, some of the souvenirs are heavy!"

I tossed my backpack up on the bed, spilling the wooden doll Megan had purchased for her sister across the end of the bed.

"We have to use the post office," I said, unzipping the bottom of my backpack, where all the unworn clothes had been stuffed. "Either that, or carry all of this crap with us through Europe."

It was settled pretty quickly; we'd pack everything up into the two boxes like we had planned, hurry to the post office, and send everything off. Hopefully, we'd be finished with our tedious errands by early afternoon, affording us enough time to lounge around our beautiful hotel. That was all I really wanted, and it hardly seemed like a lot.

By the time the two boxes had been packed full, one with our clothes and souvenirs and the other with our two sleeping bags and pads, each weighed at least fifteen pounds, a small fortune by DHL standards, I was certain. We took as much care as we could with the souvenirs in particular, packing the particular fragile items, like the animal carvings for my mother and the wooden doll, between layer after layer of clothing.

I was a bit relieved to see the attendant who advised us about DHL busy speaking to an elderly woman at the counter when we departed the hotel with one box apiece tucked safely in our arms.

Headed south on Kenyatta Avenue with Megan on my left, my vigilance as we plodded through the streets of 'Nairobbery' was at an all-time high.

The crowded streets were filled with potential suspects, whether it was the group of young guys who I thought had started following us once we passed the shoe shine stand; the lanky guy who glared at us coolly as he passed, then glancing down at the bulky box cradled in my arms, or even the well-dressed man in the suit, happily commenting on the cooler weather.

From time to time, I'd reach down to feel the bulge of my wallet, safely tucked in the front pocket of my shorts. The post office seemed further than it appeared on the deceiving map, and I was partially worried, with all of my attention devoted to rooting out criminals, that we might have walked right by it.

Nearly a half-block away, a Caucasian head with prickly blond hair standing on edge bobbed briefly over the crowd in front of us, disappearing briefly before up again over a pair of two, well-dressed African men.

"Is that who I think it is?" asked Megan, noticing the same, bobbing head. "Is that Aubrey?"

Megan's hunch proved true as the sea of crowd thinned near a department store and we saw the familiar, bouncing gate of our Dutch friend. It was Aubrey alright—wearing his yellow 'Charlie Brown' T-shirt as he hiked through the streets of Nairobi with Bill and Stacey at his side.

"Hey guys!" exclaimed Megan once we came face to face with the trio. "We missed you this morning!"

"You know how it is," Bill smiled. "We had to get up early so we just headed up here."

As comforting as it was to spot a few friendly faces on the bustling city streets, it also felt unusually awkward, marred by extended moments of silence and everyone looking like they'd rather be somewhere else. Anywhere else.

"Just headed to the post office, you know," I said, glancing at the group while wondering if Bill had taken Vernor's place in the bizarre love triangle.

"Just got back," Bill said, pointing over his shoulder. "Only a few blocks more."

"Was it expensive?"

"Not too bad," Bill said, shrugging slightly. "I sent back one of those chieftain chairs I bought in Victoria Falls. There's no way I'm going to even think about going on with all of these souvenirs."

"I told him DHL!"

Bill didn't seem like the type of guy who still had at least another year of non-stop traveling inside him. It wasn't that he couldn't do it, but I didn't see why he would want to.

"If you're ever in Chicago, look us up," Megan told him. "I don't know where we'll be, but you know...."

"Where are you staying here, Megan?" Stacey rudely interrupted, standing with arms crossed as she lightly tapped her foot against the pavement. "We left our bags at the hostel until we decide."

That was good news. I figured seeing Aubrey without his blue suitcase meant he had already been rolled.

"Oooh," bragged Megan, giving me a quick glance. "The New Stanley! It's gorgeous! Five stars!"

Stacey's eyes grew wide. Even she was impressed.

"Well, good for you!" Stacey declared, feigning good cheer. "And how much did that cost you?"

"I forget, really," I offered. "But I booked it so far ahead online that we got a great deal."

"Hmmmm..." Stacey mumbled. "We may have to check that out."

"Well," I began, glancing at my watch. "We really want to take care of this before lunch, so we have to get going."

"Remember the book!" Aubrey said boldly, shaking his finger as if he was scolding a child.

"As soon as I'm done, Aubrey," Megan returned. "I promise."

After wishing one another well and promising we'd keep in touch, we continued on to the post office. The person I envied least of all was Stacey, who was meeting up with another overland tour in a few days for another couple weeks in Uganda. Gorillas or not, I couldn't even think about it without feeling nauseous.

Hiking one final city-sized block, Megan called out when she spotted the post office on our left, tucked away in the far corner of a huge, glass office building. Aside from a few, scattered people seated in plastic chairs, the post office seemed pretty empty. I glanced at my watch.

"They may be closed for lunch," I observed. "But maybe we can hurry."

Approaching the main desk with our boxes, a seated woman directed us to a large, glass-enclosed office, where two older women sat on tiny stools crowded around a metallic desk that looked right out of high school. The woman actually behind the desk, with her hair tucked beneath a red scarf, was reading something, while the other woman knitted steadily through sleepy eyes.

"Excuse me," Megan said, after I rapped slightly on the window. "We need to send these to the United States, please."

Placing my box on the floor, Megan quickly dumped hers on top. The woman behind the desk moved slowly, closing shut the folded magazine in front of her before tucking it carefully into the top drawer.

"Sea or air?"

"I don't know—what's the price?"

As the woman behind the desk whipped out a pencil and began writing some numbers down on a sheet of scratch paper, the other woman, her knitting placed in her lap, leaned over to glance at the boxes.

"What's in there?" she curiously inquired as she placed a hand on the box. "Anything you need to declare, hmmm?"

Suddenly, I had a sinking feeling in the pit of my stomach. One that told me our packages would never make it out of the post office.

"Just old clothes," I answered quickly. "Just things we don't really want with us here."

Not looking entirely satisfied, the woman ducked behind her associate's shoulder, reviewing the pencil-scrawled numbers across the paper. Then, taking one box at a time, she weighed each on a large, digital scale by the main desk and handed the woman crunching the numbers two slips of yellow paper.

"It will cost around $70 by sea for the two," the woman said softly after hammering away briefly on the calculator. "By air, around $120."

"By sea?" I inquired, as the two women waited for our answer. "How long does that take?"

"A few months," the woman behind the desk stated matter-of-factly. "Upwards of six months. Air is two weeks."

Though neither one of us were thrilled at the prospect of our package sitting on a dock for months on end, 'sea' was the most affordable and therefore, most appealing option. The very notion was crazy—our clothes would be on vacation longer than we were.

"I told him DHL!"

"You need to wrap those boxes," the woman who had been knitting said. "In plain, brown paper with the address written on it clearly."

The woman behind the desk nodded in agreement when I looked her way.

"Can we get that here?"

"At the grocery across the street," the woman responded. "You have to hurry if you want to make it back before we leave for lunch in fifteen minutes."

"We won't be back for an hour, then," the second woman added.

The only thing missing from our sprint was the firing of the starter's pistol. With a handful of confusing forms and our boxes, we blazed a path to the main lobby.

"I'll get the paper!" Megan ordered. "Find the knife and start filling all that out!"

As I watched Megan weaving through traffic and disappear into the large grocery across the street, I dug deep into both boxes for the large hunting knife we had brought along, finally finding it after unpacking nearly everything. I could only imagine how crazy I looked to the friendly security guard, who had casually strolled over to make small talk as I sat hunched over the paperwork on the floor, my knife resting on top of the stack of boxes.

Megan returned just as I finished the last form, tossing the roll of thin, brown parcel paper to the floor as we attacked it with the knife. As delicate as it was to work with, growing frayed and nicked with the gentlest touch, the hurried wrapping job did look surprisingly professional—if you ignored the huge amounts of duct tape holding it on.

I was sweating by the time we raced back to the glass-enclosed office, where the two women almost appeared surprised we had made it back before lunch.

"Here," the woman behind the desk announced, handing me a thick black marker. "Write the shipping addresses on the package."

"Right on the paper?" Megan asked politely. "What happens if the paper rips off?"

The woman sat silently as I took the marker from her hand.

"We will put some string on it," the other woman, still knitting, offered. "It won't rip off, because the men will carry it using the string."

Catching a glimpse of Megan, looking just as frustrated as I was, only made me chuckle instead. For $70, the only thing keeping our packages from disappearing forever was a thin, paper outer shell taped to the box. And string. You can't forget the string.

"Let's do it," I said, watching as the two women tied two strings loosely around each package, one in either direction. "And hope for the best."

I put my arm around Megan as the two women, each carrying one of our packages, disappeared behind a swinging door moments later. I had more of a problem with the potential six-month wait rather than the risk of the packages never arriving at all. I mean, it was the postal service. Even if it wasn't most efficient, it had to be pretty reliable.

"Well," Megan said longing, like a parent watching her children drive off for summer camp. "There they go."

"See you in six months," I added.

After the madcap rush to get the packages off our hands, it was a tremendous relief not having to worry about it anymore. Barely after twelve in the afternoon, we now figured we had the entire day in front of us. That is, after one final stop at the currency exchange to pay for dinner that night. We hadn't expected shipping the packages would be so expensive.

Like most cities we had explored in Africa, you'd never have to look very far to find a currency exchange agent in downtown Nairobi. Along one stretch, it seemed like nearly every other storefront consisted of one, each boasting "the best rates in town." We settled on the Thomas Cook, a secure fortress with a burly security guard stationed out front and a series of doors that required you to be buzzed through each one. It doesn't get any more secure than that.

"Change, please," Megan told the dark-haired Caucasian man behind the counter as she handed him a twenty dollar bill, just enough to get us through the rest of our time in Nairobi.

"Yeah," I joked. "We just visited your post office and got robbed sending packages home."

The man's face behind the counter grew very serious—almost grave.

"The post office?" the man said in a hushed tone as he leaned closer to the glass.

"Why did you go there?"

His eyes opened wide in disbelief, the man glanced quickly at Megan and myself as he awaited his answer. He was deathly serious.

"We had packages to send back," I stated. "Nothing great, but too heavy to carry the rest of the way."

A sick feeling came over me as I recalled how we stuffed every souvenir we had purchased in Africa, minus my Cape Town painting, inside the one box. Every single one. We both stood speechless.

"Tell me," the man pressed, glancing down at the twenty dollar bill still resting on the counter. "What exactly did you send?"

Megan bit her lip slightly.

"All of our souvenirs," she stated excitedly, struggling to squelch her rising anxiety. "And our sleeping bags, some sleeping pads and some clothes we didn't need."

The man nodded his head sadly, eulogizing our packages in his mind, before leaning back and calling to a black man seated at a desk in an adjacent office.

"They sent packages home through the post office!" the man behind the counter called out to his associate. Instantly, a look of horror came over the black man's face as he raced up to the counter.

"Did you send souvenirs?" he asked with a hint of terror in his voice.

I sheepishly nodded, feeling as if I had committed a tourist faux-pas on the same level as believing Cabrini Green was a golf course, not an urban housing project in Chicago.

"You will never, ever see those packages again," the man mourned. "I am sorry."

Megan and I stood silently in disbelief for a moment, exchanging glances with one another before facing the two men again, both looking at us through pitiful eyes. There's no worse feeling than believing you've been ripped off, and I had the sinking feeling I'd one day recognize my lost clothes on the back of some indigent refugee over a CNN satellite feed one day. But it wasn't the clothes. It wasn't even the sleeping bags. It was the souvenirs, though some of them were seriously cheesy, they were mementos, nonetheless, of my past six weeks in Africa. The animal carvings for my mom I picked up in Zanzibar, the hand-carved statue of the demon spirit from Malawi, everything. And

I felt absolutely helpless, haunted by the words of the doorman at the hotel and his three favorite initials, DHL.

"Maybe not all is lost," the black man said, detecting our disappointment. "I would return to the post office right away and demand the packages back."

"You just can't do that, can you? What would you even say?" I asked.

"Just tell them you changed your mind," his dark-haired associate chimed in. "You may not get your money back, but then you will know the post office won't steal them from you!"

Megan glumly thanked the man after he had changed her $20, who returned by wishing us well as we sadly wandered back outside to the busy, downtown street. My head was spinning. Do we go back to the post office to retrieve the packages? My emotions told me to make up some story to get everything back, find a way to carry it all to Italy, and then send it home. It wouldn't be easy and definitely wouldn't be cheap, but it was a much better bet.

"So what are you thinking?" Megan asked me in a soft voice as we stood frozen on the city street.

"I just don't know," I said, frustrated. "I knew this was going to turn into an all-day thing. Now we need to run back to the post office, fight with them to get everything back, then figure out what to do with those damn boxes once we get them!"

Megan said nothing, lifting her chin slightly into a cool breeze as crowds of people rushed past us, glancing with the occasional curious look as we stayed planted in place.

"I don't even think the post office will return our packages," I said, noticing my voice getting louder as I grew more upset.

"Fuckit," Megan said calmly, grabbing my hand. "It's not in our hands anymore, and maybe those guys don't even know what they're talking about, anyway."

As much as I wanted to march back to that post office and sprint away with those two boxes, I understood the wisdom in what she was saying. Maybe it was a risk—a huge risk—that we might never see those packages again. But after six weeks of worrying about so much, from poisonous snakes, predators stalking us at night, to becoming ill with some bizarre disease, I was through. I didn't want the worry any more—I just couldn't handle it.

I looked Megan in the eyes, then noticed the sweet, tender smile slowing growing across her face. It wouldn't be easy for me, but I had to see it her way, that things were no longer in our control. Though we packed everything with care and did what we had to do, it just wasn't up to us anymore, and if embracing that notion was the only one I could enjoy the rest of my trip, then that was the way it had to be.

"Let's go back to the hotel," I told her, squeezing her hand gently in mine.

Still, I couldn't help but stop at the oval-shaped concierge stand on our way back up to our room, as I planned to survey a few more of the fine Nairobi post office I had heard so much about.

"You did not listen!" our doorman repeated as he turned to Megan. "I told him—DHL!"

The manager on duty, a sophisticated woman dressed in a sharp, black dress, offered some reassurance, at least.

"I'm not aware of the post office being bad," she stated, after hearing our plight. "If there are cases of theft, wouldn't it be more likely that incoming packages are stolen than ones being shipped out?"

She made some sense. I labored a little on her logic back in the room until Megan politely cut me off, reminding me I promised to let it go. Megan was always so much better at that than I was. But she was right. It was done.

By the time the entire shipping fiasco had run its course, our envisioned day of leisure had reached late afternoon, rife with more stress than either of us would ever have imagined. It was definitely one of those 'I just want to be left alone' moments for the both of us. Though the cooler weather still made it unwelcoming to swim in the rooftop pool, the health club did prove to be the perfect release for both of us, with Megan opting for a long steam bath while I chose to sweat my worries away in the sauna. It felt good not running through the streets of Nairobi like a madman—it was one of the few moments in the day when I could just relax and feel the tension flowing from my body.

After dinner at the Thorn Tree, a small café-style restaurant that seemed a little out-of-place overlooking the smog-choked street in front of us, the fatigue of six weeks on the road set in once again and we retreated to our room, where Megan pulled the plane tickets to Amsterdam from the far reaches from her backpack. Meanwhile, I tried to get a grip on the fact that we'd be sleeping in Italy, our final destination, the following night.

I was excited to leave Africa. After six weeks of touring, I think anyone would be, though I instantly remembered that Stacey, Aubrey and Bill still had at least a few more weeks on the continent to go.

The fact was, I was completely exhausted and didn't believe I could ever find proper rest while staying in Africa, at least not in the campground and hostel accommodations I had been dealing with since my arrival. Ultimately, everyone reaches a point where they desire a little more comfort in life. For me, that was Africa, which reminded me of how much more enjoyable things might be if I had a spacious room in a lodge and a warm bed to retire to every single evening. That's why when I think about the number of people who applauded me for making the trip, saying things like "That's awesome to do while you're young" and "Now's the perfect time." It makes me smile. As much as those words do ring true, that it is easier to pick up and go when you are younger and have few commitments to leave behind, it still puts one hell of a beating on the body.

Megan all but collapsed into a deep sleep that night as soon as she hit the bed, burying herself deep into the soft mattress while wrapping herself in the thick, white comforter. Like our stay at the lodges in the Serengeti, I wasn't so lucky, lying wide awake as my sore body seemed to be longing for something hard to sleep on. When I did finally manage to fall asleep, another vertigo attack, one that made me leap up from the bed and race down the hallway to the light switch, all but ensured I wouldn't be dozing off again anytime soon.

So much for dreaming of Italy, of sinking my teeth into authentic pizza, plate after plate of pasta, and sampling the huge assortment of gelato.

"I told him DHL!"

EPILOGUE

Fumbling through the darkness of the hotel room once the clock radio began its annoying, robotic beep, I stepped quickly to the balcony window, pulling the drapes open wide. Hoping for an invigorating blast of bright, morning sun, I instead found a city still enveloped in darkness, completely quiet save for the occasional sound of a speeding auto somewhere in the distance. It figured. We just seemed cursed, having to wake up in darkness all of the time.

With our flight leaving for Amsterdam in a few short hours, we were left with few options, especially since we were crunched for time if we hoped to make our connecting flight to Italy. It seemed silly—flying well past Italy to Amsterdam only to board another flight into Naples later that evening—but we had failed in every attempt we made to simplify things. Instead of an overland truck, we'd be spending the entire day on airplanes.

Megan and I were too busy getting ready that morning to discuss much about our time together in Africa.

At least the trip to the airport in Nairobi was pleasant. In a sharp, dark-blue Buick, it was style all the way, topped off by a smartly-dressed driver who hid his sometimes-difficult life well behind his congenial personality. Working several hours apart from his wife and kids, he grew excited when he thought aloud about earning enough money one day to send for his family to join him in Nairobi, a time which he prayed would be soon. Even as jaded as I could be, his story definitely got through to me.

The three weeks we spent traveling through Europe is a story for another time, not as fly-by-the-seat-of-your-pants as Africa, but full of too many adventurous twists and turns to brush off in a few, short paragraphs. Sleeping in beds every night through Europe was a definite plus, though I'd gladly trade it for a tent if it meant I didn't have to carry the nearly fifty pounds of gear strapped to my back whenever we changed locales. The summer heat of Italy is not kind.

By the time we had finished traveling throughout Europe, which included stops in Italy, Germany and Amsterdam, I was more than ready to return to Chicago, still exhausted, but also very homesick. The thought made me wonder if it was possible to be homesick, even if I didn't truly have a home. As we had planned, my parents' home in the suburbs proved to be an accommodating base of operations, though at times, I thought I had wandered into another episode of "All in the Family."

When we moved into our own place almost one full month later, a small apartment in the Bucktown neighborhood of Chicago, Megan began the laborious task of rooting through all of the photos she had snapped—nearly twenty rolls—in order to select the best for a website chronicling our adventures. It would be a lot of work, but it was something she wanted to do by herself, to use as a springboard for a career in web design.

I realized in looking at the stacks and stacks of photos—of lions majestically lying beneath the warm, African sun, of gently-rising Dune 45, the formidable mountain of red sand I still couldn't believe I scaled, and even some of the sillier photos, like Megan clawing around behind an unknowing tortoise on Prison Island, I missed Africa. Forgotten were the lost hours aboard Ella, the crappy, tired food and the hard ground to sleep on. That's the power of photography, I guess, which I'm convinced could make even the worst trip seem tolerable. Putting all of that aside, I always look back on my experience in Africa with Megan and the rest of the crew as a great, exciting experience, though I will never forget how exhausting and mind-numbing the trip got at times. Megan and I even talked about going back to the continent one day, though we'd strive to do so via the comfortable lodge circuit instead of tenting. Still, even suggesting we return seemed unprecedented at one time, considering how close we were to pulling ourselves off the tour in Victoria Falls like we wanted to. I will remain grateful that we never did—we would have missed out on so much.

Admittedly, I didn't fall in love with the continent like so many of the campground hosts we had met did, willing to leave their previous lives behind to start a new one in Africa. I think it was more the sensation of being in such a unique and unpredictable setting, in a land where you sensed you were the visitor on nature's domain. Though I had never felt so vulnerable at times and completely out of my element, there was also a sort of peacefulness about it, of seeing nature at its most basic—through a night sky filled with thousands of brightly dancing stars. You can only feel that in a place like Africa.

When Megan completed the website a few, short months later, I was very impressed with the finished result, a chronicle of how we both put our lives on hold for six weeks and took off to a follow a dream. With her list of e-mail addresses, Megan sent the link to everyone in our group, then urged everyone to sign the guest book she created on the site and leave a few words. Even I was excited with the prospect of hearing back from everyone.

"Nice website, guys!" Thom, as the first to report back, declared in the guest book. "Most of the pictures I have are of Bill or myself getting drunk in some bar."

Bill, then trekking through the United States, e-mailed us that he'd look us up when he came through Chicago, but then had a sudden change of plans and didn't make it. Bill hitting the row of bars and pubs in Lincoln Park would have been priceless.

We never heard from anyone from the first leg of the tour—Matt, Connor and Dominick. I got over not hearing from Matt pretty quickly, though part of me wondered what ever became of Dominick.

Helen and Abe, Mary, Stacey and Vernor were also missing, never to be heard from again. I understood Helen and Abe—they didn't seem to have a stranglehold of how e-mail worked back in Africa. And as for Mary and Stacey, who needed the aggravation? Mary could still probably manage a way to annoy via email, and all Stacey was really good for was bragging about her life in New York.

It would have been cool to hear from Vernor, but he probably did really believe the people were the worst part of the tour. His email address was something like 'Vernor's Africa Trip @ yahoo.com' so you knew he planned to cut it loose as soon as he could.

There was no way to tell the fate of Skonky, Charlie, or any of the other guides who joined us for those six weeks in Africa. If Skonky did get reprimanded or even fired, the sheer abundance of touring companies practically ensured he probably was leading a group through Africa somewhere right now. We did learn Charlie saved herself some embarrassment and didn't fly to Australia to break up Matt's wedding. And the others? All I can really do is wish Rutger and Woody, two guys who really proved something, to have the opportunity to lead tours by themselves. Oh yeah—and good health for Seth. He needed it.

And of course, there was Aubrey. Who could forget Aubrey, naïve Charlie Brown, himself? Despite his metallic blue suitcase, Megan and I were both pleased to learn he had survived Nairobi, confirmed when he fired off an e-mail to us a few months after we returned to Chicago.

"I climbed Mt. Kenya with Bill before we left the continent," Aubrey wrote. "I hope everything is good in Chicago. P.S. I need the Mandela book back."

The Mandela book. I don't think Megan even finished the thick volume. Even I took a stab at it, getting nearly a quarter of the way through before setting it down next to the side of the bed.

"We really have to send it back to him," Megan instructed. "I'll take it to work one day and mail it from there."

Going on a year-and-a-half after our tour with African Wanderer ended, Megan and I still make that same promise to one another, usually whenever we clean the bedroom and have to push the book out of the way or whenever Aubrey writes us, usually every couple of months.

"Things are great in Amsterdam," Aubrey wrote in his last email. "I think my Mandela book would really like it here."

www.ingramcontent.com/pod-product-compliance
Lightning Source LLC
Chambersburg PA
CBHW051933290426
44110CB00015B/1965